Texts and Monographs in Computer Science

Programming Methodology

A Collection of Articles by Members of IFIP WG2.3

Edited by

David Gries

Springer-Verlag
New York Heidelberg Berlin

David Gries

Cornell University
Department of Computer Science
Upson Hall
Ithaca, New York 14859
USA

AMS Subject Classifications: 68A05, 68A10, 68A20
(C.R.) Computing Classifications: 4.0, 4.2, 4.35, 5.24

Library of Congress Cataloging in Publication Data

Main entry under title:

Programming methodology.

  (Texts and monographs in computer science)
  Bibliography: p.
  Includes index.
  1. Electronic digital computers—Programming—
Addresses, essays, lectures. I. Gries, David,
1939–
QA76.6.P7516   001.6'42   78-16539
ISBN 0-387-90329-1

Printed in the United States of America.

ISBN 0-387-90329-1 Springer-Verlag New York

ISBN 3-540-90329-1 Springer-Verlag Berlin Heidelberg

Contents

Preface

This volume is being published for two reasons. The first is to present a collection of previously published articles on the subject of programming methodology that have helped define the field and give it direction. It is hoped that the scientist in the field will find the volume useful as a reference, while the scientist in neighboring fields will find it useful in seriously acquainting himself with important ideas in programming methodology. The advanced student can also study it—either in a course or by himself—in order to learn significant material that may not appear in texts for some time.

The second reason for this volume is to make public the nature and work on programming methodology of IFIP Working Group 2.3, hereafter called WG2.3. (IFIP stands for *International Federation for Information Processing*.) WG2.3 is one of many IFIP Working Groups that have been established to provide international forums for discussion of ideas in various areas. Generally, these groups publish proceedings of some of their meetings and occasionally they sponsor a larger conference that persons outside a group can attend.

WG2.3 has been something of a maverick in this respect. From the beginning the group has shunned paperwork, reports, meetings, and the like. This has meant less publicity for IFIP and WG2.3, but on the other hand it has meant that meetings could be devoted almost wholly to scientific discussions.

Moreover, meetings have not centered on formal presentation of completed, published material; instead, the emphasis has been on the presentation and discussion of research underway. Thus, members could receive their colleagues' constructive criticisms at a much earlier stage than usual. Many members feel that this mode of operation has furthered their own research endeavors, and have accordingly acknowledged WG2.3 in their publications.

This volume, then, is the first formal "output" from WG2.3. It contains articles by members of the group that are deemed to be significant and exemplary work of programming methodology and of WG2.3. Unfortunately, lack of space prohibits the incorporation of material by all members. Many have written important books, articles, and technical reports that simply could not be included.

Each of the next five Parts consists of an Introduction and a series of articles devoted to one aspect or area of programming methodology. Part I contains a number of largely nontechnical articles, many of them based on lectures, which give thoughts, opinions, and viewpoints on various aspects of the field. This Part should give the reader a definite view of where the experts think programming has been and where it is or should be going.

Parts II through V then cover four different areas of programming methodology in detail. These certainly do not define the complete field of programming methodology (which is nowhere defined), but they represent significant aspects of the subject. Part II contains articles on the use of *correctness proofs* in programming and the related topic of defining a programming language so as to facilitate proofs. Part II is the largest of the five Parts, reflecting the importance of the subject and the major role played by members of WG2.3 in its development. The articles in Part III attack the problem of *harnessing parallelism* so that it can be used effectively—particularly in operating systems. Part IV is devoted to the topic of (programmer-defined) *data types* and their use in programming. Finally, the articles in Part V deal with different aspects of creating large programs and/or systems of programs, and is entitled Software Development.

Following Part V is a list of references, which is split into two sections. The first is a WG2.3 Bibliography—a list of publications relevant to programming methodology by members of WG2.3. Most of this was compiled by Sol J. Greenspan and Jim J. Horning (see [Horning 77b*]); the reader might wish to obtain this report, which contains annotations not included here.

All the publications cited by articles in this volume are listed either in the WG2.3 Bibliography or in the second list of references following this bibliography, and all references within the text are to one of these lists. Examples will illustrate the nature of the text references: [Burstall 72b*] refers to the second (because of b) 1972 article by Burstall (Algebraic description of programs with assertions, verification, and simulation); the "*" indicates that it is to be found in the WG2.3 Bibliography. The reference [Mills 72] refers to the 1972 article by Mills (Mathematical foundations of structured programming), which appears in the second list of references (no "*" is present).

In compiling this volume, I have had the help of many people. Mike Woodger, the first chairman of WG2.3, was influential in getting this project underway and constructed an initial list of potential articles. Jim Horning, the current chairman, continued to support the project and (along with Greenspan) provided most of the references in the WG2.3 Bibliography. I have had the advice and criticism of WG2.3 members and of Jim Donahue, Greg Andrews, and Manfred Paul both on my selection of articles and on my Introductions. Needless to say, however, I take full responsibility for any mistakes, for the selection and arrangement of the articles, and for the omission of many other excellent articles in order to keep the volume to a reasonable size. It should be mentioned that the volume would not have been possible without the dedicated and creative work of the authors of the articles.

David Gries

Acknowledgments

The editor, the authors, IFIP, and the publishers acknowledge with thanks permission to reprint the copyrighted articles in this book that have been published in various journals, proceedings, and books. With a few exceptions, the articles are reprinted from *Acta Informatica*, the *Communications of the ACM*, the *Computer Bulletin*, *IEEE Trans. on Software Engineering*, *Lecture Notes in Computer Science* (Springer-Verlag), books by Academic Press and Prentice–Hall, and the *Proc. of the International Conference on Reliable Software*. Below we give the individual credits.

Brinch Hansen, P. Structured multiprogramming. By permission of the ACM, from *CACM* **15** (July 1972), 574–578.

Brinch Hansen, P. The programming language Concurrent Pascal. By permission of the Institute of Electrical and Electronics Engineers, Inc., from *IEEE Trans. Software Eng.* **1** (June 1975), 199–207.

Buxton, J. N. Software engineering. By permission of the author, from *Proc. 1974 CERN School of Computing*, CERN Rpt. No. 74-23 (Nov 1974), 394–401.

Dahl, O.-J. An approach to correctness proofs of semicoroutines. By permission of the author, from *Math. Foundations of Computer Science. LNCS* **28** (1975), 157–174.

Darlington, J. and Burstall, R. M. A system which automatically improves programs. By permission of Springer-Verlag, from *Acta Informatica* **6** (1976), 41–60.

Dijkstra, E. W. The humble programmer. By permission of the ACM, from *CACM* **15** (Oct 1972), 859–886.

Dijkstra, E. W. Correctness concerns and, among other things, why they are resented. By permission of the author, from *Proc. Int. Conf. on Reliable Software, SIGPLAN Notices* **10** (June 1975), 546–550.

Dijkstra, E. W. Guarded commands, nondeterminacy, and formal derivation of programs. By permission of the ACM, from *CACM* **18** (Aug 1975), 453–457; also appeared in Yeh, R. T. (ed.), *Current Trends in Programming Methodology I*. Prentice–Hall, 1976, 233–242.

Gries, D. On structured programming. By permission of the ACM, based on a letter to the editor by the author in *CACM* **17** (Nov 1974), 655–657.

Guttag, J. V. and Horning, J. J. The algebraic specification of abstract data types. By permission of Springer-Verlag, from *Acta Informatica*, to appear.

Hoare, C. A. R. An axiomatic basis for computer programming. By permission of the ACM, from *CACM* **12** (Oct 1969), 576–580, 583.

Hoare, C. A. R. Proof of a program: FIND. By permission of the ACM, from *CACM* **14** (Jan 1971), 39–45.

Hoare, C. A. R. Towards a theory of parallel programming. By permission of Academic Press, from Hoare, C. A. R. and Perrott, R. N. (eds.), *Operating Systems Techniques*. Academic Press, 1972.

Hoare, C. A. R. Proof of correctness of data representations. By permission of Springer-Verlag, from *Acta Informatica* **1** (1972), 271–281.

Hoare, C. A. R. Monitors: an operating system structuring concept. By permission of the ACM, from *CACM* **17** (Oct 1974), 549–557.

Hoare, C. A. R. The engineering of software: a startling contradiction. By permission of the British Computer Society, based on a note by the author in the *Computer Bulletin* (Dec 1975).

Lehman, M. M. Programs, cities, students—limits to growth? By permission of the author, from *Inaugural Lecture College Series*, Vol. 9, 1970–1974, 211–229.

Owicki, S. and Gries, D. An axiomatic proof technique for parallel programs. By permission of Springer-Verlag, from *Acta Informatica* **6** (1976), 319–340.

Parnas, D. L. On a "buzzword": hierarchical structure. By permission of the author, from *IFIP 1974*, 336–339.

Parnas, D. L. On the design and development of program families. By permission of the Inst. of Electrical and Electronics Engineers, Inc., from *IEEE Trans. Software Eng.* **1** (March 1976), 1–9.

Randell, B. System structure for software fault tolerance. By permission of the Inst. of Electrical and Electronics Engineers, Inc., from *IEEE Trans. Software Eng.* **1** (April 1975), 220–232; also appeared in Yeh, R. T. (ed.), *Current Trends in Programming Methodology I*. Prentice–Hall, 1976, 195–219.

Reynolds, J. C. Programming with transition diagrams. By permission of the author.

Reynolds, J. C. User-defined types and procedural data structures as complementary approaches to data abstraction. By permission of the author, from Schuman, S. A. (ed.), *New Directions in Algorithmic Languages 1975*, Inst. de Recherche d'Informatique et d'Automatique, Rocquencourt, 1975, 157–168.

Ross, D. T. Structured analysis (SA): a language for communicating ideas. By permission of the Inst. of Electrical and Electronics Engineers, Inc., from *IEEE Trans. Software Eng.* **3** (Jan 1977), 16–34.

Turski, W. M. Software engineering—some principles and problems. By permission of the author, from *Mathematical Structures–Computational Mathematics–Mathematical Modelling*. Publ. House of the Bulgarian Academy of Sciences, Sofia, 1975, 485–491.

Wirth, N. Program development by stepwise refinement. By permission of the ACM, from *CACM* **14** (April 1971), 221–227.

A History of IFIP WG2.3 (Programming Methodology)

M. Woodger (Chairman 1969–1976)

Origin

When ALGOL 68 was produced by WG2.1 of IFIP, in December 1968, a minority of members of that group opposed its publication, feeling that programmers needed tools other than bigger and better programming languages. The NATO Conference on Software Engineering at Garmisch in October 1968 had generated international awareness of the problems of construction and control of reliable programs, and the parent committee TC2 of IFIP approved the formation of a new working Group to cover this subject. I agreed to chair it, and the organizing meeting in Oslo, 20–22 July 1969, was attended by O.-J. Dahl, E. W. Dijkstra, M. D. McIlroy, B. Randell, G. Seegmueller, W. M. Turski, M. Woodger and M. Paul (Chairman WG2.1). D. T. Ross was also a founder member. The title Programming Methodology is due to Randell.

Purpose

The group provides an international forum for discussion and cross-fertilization of ideas between workers in this field. It avoids paper work, reports, voting, and the like, and has no explicit "product." The intention is rather that the results of this interaction will be seen in the normal scientific publications of the members. The reader of this book may perhaps judge the success of this plan. Minutes of meetings are not normally kept; they are judged to be of little value, except perhaps to those unable to attend a particular meeting yet able to follow the general course of events.

We tried to balance some conflicting influences. I mention just a few: Having too many people at a meeting delays interaction, preventing a proper exchange of views. Having too narrow or specialized a cross section of the programming community in the membership reduces the cross fertilizing effect. Having members who are not actively working in the field reduces the value of discussions. Having a rigid timetable inhibits the airing of newly produced or developing points of view.

Differences of opinion remain on the value of such a group, but the experience of these early years has convinced me that it has played a part in the development of the subject. If, in particular, experts of divergent views who seldom meet can be persuaded to listen to each other over a period of a few days, in congenial company and surroundings, then misunderstandings can be removed and a common basis for progress achieved.

Membership

It is one thing to decide who should belong to such a group. It is quite another thing to persuade them to come to meetings. We were fortunate in having the cooperation of some of the most active people in this subject. But the membership list does not indicate who took part. On the average, about half the membership manages to attend, around ten people in the early years.

The delicate matter of whom to invite to membership (bearing in mind that reversing this is difficult!) was handled by having, at most meetings, presentations from a few recommended individuals, invited as "observers"; if it was judged that their continuing contribution would benefit the group then their membership was recommended to Technical Committee 2, whose Chairman issued the official invitations. The only real difference between members and observers at a meeting was that members had a permanent right to attend. The discussions were always open to both, and their contributions were potentially of equal value.

A deliberate attempt was made to widen the area covered by the experience and background of the members, from an initial recognized bias towards "Algolists," academics, Europeans, and scientists, to include the world of commerce and industry, the USSR, and Japan. Recognizing that regular attendance by a resident of a remote country cannot be expected, it has been the practice to invite any Japanese specialist known to be in the area of the meeting.

Meetings

The group meets once or twice a year, for five days at a time, at a place selected by a host organization (generally that of a member). The dearth of funds from IFIP means that the organizations of members have to support their travel, hence all meetings until 1976 have been held in Europe.

One or two topics for discussions are decided beforehand, to orient the meeting. Otherwise no rigid rules are applied, and the use made of the available time depends on who turns up.

The following account of the meetings would be dull if it were complete, but it plots a few landmarks. The selection is mine.

The first meeting of the Group, at Regnecentralen, Copenhagen, Denmark, 16–20 March 1970, was notable for E. W. Dijkstra's presentation on structured programming, O.-J. Dahl's on the class concept of SIMULA 67, and D. T. Ross' on the use of his notion of "plex" in the design of integrated software packages. C. Strachey, C. A. R. Hoare, G. Radin, J. C. Reynolds, B. Randell, P. Brinch Hansen, M. M. Lehman, W. Teitelman, M. D. McIlroy, and J. Madey also took part.

Meeting No. 2 was at Warwick University, England, 3–7 April 1971. J. N. Buxton was host and we had Japanese and Russian participation in the persons of E. Wada and S. S. Lavrov. C. A. R. Hoare presented a school timetabling program as a realistic example to show the problems of systematic construction together with proof of correctness. M. M. Lehman described a new limitation to the growth of really large operating systems through successive releases. C. Strachey outlined D. Scott's new foundations for theoretical computer science. W. M. Turski was appointed secretary.

The third meeting, at Bristol University, England, 2–7 January 1972, was hosted by F. G. Duncan. A. S. Douglas discussed the problems of processing large volume questionnaires, and W. M. Turski explained the logic of inverted files. E. W. Dijkstra discussed levels of programming which abstract from the existence of lookahead or nonunique value representations at lower levels. He also discussed the general producer–consumer relationship and the notion of coroutines. C. A. R. Hoare commented on defects of SIMULA 67 and PASCAL.

4th meeting: Warsaw, 18–29 September 1972. R. M. Balzer described plans to use the ARPA network for interactive program building, and W. Teitelman described an existing system with exceptional user friendliness based upon LISP. D. T. Ross discussed the use in his firm of finite state machines specified by the language of "regular expressions" for generating components of compilers. M. D. McIlroy described "pipes," a novel kind of program primitive for describing communication between processes and files.

5th meeting: Munich, Germany, 1–6 April 1973, host G. Seegmueller. This meeting was notable for the introduction by E. W. Dijkstra of his axiomatic definition of the semantics of a program by "predicate transformers." A predicate transformer operates on a predicate describing the final state of the machine and yields the "weakest precondition," i.e., the complete set of corresponding initial states. Rules for the construction of predicate transformers then define the semantics of the programming language. He also introduced a new way of handling deadlocks by a constraint on a violation count. N. Wirth described the stages of definition and implementation of a structured compiler for PASCAL. C. A. R. Hoare introduced "monitors" as a method of structuring operating systems. D. T. Ross, M. M. Lehman, J. C. Reynolds, J. N. Buxton, D. L. Parnas, and C. Jones also took part.

6th meeting: Blanchland, Northumberland, England, 21–26 October 1973, host B. Randell. This was memorable for M. A. Jackson's account of commercial programming and his technique of matching program structure to file structure. R. M. Burstall described work with J. Darlington on automatic program transformation. E. W. Dijkstra developed many ideas during the week, principally those behind "guarded commands" and a uniform treatment of multi- and uniprogramming. D. J. Pearson described ICL's CADES system. H. D. Mills and J. D. Roberts also took part.

7th meeting: Boldern, Zurich, Switzerland, 29 April–4 May 1974, host N. Wirth. D. L. Parnas spoke on program hierarchies; D. T. Ross presented "structured analysis"; B. W. Lampson, J. J. Horning, C. Bron, and P. Naur took part. E. W. Dijkstra presented a new virtual storage management system in which page allocation was done per program rather than for all programs together. C. A. R. Hoare attacked the use of "pointers" or references in programming languages. O.-J. Dahl discussed the concept of the "history of a variable"—the external effect of any piece of program should be regarded as an assignment to some variables or their histories.

8th meeting: Munich, 8–13 December 1974, host G. Seegmueller. B. Randell reported work on error recovery, using automatic selection of alternative algorithms on failure. N. Wirth dealt with criticisms of PASCAL, and agreed that "union of types" should be avoided. D. Gries described joint work with S. Owicki on proofs of programs involving parallel processes. C. A. R. Hoare discussed protection and checking of constraints in multilayered designs of operating systems, and how to do much of this at compile time. P. Naur and J. J. Horning reported on experiments on the teaching of programming.

9th meeting: Baden-bei-Wien, Austria, 1–5 September 1975, host C. Jones. E. W. Dijkstra developed a new freedom from past attitudes to programming typified by the terms "sequential" and "parallel." He showed programs that could be interpreted in three ways: as sequential algorithms for a single machine; as partially nondeterministic algorithms, controlling the creation of and communication between a host of auxiliary virtual machines; and as algorithms describing a data driven machine. I crossed swords with him over a detail: the confusion of levels of detail in the specification of a twin process "on the fly" garbage collector.

C. A. R. Hoare introduced "traces"—the execution history of a program (both actions and assertions) treated in abstraction from the notion of a machine state—as a basis for defining a programming language. Types of variables and their values, real and abstract, were discussed at length, with help from J. C. Reynolds. D. L. Parnas described experiments in the design of a family of operating systems, L. Belady discussed IBM's system development process, and M. A. Jackson displayed shortcomings of "JCL" and IBM's version of structured programming.

10th meeting: Cazenovia, near Syracuse, New York state, 5—9 July 1976, host J. C. Reynolds. At this, the first meeting outside Europe, we had notable contributions by J. W. Backus on "functional programming without variables" and by A. W. Holt on modelling of state and event choices by Petri nets. This latter approach excited plenty of interest and discussion in and out of session. G. Mealy developed a formalization of data types. D. T. Ross discussed "a variable as an object," showing a new interpretation of A. Tarski's definition of conjunction in terms of equivalence in logic. Other contributions were made by R. Balzer, B. Liskov, G. Veillon, S. Owicki, H. Kopetz, J. Stoy, and M. Sintzoff.

Under a bylaw of IFIP I had to relinquish the Chair at this meeting, having served for six years. The new Chairman is J. J. Horning, and I am Vice-Chairman.

PART I

VIEWPOINTS ON PROGRAMMING

The articles in this Part give various viewpoints on aspects of programming —on programming methodology, software engineering, structured programming, and related topics. Several of them are based on lectures. None of them are very technical, but all of them are worthwhile. Together, they should provide several hours of pleasant but informative and thought-provoking reading.

First is Edsger W. Dijkstra's 1972 ACM Turing Award Lecture, The Humble Programmer. *In his lecture, Dijkstra describes his view of the past history of computer science, sketches a vision of programming in the future, and discusses three major conditions that must be fulfilled in order for this vision to become reality. Preceding this article is an extract from the Turing Award Citation read by M. Douglas McIlroy.*

The next three articles deal with software engineering. John N. Buxton's paper, taken from lecture notes for a summer course on computing given at CERN (Centre Européan de Recherche Nucléaire, in Switzerland), in 1974, outlines several views on how software should be designed and built and briefly describes "design methodologies." Wladyslaw M. Turski's article, written in 1973 and published in 1975, discusses some principles and problems of software engineering. C. A. R. (Tony) Hoare's short but thought-provoking note compares the ideals of the professional engineer with those of today's programmer and questions whether we should be linking together the terms software and engineering. All three articles should cause the reader to sit back and reflect on his own programming principles and practices.

The title of Manny M. Lehman's article, Programs, Cities, Students— Limits to Growth?, *comes from a short poem found at the end of the article. Lehman is interested in system growth—especially of software systems—and discusses various laws governing programming system life dynamics and statistical models of their growth. The article, Lehman's inaugural lecture as Professor of Computing Science at the University of London, deserves attention by those interested in large systems.*

The final note, by David Gries, is based on a letter to the editor that appeared in the Communications of the ACM *[Gries 72b*]. It attempts to shed some light on a term that has been used with a wide variety of meanings: structured programming.*

[*Extract from the Turing Award Citation read by M. D. McIlroy, chairman of the ACM Turing Award Committee, at the presentation of this Turing Award lecture on August 14, 1972, at the ACM Annual Conference in Boston.*]

The working vocabulary of programmers everywhere is studded with words originated or forcefully promulgated by E. W. Dijkstra—display, deadly embrace, semaphore, go-to-less programming, structured programming. But his influence on programming is more pervasive than any glossary can possibly indicate. The precious gift that this Turing Award acknowledges is Dijkstra's *style*: his approach to programming as a high, intellectual challenge; his eloquent insistence and practical demonstration that programs should be composed correctly, not just debugged into correctness; and his illuminating perception of problems at the foundations of program design. He has published about a dozen papers, both technical and reflective, among which are especially to be noted his philosophical address at IFIP [Dijkstra 62a*], his already classic papers on cooperating sequential processes [Dijkstra 65b*], and his memorable indictment of the go-to statement [Dijkstra 68d*]. An influential series of letters by Dijkstra have recently surfaced as a polished monograph on the art of composing programs [Dijkstra 71b*].

We have come to value good programs in much the same way as we value good literature. And at the center of this movement, creating and reflecting patterns no less beautiful than useful, stands E. W. Dijkstra.

1
The Humble Programmer[1]

Edsger W. Dijkstra
Burroughs Corporation

As a result of a long sequence of coincidences I entered the programming profession officially on the first spring morning of 1952, and as far as I have been able to trace, I was the first Dutchman to do so in my country. In retrospect the most amazing thing is the slowness with which, at least in my part of the world, the programming profession emerged, a slowness which is now hard to believe. But I am grateful for two vivid recollections from that period that establish that slowness beyond any doubt.

After having programmed for some three years, I had a discussion with van Wijngaarden, who was then my boss at the Mathematical Centre in Amsterdam—a discussion for which I shall remain grateful to him as long as I live. The point was that I was supposed to study theoretical physics at the University of Leiden simultaneously, and as I found the two activities harder and harder to combine, I had to make up my mind, either to stop programming and become a real, respectable theoretical physicist, or to carry my study of physics to a formal completion only, with a minimum of effort, and to become..., yes what? A programmer? But was that a respectable profession? After all, what was programming? Where was the sound body of knowledge that could support it as an intellectually respectable discipline? I remember quite vividly how I envied my hardware colleagues, who, when asked about their professional competence, could at least point out that they knew everything about vacuum tubes, amplifiers and the rest, whereas I felt that, when faced with that question, I would stand empty-handed. Full of misgivings I knocked on van Wijngaarden's office door, asking him whether I could speak to him for a moment; when

I left his office a number of hours later, I was another person. For after having listened to my problems patiently, he agreed that up till that moment there was not much of a programming discipline, but then he went on to explain quietly that automatic computers were here to stay, that we were just at the beginning and could not I be one of the persons called to make programming a respectable discipline in the years to come? This was a turning point in my life and I completed my study of physics formally as quickly as I could. One moral of the above story is, of course, that we must be very careful when we give advice to younger people: sometimes they follow it!

Two years later, in 1957, I married, and Dutch marriage rites require you to state your profession and I stated that I was a programmer. But the municipal authorities of the town of Amsterdam did not accept it on the grounds that there was no such profession. And, believe it or not, but under the heading "profession" my marriage record shows the ridiculous entry "theoretical physicist"!

So much for the slowness with which I saw the programming profession emerge in my own country. Since then I have seen more of the world, and it is my general impression that in other countries, apart from a possible shift of dates, the growth pattern has been very much the same.

Let me try to capture the situation in those old days in a little bit more detail, in the hope of getting a better understanding of the situation today. While we pursue our analysis, we shall see how many common misunderstandings about the true nature of the programming task can be traced back to that now distant past.

The first automatic electronic computers were all unique, single-copy machines and they were all to be found in an environment with the exciting flavor of an experimental laboratory. Once the vision of the automatic computer was there, its realization was a tremendous challenge to the electronic technology then available, and one thing is certain: we cannot deny the courage of the groups that decided to try to build such a fantastic piece of equipment. For fantastic pieces of equipment they were: in retrospect one can only wonder that those first machines worked at all, at least sometimes. The overwhelming problem was to get and keep the machine in working order. The preoccupation with the physical aspects of automatic computing is still reflected in the names of the older scientific societies in the field, such as the Association for Computing Machinery or the British Computer Society, names in which explicit reference is made to the physical equipment.

What about the poor programmer? Well, to tell the honest truth, he was hardly noticed. For one thing, the first machines were so bulky that you could hardly move them and besides that, they required such extensive maintenance that it was quite natural that the place where people tried to use the machine was the same laboratory where the machine had been developed. Secondly, the programmer's somewhat invisible work was without any glamour: you could show the machine to visitors and that was several orders of magnitude more spectacular than some sheets of coding. But most important of all, the programmer himself had a very modest view of his own work: his work derived all its significance from the existence of that wonderful machine. Because that was a unique machine, he knew only too well that his programs had only local significance, and also because it was patently obvious that this machine would have a limited lifetime, he knew that very little of his work would have a lasting value. Finally, there is yet another circumstance that had a profound influence on the programmer's attitude toward his work: on the one hand, besides being unreliable, his machine was usually too slow and its memory was usually too small, i.e. he was faced with a pinching shoe, while on the other hand its usually somewhat queer order code would cater for the most unexpected constructions. And in those days many a clever programmer derived an immense intellectual satisfaction from the cunning tricks by means of which he contrived to squeeze the impossible into the constraints of his equipment.

Two opinions about programming date from those days. I mention them now; I shall return to them later. The one opinion was that a really competent programmer should be puzzle-minded and very fond of clever tricks; the other opinion was that programming was nothing more than optimizing the efficiency of the computational process, in one direction or the other.

The latter opinion was the result of the frequent circumstance that, indeed, the available equipment was a painfully pinching shoe, and in those days one often encountered the naive expectation that, once more powerful machines were available, programming would no longer be a problem, for then the struggle to push the machine to its limits would no longer be necessary and that was all that programming was about, wasn't it? But in the next decades something completely different happened: more powerful machines became available, not just an order of magnitude more powerful, even several orders of magnitude more powerful. But instead of finding ourselves in a state of eternal bliss with all programming problems solved, we found ourselves up to our necks in the software crisis! How come?

There is a minor cause: in one or two respects modern machinery is basically more difficult to handle than the old machinery. Firstly, we have got the I/O interrupts, occurring at unpredictable and irreproducible moments; compared with the old sequential machine that pretended to be a fully deterministic automaton, this has been a dramatic change, and many a systems programmer's grey hair bears witness to the fact that we should not talk lightly about the logical problems created by that feature. Secondly, we have got machines equipped with multilevel stores, presenting us problems of management strategy that, in spite of the extensive literature on the subject, still remain rather elusive. So much for the added complication due to structural changes of the actual machines.

But I called this a minor cause; the major cause is · · · that the machines have become several orders of magnitude more powerful! To put it quite bluntly: as long as there were no machines, programming was no problem at all; when we had a few weak computers, programming became a mild problem, and now we have gigantic computers, programming has become an equally gigantic problem. In this sense the electronic industry has not solved a single problem, it has only created them—it has created the problem of using its products. To put it in another way: as the power of available machines grew by a factor of more than a thousand, society's ambition to apply these machines grew in proportion, and it was the poor programmer who found his job in this exploded field of tension between ends and means. The increased power of the hardware, together with the perhaps even more dramatic increase in its reliability, made solutions feasible that the programmer had not dared to dream about a few years before. And now, a few years later, he *had* to dream about them and, even worse, he had to transform such dreams into reality! Is it a wonder that we found ourselves in a software crisis? No, certainly not, and as you may guess, it was even predicted well in advance; but the trouble with minor prophets, of course, is that it is only five years later that you really know that they had been right.

Then, in the mid sixties something terrible happened: the computers of the so-called third generation made their appearance. The official literature tells us that their price/performance ratio has been one of the major design objectives. But if you take as "performance" the duty cycle of the machine's various components, little will prevent you from ending up with a design in which the major part of your performance goal is reached by internal housekeeping activities of doubtful necessity. And if your definition of price is the price to be paid for the hardware, little will prevent you from ending up with a design that is terribly hard to program for: for instance the order code might be such as to enforce, either upon the programmer or upon the system, early binding decisions presenting conflicts that really cannot be resolved. And to a large extent these unpleasant possibilities seem to have become reality.

When these machines were announced and their functional specifications became known, many among us must have become quite miserable; at least I was. It was only reasonable to expect that such machines would flood the computing community, and it was therefore all the more important that their design should be as sound as possible. But the design embodied such serious flaws that I felt that with a single stroke the progress of computing science had been retarded by at least ten years; it was then that I had the blackest week in the whole of my professional life. Perhaps the most saddening thing now is that, even after all those years of frustrating experience, still so many people honestly believe that some law of nature tells us that machines have to be that way. They silence their doubts by observing how many of these machines have been sold, and derive from that observation the false sense of security that, after all, the design cannot have been that bad. But upon closer inspection, that line of defense has the same convincing strength as the argument that cigarette smoking must be healthy because so many people do it.

It is in this connection that I regret that it is not customary for scientific journals in the computing area to publish reviews of newly announced computers in much the same way as we review scientific publications: to review machines would be at least as important. And here I have a confession to make: in the early sixties I wrote such a review with the intention of submitting it to Communications, but in spite of the fact that the few colleagues to whom the text was sent for their advice urged me to do so, I did not dare to do it, fearing that the difficulties either for myself or for the Editorial Board would prove to be too great. This suppression was an act of cowardice on my side for which I blame myself more and more. The difficulties I foresaw were a consequence of the absence of generally accepted criteria, and although I was convinced of the validity of the criteria I had chosen to apply, I feared that my review would be refused or discarded as "a matter of personal taste." I still think that such reviews would be extremely useful and I am longing to see them appear, for their accepted appearance would be a sure sign of maturity of the computing community.

The reason that I have paid the above attention to the hardware scene is because I have the feeling that one of the most important aspects of any computing tool is its influence on the thinking habits of those who try to use it, and because I have reasons to believe that that influence is many times stronger than is commonly assumed. Let us now switch our attention to the software scene.

Here the diversity has been so large that I must confine myself to a few stepping stones. I am painfully aware of the arbitrariness of my choice, and I beg you not to draw any conclusions with regard to my appreciation of the many efforts that will have to remain unmentioned.

In the beginning there was the EDSAC in Cambridge, England, and I think it quite impressive that right from the start the notion of a subroutine library played a central role in the design of that machine and of the way in which it should be used. It is now nearly 25 years later and the computing scene has changed dramatically, but the notion of basic software is still with us, and the notion of the closed subroutine is still one of the key concepts in programming. We should recognize the closed subroutine as one of the greatest software inventions; it has survived three generations of computers and it will survive a few more, because it caters for the implementation of one of our basic patterns of abstraction. Regrettably enough, its importance has been underestimated in the design of the third generation computers, in which the great number of explicitly named registers of the arithmetic unit implies a large overhead on the subroutine mechanism. But even that did not kill the concept of the subroutine, and we can only pray that the mutation won't prove to be hereditary.

The second major development on the software scene that I would like to mention is the birth of FORTRAN. At that time this was a project of great temerity, and the people responsible for it deserve our great admiration. It would be absolutely unfair to blame them for shortcomings that only became apparent after a decade or so of extensive usage: groups with a successful look-ahead of ten years are quite rare! In retrospect we must rate FORTRAN as a successful coding technique, but with very few effective aids to conception, aids which are now so urgently needed that time has come to consider it out of date. The sooner we can forget that FORTRAN ever existed, the better, for as a vehicle of thought it is no longer adequate: it wastes our brainpower, and it is too risky and therefore too expensive to use. FORTRAN'S tragic fate has been its wide acceptance, mentally chaining thousands and thousands of programmers to our past mistakes. I pray daily that more of my fellow-programmers may find the means of freeing themselves from the curse of compatibility.

The third project I would not like to leave unmentioned is LISP, a fascinating enterprise of a completely different nature. With a few very basic principles at its foundation, it has shown a remarkable stability. Besides that, LISP has been the carrier for a considerable number of, in a sense, our most sophisticated computer applications. LISP has jokingly been described as "the most intelligent way to misuse a computer." I think that description a great compliment because it transmits the full flavor of liberation: it has assisted a number of our most gifted fellow humans in thinking previously impossible thoughts.

The fourth project to be mentioned is ALGOL 60. While up to the present day FORTRAN programmers still tend to understand their programming language in terms of the specific implementation they are working with—hence the prevalence of octal or hexadecimal dumps—while the definition of LISP is still a curious mixture of what the language means and how the mechanism works, the famous Report on the Algorithmic Language ALGOL 60 is the fruit of a genuine effort to carry abstraction a vital step further and to define a programming language in an implementation-independent way. One could argue that in this respect its authors have been so successful that they have created serious doubts as to whether it could be implemented at all! The report gloriously demonstrated the power of the formal method BNF, now fairly known as Backus-Naur-Form, and the power of carefully phrased English, at least when used by someone as brilliant as Peter Naur. I think that it is fair to say that only very few documents as short as this have had an equally profound influence on the computing community. The ease with which in later years the names ALGOL and ALGOL-like have been used, as an unprotected trademark, to lend glory to a number of sometimes hardly related younger projects is a somewhat shocking compliment to ALGOL's standing. The strength of BNF as a defining device is responsible for what I regard as one of the weaknesses of the language: an over-elaborate and not too systematic syntax could now be crammed into the confines of very few pages. With a device as powerful as BNF, the Report on the Algorithmic Language ALGOL 60 should have been much shorter. Besides that, I am getting very doubtful about ALGOL 60's parameter mechanism: it allows the programmer so much combinatorial freedom that its confident use requires a strong discipline from the programmer. Besides being expensive to implement, it seems dangerous to use.

Finally, although the subject is not a pleasant one, I must mention PL/1, a programming language for which the defining documentation is of a frightening size and complexity. Using PL/1 must be like flying a plane with 7,000 buttons, switches, and handles to manipulate in the cockpit. I absolutely fail to see how we can keep our growing programs firmly within our intellectual grip when by its sheer baroqueness the programming language—our basic tool, mind you!—already escapes our intellectual control. And if I have to describe the influence PL/1 can have on its users, the closest metaphor that comes to my mind is that of a drug. I remember from a symposium on higher level programming languages a lecture given in defense of PL/1 by a man who described himself as one of its devoted users. But within a one-hour lecture in praise of PL/1 he managed to ask for the addition of about 50 new "features," little supposing that the main source of his problems could very well be that it contained already far too many "features." The speaker displayed all the depressing symptoms of addiction, reduced as he was to the state of mental stagnation in which he could only ask for more, more, more.... When FORTRAN has been called an infantile disorder, full PL/1, with its growth characteristics of a dangerous tumor, could turn out to be a fatal disease.

So much for the past. But there is no point in making mistakes unless thereafter we are able to learn from them. As a matter of fact, I think that we have learned so much that within a few years programming can be an activity vastly different from what it has been up till now, so different that we had better prepare ourselves for the shock. Let me sketch for you one of the possible futures. At first sight, this vision of programming in perhaps already the near future may strike you as utterly fantastic. Let me therefore also add the considerations that might lead one to the conclusion that this vision could be a very real possibility.

The vision is that, well before the seventies have run to completion, we shall be able to design and implement the kind of systems that are now straining our programming ability at the expense of only a few percent in man-years of what they cost us now, and that besides that, these systems will be virtually free of bugs. These two improvements go hand in hand. In the latter respect software seems to be different from many other products, where as a rule a higher quality implies a higher price. Those who want really reliable software will discover that they must find means of avoiding the majority of bugs to start with, and as a result the programming process will become cheaper. If you want more effective programmers, you will discover that they should not waste their time debugging—they should not introduce the bugs to start with. In other words, both goals point to the same change.

Such a drastic change in such a short period of time would be a revolution, and to all persons that base their expectations for the future on smooth extrapolation of the recent past—appealing to some unwritten laws of social and cultural inertia—the chance that this drastic change will take place must seem negligible. But we all know that sometimes revolutions do take place! And what are the chances for this one?

There seem to be three major conditions that must be fulfilled. The world at large must recognize the need for the change; secondly, the economic need for it must be sufficiently strong; and, thirdly, the change must be technically feasible. Let me discuss these three conditions in the above order.

With respect to the recognition of the need for greater reliability of software, I expect no disagreement anymore. Only a few years ago this was different: to talk about a software crisis was blasphemy. The turning point was the Conference on Software Engineering in Garmisch, October 1968, a conference that created a sensation as there occurred the first open admission of the software crisis. And by now it is generally recognized that the design of any large sophisticated system is going to be a very difficult job, and whenever one meets people responsible for such undertakings, one finds them very much concerned about the reliability issue, and rightly so. In short, our first condition seems to be satisfied.

Now for the economic need. Nowadays one often encounters the opinion that in the sixties programming has been an overpaid profession, and that in the coming years programmer salaries may be expected to go down. Usually this opinion is expressed in connection with the recession, but it could be a symptom of something different and quite healthy, *viz.* that perhaps the programmers of the past decade have not done so good a job as they should have done. Society is getting dissatisfied with the performance of programmers and of their products. But there is another factor of much greater weight. In the present situation it is quite usual that for a specific system, the price to be paid for the development of the software is of the same order of magnitude as the price of the hardware needed, and society more or less accepts that. But hardware manufacturers tell us that in the next decade hardware prices can be expected to drop with a factor of ten. If software development were to continue to be the same clumsy and expensive process as it is now, things would get completely out of balance. You cannot expect society to accept this, and therefore we *must* learn to program an order of magnitude more effectively. To put it in another way: as long as machines were the largest item on the budget, the programming profession could get away with its clumsy techniques; but that umbrella will fold very rapidly. In short, also our second condition seems to be satisfied.

And now the third condition: is it technically feasible? I think it might be, and I shall give you six arguments in support of that opinion.

A study of program structure has revealed that programs—even alternative programs for the same task and with the same mathematical content—can differ tremendously in their intellectual manageability. A number of rules have been discovered, violation of which will either seriously impair or totally destroy the intellectual manageability of the program. These rules are of two kinds. Those of the first kind are easily imposed mechanically, *viz.* by a suitably chosen programming language. Examples are the exclusion of goto-statements and of procedures with more than one output parameter. For those of the second kind, I at least—but that may be due to lack of competence on my side—see no way of imposing them mechanically, as it seems to need some sort of automatic theorem prover for which I have no existence proof. Therefore, for the time being and perhaps forever, the rules of the second kind present themselves as elements of discipline required from the programmer. Some of the rules I have in mind are so clear that they can be taught and that there never needs to be an argument as to whether a given program violates them or not. Examples are the requirements that no loop should be written down without providing a proof for termination or without stating the relation whose invariance will not be destroyed by the execution of the repeatable statement.

I now suggest that we confine ourselves to the design and implementation of intellectually manageable programs. If someone fears that this restriction is so severe that we cannot live with it, I can reassure him: the class of intellectually manageable programs is still sufficiently rich to contain many very realistic programs for any problem capable of algorithmic solution. We must not forget that is *not* our business to make programs; it is our business to design classes of computations that will display a desired behavior. The suggestion of confining ourselves to intellectually manageable programs is the basis for the first two of my announced six arguments.

Argument one is that, as the programmer only needs to consider intellectually manageable programs, the alternatives he is choosing from are much, much easier to cope with.

Argument two is that, as soon as we have decided to restrict ourselves to the subset of the intellectually manageable programs, we have achieved, once and for all, a drastic reduction of the solution space to be considered. And this argument is distinct from argument one.

Argument three is based on the constructive approach to the problem of program correctness. Today a usual technique is to make a program and then to test it. But: program testing can be a very effective way to show the presence of bugs, but it is hopelessly inadequate for showing their absence.

The only effective way to raise the confidence level of a program significantly is to give a convincing proof of its correctness. But one should not
first make the program and then prove its correctness, because then the
requirement of providing the proof would only increase the poor programmer's burden. On the contrary: the programmer should let correctness
proof and program grow hand in hand. Argument three is essentially based
on the following observation. If one first asks oneself what the structure of
a convincing proof would be and, having found this, then constructs a
program satisfying this proof's requirements, then these correctness concerns turn out to be a very effective heuristic guidance. By definition this
approach is only applicable when we restrict ourselves to intellectually
manageable programs, but it provides us with effective means for finding a
satisfactory one among these.

Argument four has to do with the way in which the amount of
intellectual effort needed to design a program depends on the program
length. It has been suggested that there is some law of nature telling us that
the amount of intellectual effort needed grows with the square of program
length. But, thank goodness, no one has been able to prove this law. And
this is because it need not be true. We all know that the only mental tool
by means of which a very finite piece of reasoning can cover a myriad of
cases is called "abstraction"; as a result the effective exploitation of his
powers of abstraction must be regarded as one of the most vital activities
of a competent programmer. In this connection it might be worthwhile to
point out that the purpose of abstracting is *not* to be vague, but to create a
new semantic level in which one can be absolutely precise. Of course I
have tried to find a fundamental cause that would prevent our abstraction
mechanisms from being sufficiently effective. But no matter how hard I
tried, I did not find such a cause. As a result I tend to the assumption—up
till now not disproved by experience—that by suitable application of our
powers of abstraction, the intellectual effort required to conceive or to
understand a program need not grow more than proportional to program
length. A by-product of these investigations may be of much greater
practical significance, and is, in fact, the basis of my fourth argument. The
by-product was the identification of a number of patterns of abstraction
that play a vital role in the whole process of composing programs. Enough
is known about these patterns of abstraction that you could devote a
lecture to each of them. What the familiarity and conscious knowledge of
these patterns of abstraction imply dawned upon me when I realized that,
had they been common knowledge 15 years ago, the step from BNF to
syntax-directed compilers, for instance, could have taken a few minutes
instead of a few years. Therefore I present our recent knowledge of vital
abstraction patterns as the fourth argument.

Now for the fifth argument. It has to do with the influence of the tool
we are trying to use upon our own thinking habits. I observe a cultural
tradition, which in all probability has its roots in the Renaissance, to

ignore this influence, to regard the human mind as the supreme and autonomous master of its artifacts. But if I start to analyze the thinking habits of myself and of my fellow human beings, I come, whether I like it or not, to a completely different conclusion, *viz.* that the tools we are trying to use and the language or notation we are using to express or record our thoughts are the major factors determining what we can think or express at all! The analysis of the influence that programming languages have on the thinking habits of their users, and the recognition that, by now, brainpower is by far our scarcest resource, these together give us a new collection of yardsticks for comparing the relative merits of various programming languages. The competent programmer is fully aware of the strictly limited size of his own skull; therefore he approaches the programming task in full humility, and among other things he avoids clever tricks like the plague. In the case of a well-known conversational programming language I have been told from various sides that as soon as a programming community is equipped with a terminal for it, a specific phenomenon occurs that even has a well-established name: it is called "the one-liners." It takes one of two different forms: one programmer places a one-line program on the desk of another and either he proudly tells what it does and adds the question, "Can you code this in less symbols?"—as if this were of any conceptual relevance!—or he just says, "Guess what it does!" From this observation we must conclude that this language as a tool is an open invitation for clever tricks; and while exactly this may be the explanation for some of its appeal, *viz.* to those who like to show how clever they are, I am sorry, but I must regard this as one of the most damning things that can be said about a programming language. Another lesson we should have learned from the recent past is that the development of "richer" or "more powerful" programming languages was a mistake in the sense that these baroque monstrosities, these conglomerations of idiosyncrasies, are really unmanageable, both mechanically and mentally. I see a great future for very systematic and very modest programming languages. When I say "modest," I mean that, for instance, not only ALGOL 60's "for clause," but even FORTRAN'S "**do** loop" may find themselves thrown out as being too baroque. I have run a little programming experiment with really experienced volunteers, but something quite unintended and quite unexpected turned up. None of my volunteers found the obvious and most elegant solution. Upon closer analysis this turned out to have a common source: their notion of repetition was so tightly connected to the idea of an associated controlled variable to be stepped up, that they were mentally blocked from seeing the obvious. Their solutions were less efficient, needlessly hard to understand, and it took them a very long time to find them. It was a revealing, but also shocking experience for me. Finally, in one respect one hopes that tomorrow's programming languages will differ greatly from what we are used to now: to a much greater extent than hitherto they should invite us to reflect in the structure of what we write down all abstractions needed to cope conceptually with the complexity of what we are designing. So much for the greater adequacy of our future tools, which was the basis of the fifth argument.

As an aside I would like to insert a warning to those who identify the difficulty of the programming task with the struggle against the inadequacies of our current tools, because they might conclude that, once our tools will be much more adequate, programming will no longer be a problem. Programming will remain very difficult, because once we have freed ourselves from the circumstantial cumbersomeness, we will find ourselves free to tackle the problems that are now well beyond our programming capacity.

You can quarrel with my sixth argument, for it is not so easy to collect experimental evidence for its support, a fact that will not prevent me from believing in its validity. Up till now I have not mentioned the word "hierarchy," but I think that it is fair to say that this is a key concept for all systems embodying a nicely factored solution. I could even go one step further and make an article of faith out of it, *viz.* that the only problems we can really solve in a satisfactory manner are those that finally admit a nicely factored solution. At first sight this view of human limitations may strike you as a rather depressing view of our predicament, but I don't feel it that way. On the contrary, the best way to learn to live with our limitations is to know them. By the time that we are sufficiently modest to try factored solutions only, because the other efforts escape our intellectual grip, we shall do our utmost to avoid all those interfaces impairing our ability to factor the system in a helpful way. And I can not but expect that this will repeatedly lead to the discovery that an initially untractable problem can be factored after all. Anyone who has seen how the majority of the troubles of the compiling phase called "code generation" can be tracked down to funny properties of the order code will know a simple example of the kind of things I have in mind. The wider applicability of nicely factored solutions is my sixth and last argument for the technical feasibility of the revolution that might take place in the current decade.

In principle I leave it to you to decide for yourself how much weight you are going to give to my considerations, knowing only too well that I can force no one else to share my beliefs. As in each serious revolution, it will provoke violent opposition and one can ask oneself where to expect the conservative forces trying to counteract such a development. I don't expect them primarily in big business, not even in the computer business; I expect them rather in the educational institutions that provide today's training and in those conservative groups of computer users that think their old programs so important that they don't think it worthwhile to rewrite and improve them. In this connection it is sad to observe that on many a university campus the choice of the central computing facility has too often been determined by the demands of a few established but expensive applications with a disregard of the question, how many thousands of "small users" who are willing to write their own programs are going to suffer from this choice. Too often, for instance, high-energy physics seems to have blackmailed the scientific community with the price of its remaining experimental equipment. The easiest answer, of course, is a flat denial of the technical feasibility, but I am afraid that you need pretty strong arguments for that. No reassurance, alas, can be obtained from the remark that the intellectual ceiling of today's average programmer will prevent the revolution from taking place: with others programming so much more effectively, he is liable to be edged out of the picture anyway.

There may also be political impediments. Even if we know how to educate tomorrow's professional programmer, it is not certain that the society we are living in will allow us to do so. The first effect of teaching a methodology—rather than disseminating knowledge—is that of enhancing the capacities of the already capable, thus magnifying the difference in intelligence. In a society in which the educational system is used as an instrument for the establishment of a homogenized culture, in which the cream is prevented from rising to the top, the education of competent programmers could be politically unpalatable.

Let me conclude. Automatic computers have now been with us for a quarter of a century. They have had a great impact on our society in their capacity as tools, but in that capacity their influence will be but a ripple on the surface of our culture compared with the much more profound influence they will have in their capacity of intellectual challenge which will be without precedent in the cultural history of mankind. Hierarchical systems seem to have the property that something considered as an undivided entity on one level is considered as a composite object on the next lower level of greater detail; as a result the natural grain of space or time that is applicable at each level decreases by an order of magnitude when we shift our attention from one level to the next lower one. We understand walls in terms of bricks, bricks in terms of crystals, crystals in terms of molecules, etc. As a result the number of levels that can be distinguished meaningfully in a hierarchical system is kind of proportional to the logarithm of the ratio between the largest and the smallest grain, and therefore, unless this ratio is very large, we cannot expect many levels. In computer programming our basic building block has an associated time grain of less than a microsecond, but our program may take hours of computation time. I do not know of any other technology covering a ratio of 10^{10} or more: the computer, by virtue of its fantastic speed, seems to be the first to provide us with an environment where highly hierarchical artifacts are both possible and necessary. This challenge, *viz.* the confrontation with the programming task, is so unique that this novel experience can teach us a lot about ourselves. It should deepen our understanding of the processes of design and creation; it should give us better control over the task of organizing our thoughts. If it did not do so, to my taste we should not deserve the computer at all!

It has already taught us a few lessons, and the one I have chosen to stress in this talk is the following. We shall do a much better programming job, provided that we approach the task with a full appreciation of its tremendous difficulty, provided that we stick to modest and elegant programming languages, provided that we respect the intrinsic limitations of the human mind and approach the task as Very Humble Programmers.

2
Software Engineering

J. N. Buxton
University of Warwick

1 Introduction

This paper summarizes briefly the content of a course of lectures held in Switzerland in 1974 on the general topic of software engineering. The course could have been subtitled "A series of talks across the academic–practical user interface: An area of computing characterized not so much by an interface as by a morass of misunderstanding."

Software, in this context, is taken to mean large programs of some generality and with many users—so it includes substantial applications programs as well as suppliers' basic software. What are the desirable properties of software? For example, generality, flexibility, reliability, efficiency; more precisely, working reliably to specification, on time, and for a reasonable cost. The present state of affairs is otherwise. In many sensitive areas, software is late, expensive, unreliable and does not work to specification. This is known as the "software crisis."

The importance of the situation can be shown by quoting a few figures. Overall software costs in the U.S.A. are estimated to be of the order of one thousand million dollars per year, or more than 1% of the Gross National Product. Some individual projects: the "man in space" project software costs from 1960–1970 were about one thousand million dollars; the development cost of OS 360 to 1969 was about two hundred million dollars. The indirect costs of late delivery and poor performance are hard to quantify, but are probably at least as great. So, the problem of how to improve software is very real and practical.

2 History

Relatively speaking, 15 or so years ago there were no big software problems: also, there was no big software. In 1961 the released software for the IBM 709 amounted to about 100K words of program. Software was built by small groups of highly qualified people and in many cases was the result of close, if informal, cooperation between university and industry. Looking back it seems like a "golden age"—however, the seeds of future problems were becoming apparent. Software was normally undocumented and bugs could only be fixed by the man who built it originally. It was inflexible and normally inextensible.

A software industry was beginning to grow up and meet its first real problems. One of these was the problem of overpersonalized and undocumented design in an industry which quickly became one of high mobility. Another, in a rapidly growing business, was the problem of using less well-trained staff. High level languages were regarded as the solution to this problem as well as an aid to productivity.

In the early 1960s two major steps occurred and in these steps in particular I think we can see the origins of the software crisis. The first step was the early attempts to tackle the really big problems—for example, in aerospace and real-time control. These problems often combined massive data processing with stringent real-time complexity and they greatly overextended the technology of the day. The second big step was the introduction of the first big comprehensive machine ranges—in particular, System 360. This set the software designers a problem two orders of magnitude harder than before —both to handle a configuration range from tiny to elephantine and also to provide a functional range covering computing from data processing through scientific applications to the edges of realtime control.

The magnitude of the problems of software was discussed at length in the NATO conferences held in 1968 and 1969. During the last few years I think it is possible to distinguish three main lines of thought as to how software should be designed and built, which I characterize as the cottage industry, heavy engineering, and applied logic approaches.

3 Cottage industry

This starts from the observation that most good software in general use has been developed by small groups. Furthermore, its aims are probably limited to giving good service in rather narrow areas. At first, such software often came from universities with little documentation and less support. However, this is no longer the case, and much good and well-supported work is produced, in particular by small software houses often with strong university connections. The main limitations on the cottage industry approach is that it does not help us to face the really big problems, where we must deploy massive resources to make any real impact. The cottage industry approach probably only works with projects which can be done by tightly organized groups within less than 20 man-years.

4 Heavy engineering

This leads us to the view that software designers and constructors must use the techniques of a big and complex technological industry to tackle the really big problems. Such large scale projects demand consideration of, for example, the management techniques appropriate to organizations of hundreds or even thousands of engineers. Problems arise partly in control and also in recording or documentation of the work. Both are severe and costly but not insuperable, and the heavy engineering approach has some outstanding successes—for example, the Apollo project.

Some suggested principles can be extracted as possible guidelines for such an industry—for example:

(i) Software is incompressible in time—if a project is running late it is usually disastrous to take on more people to help.
(ii) Design the system to use not more than 75% of the available resources —then you have something in hand to implement design changes.
(iii) Employ good staff.
(iv) Keep them gaining experience on similar work—this was one of the keys to the Apollo success.

But one crucial problem is begged in this analysis—how do you actually design a big system? It seems that the most successful examples of systems are not so much designed as evolved through many iterations by a process of Darwinian selection. Unfortunately, economic pressures on the industry are often such that we cannot wait that long, and so the dinosaurs go into service rather than quietly being allowed to fade away.

5 Applied logic

According to this approach, software is an abstract product whose behaviour is governed by the laws of logic. The construction of software is therefore determined by the rules of applied computer science in the same way as the design of an aeroplane is bounded by the laws of materials science and of aeronautics. Unfortunately, we do not yet know all the laws, and until our theoretical knowledge has advanced further, we are limited in the size and complexity of the software projects which we should undertake. We do have rules in the structured programming field and we do have some useful theorems to guide us, but their application is slow and arduous.

For some time we have suffered from a basic dichotomy of view as to the nature of software, whether it is an abstract product subject to logic or an engineering product subject in some way to less rigid laws. I suggest the dilemma can be resolved as follows. Software, on an ideal machine, is indeed abstract. However, a software system on a real machine, with interfaces involving people, is not fully abstract and so has some characteristics which have analogies in the indeterminacy principles of physics and in biology. So, in a sense, both parties to the argument are correct. Where possible, and in an increasing area, we need to apply rigour and proofs. Elsewhere we apply typically biological techniques, such as redundancy or drastic reinitialization to rescue a system drifting into trouble.

6 Systems Design

Let us now take up the basic problem—how should one design big systems? There are no shortcuts to success—design is a question of style and of the designer's ability and experience. The basic purpose of a system is to perform to its functional specification in an economical and reliable way. Our thesis is that to be economical, it must be reliable, and in designing reliable systems lies the difficulty. We can only establish reliability by testing to the full, and we can only do this if we can design systems for which we can specify an exhaustive set of test cases small enough to be tested.

Big systems are large and complex and the basic design principle is that of "divide and rule." Divide the system into modules by the process of systems design, eventually validated by system tests. Then program the modules, for example by structured programming, validated by module tests. The problem we now face is that of how to divide the system into modules.

Modularization was first used as a managerial device to break the work of a big project up into controllable units, and apparently for this purpose the details of the division are not very important. To produce a testable system, however, the splitting up is crucial. It must be done so as to minimize, to order, and to make explicit the connection between the modules. The key to producing a system which can be validated is to massively reduce and to order the system connectivity.

7 Design methodology

There are no rules on how to do this, but some helpful methodological guidelines have been developed in recent years. The keynote behind these guidelines is that of hierarchical ordering as a technique, and possibly the only technique, to control complexity. The principles discussed here have hierarchical ordering as their aim; they overlap considerably and in some respects they are different ways of expressing the same ideas. An unstructured multiply connected network is a good model for many classically designed systems—and a hierarchical structure is orders of magnitude more accessible. The design effort needed to produce a well-ordered system may well seem at first to be much greater, but the improvement in quality is in the long run far more important.

The first idea is that of "levels of abstraction" due to Dijkstra. The modules in the system are ordered into levels in a tree structure. The basic principles are that modules in a particular level may only call on the services of modules at lower levels, and that resources used by modules on one level are hidden from modules at higher levels. Each level in effect specifies an "abstract machine": the lowest level is the hardware—or the software provided by the manufacturers—and the highest level is an abstract machine whose functions are precisely those required by the system specification. Each intermediate level specifies one important level of abstraction in the process of converting the given hardware to the required system. How do you divide up the system functions into well-ordered abstract machines? Well, by practice and experience, and by doing it wrong a few times first!

An alternative way of looking at the problem has been given by Parnas, who proposes "information hiding" as the criterion for division into modules. The idea is that every module encapsulates a design decision which it conceals from all other modules. This is a direct attack on the problem of system flexibility—if a design decision needs to be changed then it is the affair of only one module. All other modules communicate only by explicit function calls and parameters and so, if a module is changed, implicit effects of the change are not propagated throughout the system.

A third and composite approach aims to minimize the overall connectivity. System functions are grouped into modules, and generalized where necessary, so as to produce a minimum number of connections while retaining modules of manageable size and internal structure.

The study of design methodologies is clearly in its early days, when much discussion is really about terminology rather than facts, and when few clear principles have emerged. Nevertheless, what is already available can in practice be effective and useful.

8 The chief programmer team

In conclusion I wish to draw together the following ideas:

(i) that design is an affair of individual style and experience, like architecture, and so the ultimate responsibility for a computing system design should be in the hands of an identifiable individual;
(ii) that the structure of the group building a system should reflect the structure of the system design, not the other way round;
(iii) that in the vast majority of cases it is economically far more effective to produce a structured and rigorously testable design in the beginning, rather than to save on design effort and hope to debug it later.

These threads are brought together in the "chief programmer teams" experiments carried out by Harlan Mills at IBM. The best known is the N.Y. Times Information Bank system, which Mills undertook to build as a substantial databank system for a real customer. The design was done in top-down style, specifying the total system first with "program stubs" representing subsidiary modules or subsystems. Structured programming was used as the implementation technique. The team consisted of a nucleus with Mills as chief programmer, a backup or reserve chief programmer, an administrator to handle contractual interfaces, and a program librarian to administer the program and documentation texts. Specialist programmers were called in as required to complete the "program stubs": the analogy is with a surgical team under the control of one responsible surgeon but with specialist help as needed.

The result of the experiment was markedly successful. The system was delivered on time, working to specification and within the budget. The quality was exceptionally high and the system contained no serious errors and very few minor ones. The overall programmer productivity was estimated to be about double that obtainable by conventional techniques.

Of course, the success of one experiment is not a complete justification for a new approach, but clearly this line is well worth further investigation. In my view, a combination of the chief programmer team organization with design methodology and structured programming is the best way to proceed at present with a software project.

9 Bibliography

[Baker 72; Buxton 75*; Dijkstra 71b*; Liskov 72; Parnas 72f*; Wirth 71a*]

3
Software Engineering—
Some Principles and Problems*

W. M. Turski
Institute of Informatic
Warsaw University, Poland

Software engineering is a relatively new name coined to denote a rapidly growing body of knowledge concerned with computer-program design, composition and production. The art of programming is, of course, much older than software engineering of which it is an essential ingredient; many principles of good programming are considered as cornerstones of software engineering. It is not, however, a case of total immersion: not all time-honoured practices of "clever" programmers could be included among the techniques recommended to a software engineer. To quote but two examples: tricky programming in which an expert programmer takes advantage of his intimate knowledge of the machine code of the computer for which he programs in order to use certain bit patterns for two or more different purposes (e.g., as an instruction and as a constant) is an antithesis of the entire software engineering philosophy. Similarly, once highly fashionable overall code optimization in computer produced programs (like in compiler produced object codes) is considered almost a waste of time by software engineering; in case of compilers and other code generating programs, it is recommended instead to aim for satisfactory code first and restrict the fine tuning (local optimization) to such portions of the code which are found to be executed most frequently or for the longest periods of time.

Software engineering is equally concerned with the quality of the programmer's products and with the efficiency of the process of getting this product.

*This paper is dedicated to Academician L. Iliev on his 60th birthday.

While exact standards of program quality are not as yet established, one can list at least some components of this notion.

1. A good program should be *correct*. This requirement is neither trivial nor easy to satisfy. First of all, it is by no means clear what the meaning of the expression "correct program" is. As the popular saying goes: "there are no incorrect programs—they are just other programs". A software engineer tends to understand that "correct program" means a "program which acting upon data satisfying given conditions C_1 will eventually produce results satisfying conditions C_2." In other words, a correct program for a given transformation of data is any one about which it can be proven that it indeed performs this transformation. Thus, for any given problem there may exist a whole class of correct programs and correctness alone cannot be taken as a hallmark of quality; properties required in the following points indicate some of the other attributes of this notion.

It should be pointed out, however, that the above definition of correctness is in the majority of cases oversimplified, and nearly always too primitive. A more realistic definition requires that a program S is correct if, given condition C_1 (which is a statement about initial state), program S will terminate in a state satisfying another given condition C_2 and at all observable states during the program execution a specified relation (perhaps a composite one) will be observed; such relations are often called invariants. Conditions C_1 are known as preconditions, C_2 as postconditions of S. Now, it is virtually impossible to test the correctness of any but the simplest programs by case examples. Consider, for instance, a program for evaluation of an integer-valued function F of integer, but otherwise unrestricted, arguments; assume further that it is required of F to take only non-zero values. No matter how many test cases are evaluated, we can never be assured—on the strength of these tests alone—that F indeed does not take the value zero for some argument.

A very profound observation on this subject has been formulated by E. W. Dijkstra: "testing may show a presence of an error, never the absence of errors". This is not to say that test cases are completely useless: they may provide useful information about the pattern of program evolution (e. g. the time characteristics), but we have to look for other methods of establishing correctness. These methods must necessarily be similar to mathematical proof techniques since the assertions which are proven are usually expressed in a manner similar to mathematics. A number of important lessons follow from this observation:

(i) In order to ease the task of correctness proving, programs should be decomposed into smaller units in such a way that
a. corresponding initial and final conditions would be easily deriveable from C_1 and C_2;
b. there would be known rules of inference permitting derivation of assertions about entities composed in a given way from smaller units;

c. the decomposition should be applicable recursively until primitive units are obtained.

(ii) A body of theorems should be assembled, such that

a. properties of primitive units into which programs decompose are established;

b. rules of inference referred to in (i) are formulated in a rigorous fashion;

c. a sufficiently rich class of correct programs can be constructed from primitive units by inference rules.

(iii) Our ability to prove correctness of programs critically depends on rigorous formulation of postconditions and preconditions, i.e., on our ability to give rigorous specification for the programmers task.

As a practically important consequence of this insight into the program correctness issue, the software engineering approach requires that the correctness of a program should be established along with the program construction and not be left to a later stage; it turns out that including the correctness consideration in the programming process provides an invaluable aid in achieving a given goal in an overall better way. Thus we see that considerations about the quality of the product lead to recommendations with respect to the process of obtaining this product.

The decomposability of programs—*modularity* as it is often called—is not only a means to prove their correctness and a means to conquer complexity, but also a very useful tool to achieve other properties of good programs.

2. A good program should be *adaptable*. Construction of a large program is an expensive undertaking in terms of human effort (and other resources) used. It is also a lengthy process. Often, while a program is being constructed, its specifications, i.e., stated objectives, will be changed, sometimes quite substantially. Of course, with a very drastic change of specifications one cannot expect a programming project to be completed without fundamental changes; there is, however, a class of changes in specifications which can be catered for by suitable changes in the project undertaken. It is not generally known how "large" the class of admissible specification changes is, neither do we know, in general, how to introduce changes in the program being constructed; research in this direction belongs to the most interesting and important areas of computing science.

Nevertheless, we know already that a modular structure of programs helps considerably to introduce at least a measure of adaptability. A simple example will illustrate this point. Assume that the problem to be solved is a compiler for a programming language. The modular approach dictates that the compiler will consist of a hierarchy of well-defined parts, each having a prescribed functional behaviour in terms used by its "superior" modules and calling on "subservient" modules for execution of subtasks which are refined, i.e., developed into smaller units on a lower level. Of course, a concrete set of modules used in a compiler will depend on many programming decisions, but it is quite likely that among the modules there will be one, called, e.g., Lexical Preprocessor, whose task is to read a stream of input characters and convert it into a stream of tokens of which statements of the language being compiled are composed. The task of the Lexical Preprocessor may, e.g., consist is deleting blanks and other display features of the source text, suppressing comments and condensing the so-called fat characters (as, for example, **begin, else** in ALGOL 60) into single tokens. Other modules of the compiler may use operation "get next token" which is expanded by the Lexical Preprocessor into "read" and "skip" operations, where "skip" is a controlled loop consisting in, depending on the case in hand, either reading and "forgetting" blanks, or reading and forgetting characters of a comment, or reading and "forgetting" consecutive characters of a "fat" character. A concrete implementation of the Lexical Preprocessor will, naturally, include code table geared to the representation of input characters. If now specification for the compiler changed in such a way that instead of "compact binary" representation on magnetic tape the input will be presented in ISO Code on paper tape, it is sufficient to change only the Lexical Preprocessor (and then perhaps only a part of it), leaving the remaining modules of the compiler unchanged.

3. A good program should be *robust*. It is not sufficient that a program is correct (in the sense explained above on p. 30). It should also behave in a predictable fashion when faced with unforseen initial conditions. One cannot expect a program to work according to specifications if its preconditions are not satisfied, but a good program should recognize the case and signal it in an unambiguous way. As an example, consider a program used for displaying characters on a monitor, and assume for simplicity that it displays only 26 letters and a blank, i.e., a total of 27 different characters. Assume further that, as input, this program gets a five-bit signal, which means that there are 32 different combinations representable by the signal. Correct program will display desired character in 27 valid cases, a robust program will not only do this, but also actively notify if given one of the illegal combinations. Of course, no module using our display program should send such an illegal combination, and *their* correctness requires that only legal combinations are sent; it is not only cheaper, however, but also safer to check this fact on input to the display program. As a corollary, consider that the display program module may be used in another environment, where signals to be displayed are obtained, e.g., by truncating to 5 bits longer messages and correctness criteria apply there only to the latter.

Frequent checks, even of the most obviously true facts, are symptoms of a well-engineered software and form error-proof barriers. Hardware designers may very well infer from this a hint that it would be very desirable to have a cheap method of performing checks which with high probability give positive answers (rather like overflow checks which, in most cases, cost nothing and cause interrupt only when an overflow occurs).

4. A good program should be *stable*. Stability of programs is a notion similar to robustness and adaptability and is the property of a program which can cope with large classes of data. We refer to this property essentially because it is often impossible to verify that data supplied satisfy preconditions of a program (e.g., large volumes of numeric values), since the validation process may be of the same complexity as the program itself. The program is expected to work properly only for data satisfying the precondition, but if the data deviate from the desired precondition only a little, the program should give an almost satisfactory performance. It is relatively easy to satisfy this requirement in numerical applications (where it is quite often reduced to numerical stability of the algorithm), but an example from an entirely different field will, hopefully, illustrate a more general point. Consider a large program monitoring a complex real-time object (e.g., a Lunar mission). Under normal circumstances this program receives a great many inputs from sensors and telemetric installations and performs many different functions. Under adverse circumstances some of these inputs may be subject to severe distortion and some may be totally absent. A stable program should nevertheless function, in a sense selecting these modules which can work correctly and perhaps activating emergency routines in others.

A well-engineered software product should not fail completely on account of a single input error; if it degrades (and degrade it must if preconditions are not satisfied), it should do so smoothly.

Having established correctness, adaptability, robustness and stability requirements, we may proceed to the next stage, namely to *program optimality*. Of course, it is rather meaningless to talk about optimality at large, global optimality; clearly, there are too many aspects of this notion, and quite often they are conflicting. Thus it would be much more reasonable to consider only conditional or relative optimality, i.e., optimality with respect to a chosen attribute of a good program. Obvious candidates for such attributes are: time economy, storage economy, fast response to on-line queries, minimal average service queue. One can multiply examples of such secondary requirements no end, but the real point is that they are viewed as secondary only, yielding priority to considerations outlined before. In this connection it is very appropriate to quote P. Landin: why should we spend a lot of time trying to program optimally, only to discover that we do not have a working program, rather than getting it working correctly first and worry about any improvements later? (this quotation —as all others in this paper is based on recollection rather than actual papers, thus some inadverent twists of the wording are quite possible).

A typical problem raised by software engineering with respect to the construction of modules is the one of *module size*. Using a simplified model and an analogy to building blocks with which our children play so keenly, this problem can be stated as follows. With small modules a lot of information needs to be distributed to modules forming up a program thus causing a considerable information traffic within the system. The larger the modules are, the more information becomes localized to blocks and, on the average, the information traffic within the system becomes less dense. One can even consider—as limiting cases—a maximum size of a module, i.e., a whole program in which case there is no information traffic within the system (of course, this by no means excludes the input/output traffic), and a minimum size of a module, a single machine instruction, to which no information is local and thus, as if it were, whole current state is handed over (and in these terms it becomes indeed a very heavy traffic). On the other hand, assuming a small size of modules we gain considerable flexibility (cf. kids' building blocks) which decreases with the growth in size of an average module. There is also a third pertinent point of view, i.e., the considerations of "intermodular friction": smaller modules tend to be interfaced one with another by "larger surfaces," replacement of a module with large interface causes considerable "friction," requiring perhaps adjustment in other models interfaced to it; when this phenomenon reaches a certain level, a change in a module may lead to a rewrite of all, or nearly all, remaining blocks (this is known as system explosion, and can be seen in the growing number of individual module handlings between consecutive releases of, e.g., OS360, resulting in a fission process—two operating systems being a replacement of one; justification of this remark is supplied by results due mostly to M. M. Lehman).

While no general results in this field are yet available, it seems that paradoxes can be best avoided by consistent application of hierarchical structuring rather than by flat structures of a great many equal subordinates to one control subroutine. By hierarchical decomposition we almost achieve the best of both approaches: we start with relatively large modules and decompose them into smaller ones to be further decomposed.

The discussion presented in the last few paragraphs indicates how the software engineering approach leads to the study of programs as physical objects; important results are to be expected in this area from application of notions and techniques of statistical physics and information theory.

The second class of problems to which a software engineer addresses himself in a way different from that of a traditional programmer is concerned with *data structures*.

From the data handling point of view, traditional programming could be characterized by saying that data structuring was both process- and machine-dependent. By this I mean that data structures were declared within a program and declarations (or data specification parts in more general sense) were highly dependent on the characteristics of particular storage media available within the system. This approach turned out to be quite insufficient when systems dealing with very large collections of data came into being. Practical considerations forced a reevaluation of adopted models, which permitted much cleaner and intellectually more satisfying ideas to be formulated and—to some extent—implemented.

Software engineering recognizes the existence of *data morphology*, i.e., structures in data aggregates, independently of any processing to be undertaken over such data. Morphology of data aggregates can (and should) be described in terms which are related only to the data and ordering relations defined on data. On the other hand, storage media have structures of their own, induced by hardware characteristics and by the software addressing mechanism.

An implementation, or data representation, is obtained by mapping data structures into storage structures. This map can be considered as an interface in two different senses:

1. It is an interface between two levels of abstraction: on one side of this interface we find the relations existing in data aggregates, on the other side —relations between storage locations (and their groupings, such as cylinders or tracks) occupied by data representations in the storage medium.

2. Second interpretation of the interface relates it to the machine-and process-independence. Identical data description can be used by many installations, and, which is even more important, by many different programs (this is the fundamental idea of the so-called data banks). By a suitable mapping this "abstract" description is transformed into a "concrete" one, taking into account specific features of the program or of the hardware installation.

The most important advantage of the treatment described consists in the separation of features specific to data proper from features specific to data representation in storage. A programmer can now use the first set of properties in composing the structure of his program and in establishing its correctness, adaptability and stability. Only when going to a more detailed description of the computation, in expanding his program so as to take into account implementational features, does he include the mapping of data structures into storage structures, much in the same way as he maps, e.g., operations of an external language into operations of the machine code; thus most of the *problem solving* is carried out without cluttering his reasoning with unnecessary details of concrete representation of data. (The reader will note, however, that the robustness considerations were conspicuously left out from the list of program characteristics established on the level not involving the interface; the display program example, considered above, gives an ample justification for this omission.)

The general concept of levels of abstraction or, looking from the other point of view: "levels of detail", is this inherent feature of software engineering approach which is all-important in data handling by information processing systems. Violation of this principle by software designers—patently evident in some systems delivered by computer manufacturers—has an excruciatingly painful effect: the implementational considerations, injected into an inappropriately high level of abstraction, form an opaque medium in which the program structure cannot be seen, while proliferation of details makes it virtually impossible to establish any properties of the program.

It should be emphasized that it is not only when dealing with large volumes of data that the morphological properties ought to be treated separately from implementational ones; also when the morphology is complex (and this could be the case even with data aggregates of a very modest size) mixing it with the specificities of the implementation cannot but obscure the problem. Hence, the software engineering advises the following scheme: the data is described by its morphological (i.e., identifying and relational) features, programming languages provide means to map these features into syntactical constructs (of which the morphological properties will be the semantic interpretation); the syntactical constructs are then refined ("further specified", "defined in more detail") by the implementation of the mapping from data structures to storage structures. Only the last part of the model is hardware oriented.

It is, of course, quite a difficult problem: how to design syntactical constructs to be used in programming languages in such a way that sufficiently rich variety of morphological features could be expressed by these constructs; it is evidently clear that we shall not succeed if we do not study the morphology of data and restrict our attention to such cases which could be mapped into constructs already available in the existing languages.

Acknowledgment. Even though no references in this paper are explicitly given, it is my pleasant duty to thank my Colleagues in IFIP Working Group 2.3 (Programming Methodology) for being a constant source of inspiration for thoughts expressed in the above contribution.

4
The Engineering of Software: A Startling Contradiction

C. A. R. Hoare
University of Oxford

The comparison of ideals

If words could cure the ills of our profession of programming, what a healthy and highly respected profession it would now be! We have had "modular programming"; the craze for "structured programming" has hardly yet reached the height of its commercial profitablity; and already we have a newcomer to the charts—the theme we have all so long been waiting for—yes, it's "SOFTWARE ENGINEERING". The experienced programmer will greet the gladsome tidings with a stifled yawn, and turn to more urgent and important tasks. But perhaps there is something he could learn from these catch phrases on their passage from popularity to oblivion. Certainly, the latest combination of the new but already tarnished word "software" with the old and respected profession of engineering is such a startling contradiction that it should give us pause. Let us compare the ideals of the professional engineer with those adopted by some programmers of the present day.

Ability and understanding

One outstanding characteristic of the professional man, be he a doctor, architect, or engineer, is that he understands the real needs of his client or employer, often very much better than the client himself; and he has the ability and status to persuade the client to recognise his own interests and to abandon his less useful flights of fancy.

Professional integrity

Then he has the professional skill to recommend from a range of known and trusted techniques those methods that in the given circumstance will achieve the required effect at minimum cost and inconvenience to the client. And finally, he has the professional integrity to resign his post or commission if his recommendations are not accepted.

Resignation when advice not taken

I fear that there is a sad contrast with some programmers, whose only wish is that their client should "make up his mind what he wants," and who will welcome his most elaborate fancies as a challenge to their programming ingenuity. How many of them are ignorant of, or prefer to ignore, the known techniques used successfully by others, and embark on some spatchcocked implementation of their own defective invention? And I know only one programmer who resigned on the spot when his advice was not taken by his less technically competent manager.

Reducing costs and increasing reliability

A second characteristic of the good engineer is his vigilance in seeking every opportunity to reduce the costs and increase the reliability of his product. He realizes that the conflict between these two objectives can be resolved only by preserving the utmost simplicity of concept, specification, design, and implementation. Above all, he insists that he shall have a complete understanding and control over every aspect of his project—and the more difficult his project, the more firmly will he insist on the simplicity without which he cannot understand what he is doing. Here again, we find exactly the opposite characteristic in some of our best programmers, who deliberately avoid simplified solutions; they obtain satisfaction from the sophistication of their designs and methods, and derive excitement from engaging in projects of a complexity slightly beyond their ability to understand and control. They may well succeed once; but on the next occasion they may discover that there is no way of distinguishing (in advance) between what is slightly and what is totally beyond their comprehension.

Sound theories and techniques

A great advantage of the present day engineer is that his designs are based on sound mathematical theories and computational techniques, discovered over the years by his brilliant predecessors, and now enshrined in textbooks and undergraduate teaching, in mathematical tables, and in standard codes of practice. But in spite of the soundness of his theory, he still has many causes for worry that his abstractions (and his product) may break down—a faulty casting, a defective batch of components, a lazy workman, or an unpredictable natural hazard.

The computer programmer has little worry of this kind: his working material is the hardware of the computer itself, and its reliability can usually be taken for granted. Certainly, by far the most significant cause of failure in software are the errors and oversights of the programmer himself. But here perhaps he is not wholly to blame, since he has no widely accepted mathematical or theoretical foundation for his work. This is a most urgent topic of research at our universities and elsewhere, and it is to be hoped that the results will be most widely and most rapidly propagated.

Mastery of tools

A final point of contrast lies in the working tools of the profession. An engineer naturally demands of his tools the highest quality and precision, reliability, convenience, and cheapness in use. In many professions, the tools are quite simple; in others they are more complex. But in either case the engineer has developed an intuitive understanding and ingrained mastery of their proper uses; and this frees him to devote his whole intellectual effort to the understanding and solution of his clients' problems.

The basic tools of the programmer are the programming languages and compilers, job control languages and operating systems, utilities and other software supplied in profusion by the manufacturer of his computer. But what a sorry comparison with the tools of other professions! That they are unreliable, that they are profligate of computer time and storage, that they are inconvenient in operation—these are facts that have been long recognized and widely suffered.

Complexity...

Perhaps the worst symptom (and also a large part of the cause of the trouble) is their extraordinary and still increasing complexity, which totally beggars the comprehension of both user and designer. Among manufacturers' software one can find what must be the worst engineered products of the computer age. No wonder it was given away free—and a very expensive gift it was, to the recipient!

Masquerading as power...

But still we have some experienced programmers and managers who actually welcome the stuff, praise it, want more of it, and even pay for it. Here perhaps the fatal attraction is the very complexity, which would revolt the instincts of any engineer, but which, to the clever programmer, masquerades as power and sophistication. He may have even less creditable motives: the use of unreliable tools both increases and excuses the unreliability of his programs; the use of inefficient tools both increases and excuses the inefficiency of his programs; and the complexity of his tools can protect him from close scrutiny or control of his client or employer.

Resulting in perpetuation

And finally, after a few years experience of some particular product, the programmer finds that even his partial understanding of it can command a high salary; and he has the strongest motive for refusing to learn something new, and for rejecting the idea that it might possibly be an improvement. And his manager who committed himself to that product many years ago has an even stronger personal and financial interest in its perpetuation.

A discipline of software engineering

The attempt to build a discipline of software engineering on such shoddy foundations must surely be doomed, like trying to base chemical engineering on the phlogiston theory, or astronomy on the assumption of a flat earth. But the study of manufacturers' software is an excellent way to sharpen our understanding of the principles of software engineering, both because of its consistent violation of those principles, and because it makes a serious and creditable attempt to define the working tools of the software engineer.

It is important to take an optimistic, practical and forwardlooking approach. There are many ways in which existing tools can be used more effectively—by adoption of supplementary software packages, by instrumentation and tuning, by program editors and preprocessors, by structured programming aids, training manuals and courses, and by standards of programming practice. It is desirable to survey the range of methods which are immediately available for practical use, and to look slightly further ahead, and describe some of the possibilities of further improvement that are now being opened up by fundamental and applied research. Even if the practical difficulties of change delay the widespread application of results of new research, it is important that programmers and managers should understand now what they are; so that they are never again led astray by the specious promise of sophistication and complexity.

Evidence?

In this short sermon on the theme of software engineering, I have made many allegations against the quality of software, and against the competence, intelligence, and integrity of programmers. But I have not given a single example to support my case, nor have I named a single name. Let me do so now: I name the guilty man: I name myself. Within myself I have discovered all the faults which I have ascribed to programmers in general. If my remarks carry any conviction, it can only be because my reader has made a similar discovery.

5
Programs, Cities, Students— Limits to Growth?

M. M. Lehman
University of London

The battlefield of programming

In an invited lecture to the 1971 IFIP Congress [Randell 71b*], Brian Randell of the University of Newcastle typified the situation current in the design, implementation and maintenance of computer software systems by showing a slide (Plate I)[1] of a medieval battlefield with ranks aligned but carnage abounding and devastation everywhere.

The situation today is really very little different. The programming systems world is a little older, perhaps a little wiser, but has in its practice not learnt much from the experiences of the last ten years. Many still ride bravely into battle (Plate IIa) determined to master the system that they wish to create or maintain. Most in one way or another fall by the wayside (Plate IIb). And programming expenditure goes up and up and up.

The total picture is however not completely bleak. Some dragons have been slain (Plate III). The need for a discipline of software engineering is recognized [Naur 69b*]. The formulation of concepts of programming methodology exemplified by Dijkstra's concept of structured programming [Dijkstra 72d*] strikes at the roots of the problem. The realization that a program, much as a mathematical theorem, should and can be provable and proven correct as it is developed and maintained [Dijkstra 68e*] and before its results are used will ultimately change the nature of the programming task and the face of the programming world.

[1] My thanks are due to the management of the Alte Pinakothek Museum in Munich for permission and facilities to produce the first three slides, to Mr. P. Young of the Victoria and Albert Museum for the loan of slide four and to the Directors of both museums for permission to reproduce the slides in the published version of the lecture. Also to Professor G. Seegmueller for his assistance in the preparation of the slides.

Plate I

Randell's depiction of the software crisis. (Detail from *Die Alexanderschlacht*, Albrecht Altdorfer, by courtesy of the Alte Pinakothek Museum, Munich.)

Plate II

(a) Ride into Battle. (Detail from *Die Alexanderschlacht*, Albrecht Altdorfer, by courtesy of the Alte Pinakothek Museum, Munich.)

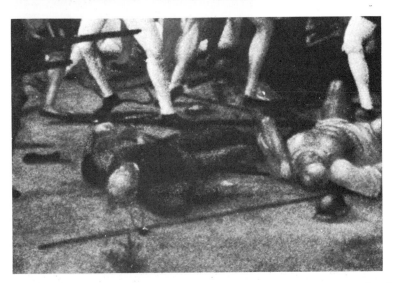

(b) Fallen by the Wayside. (Detail from *Belagarung Von Alexia*, Feselen, by courtesy of the Alte Pinakothek Museum, Munich.)

Plate III

Some Dragons Slain. (Panel from *Altar-piece with scenes from the life of St. George* attributed to Marzal de Sas, by courtesy of the Victoria and Albert Museum, London.)

Plate IV

(a) The Top-down Approach. (Photo-montage on *Die Alexanderschlacht*, Albrecht Altdorfer, by courtesy of the Alte Pinakothek Museum, Munich.)

(b) The anti-regressive ant.

Clearly these developments are of fundamental importance. They offer the only long-term solution to the creation of the masses of programming material that the world appears to require; or at least that computer manufacturers and software houses think the world requires. Nevertheless we must face the fact that progress in mastering the science of program creation, maintenance and expansion will be painful and slow.

The systems approach

Such progress as is currently being made stems primarily from the personal involvement of the researchers and the developers in the programming process at a detailed level. Often they only tackle one problem area: algorithm development, language, structure, correctness proving, code generation, documentation, testing. Others view the process as a whole but are still primarily concerned with the individual steps that, together, take one from concept to computation. And this type of study is clearly essential if real insight is to be gained and progress made.

But application of the scientific method has achieved progress in revealing the nature of the physical world by also pursuing a course other than studying individual phenomena in exquisite detail. A system, a process, a phenomenon, may be viewed in the first place from the outside, observing, clarifying, measuring and modelling identifiable attributes, patterns and trends. From such activities one obtains increasing knowledge and understanding based on the behavior of both the system and its sub-systems, the process and its sub-processes. Following through developing insight in structured fashion, this outside-in approach in due course leads to an understanding of, and an ability to control, the individual phenomena but in the context of their total environments.

In terms of the previous analogy one may overfly (Plate IV) a battle, study it using all available observational tools. Thereby one would observe its ebb and flow identifying the location, global characteristics and, on closer and closer inspection, the nature of the main points of advance, or of chaos and destruction. Having succeeded in this, one may hope to better understand, and hence modify and control, what is going on.

In my present area of interest and concern I have adopted such a structured analysis approach to study the programming process. I shall be showing you samples of data that support this systems approach to the study of the process. One need not search too hard for its conceptual justification. A programming project can involve many hundreds of people and many tens of managers. Many millions of pounds or dollars may be spent on it. Thus individual decisions of almost any form make very little impact on the overall trend. It is really the inertia of people and habits, the momentum of practices and budgets, the general smoothing effect of organizations, that determine the rate of progress and fate of a project.

The roots of the study

Some years ago I undertook a study of the programming process in one particular environment [Lehman 70*]. As part of the study I obtained project statistics of a programming system which had already survived a number of versions or releases. The data for each release of the system included measures of the size of the system, the number of modules added, deleted or changed, the release dates, information on manpower and machine time used and costs involved in each release. In general there were large, apparently stochastic, variations in the individual data items from release to release. But overall the data indicated a general upward trend in the size, complexity and cost of the system and the maintenance process (Figure 1).

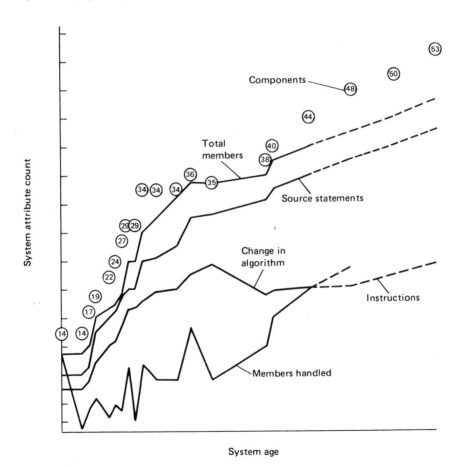

Figure 1   Early data.

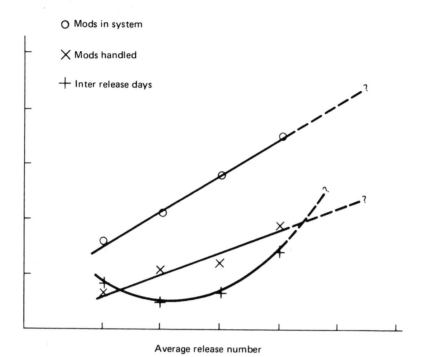

Figure 2   Initial data averaged.

As a first step in my study of this data I averaged the various parameters. The intent was of course to expose any specific trends. And expose them it did. When the averaged data was plotted the previously erratic data had become strikingly smooth (Figure 2).

Some time later additional data (Figure 3) confirmed previous suspicions of nonlinear, possibly exponential, complexity growth. Moreover, extrapolation of the plots suggested further growth trends significantly at odds with the then current project plans. The data was also highly erratic (Figure 4) with major but apparently serially correlated (Figure 5) fluctuations from release to release. Nevertheless almost any form of averaging led to the display of very clear trends (Figure 6). Thus it was natural to apply uni- and multi-variate regression and auto-correlation techniques to fit appropriate regression and time-series models to represent the process for purposes of planning, forecasting and improving it in part or as a whole. In general there was definite evidence that one might consider a software maintenance and enhancement project as a self-regulating organism subject to apparently random shocks, but overall obeying its own specific conservation laws and internal dynamics.

All in all these first observations encouraged me to search for laws that governed the behavior, the dynamics, of the meta-system of organization, people and program material involved in the creation and maintenance process, in the evolution of programming systems.

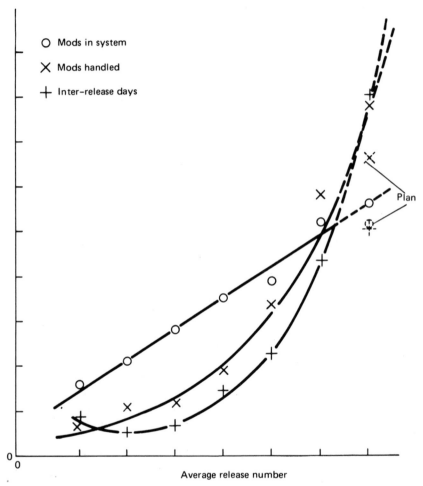

Figure 3   Later data.

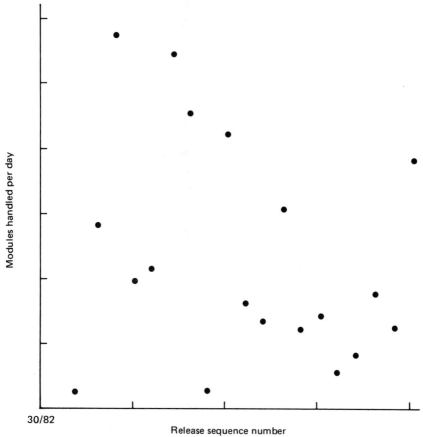

Figure 4   Scattered data.

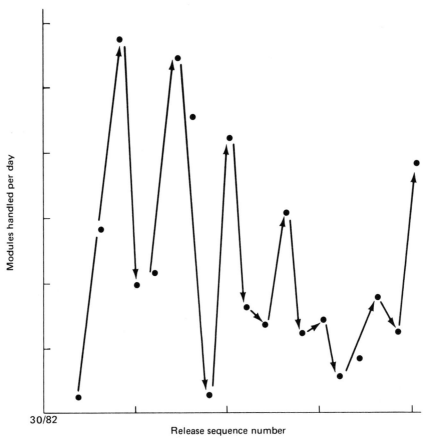

Figure 5 Serial correlation.

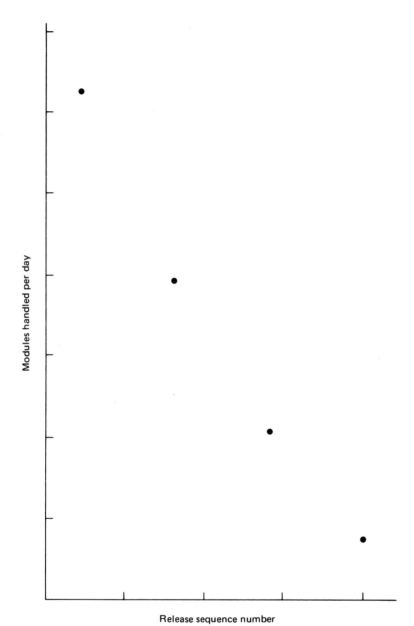

Figure 6   Overall smoothness.

Laws of programming-system life dynamics

It is perhaps necessary to explain here why I repeatedly refer to the continuous creation, maintenance and enhancement of programming systems. It is the actual experience of all who have been involved in the utilization of computing equipment and the running of large multiple-function programs that the latter demand continuous repair and improvement. Thus I postulate as a *First Law* (Figure 7) of Program Evolution Dynamics:

THE LAW OF CONTINUING CHANGE

Software does not face the physical decay problems that hardware faces. But the power and logical flexibility of computing systems, the extending technology of computer application, ever-evolving hardware and the pressures for the exploitation of new application areas all make users demand, and manufacturers encourage, continuous adaptation of programs to keep in step with increasing skill, insight, ambition and opportunity. Thus a programming system undergoes never-ending maintenance and development, driven by the potential difference between current capability and the demands of the environment.

As a system is changed it inevitably becomes more complex and unmanageable. Hence I also postulate a *Second Law*:

THE LAW OF INCREASING ENTROPY

This law too is supported by universal experience and in conjunction with the evidence deduced from such programming project data as has been available and studied, has led me to the formulation of a *Third Law*:

THE LAW OF STATISTICALLY SMOOTH GROWTH

The system and its metasystem, the project organization developing it, constitute an organism constrained by conservation laws. These may be locally overcome, but they direct, constrain and control the long-term growth and development patterns and rates. It is the study of one aspect of this third law, and its generalization, that forms the underlying theme of the remainder of my talk.

I Law of continuing change

A system that is used undergoes continuing change until it becomes more economical to replace it by a new or restructured system

II Law of increasing entropy

The entropy of a system increases with time unless specific work is executed to maintain or reduce it

III Law of statistically smooth growth

Growth trend measures of global system attributes may appear stochastic locally in time and space but are self-regulating and statistically smooth

---

Figure 7   Laws of program evolution dynamics.

Statistical models of system growth

These laws, as formulated now, have gradually evolved as we have pursued our study of the programming task. In the first instance my observations simply led to the conception of an area of study which, at the time, we termed Programming Systems Growth Dynamics [Lehman 71*] but which we now prefer to refer to as 'Evolution Dynamics'. In close association with a colleague, L. Belady (who I am happy to say is here this evening as an SRC-sponsored Senior Visiting Research Fellow) it has also led to the development of statistical and theoretical models, such as those that I shall discuss, and to an ever-increasing understanding of the nature and dynamics of the programming process.

Let me give just one, very significant, illustration of the statistical models. Figure 8 plots the size of the system as measured in modules. Clearly the growth measured as a function of release numbers has been strictly linear. This growth is really very steady. However closer examination of the plot reveals a superimposed ripple (Figure 9). To control engineers this may suggest a self-stabilizing, multi-loop feedback system. Positive feedback arises, for example, from the desire of users to get more

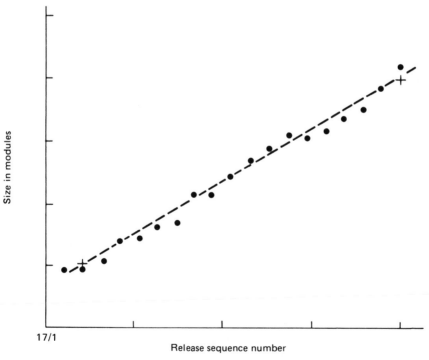

Release sequence number

Figure 8   Linear growth.

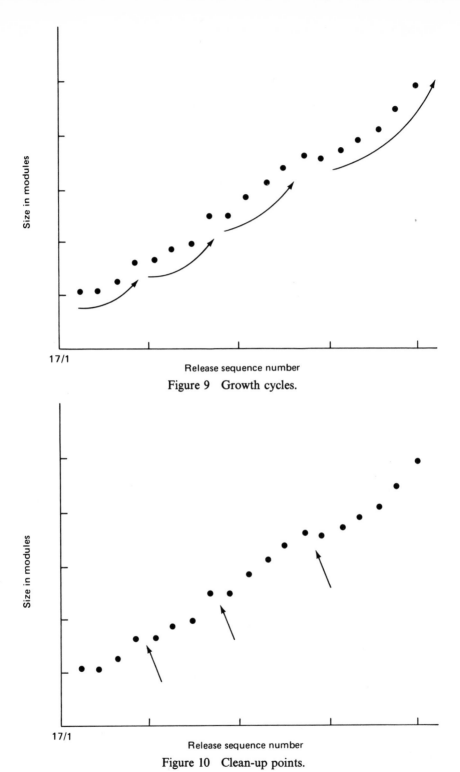

Figure 9   Growth cycles.

Figure 10   Clean-up points.

function, more quickly. This creates the pressures that cause the rate of systems growth to increase.

But a compensating negative feedback every now and again causes a decline (Figure 10). As attempts are made to speed up the growth process, design and implementation may become sloppy, short cuts are adopted, testing is abbreviated, documentation falls behind, errors are made and the fault rate builds up. Changes to the code become progressively more difficult. Project and system entropies have become large, their structures

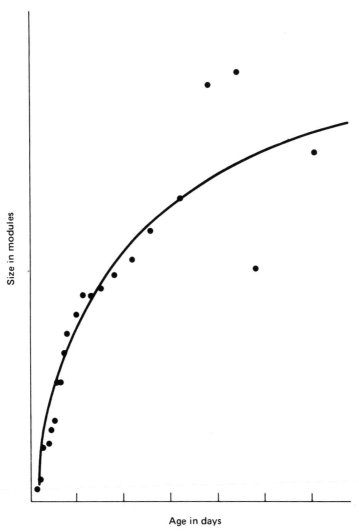

Figure 11   Limit to growth?

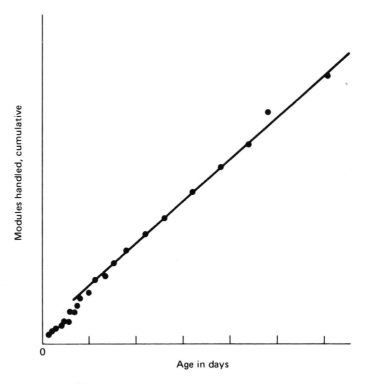

Figure 12   Constant rate of work-output.

have become hazy. The net result is that the growth rate declines. Both systems must be cleaned up, their structures improved, their entropy reduced, before enhancement of the system can be resumed.

Incidentally it may appear strange that apparently valid statistical models are obtained using an arbitrarily assigned 'Release Number' as one of the variables. Its use as a 'pseudo-time' variable can be justified by the 'Principle of Parsimony' [Box 70], the simplicity and regularity of the models that its use yields. A more fundamental justification follows from a fuller understanding of the role of the system release point as a stabilizing or anchor point in the programming process and for the programming organization. In fact what we have termed the 'release number' must really be viewed as the release 'sequence' number, which may well differ from the former and which, quite naturally, forms a basis for the time-series type of analysis [Cox 66]. And there can be no question that results to date fully substantiate the claim that release-based project data provides a useful and powerful planning tool. Used in conjunction with real-time based models (Figure 11, 12) it is also beginning to yield insight into the programming process, insight that will eventually permit its improvement.

The macro models

The Yorktown model

The statistical analysis represents, at most, a tool to guide our understanding, and hence mastery, of the intellectual and organizational effort that really underlies the programming process. In parallel with that analysis Belady and I looked at fundamental aspects of the programming process, searching for representative theoretical models. It is not possible to elaborate on the details of the resultant sequence of models in the present lecture. I will nevertheless show you the forms of two of the earlier ones, without however interpreting all their terms, to give some idea of the approach taken.

As a first approach [Lehman 71*] we developed a model to represent the communication cost of such a project. We showed [Lehman 72*] that in general the cost W_{i+1} of taking a programming system from release i to release $(i+1)$ can be represented as:

$$W_{i+1} = W(B_i) + wH_i^2 \cdot 2^{2G_i \cdot i - DAL_i} \qquad [1]$$

Briefly the coefficient H represents the entropy, the degree of unstructuredness, of the program itself. G represents the entropy of the project. It measures the communication effort required at all times for coordination between the groups and individuals maintaining and updating the system. Finally the factor DAL represents the state of knowledge of systems and meta-system capability structure and content, the correctness, completeness and accessability of system and project documentation.

This macro model is static and does not express any controlling feedback relationships. It merely indicates that one source of exponential cost growth is the ever-increasing difficulty of ensuring that changes to the code are compatible with its past definition and behavior. Changes to the system today must not undo yesterday's work or prevent a repeat of yesterday's usage. Nor must they conflict with activities occurring elsewhere in the organization, today.

Any tendency to diverge may be minimized and controlled by creating and maintaining a well-structured system (H small) and/or by having a well-structured, strongly communicating, project organization (G small). Additionally, specification and documentation accuracy and program clarity must be maintained, so as to ensure that all questions about the meaning, intention or effect of code can easily and unambiguously be answered and, ideally, so that the code can be proven correct. The exponential growth trend would be suppressed given perfect system structure, perfect project structure or perfect documentation but in practice these cannot be achieved or maintained.

The Berkeley model

We now leave this primitive model and turn to one that displays the dynamics of the process. A dynamic macro model may be developed directly [Lehman 72b*], applying the techniques of structured analysis, to yield as a simple example at the highest level and where all parameters are assumed to be functions of time:

$$W = u{\cdot}F + M{\cdot}v{\cdot}K{\cdot}F + N{\cdot}w{\cdot}E + P{\cdot}x{\cdot}R \qquad [2]$$

In any programming project there will be activity related to the design and creation of new code and the modification of existing code. This is represented in [2] by a factor F. All such activity must be accompanied by additional activity, $K{\cdot}F$, to document and record it, and both activity measures must be multiplied by expenditure rates of factors u, v say, to yield the actual cost rate or cost terms.

There is also the activity represented by the exponential term in the previous model and now abbreviated to E, yielding a model term $w{\cdot}E$. Finally, in any project, there should be concern to improve the quality of the product and the productivity of its participants. The expenditure rate or expenditure of such activity is modelled by a term $x{\cdot}R$. This therefore represents that part of the budget applied to methodology improvement and tool development.

We observe that the level of productive activity F and its division between, for example, repair (F_1) functional improvement (F_2) and the creation of new capabilities (F_3) is a management judgment based on fault rates, business considerations and pressures from users. But once their average rate or level has been set, that of the activities represented by the other terms is predetermined if the system is to remain healthy—that is, usable, maintainable and enhanceable.

In practice, however, under the pressures of continuous demand and imminent completion dates, the work whose neglect has no immediate consequence is pushed aside. Thus the average level of activities represented by the last three terms will often fall below the level required to match program creation and modification. This reduction, a consequence of conscious or unconscious management decisions, is reflected in the model by the addition of management factors M, N, P that are, in general, less than 1.

The inter-parameter relationships

We have noted that all the variables and parameters in [2] are themselves time dependent. Additionally there will be time-dependent relationships between them. A complete model must express these relationships. Thus, as an example, if documentation is neglected ($M < 1$), the cost term u will increase in the future as knowledge of the state of the system declines and it becomes increasingly difficult to understand the content, intention or meaning of a piece of code. Moreover errors or defects in the system will increase, that is the ratio of repair activity (F_1) to enhancement (F_2 and F_3) will increase, an effect which is critical (and observable) in the dynamics of the process. Possible sets of relationships, the families of differential equations they lead to and the relationships between the solutions of these equations, available project and program data and our understanding of the programming process, are now being studied in our SRC supported research project under the title Systems Engineering (Growth Dynamics), and in a project 'Program evolution dynamics' led by L. Belady at the IBM Yorktown Heights Research Laboratories.

Progressive activities

Much more could be said about this family of models. For now, however, I draw attention to just one of its characteristics. If we examine the four terms of [2] we find that the first is concerned with activity undertaken because of its assessable value to the organization and the user. It produces code, hopefully usable code. We have added as it were to the store of potential energy in the system, to its power. We have increased the value of the system. I term activity of this type *progressive*.

Anti-regressive activities

The other three terms on the other hand do not, by and large, have a direct or immediate effect on the power or value of the system. System documentation, for example, must be undertaken while the work is being done or shortly thereafter. But it will be used only at some future time when it becomes necessary to modify the system. If it is there, well and good. If not trouble lies ahead. The system will be difficult to repair, to change. It may not be possible to keep the system in harmony with a changing environment. Relative to its environment, it will have begun to decay.

The prime purpose of the expenditure represented by the E term is to prevent the insertion or perpetuation of a fault in the system that will, at some future time, result in undesirable or incorrect operation. Ideally it relates to the activity that would be required to re-prove correctness of the system each time it is changed. Since in the present state of the art this cannot, in general, be done, the term can equally be interpreted to represent testing activity which serves as a poor, but as yet essential, substitute. Thus all in all the term models the effort to minimize the number of undiscovered faults in the system. It too represents an investment in the future.

Finally the fourth term, modelling the cost of methodology and tool development, also represents a long-range investment. It is concerned with maintaining a capability to cope with system development and maintenance despite increasing size and complexity.

In general these three elements of the model represent the cost of effort that I term *anti-regressive*. They are concerned not with increasing the value of the system immediately but with the investment of activity today to prevent system unmaintainability, and hence decay, in the future.

Unbalanced productivity growth

Baumol's Principle and its generalization

It is my thesis that the complementarity of progressive and anti-regressive activity is fundamental to all human activity.

In 1967, [Baumol 67] discussed the consequences of unbalanced productivity growth. His principle conclusion was that areas in which there is an intrinsic barrier to productivity increases must ultimately be priced out of commercial existence. But is this effect limited to instances where the obstacle to productivity increases is intrinsic? Any politician, administrator, manager, or even individual will be prepared to make an investment or an effort now, if the return is immediate or at least demonstrable. However to invest now so that in the future decay can be avoided or some other activity will be more efficient is quite a different matter. Thus there is inherent psychological pressure for productivity to increase faster in progressive than in the anti-regressive areas. I suggest now that a Baumol-like effect will occur also in this case despite the fact that there is no intrinsic barrier to productivity growth.

What is the consequence of this? In general all progressive activity must be accompanied by some anti-regressive activity. As progressive activity and productivity grow so does the demand for anti-regressive activity. But so does the cost of labour in both areas. Therefore more and more anti-regressive activity, costing more and more, is required and until something is done about productivity in the anti-regressive area one of two things may happen. Resources may be diverted from the progressive to the anti-regressive area. Progressive activity must then fall, growth rates decline and ultimately actual recession may set in.

Alternatively anti-regressive activity may be neglected. In that event, inevitably, sooner or later further growth grinds to a halt. In a programming system, for example, this occurs when the fault rate becomes so high that the system must be cleaned up before further developments can proceed, an effect clearly visible in Figures 10 and 11.

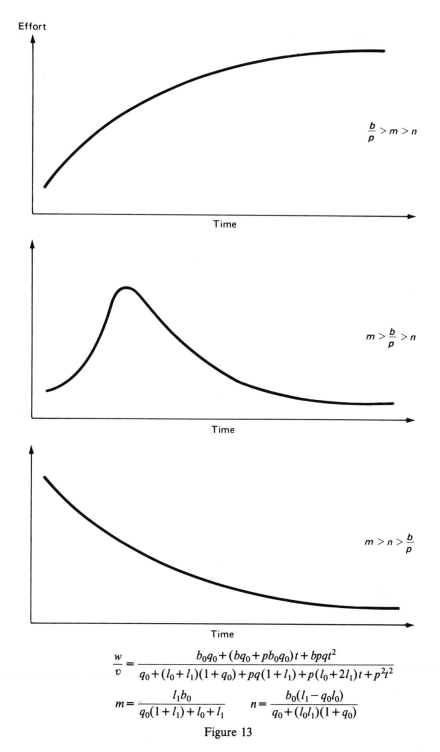

$$\frac{w}{v} = \frac{b_0 q_0 + (bq_0 + pb_0 q_0)t + bpqt^2}{q_0 + (l_0 + l_1)(1 + q_0) + pq(1 + l_1) + p(l_0 + 2l_1)t + p^2 t^2}$$

$$m = \frac{l_1 b_0}{q_0(1 + l_1) + l_0 + l_1} \qquad n = \frac{b_0(l_1 - q_0 l_0)}{q_0 + (l_0 l_1)(1 + q_0)}$$

Figure 13

The London model

The preceding discussion suggests a further abstraction of our dynamic model. We may in fact model the dynamics of the programming process as a function of the interaction between progressive and anti-regressive activity, work output and system growth or evolution. By presenting a higher level view of the process, such a model may provide a more concise summary of its time-behavior.

Also by abstracting in appropriate terms, the model may yield a wider interpretation, and therefore be used to describe a more universal phenomenon.

It is unfortunately not possible to present here a precise definition of the concepts of Progressive (P) and Anti-regressive (AR) activities, as would be required to develop such a model. Instead I shall simply outline, in terms of more primitive concepts, a model that results from some simple assumptions about the relationships between them and suggest one consequence that appears to relate to Growth and the Limits to Growth.

The primary assumption will be that productivity increases more rapidly in the progressive areas than it does in the anti-regressive.

With an additional assumption of linear productivity growth, the resultant models of manpower allocation and work output take the form of rational polynomial functions of the time variable t (Figure 13). We cannot

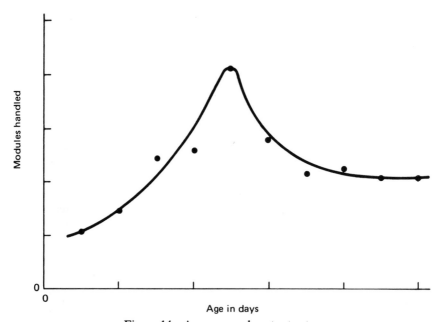

Age in days

Figure 14   Average work-output rates.

examine these models fully here, but a sample system output shows clearly that, at best, under a set of rather unlikely conditions, the output grows to an asymptotic limit. In practice however output can ultimately be expected to decline. This is entirely due to the progressive and anti-regressive productivity imbalance and can therefore only be mastered by careful control of that balance. And this effect is very real, as can be seen from the behavior of a derived rate-of-work measure taken from actual programming project data (Figure 14).

Generalization

Progressive and anti-regressive activities in city life

The high-level model that has been outlined was suggested by the earlier model of the programming process. I now suggest that it may also be interpreted within the context of sociological and economic systems. In a city, for example, we may identify as progressive (as previously defined) work output that contributes positively to the growth of the standard of living and the quality of life of the community.

But a community also undertakes anti-regressive activities. Collecting garbage, for example, does not increase the value of life in the city, it merely maintains the status quo. It is the neglect of that activity that leads to decay. Similarly police action is primarily directed to the prevention of deterioration of life in the city as a result of increasingly disordered traffic, breakdown in communications, criminal activity. It is strictly anti-regressive.

Unless the problem of productivity imbalance between these progressive and anti-regressive activities is mastered, the previous model suggests that sooner or later the economics of a city will be dominated by the cost of the latter. And once again the underlying, psychological, cause for the resultant consequences is clearly understandable. Unless an electorate is very far-sighted, very sophisticated, the city fathers, the politicians who face re-election, the managers who seek promotion, are concerned with short-range profitability, not long-range preservation. They will in general tend to favour progressive expenditure and investment over the anti-regressive. But any such consistent bias will ultimately but inevitably lead to slowed growth and then to decay. Indeed, as we have so recently seen, only immediate chaos and decay forces the adoption of adequate levels of anti-regressive measures.

Non-uniqueness of the P and AR assignation

To avoid confusion I should perhaps stress here that the distinction between progressive and anti-regressive activity is not always clear cut.

De-pollution activity, for example, is progressive and officials can support, even encourage, it without fear of losing their office in the next election or the next shareholders meeting. The control and prevention of pollution however before its effects are felt (or, I fear, when its effects are no longer felt) is a very different matter. This is something for next year, for the next generation, to worry about. This is something for the future. The same activity is progressive when it cleans up something that has already occurred and accumulated, but is strictly anti-regressive when it is directed towards preventing the same thing from occurring.

Progressive-Anti-regressive conflict and balance

The preceding discussion can have given only the barest outline of the concepts and phenomena we are investigating. In fact we hypothesize that the life cycle of any complex, dynamic system is, at least in part, governed by the conflicting resource demands of progressive and anti-regressive activities. There will be an ever-increasing demand for the latter at a cost per unit of work that increases relative to the cost of the former.

There are three classical ways to deal with this problem. One may bring in resources from outside. In the United States, for example, an increasing number of State and City preservation projects are requesting and receiving Federal aid. But then the external source and the old system become one, enlarged, system, which too must ultimately limit, possibly decline. Alternatively one may divert resources from the progressive to the anti-regressive. This too implies a constraint on growth. A third alternative simply ignores the need for anti-regressive activity. But this is decay, even if it is not immediately visible. Thus individually or in combination these approaches all inevitably lead to a limitation to growth and hence to decay.

The way out exists. We must recognize that systems have content, structure and complexity. Consequent inertial and momentum effects result in limits on the rate of growth and of change, but not necessarily to growth itself. If one part of a system is caused to grow too fast another must grow more slowly or even decline. If at one time a system grows too fast, that must be followed by a standstill or even a decline. So the average growth rate is best restricted to its 'natural' value. Even more importantly the integrals of P and AR activity and their productivity growth must, on the average, be relatively balanced, however tempting it may be to leave the latter for future generations.

Anti-regressive activity in organizations

Before passing to the final theme of this evening's talk I would briefly mention two further points. First let me describe this same conflict as seen in the life of almost any organization. In a large business, for example, there are basically three levels of activity. The progressive rank and file engage in the activity that yields the revenue that enables the business to exist and to grow. Executive management develops and initiates the policies and strategies that enable the business to prosper. This is also progressive. Finally one has middle management. The function of middle management is to act as a communication link, vertically and horizontally. They transmit, interpret, coordinate, protect and generally prevent the development of misunderstandings, harmful competition and internal conflicts between different sub-organizations and products.

Middle management is a strictly anti-regressive, communications, responsibility. As such it will tend to grow more rapidly than the progressive sectors of the organization in both activity and unit cost. Moreover feedback analysis of the mechanisms of promotion, demotion and resignation from an organization shows that the average level of competence in the middle management ranks of an organization may be expected to decline with time [Lehman 68*]. Unless carefully and consciously controlled, middle management will tend to be a growing but increasingly mediocre organism. Thus a business, a government, even an educational institution, will get choked by its bureaucracy, the anti-regressive middle management, unless structure, function and productivity are carefully balanced. In particular it is vital that adequate resources for productivity development are correctly allocated over the organization, so that at all times productivity in the middle management area balances that of the remainder of the organization.

The Club of Rome

Let me also make very brief reference to the Club of Rome report on the Limits to Growth [Meadows 72]. In their summary (Figure 15) of the problems whose solution would help conquer the problems of growth limitation, all except one would be classified by me as anti-regressive. The fundamental oversight of the team was, perhaps, identification of resource exhaustion as the primary cause of the immediate danger. In my judgement it is, in fact, primarily a symptom. The phenomena which they discuss appear to represent just another special case of my general rule.

The problem in this instance is that mankind has, by and large, not been willing to invest sufficiently in the anti-regressive activity of long-range research and development, to find materials and techniques to replace currently conventional sources of energy and raw materials when

THE LIMITS TO GROWTH
The State of Global Equilibrium

Technological advance would be both necessary and welcome in the equilibrium state. A few obvious examples of the kinds of practical discoveries that would enhance the workings of a steady state society include:

ANTIREGRESSIVE → • new methods of waste collection, to decrease pollution and make discarded material available for recycling;

• more efficient techniques for recycling, to reduce rates of resource depletion;

• better product design to increase product lifetime and promote easy repair, so that the capital depreciation rate would be minimized;

• harnessing of incident solar energy, the most pollution-free power source;

• methods of natural pest control, based on more complete understanding of ecological interrelationships;

• medical advances that would decrease the death rate;

• contraceptive advances that would facilitate the equalization of the birth rate with the decreasing death rate.

Figure 15   The true limiter of growth.

these are exhausted. The disastrous consequences of the exhaustion of specific resources is a direct consequence of the universal tendency to neglect apparently unprofitable anti-regressive activity, to prefer immediate profit to long-term security.

The sun, the atmosphere, the tides, for example, form an almost inexhaustible but as yet barely exploitable energy source. And given energy and mankind's ingenuity and creativeness, material shortages can always be overcome, provided that there is no practical limit to the growth of mankind's collective intellect. And that is the topic to which we now turn.

Limits to growth through the educational process

Knowledge or understanding

In education too there is the progressive and the anti-regressive. And, in my judgement, the same error, the analogous unbalance, exists and unfortunately increasingly so.

But let me explain. The global objectives of an educational system are rarely stated or even recognized. One may hear talk of local or immediate objectives but the really fundamental goal is not discussed. In my wanderings through the world I have experienced various educational systems, as a student, as a parent, as a manager, as a teacher. Some have stressed knowledge, others understanding. The implications of this difference reach down into the very structure and heart of the society in which these systems operate. Educational systems may, in fact, be classified by the extent of their orientation to *knowledge* and to *understanding*.

In the limit, the objectives implied by these orientations are orthogonal, at times even contradictory, in terms of the methodology they imply and the results that they yield. Orthogonality does not, of course, imply exclusion. Most systems contain, and need to contain, elements oriented to and supporting both knowledge and understanding. But what we are seeking here is correct balance between them, for the individual and for society.

Knowledge

An educational system may primarily seek to transfer to its students some selected portion of the reservoir of human knowledge, as well as the means whereby this reservoir may be further accessed. Thus the knowledge which has been accumulated over millenia will be explicitly carried forward into the future.

The drift to knowledge-oriented education occurs because its pay-off is immediate. The child comes out of kindergarten, is ready to go into school to absorb more knowledge there. It comes out of school and is able either to take a job and earn its living or to go forward to higher education and then earn its living. This is progressive. Each quantum of knowledge that is gained becomes the basis for further learning or for other activities as required by society. Moreover in this era of democracy and human equality a common standard of knowledge acts as the great leveller; it provides a definable standard against which egalitarianism can measure its success.

Understanding

At the other extreme, the pure understanding-oriented system seeks to instill insight; not so much the facts themselves as the relationships between the facts, valid analogies, cause and effect. An essential ingredient of this educational process is the development of analytic powers, self-expression and creative thinking, with the ability to seek out and elucidate new knowledge as required. Assessment of the degree of success achieved in the process is a matter of judgement, even viewpoint and opinion.

An understanding-oriented system is primarily anti-regressive. Its graduates cannot normally apply their insight and creative skills directly. Real life requires facts. But only a person with understanding can discard surplus or outdated knowledge. Only he or she can replace large depositories of knowledge by algorithms for their retrieval. It requires true understanding to develop new methodologies and to guide the knowledgeable to new horizons when the old ones become outdated or exhausted.

Attributes of the two systems

What are the attributes and hallmarks of these alternative systems? How does one determine in which direction a particular system is oriented? How can one structure a system and adopt appropriate methodologies to achieve a best balance between understanding and knowledge for the individual, for a community and for mankind at large?

The knowledge-oriented system is typified by excessive emphasis on self-learning and homework, grades and credits. It relies heavily on frequent examinations that test the extent of a student's knowledge on the completion of each quantum of study. High pass marks and high scores result from a precise definition of what was to have been learned, and from the statistical reliability of large numbers of multiple choice questions.

In the understanding-oriented system on the other hand emphasis must be quite different. Self-study and home learning start much later and the emphasis in marking will be on *how* a complex question was approached, not only on the correctness of the final solution. The award of a degree is not the sum of a large number of credits in different subjects each of which has been obtained immediately after a course has been taught. It follows from the completion of a course of study, for a demonstration of the nature and extent of the understanding that has been gained, of the meaning and the significance of what has been learnt. Multiple choice questions are of no use at all here. A student cannot express his understanding by marking a square black. His insight and ability is revealed by his choice of words, by the way in which he approaches a problem. We are interested to see *how* he has understood the facts and the concepts to which he has been exposed, what he can *do* with them, not so much in his ability to reproduce them.

Consequences of knowledge orientation

In a society in which education is knowledge-oriented the teacher adjusts his rate of teaching to the average absorptive capability of the class. Thus there will emerge a group of people clustered around a level of knowledge determined by their average absorptive capacity. The weaker ones will have been helped forward and this indeed is a good feature of the system. Those with more powerful intellects, a greater potential for creative thinking, will have been held back. They will not have been taught to express their own ideas but merely to repeat what they have heard from their teachers.

The consequences will be a society in which achievement must be obtained through teamwork. A knowledge-oriented society will be a technology-based society in which known facts are produced from the joint encyclopaedic memories of a team and applied to achieve specified and known to be achievable objectives, great works of technology. In themselves these works do not foster creative inventiveness or the development of new concepts or deeper insights.

Such a society must possess the capability to get people to work together, the ability to manage teams of people and guide them towards a common objective. It is knowledge orientation that leads to the need for management science. Thus it is not in the least surprising that the USA with its 'melting-pot' society and, as a consequence, its knowledge-based, materialistic, orientation is the undoubted world leader in technology and in management.

And those of understanding

When we now consider the understanding-oriented system, the first thing to be noticed is that one needs more gifted teachers. Each student will interpret the teacher somewhat differently. If the teacher in turn understands the educational process, he can take each student to the limits of his individual ability. Inevitably some people will be left behind because they do not have the motivation or the ability to understand. Higher education will be more restricted and in the output of the overall educational system one finds a wide spectrum of knowledge, skills and creative ability, rather than the cluster produced by the knowledge-oriented system.

At one end of the spectum will be highly motivated, creative, thoughtful individuals able to express themselves, to develop and to exploit new concepts. They will not require to interact strongly and intimately with others to achieve their inspiration because they have learnt to achieve results on their own or in very small groups. The demand for strong, effective management, and the ability to provide it, will not be so well developed and ultimately that may prove to be to the detriment of that society. It will, for example, tend to be scientifically creative rather than technologically productive: able to produce concepts, fresh viewpoints, new inventions and methodologies, but less able to develop and control their mass exploitation.

Mankind's intellectual growth

I should not like these remarks to be in any way misunderstood. Mankind needs both systems. The challenge today is not which way to go but how to provide the correct balance between the progressive and anti-regressive in education, as elsewhere. Knowledge alone will not suffice to ensure survival of humanity. Nor can we hope to retain all the knowledge that humanity has gathered over the last five thousand years. What must be done is to ensure that forgotten knowledge can be reproduced when required. New ideas must be produced faster than the older ones may be forgotten. Understanding-oriented education is an investment in the future. It ensures that there will always exist those creative minds that can think for themselves, that produce and explore new concepts, that provide a sense of direction, creative inspiration and action, possibly even a little bit of sanity, in this fact-oriented, technology-based, profit-seeking world. But knowledge is also required. At any given moment in time only a knowledge-oriented technological society can solve the immediate problems that face a community, a nation and mankind as a whole.

We have analyzed education in terms of the progressive and anti-regressive system concepts. If the same laws of growth apply we can ensure continued growth only by achieving the correct balance between progressive and anti-regressive education. Thus I would like to think that we here at Imperial College will help counter-balance a worldwide trend to knowledge-oriented education, by maintaining and emphasizing the traditional understanding-orientation of British education. The new Computer Science course that we have set up has been carefully designed and structured to yield a student who understands and not just knows his subject. Thus I trust that we shall be playing our part in ensuring the continued intellectual growth of mankind and through that also its physical progress—progress in which computer systems and computer science will play a major role.

Conclusion

Finally may I be permitted to follow ancient Jewish practice and conclude my talk with a biblical viewpoint of the concepts I have presented. The author of *Proverbs* also recognized the potential conflict between progressive temptation and anti-regressive needs (Plate IVb):

'Go to the ant, thou sluggard, consider her ways and be wise. Though having no officer, overseer or ruler, she prepareth her bread in the summer, gathereth her food in the harvest.' [Solomon, *Proverbs* 6, verses 6 – 8.]

One might ask why the author here places bread preparation in summer *before* food gathering in the harvest when in fact in the Middle East the harvest is gathered in spring. The Malbim, a 19th century commentator, remarks that the meaning of this text is that the ant eats in the winter because she has previously prepared her food in the summer. This she can do because during the spring harvest she is willing to store her collection rather than to eat it all. She works for a future that she may never live to see and this voluntary action occurs despite the absence of pressure from rulers or overseers. The anti-regressive is so integrated into the progressive that the two remain balanced and in step at all times.

There is clearly no need to add anything further to these ancient words of wisdom except a final overall summary:

> Programs and Cities and Students
> All have the potential to grow.
> With P and AR action balanced
> There need be no Limit to Growth.

Acknowledgments. I would like to acknowledge the loyal support, the patience and the constructive criticism that I have received from my colleagues in the Computing Science section of the Department of Computing and Control over the last two years and during the preparation of this paper. In particular I single out the many thought-provoking discussions with A. L. Lim. Equally I must mention and gratefully acknowledge all I have learned and am continuing to learn from my colleagues in the IFIP working group WG2.3. Above all, however, I want to acknowledge the close and continuing association with L. A. Belady who, but for the nature of this paper, would surely have been a co-author. Last, but certainly not least, I want to thank my wife Chava for her artistic contributions to this lecture and for her constant and continuing support and encouragement which have made my work and this lecture possible.

6
On Structured Programming

David Gries
Cornell University

What is structured programming?

The term *structured programming* (hereafter abbreviated *sp*) has been used with many different meanings since Edsger W. Dijkstra first coined the term. Actually, the term appeared in the title of his monograph Notes on structured programming [Dijkstra 72d*], but as far as I can determine not in the monograph itself! The lack of a precise definition has allowed, even encouraged, people to use it as they wished, to attribute to sp what they themselves learned from reading Notes on structured programming, however different this might have been from Dijkstra's intent. Taken out of context or viewed in the wrong light, some of the resulting definitions of sp that have appeared in the literature seem stupid (e.g., sp is programming without **gotos**), and it is quite understandable that programmers have looked askance when asked to learn and practice it. The matter has gotten so out of hand that some programmers and managers feel that sp is an attempt to "deskill" the profession—to put so many restrictions on the programmer that his task becomes trivial and can be performed by almost any person.

In discussing sp in [Denning 73], Peter Denning found the first five of the following impressions people seem to have of sp; I found the following eight. Taken together, they give a good general view of the subject.

1. It is a return to common sense.
2. It is the general method by which our leading programmers program.
3. It is programming without the use of **goto** statements.
4. It is the process of controlling the number of interactions between a

given local task and its environment so that the number of interactions is some linear function of some parameter or parameters of the task.

5. It is top-down programming.

6. sp theory deals with converting arbitrarily large and complex flowcharts into standard forms so that they can be represented by iterating and nesting a small number of basic and standard control logic structures (these usually being sequencing, alternation, and iteration) [Mills 71].

7. sp is a manner of organizing and coding programs that makes the programs easily understood and modified [Donaldson 73].

8. The purpose of sp is to control complexity through theory and discipline [Mills 72].

9. sp should be characterized not by the absence of **goto**s, but by the presence of structure [Mills 72].

10. A major function of the structuring of the program is to keep a correctness proof feasible [Dijkstra 72d*].

11. A fundamental concept (of sp) is a proof of correctness [Karp 1974].

12. sp ... allows verification of the correctness of all steps in the design process and, thus, automatically leads to a *self-explicable* and *self-defensive* programming style [Bauer 73].

13. sp is no panacea—it really consists of a formal notation for orderly thinking, *an attribute not commonly inherent in programmers or any other type* (my emphasis). It is a discipline which must be acquired and continuously reinforced through conscious effort. It is worth the trouble [Butterworth 1974].

Let me give C. A. R. Hoare's definition, which I feel captures the essence of sp: "The task of organizing one's thought in a way that leads, in a reasonable time, to an understandable expression of a computing task, has come to be called sp."

I would add to this that one should always strive for simplicity and elegance. The simplest solution is always the easiest to understand. This does not mean that one must sacrifice efficiency; indeed, it is often only when we understand a problem and a solution that we can develop a more efficient one. Computer science already has its complexity theory; we might call sp the "art of simplicity" or "simplicity theory."

Research in structured programming

I think the reader will have a better understanding of sp if he understands the various areas of research on the subject. Research in sp involves four closely related topics: programming methodology, program notation, program correctness, and program verification. I shall discuss each of these.

1.*Programming methodology*. The goals are to devise orderly, efficient methods for developing readable correct programs, to identify and explain tools and techniques for solving programming problems (or any problems for that matter), and to find out how to think clearly when programming. Some of the current buzz terms are: levels of abstraction, stepwise refinement, top-down programming, "solve a simpler problem first," and "find a related problem." But these buzz terms mean little by themselves; the only way to really understand what has been done so far is to study some of the discussions on the subject, most notably [Dijkstra 72d*].

It must be made clear that one technique will never suffice (for example, top-down programming). A programmer needs a bag of tricks, a collection of methods for attacking a problem. Secondly, if we are to raise the level of programming, each programmer (no matter how good he feels he is) must become more conscious of the tools and techniques he uses. It is not enough to just program; we must discover how and why we do it. Programming methodology is concerned with how we should program and why.

We *must* realize that programming is a difficult task, and we must be more receptive to new ideas; even the best programmer can learn to program more efficiently.

Computer science is in the *unique* position of trying to teach general problem solving to a large number of students. When a student finishes a programming course we expect him to be able to program any problem in an area in which he is knowledgeable. Yet it is fair to say that almost none of the elementary programming books say anything about problem solving, about orderly thinking, about expressing algorithms clearly and simply. The only conclusion to draw is that the students are not being taught how to program; they are only being taught a programming language.

Teaching a programming methodology means that we ourselves must understand the programming process and how it can be made more orderly and efficient. Someone must isolate and explain the tools that are available, must give examples of their use, must try to determine why one way of looking at a problem may be more useful than another. Thus, it is not fair to criticize work in this area by saying, "That's obvious, I always program that way."

When teaching programming, I am interested in explaining problem solving ideas, in teaching orderly thinking, in getting across a sense of simplicity, elegance, and style. The language that best suits my needs is one which is itself "clean," which has the control structures I feel are most useful in programming, and which can be taught in a modular fashion. Here FORTRAN is at a distinct disadvantage to ALGOL, ALGOL W, Pascal, and a limited subset of PL/1, and if a reasonably efficient implementation of any of these is available, I fail to see why anyone would pick FORTRAN. (We are of course partially limited in choice since others outside computer science often have a voice in the matter; because of this, for example, Cornell teaches a subset of PL/1 instead of Pascal or ALGOL W.) But anyone who has been taught programming (as opposed to a programming language) should be able to become fluent in FORTRAN, PL/1, ALGOL, etc., with relative ease.

2. *Program notation.* Language shapes the thought and culture of those who use it, Benjamin Whorf said; and this is certainly true in programming. A cluttered programming language can hinder us from thinking clearly; a restricted language can hide the best algorithm from us. Research in this area of sp is devoted to improving notation (1) by looking for better notation and language features which can help simplify the programming process, (2) by determining which control structures are best suited for describing algorithms correctly and clearly, and (3) by learning how to describe data structures in a cleaner fashion.

A restricted notation puts a programmer at a severe disadvantage. A prime example of this is the **do** $I = 1$ ... loop notation. Even on some very simple problems, programmers with the **do** $I = 1$ ... mentality do not find the simplest, most efficient solution because their idea of iteration is so limited.

This does not mean one shouldn't use FORTRAN. Sp methodology tells us not to program *in* a programming language, but *into* it. Express the algorithm in a notation that best fits the problem, then refine this algorithm into the programming language. Use any notation that fits the problem, and then use whatever is necessary—including **goto**s—to *simulate* that notation in the programming language, taking care of course to describe your intent in the program itself. This is often harder to do with FORTRAN, but there is no harm in it as long as you do not restrict your algorithmic thoughts to FORTRAN concepts.

3. *Program correctness.* The first 25 years of programming saw little emphasis on initial correctness and too much emphasis on debugging. But debugging can never show the absence of errors, only their presence. Current sp methodology suggests that one should try to develop a program and its proof of correctness hand in hand.

What is a proof? The broadest definition would allow any informal discussion that convinces at least one person (besides the author), and the narrowest would require a strictly formal, detailed analysis leading from a set of axioms to the theorem. To be *practical*, we want something that falls between these two extremes.

Most of the work on proving correctness has been quite formal and mathematical and is as yet of no use to the programmer. But some important *practical* ideas have arisen in the research on axiomatic approaches to programming language definition. One such idea is that we should not look so much at how a program changes values of variables, but instead at how relations among the variables remain the same.

The fact that one can prove a program correct using a mathematical definition of correctness, without reference to how a program is executed, is extremely valuable and insightful. It allows the programmer to separate his two main concerns—efficiency and correctness—and deal with each in turn. A significant advance is Hoare's invariant relation axiom for **while** loops. This axiom gives us finally a practical approach to understanding iteration; it bridges the gap between the static aspect of a loop (how we read it) and its dynamic aspect (how it gets executed).

The invariant relation axiom is practical enough to be used by any programmer willing to spend some time studying it. For more information read [Dijkstra 72d*; Wirth 73a*; Gries 73a*].

4. *Program verification.* No matter how hard we try to prove the correctness of a program there will be mistakes in it. Most of these will be syntactic mistakes; we have proven the correctness of the algorithm, and not its representation as a program. Thus there is still need for program verification.

I hesitate to call this phase of programming "debugging," for this seems to imply that mistakes are to be expected. Syntax mistakes, perhaps, but not logical mistakes. The attitude of "I'll just run it, find the bugs, and fix them" has caused much trouble.

Research is being done in this area (see for example [Hetzel 73]), but I feel that at this stage the other three areas of sp are more important.

Conclusion

Structured programming, then, is an approach to understanding the complete programming process. While it is true that some people go overboard on their belief in the preliminary results (don't ever use a **goto**, you must use only the conditional and while statements!), the majority of the people involved in sp are interested only in learning how to program better. sp research will have an important and lasting impact on computing because it will lead to a better understanding of programming.

If you are interested in learning more about what sp really is, I can give some suggestions. The first is to study the readings given below with an open mind; the second is to actually try to write several programs using the principles that have emerged from sp research. You will find it hard work, because you will have to be continually aware of your thought processes, and you will have to think differently than you're used to. If after this study (and only then) you disagree with the principles, you are entitled to say they are not for you, and you are invited to propose your own principles.

I suggest you read several things: Polya's paperback entitled *How to Solve It* [Polya 71], and [Dijkstra 72d*; Gries 73*; Wirth 73*; Dijkstra 76*].

PART II

THE CONCERN FOR PROGRAM CORRECTNESS

Proofs

This Part is concerned with proving programs correct, with developing programs and their proofs hand in hand, and with defining programming languages in a manner that supports correctness proofs. The word proof *has unpleasant connotations for many, especially when it is connected with the word* mathematics, *and it will be helpful to explain just what is meant by a proof of correctness of a program and to explain why the material presented here is so important.*

According to Webster's Third New International Dictionary, a proof *is "the cogency of evidence that compels acceptance by the mind of a truth or a fact."[1] Thus a proof is an argument that convinces the reader (or listener) of the truth of a statement. Note that the definition says nothing about the language in which the proof is written. Proofs may be written in (im)pure English (or some other natural language), in mathematical notation, in a mixture of the two, or in any convenient notation.*

One possible proof is, "The statement is obviously true," which might be convincing either because of the stature of the person making the claim ("His word is proof enough for me!"), or because of the simplicity of the statement. On the other hand, we have proofs in a formal logic, which can be characterized as follows. The logical system is a set of basic assumptions, or axioms, *and a set of* inference rules *which can be used to infer consequent truths or* theorems. *A proof of a statement is a finite sequence of statements, ending with the statement to be proved, each of which is an axiom or is easily*

---

[1] A fact is, according to the dictionary, something presented rightly or wrongly as having objective reality.

and obviously derived from earlier statements by the application of an inference rule.

Generally, proofs fall between these two extremes.

A proof must be convincing. After digesting a proof, a reader should believe that the statement is true, and he should have a good understanding of why it is true. An argument may not be convincing because there are too few "steps" in it and because the mental leap from step to step is too great. Or the argument may contain so many detailed steps that the reader loses interest, becomes exhausted, and is overwhelmed by the detail. A good proof draws a balance between these two extremes. It emphasizes the ideas that provide insight and understanding, and suppresses those details that the reader can easily fill in himself. Organizing a proof to provide understanding with as little effort as possible on the part of a reader is indeed a difficult art to master.

There is also the chance that a reader does not understand a proof simply because he does not have the necessary knowledge; the arguments used are just too sophisticated or advanced for him. In this case, the only solution for the reader who wants to understand the proof is to educate himself.

A proof can be faulty and yet convincing. One proof of the famous four color conjecture, published in 1879, was believed to be correct for 11 years until a mistake was discovered in it, at which time it was no longer convincing and no longer a proof. Proofs are written by humans; hence many of them will contain a mistake of one sort or another.

Currently, each programmer tries to prove his program correct, in that he reasons to himself that it is so and may even write documentation aimed at convincing any reader. Unfortunately, most programmers are not at all adept at this, as can be determined by looking at how much time is spent "debugging." The problem, which is not the fault of the programmer, is that he does not as yet possess the requisite tools for producing correct programs. His reasoning is based solely on his understanding of how programs are executed on a machine, and he usually attempts to argue about correctness based on a number of test cases that he has hand simulated or run on a computer. His understanding is based more on intuition than on fact, and his mental tools are inadequate to handle the mass of detail.

A programmer attempts to reason about programs—about their correctness, effieiency, and so forth. In order to learn how to reason about programs it seems appropriate to turn to mathematics or other fields where reasoning is studied. Logic, the branch of mathematics of particular interest to us, has often been called the science and art of reasoning. Thus it seems appropriate for the scientist who wants to develop a theory of reasoning about programs to turn to formal logic for knowledge and insight, and it makes sense for a programmer, or anyone who wants to develop the art of writing convincing arguments for that matter, to learn some formal logic.

The notion that mathematics could help us in programming has been around for some time. For example, in [McCarthy 63] John McCarthy said that, instead of trying out computer programs on test cases until they are debugged, one should prove that they have the desired properties and that it was *reasonable to hope that the relationship between computation and mathematical logic would be fruitful.*

The current thoughts on correctness proofs for programs rest on three papers that were published in the late 1960s. Peter Naur's paper [Naur 66*] emphasized the importance of program proofs and described an informal technique for providing them. Robert Floyd's paper [Floyd 67] discussed "assigning a meaning" to a program by inserting assertions at various points in a flowchart of the program and showing that the assertions do hold at those points. He also suggested that the specification of proof techniques could provide an adequate formal definition of a programming language. The paper most often cited on this subject is [Hoare 69*], which is reproduced in this part. This paper gives a logical system of axioms and inference rules that defines a small programming language, gives a formal proof in the logical system, and discusses the advantages that may follow from further pursuit of the topic.

Since the initial foundations were laid by these three, we have been progressing at a rapid rate. We have seen the development of logical systems for reasoning about all sorts of programming language concepts and constructs—such as iteration, coroutines, data types, and parallelism. And, as we shall see in Edsger W. Dijkstra's second article in this Part, we are learning how correctness proof ideas can be used to guide the development of a program hand in hand with its correctness proof.

What does this mean for the average professional programmer? In order to learn to reason effectively about programs, he needs to study some logic and mathematics, and to master material such as that presented in this Part. (Of course, this material is not the end result, and there will be better expositions of the material as time goes on.) This does not mean that he will be expected to formally *prove his programs correct, but he should begin to use the ideas and insight gained by the research on formal theory of correctness of programs. A mathematical foundation is being laid for the task of programming, and those seriously interested in that task should master it.*

There is another reason for turning to mathematics in order to learn more about programming, and that is the concern in mathematics for simplicity, elegance, and naturalness of notation. G. Polya, in his book How To Solve It, *says that the use of signs is indispensable to the use of reason, and calls mathematical notation a precise, concise language, with rules that suffer no exception. The language of mathematical symbols can indeed assist the mind in its search for understanding, and in fact we often understand something only when we have developed a good notation for expressing it.*

The programmer is constantly developing notation or deciding upon notation for expressing his algorithmic ideas. When programming, he attempts to use a notation that fits the problem, and then gradually to work that notation into the programming language at hand. Thus, it is important that he realize the advantages of a good, crisp notation over a more awkward one.

To realize the advantages of a well-chosen notation, try to add a few large numbers using only Roman numerals instead of our decimal notation. Examples of good and bad notation abound in computer science. A good example is the notation *BNF (Backus Naur Form), which was used to define the syntax of ALGOL 60 and which has had such an enormous influence on programming language design and compiler construction. In terms of programming language constructs, the FORTRAN concept and notation of iteration, the indexed **do** loop, severely restricts the possibilities for algorithmic expression, while the more general **while** loop is much more flexible. Dijkstra's guarded command loop (see the seventh paper in this Part) is even more convenient and elegant, and allows the simple expression of some algorithms that would appear awkward using the **while** loop.*

The articles in Part II

What better beginning to a section on correctness of programs than an article entitled Correctness concerns and, among other things, why they are resented. *Written by Edsger W. Dijkstra in his inimitable style, this article provides a historical perspective that, together with the Introduction to this Part, should prepare the reader to understand and evaluate the theoretical results that follow.*

The second article, An axiomatic basis for computer programming *by C. A. R. (Tony) Hoare, has stimulated much of the current research in programming methodology and programming language design. This paper provides a definition of a programming language in terms of how a program should be proved correct rather than in terms of how it should be executed. It provides for what Dijkstra has called the* separation of concerns *for correctness and efficiency; each can now be treated in relative isolation, in its own domain. Every computer scientist and programmer should study this article for its perspective and historical value.*

Hoare's article, "Proof of a program: FIND," *gives a detailed proof of a nontrivial algorithm using the method suggested in the previous article. It is hard work to study and understand this paper if one is not familiar with the notation and conventions, but this should not deter the reader. It is also not suggested that every program be proved correct in this amount of detail; nevertheless, the process of reading and understanding such proofs (and then attempting to write a proof oneself) can be extremely interesting, educational, and illuminating. Note that Hoare suggests in this paper that construction of a proof as part of the coding process is hardly more laborious than the traditional practice of program testing. Provided the programmer has the education and experience, I am more than inclined to agree with him.*

Hoare received the ACM 1973 Programming Languages and Systems Award for his sequence of papers on axiomatically defining languages (which includes the two included in this volume).

The axiomatic definitional method is a powerful tool used in designing programming languages. If one accepts the assumption that understanding a proof of correctness of a program is synonymous with understanding the program, then it makes sense to define constructs and to imbed them in a language so as to arrive at simple, easy to use "proof rules." The fourth paper in this Part, "An approach to correctness proofs of semicoroutines," *by Ole-Johan Dahl, is based on such considerations. The paper also provides a proof of correctness of a nontrivial program in order to illustrate the approach.*

In the same vein, Susan Owicki and David Gries discuss "An axiomatic proof technique for parallel programs" *in the fifth paper in this Part. Here the reader will find that formal theory can indeed provide practical insight into difficult problems. Gries and Owicki received the ACM 1977 Programming Languages and Systems Award for this paper.*

The sixth paper, "Programming with transition diagrams," *by John Reynolds, has not been previously published. In this paper, in order to handle situations where avoidance of the* **goto** *would seem inhibiting, Reynolds methodically constructs programs without restricting himself to just sequencing, alternation, and iteration, but paying close attention to correctness proof ideas. The exercise is interesting and he succeeds, but please note the pessimistic afterthought at the end of the paper!*

Up to this point, the articles in this Part have considered proofs of correctness of programs, but no methods have been given for producing a proof and program hand in hand. This Dijkstra does in his paper, "Guarded commands, nondeterminacy and formal derivation of programs." *His guarded commands—a notation that is elegant, simple and useful—and his concept of a "predicate transformer" merge together to form a formal calculus for guiding the derivation of programs. After reading this article, the reader will want to turn to Dijkstra's book* A Discipline of Programming *[Dijkstra 76a*], which treats the subject in more detail.*

The last article, "A system which automatically improves programs," *by John Darlington and Rod Burstall, approaches the problem of developing programs in an entirely different manner. While Dijkstra's emphasis is on providing the programmer with adequate mental tools, Darlington and Burstall attempt to place much of the burden on the computer. Given a correct but intentionally naive program, the system should transform it into a more efficient one. The techniques described in this paper go far beyond those provided in the usual "optimizing compiler."*

7
Correctness Concerns and, among Other Things, Why They Are Resented

Edsger W. Dijkstra
Burroughs Corporation

Abstract   *A historical perspective is provided on issues concerning the correctness of programs.*

According to Webster's definition of a tutorial: "a paper and esp. a technical paper written to give practical information about a specific subject," this paper is *not* worthy of the name "tutorial," because I would never describe what I intend to do as "giving practical information". On the contrary: I intend to give as little "practical information" as I possibly can. I am not going to enumerate facts, results and theories, for those you can find—in abundance, I am tempted to add—in the published literature. What I do hope to achieve, however, is helping you to understand and evaluate those facts, results and theories when you encounter them in the literature. I intend to do so by providing you with a historical perspective, be it—in more than one sense—a partial one. It is a lucky circumstance that the amateur historian, like myself, can always come away with very few facts: the fewer the facts, the greater our freedom of interpretation, and it is that freedom that I intend to enjoy.

For a short while we have to go back to the scientific climate at the beginning of this century, for there we seem to find the roots of the philosophical opinions that prevailed a few decades later. And these philosophical opinions, in turn, seem to be the source of today's tacit assumptions. By being tacit, these assumptions tend to escape being challenged and that is bad, because they are third-generation off-spring of scientific hopes that, in the mean time, have been shown to have been unjustified, they express everyman's image of a goal that, in the mean time, has been proved to be unattainable.

The scientific optimism of the late 19th century is responsible for the common opinion that "the greater our knowledge, the more perfect our understanding." This assumption is the ultimate justification for so many of our university curricula, that one can hardly challenge it without running the risk of being accused of preaching the virtues of ignorance. Yet I challenge it: the greater our knowledge, the more perfect our understanding...what sheer nonsense! Think about the wealth of information that the modern communication media give us about the world and its inhabitants: never before has Mankind been so confused about itself as today! The overpowering flood of conflicting impressions leaves many of us so bewildered that, in utter despair, they seek salvation in cheap mysticism or a narrowminded ideology: the greater knowledge has not created greater understanding, it has created extremism instead.[1]

What, you may ask, has all this to do with Computing Science? Well, everything. In perfect analogy to the belief that our understanding was imperfect, because we did not know enough, it was also felt that many goals were not reached, because what had to be done for that purpose could not be done fast enough. The usual explanation of the successful advent of the automatic computer refers to Babbage's technical failure to make one with mechanical means, and observes that, at last, electronic technology had made its construction feasible. I would like to offer another explanation: at last there was a cultural climate in which the attitude of "the more, the better" was such a predominant one that we were willing to accept the gimmick as the obvious tool for our salvation. And if you do not believe this explanation, try to imagine, how Confucius, Buddha, Jesus, Mohammed or Homer would have reacted when they had been offered a UNIVAC 1.... Who of us doesn't remember the advertisements for the first electronic businessmachines, proudly announcing that "our machines will make for you more than a hundred thousand decisions a second!". The advertisement did not warn the reader that they were all trivial, nor that in this connection the use of the term "decision" is misleading, but to that misleading terminology I shall return later. Speed was the key issue and, in the thinking of many, it still is.

The first warnings that with faster and faster machines, the conceptual problem of designing those wonderful computations for which tomorrow's machines would be powerful enough, would at least grow in proportion, were not taken in gratitude. They were not even heard, for they would have spoiled a dream.... Babbage's daydream had first to become a fully transistorized nightmare. And has the latter traumatic experience cured all of us from confusing daydreams with attainable reality? I am afraid not: the distorting spell of speed still seems to make its victims. We see automatic theorem provers proving toy theorems, we see automatic program verifiers verifying toy programs and one observes the honest expectation that with faster machines with lots of concurrent processing, the life-size problems will come within reach as well. But, honest as these expectations may be, are they justified? I sometimes wonder....

[1] "For in much wisdom is much grief; and he that increaseth knowledge increaseth sorrow" Ecclesiastes I:18.

Another path via which the last century's unwarranted scientific optimism has influenced our trade is psychology. In an effort to understand Man, the early psychologists decided to study Rat first. They designed a crude model of the Rat's behavior, that showed some, be it superficial, resemblance to the behavior of the true, average Rat. But in the scientific optimism of those days, that superficiality did not disturb anybody: the beginning, full of promise, was there, in principle the modelling worked and from now onwards it was only a question of refining the model. Once we should have a fully acceptable model of Rat, from there to a model of Man would then only be a next step. Modern psychology has recognized the limitations of this approach, but the somewhat ratomorphic image of Man lingers on....

What, one may ask again, has this to do with our trade? Well, as I hope to explain: everything. At the beginning of the computer revolution a book appeared with the ominous title "Giant brains, or machines that think". Once at a time I was tempted to write a compensating companion to it under the title "Giant hearts, or machines that fall in love", but I did not do so, when I realized that the title about the giant brains was more symptom than cause. To the somewhat excited hopes as to what machines can do had been added a somewhat simplified image of Man.

Extreme consequences of that attitude can be found in all efforts aimed at developing "natural language programming systems," a theme that recurs with the same regularity as influenza epidemics. It is observed that without considerable dedication people have a hard time expressing themselves precisely in a formal system as provided by a programming language. Man at large being rather education resistant in that view, the problem is solved by letting him express himself in a way that precludes precision. By posing smart questions about the Man's intentions—the Man in this connection always being denoted as "the user"—the system will eventually guess his intentions. Interactive facilities have added a new dimension to this game and ultimately the "user" will produce his design specifications as a kind of Pavlovian slobber.

These are, of course, extreme cases. But even efforts to prove mechanically a posteriori the correctness or—because for the latter there seems to be a bigger market—the incorrectness of programs, efforts to guess mechanically invariant relations for repetitive constructs—because most programmers are supposed to be too lazy or too stupid to write them down themselves—, they all have something of that condescending flavour. Just because a machine is very good at a few things we are poor at, it does not follow that ultimately the machine will be very good at something, just because we, ourselves, find it difficult. Yet, the euphoric pressure to believe so is still very strong.

Although not directly connected with the theme "software reliability", I cannot resist the temptation to draw from the wider field of Computing Science a few further examples. The desire to understand Man in terms of

Machine has—as is only to be expected—its counterpart, viz. the desire to understand the Machine in terms of Man: in computing science the terminology is shockingly anthropomorphic. What with Babbage was still called "a store" is now "a memory," what used to be called "an instruction code" is now called "a programming language." I picked up the sentence: "When this guy wants to talk to that guy...", while the speaker referred to distant components of a computer network, components, which indulged in "handshaking." I contend that this preponderance of anthropomorphic terminology is the symptom of a wide-spread confusion, a confusion without which, for instance, so-called "conversational programming" would never have enjoyed the glamour that, at one time, it did enjoy. Finally: the traces of the superstition "the more, the better" can be found in the awe for so-called "powerful" programming languages, with all their bells and whistles; and does the belief "the greater our knowledge, the better our understanding" not find its ultimate confirmation in today's cult of large data bases?

I would not like to leave you with the impression that Computing Science has developed along 30 years of foolish projects: such a distortion of the truth would be too gross even for the worst amateur historian! With respect to Software Reliability a lot has happened, insights of lasting value seem to have been gained, and all that took place in a relatively short period of time!

The first expression of serious concern about the confidence level of our programs that I could find in the open literature dates from 1961. In 1965, at the IFIP Congress, it is voiced by more. Stanley Gill, for instance, remarks: "Another practical problem, which is now beginning to loom very large indeed and offers little prospect of a satisfactory solution, is that of checking the correctness of a large program.", certainly an expression of serious concern! John McCarthy opens his introduction with: "The prize to be won if we can develop a reasonable theory of computation is the elimination of debugging. Instead, a programmer will present a computer-checked proof that a program has the desired properties." Here, the reader is left in doubt as to whether McCarthy's main concern is really the ultimately attainable confidence level or only the great expense of the debugging process, but serious concern is in any case voiced. In passing we note—we shall return to this later—that neither speaker mentions any alternative for a posteriori verification.

Were these quotations two fairly isolated examples taken from the 1965 Conference Proceedings, in 1968 the climate has changed drastically. In October 1968 the NATO Conference on Software Engineering created a sensation by its open admission of the software crisis. Anyone doubting, that much has changed since then, should read those conference proceedings! One now very well-known professor of Computing Science confessses that "the word "proof"causes him to have a sort of mental hiccough," another very well-known professor of Computing Science calls the notion of proof "idyllic" and nowhere does one find a reference to R. W. Floyd's article that by that time is already one year old! While that NATO Conference was perhaps technically not very significant, its political impact can hardly be underestimated: the most significant work has happened since!

After the above sketches of the intellectual climate, we turn in a little bit more detail to some of the more technical aspects: obviously we do so without any claim to completeness.

One of the, in retrospect, most striking things is that for many years the correctness problem was solely viewed as a posteriori verification of given programs. Given a program and given a set of requirements, does the given program meet the given requirements? Phrased as a question that could be answered by "Yes" or "No", it was apparently not without appeal for the mathematicians of that period. I think that a specific tradition pushed them—many of them not being programmers—into tackling the correctness problem from that side, and that is the tradition that got its pronounced form with the work of Alan M. Turing. It is the approach in which a—hopefully well-understood!—mechanism is started and we are invited to figure out whether we can prove something about the class of ensuing happenings, corresponding to the class of initial states in which the mechanism may be started. We can ask ourselves whether it will terminate or not, or, if that is too difficult, whether we can say something about the final state provided the activity terminates, and so on. It is the mechanistic, operational point of view which regards the "answer" to be *defined* as the last one of a long sequence of successive machine states. Turing's work and the branch of mathematics that emerged from it were so impressive that they caused a strong bias in the earlier work on program correctness, a bias, which, in retrospect, I do not consider as wholly fortunate. Its main consequences seem to have been the following.

Firstly, nearly all through the sixties, efforts at giving a formal definition of the semantics of programming languages have been in the form of writing an interpreter, i.e. designing an abstract machine, for such a programming language. Developing means for describing the intermediate states of such an abstract machine soon became a major concern.

Secondly, the unsolvability of the halting problem, combined with an early desire to mechanize correctness proving, has caused many to restrict themselves to proving partial correctness only, i.e. proving only that an acceptable answer will be produced under the additional assumption that the computational process terminates.

Since the late sixties we distinguish, however, a process for which "shedding the shackles of automata theory" could be an appropriate—be it perhaps too vivid—description. Two things started to happen in parallel, initially, as far as I can see, rather independently of each other.

The first development was the result of challenging the choice of a posteriori verification of given programs as the most significant problem, the argument against that choice being, that programs are not "given", but must be designed. Instead of trying to find out which known proof-patterns are applicable when faced with a given program, the program designer can try to do it the other way round: by first choosing the proof-pattern that he wants to be applicable, he can then write his program in such a way as to satisfy the requirements of that proof. This "inversion" of the problem of program correctness was one of the cornerstones of the field of activity which, about fives years ago, became known as "programming methodology". Correctness proofs began to play in that field two significant roles: firstly, in the constructive approach to the problem of program correctness, proof-patterns provided an important heuristic guidance during the programming process, secondly, the length of the correctness proof required was generally accepted as an objective measure for the "elegance" of programs and for the "adequacy" of proposed language features. This objectivity has probably been more effective in reaching a comfortable consensus among many than anything else, certainly more effective than eloquence could ever have been. I mention this consensus explicitly, because it has been so important: it was the only way in which we could hope to raise language design from the political and commercial level, aimed at "user satisfaction", to the level of a scientific activity.

In parallel to the exploration of programming methodologies, the methods for proving program correctness and their foundations slowly divorced themselves from the operational point of view. Naur's article of 1966 and Floyd's article of 1967 are the beginning, but Hoare's article of 1969 presents a firmer step away from that point of view, as he suggests that "axioms may provide a simple solution to the problem of leaving certain aspects of a language undefined". This remark is deeper than the primarily suggested applications such as leaving wordlength or precise rounding rules unspecified. Hoare's rules for the repetitive construct rely on the fact that the repeatable statement leaves a relevant relation invariant. As a result, the same macroscopic proof is applicable to two different programs that only differ in the form of the repeatable statements $S1$ and $S2$, provided that both $S1$ and $S2$ leave the relation invariant (and ensure progress in the same direction). But then the same proof applies to a non-deterministic machine in which a daemon decides quite arbitrarily at each repetition, whether $S1$ or $S2$ will be chosen! The fact that the obvious way was shown for dealing with at least some very common and desirable forms of non-determinacy, although obvious in retrospect, only came to be exploited systematically a few years later. From the operational point of view, such daemons seem to create problems: they must be assumed to supply some "ghost-input" to the mechanism that, assumed to be deterministic, otherwise would not know which way to go. Reasoning from the other end and starting with the functional specificatons, the daemons only enter the picture by the time that we start thinking about implementations: they appear as the freedom of the implementation, viz. whenever the choice does not matter.

I now skip the enumeration of a long series of important publications, successful development projects and promising research efforts, and would like to round up by drawing your attention to two side-effects of all these efforts, the final impact of which still lies in the future.

The first one is that most techniques for proving the correctness of a program treat the program text as a static, rather formal mathematical object, that can be dealt with independently of the fact that there may exist machines that could execute such a program. As such, a clear *separation of concerns* emerges: we might call them the mathematical concerns about correctness and the engineering concerns about efficiency. In contrast to correctness concerns, the efficiency concerns are only meaningful in relation to implementations and it is only while concerned with efficiency that we need to remember that the program text is intended to evoke computational processes. Both the mathematical and the engineering concerns have, of course, always been with us, but once they used to be dealt with inextricably intertwined. The discovery how to separate them rigorously in our thinking is relatively young, and even when aware of this possibility, we often fall back into our old bad habits. But I guess that this discovery will have profound consequences, which will become fully apparent when new generations of programmers have been educated, who separate these concerns more naturally than we do, unhampered as they are by our obsolete experience and our wornout habits.

The second side-effect concerns the bells and whistles of yesterday's programming languages. When the correctness guys started their efforts, they used at first very simple programming languages, mini-languages, one might say. For the programmers who lived in "the real world of computing", this restriction was sometimes a reason for some scorn: "Toy-problems, solved by toy-programs, written in toy-languages: what has that to do with us?"

But things, again, are changing. People decided to try to program without goto-statements, and it did not do much harm to the efficiency of their programs, quite often to the contrary even. People decided to do away with "controlled variables" as we know them from FORTRAN's **do**-loops or ALGOL 60's **for**-statements, and this did not impair the efficiency either. But after a while, these "restrictions" turned out to bear unexpected fruits: for instance, people who had trained themselves in using a very simple, but elegant repetitive construct, could discover algorithms that turned out to be much harder to find by a programmer in whose mind repetition was irrevocably connected with a "controlled variable": the latter's abolishment turned out to be a gain! And this process seems to be continuing: the correctness guys still have a tendency to use minilanguages, but in the mean time their experience in using them is no longer restricted to toy-problems. On the contrary.

I would like to end this talk by relating a recent personal experience that may be exemplary for the kind of surprises that the use of such mini-languages still may have in store for us. I had been exploring programming methodologies and as a carrier for my investigations I had used a mini-language without recursion (although, intuitively, I was fully familiar with recursive programs for about fifteen years). I just did not feel tempted to introduce recursion at that stage, because my mini-language did contain extensible arrays and, when tempted to use recursion, I felt that, at least for the time being, I could always try "to program around it".

For a problem that was new for me, I developed (as a matter of fact without feeling the need for recursion) without much hesitation in a few steps a beautiful algorithm, clear, compactly coded and surprisingly efficient in terms of number of operations needed. Some months later I discovered that for exactly that problem an algorithm had been published, that had the same efficiency characteristics, but was not too easy to understand and—probably as a result—was generally considered as a great intellectual achievement: it has been called "a deep algorithm". For the difference in clarity and the ease of discovery I can only offer one explanation. My program manipulates explicitly—they entered the design quite naturally, one after the other—four independent stacks, most of them growing and shrinking asynchronously with respect to each other. The published version, however, was a recursive program, by its very nature favouring a solution with *one* (anonymous) stack, and having to squeeze a four-stack algorithm into *that* straightjacket may indeed make its discovery a "great intellectual achievement".

Some time before I had met another occasion for reappraisal of recursive solutions. As part of the solution to a much larger problem I had written an algorithm for what boiled down to the construction of a transitive closure: a given "starting set" belongs to the transitive closure and, if an element belongs to the transitive closure, so do its given "successors". My repetitive algorithm satisfied me completely: besides building up the set of elements belonging to the closure, it kept track of a subset of them, the so-called "candidates", i.e. those elements that still could have successors leading outside the current closure. It was only after completion of this algorithm when I realized that the time-honoured recursive solution for the traversal of a (rooted) binary tree was a special case, in which the absence of cycles permitted the omission of a membership test. But thanks to that, the set of candidates could remain anonymous, and in the recursive solution for the tree traversal its role is taken over by the anonymous stack. Moreover, the fact that the recursive solution grows its anonymous candidate set on a last-in-first-out basis turns out to be totally irrelevant! The discovery that doubts can be cast upon the central position of recursion—in Computing Science for more than a decade the hallmark of academic respectability!—was something of a shock for me!

And now we see the nature of the surprises that the future still may hold in store for us. A number of our established "powerful" programming language features, even beloved ones, could very well turn out to belong to "the problem set", rather than to "the solution set". And even if such refreshing conclusions were the only lasting contribution of the work of the correctness guys, their efforts seem already well-rewarded!

8
An Axiomatic Basis for Computer Programming[1]

C. A. R. Hoare
University of Oxford

Abstract   *In this paper an attempt is made to explore the logical foundations of computer programming by use of techniques which were first applied in the study of geometry and have later been extended to other branches of mathematics. This involves the elucidation of sets of axioms and rules of inference which can be used in proofs of the properties of computer programs. Examples are given of such axioms and rules, and a formal proof of a simple theorem is displayed. Finally, it is argued that important advantages, both theoretical and practical, may follow from a pursuance of these topics.*

1 Introduction

Computer programming is an exact science in that all the properties of a program and all the consequences of executing it in any given environment can, in principle, be found out from the text of the program itself by means of purely deductive reasoning. Deductive reasoning involves the application of valid rules of inference to sets of valid axioms. It is therefore desirable and interesting to elucidate the axioms and rules of inference which underlie our reasoning about computer programs. The exact choice of axioms will to some extent depend on the choice of programming language. For illustrative purposes, this paper is confined to a very simple language, which is effectively a subset of all current procedure-oriented languages.

2 Computer arithmetic

The first requirement in valid reasoning about a program is to know the properties of the elementary operations which it invokes, for example, addition and multiplication of integers. Unfortunately, in several respects computer arithmetic is not the same as the arithmetic familiar to mathematicians, and it is necessary to exercise some care in selecting an appropriate set of axioms. For example, the axioms displayed in Table I are rather a small selection of axioms relevant to integers. From this incomplete set of axioms it is possible to deduce such simple theorems as:

$$x = x + y \times 0$$

$$y \leqslant r \supset r + y \times q = (r - y) + y \times (1 + q)$$

The proof of the second of these is:

A5	$(r-y)+y\times(1+q)=(r-y)+(y\times 1+y\times q)$
A9	$=(r-y)+(y+y\times q)$
A3	$=((r-y)+y)+y\times q$
A6	$=r+y\times q$ provided $y \leqslant r$

The axioms A1 and A9 are, of course, true of the traditional infinite set of integers in mathematics. However, they are also true of the finite sets of "integers" which are manipulated by computers provided that they are confined to *nonnegative* numbers. Their truth is independent of the size of the set; furthermore, it is largely independent of the choice of technique applied in the event of "overflow"; for example:

(1) Strict interpretation: the result of an overflowing operation does not exist; when overflow occurs, the offending program never completes its operation. Note that in this case, the equalities of A1 to A9 are strict, in the sense that both sides exist or fail to exist together.
(2) Firm boundary: the result of an overflowing operation is taken as the maximum value represented.
(3) Modulo arithmetic: the result of an overflowing operation is computed modulo the size of the set of integers represented.

Table I

A1	$x+y=y+x$	addition is commutative
A2	$x\times y=y\times x$	multiplication is commutative
A3	$(x+y)+z=x+(y+z)$	addition is associative
A4	$(x\times y)\times z=x\times(y\times z)$	multiplication is associative
A5	$x\times(y+z)=x\times y+x\times z$	multiplication distributes through addition
A6	$y\leqslant x\supset(x-y)+y=x$	addition cancels subtraction
A7	$x+0=x$	
A8	$x\times 0=0$	
A9	$x\times 1=x$	

Table II

			1.	Strict Interpretation					
+	0	1	2	3		×	0	1	2	3
0	0	1	2	3		0	0	0	0	0
1	1	2	3	*		1	0	1	2	3
2	2	3	*	*		2	0	2	*	*
3	3	*	*	*		3	0	3	*	*

*nonexistent

			2.	Firm Boundary					
+	0	1	2	3		×	0	1	2	3
0	0	1	2	3		0	0	0	0	0
1	1	2	3	3		1	0	1	2	3
2	2	3	3	3		2	0	2	3	3
3	3	3	3	3		3	0	3	3	3

			3.	Modulo Arithmetic					
+	0	1	2	3		×	0	1	2	3
0	0	1	2	3		0	0	0	0	0
1	1	2	3	0		1	0	1	2	3
2	2	3	0	1		2	0	2	0	2
3	3	0	1	2		3	0	3	2	1

These three techniques are illustrated in Table II by addition and multiplication tables for a trivially small model in which 0, 1, 2, and 3 are the only integers represented.

It is interesting to note that the different systems satisfying axioms A1 to A9 may be rigorously distinguished from each other by choosing a particular one of a set of mutually exclusive supplementary axioms. For example, infinite arithmetic satisfies the axiom:

A10$_I$ $\qquad\qquad\qquad\qquad$ $\neg \exists x \forall y \qquad (y \leqslant x)$,

where all finite arithmetics satisfy:

A10$_F$ $\qquad\qquad\qquad\qquad\qquad$ $\forall x \qquad (x \leqslant \text{max})$

where "max" denotes the largest integer represented.

Similarly, the three treatments of overflow may be distinguished by a choice of one of the following axioms relating to the value of max + 1:

A11$_S$ $\qquad\qquad$ $\neg \exists x \qquad (x = \text{max} + 1)$ $\qquad\qquad$ (strict interpretation)

A11$_B$ $\qquad\qquad$ max + 1 = max $\qquad\qquad\qquad$ (firm boundary)

A11$_M$ $\qquad\qquad$ max + 1 = 0 $\qquad\qquad\qquad\quad$ (modulo arithmetic)

Having selected one of these axioms, it is possible to use it in deducing the properties of programs; however, these properties will not necessarily obtain, unless the program is executed on an implementation which satisfies the chosen axiom.

3 Program execution

As mentioned above, the purpose of this study is to provide a logical basis for proofs of the properties of a program. One of the most important properties of a program is whether or not it carries out its intended function. The intended function of a program, or part of a program, can be specified by making general assertions about the values which the relevant variables will take *after* execution of the program. These assertions will usually not ascribe particular values to each variable, but will rather specify certain general properties of the values and the relationships holding between them. We use the normal notations of mathematical logic to express these assertions, and the familiar rules of operator precedence have been used wherever possible to improve legibility.

In many cases, the validity of the results of a program (or part of a program) will depend on the values taken by the variables before that program is initiated. These initial preconditions of successful use can be specified by the same type of general assertion as is used to describe the results obtained on termination. To state the required connection between a precondition (P), a program (Q) and a description of the result of its execution (R), we introduce a new notation:

$$P\{Q\}R.$$

This may be interpreted "If the assertion P is true before initiation of a program Q, then the assertion R will be true on its completion." If there are no preconditions imposed, we write **true** $\{Q\}R.$[1]

The treatment given below is essentially due to [Floyd 67] but is applied to texts rather than flowcharts.

3.1 Axiom of assignment

Assignment is undoubtedly the most characteristic feature of programming a digital computer, and one that most clearly distinguishes it from other branches of mathematics. It is surprising therefore that the axiom govern-

---

[1] If this can be proved in our formal system, we use the familiar logical symbol for theoremhood: $\vdash P\{Q\}R.$

ing our reasoning about assignment is quite as simple as any to be found in elementary logic.

Consider the assignment statement:

$$x: =f$$

where

x is an identifier for a simple variable;
f is an expression of a programming language without side effects, but possibly containing x.

Now any assertion $P(x)$ which is to be true of (the value of) x *after* the assignment is made must also have been true of (the value of) the expression f, taken *before* the assignment is made, i.e. with the old value of x. Thus if $P(x)$ is to be true after the assignment, then $P(f)$ must be true before the assignment. This fact may be expressed more formally:

D0   Axiom of Assignment

$$\vdash P_0\{x: =f\}P$$

where

x is a variable identifier;
f is an expression;
P_0 is obtained from P by substituting f for all occurrences of x.

It may be noticed that D0 is not really an axiom at all, but rather an axiom schema, describing an infinite set of axioms which share a common pattern. This pattern is described in purely syntactic terms, and it is easy to check whether any finite text conforms to the pattern, thereby qualifying as an axiom, which may validly appear in any line of a proof.

3.2 Rules of consequence

In addition to axioms, a deductive science requires at least one rule of inference, which permits the deduction of new theorems from one or more axioms or theorems already proved. A rule of inference takes the form "If $\vdash X$ and $\vdash Y$ then $\vdash Z$", i.e. if assertions of the form X and Y have been proved as theorems, then Z also is thereby proved as a theorem. The simplest example of an inference rule states that if the execution of a program Q ensures the truth of the assertion R, then it also ensures the truth of every assertion logically implied by R. Also, if P is known to be a precondition for a program Q to produce result R, then so is any other assertion which logically implies P. These rules may be expressed more formally:

D1   Rules of Consequence

If $\vdash P\{Q\}R$ and $\vdash R \supset S$ then $\vdash P\{Q\}S$

If $\vdash P\{Q\}R$ and $\vdash S \supset P$ then $\vdash S\{Q\}R$

3.3 Rule of composition

A program generally consists of a sequence of statements which are executed one after another. The statements may be separated by a semi-colon or equivalent symbol denoting procedural composition: $(Q_1; Q_2; \cdots ; Q_n)$. In order to avoid the awkwardness of dots, it is possible to deal initially with only two statements $(Q_1; Q_2)$, since longer sequences can be reconstructed by nesting, thus $(Q_1; (Q_2; (\cdots (Q_{n-1}; Q_n)\cdots)))$. The removal of the brackets of this nest may be regarded as convention based on the associativity of the ";-operator", in the same way as brackets are removed from an arithmetic expression $(t_1+(t_2+(\cdots (t_{n-1}+t_n)\cdots)))$.

The inference rule associated with composition states that if the proven result of the first part of a program is identical with the precondition under which the second part of the program produces its intended result, then the whole program will produce the intended result, provided that the precondition of the first part is satisfied.

In more formal terms:

D2   Rule of Composition

If $\vdash P\{Q_1\}R_1$ and $\vdash R_1\{Q_2\}R$ then $\vdash P\{(Q_1; Q_2)\}R$

3.4 Rule of iteration

The essential feature of a stored program computer is the ability to execute some portion of program (S) repeatedly until a condition (B) goes false. A simple way of expressing such an iteration is to adapt the ALGOL 60 **while** notation:

while B **do** S

In executing this statement, a computer first tests the condition B. If this is false, S is omitted, and execution of the loop is complete. Otherwise, S is executed and B is tested again. This action is repeated until B is found to be false. The reasoning which leads to a formulation of an inference rule for iteration is as follows. Suppose P to be an assertion which is always true on completion of S, provided that it is also true on initiation. Then obviously P will still be true after any number of iterations of the statement S (even no iterations). Furthermore, it is known that the controlling condition B is false when the iteration finally terminates. A slightly more powerful formulation is possible in light of the fact that B may be assumed to be true on initiation of S:

  D3 Rule of Iteration

  If $\vdash P \wedge B\{S\}P$ then $\vdash P\{\textbf{while } B \textbf{ do } S\} \neg B \wedge P$

3.5 Example

The axioms quoted above are sufficient to construct the proof of properties of simple programs, for example, a routine intended to find the quotient q and remainder r obtained on dividing x by y. All variables are assumed to range over a set of nonnegative integers conforming to the axioms listed in Table I. For simplicity we use the trivial but inefficient method of successive subtraction. The proposed program is:

$$((r:=x; q:=0); \quad \textbf{while} \quad y \leqslant r \textbf{ do } (r:=r-y; q:=1+q))$$

An important property of this program is that when it terminates, we can recover the numerator x by adding to the remainder r the product of the

Table III

Line number	Formal proof	Justification
1	$\textbf{true} \supset x = x + y \times 0$	Lemma 1
2	$x = x + y \times 0\{r:=x\}x = r + y \times 0$	D0
3	$x = r + y \times 0\{q:=0\}x = r + y \times q$	D0
4	$\textbf{true}\{r:=x\}x = r + y \times 0$	D1 (1, 2)
5	$\textbf{true } \{r:=x; q:=0\}x = r + y \times q$	D2 (4, 3)
6	$x = r + y \times q \wedge y \leqslant r \supset x = (r-y) + y \times (1+q)$	Lemma 2
7	$x = (r-y) + y \times (1+q)\{r:=r-y\}x = r + y \times (1+q)$	D0
8	$x = r + y \times (1+q)\{q:=1+q\}x = r + y \times q$	D0
9	$x = (r-y) + y \times (1+q)\{r:=r-y; q:=1+q\}x = r + y \times q$	D2 (7, 8)
10	$x = r + y \times q \wedge y \leqslant r\{r:=r-y; q:=1+q\}x = r + y \times q$	D1 (6, 9)
11	$x = r + y \times q\{\textbf{while } y \leqslant r \textbf{ do } (r:=r-y; q:=1+q)\}$ $\neg y \leqslant r \wedge x = r + y \times q$	D3 (10)
12	$\textbf{true } \{((r:=x; q:=0); \textbf{while } y \leqslant r$ $\textbf{do } (r:=r-y; q:=1+q))\} \neg y \leqslant r \wedge x = r + y \times q$	D2 (5, 11)

1. The left hand column is used to number the lines, and the right hand column to justify each line, by appealing to an axiom, a lemma or a rule of inference applied to one or two previous lines, indicated in brackets. Neither of these columns is part of the formal proof. For example, line 2 is an instance of the axiom of assignment (D0); line 12 is obtained from lines 5 and 11 by application of the rule of composition (D2).

2. Lemma 1 may be proved from axioms A7 and A8.

3. Lemma 2 follows directly from the theorem proved in Sec. 2.

divisor y and the quotient q (i.e. $x = r + y \times q$). Furthermore, the remainder is less than the divisor. These properties may be expressed formally:

$$\textbf{true} \; \{ Q \} \, \neg y \leqslant r \land x = r + y \times q$$

where Q stands for the program displayed above. This expresses a necessary (but not sufficient) condition for the "correctness" of the program.

A formal proof of this theorem is given in Table III. Like all formal proofs, it is excessively tedious, and it would be fairly easy to introduce notational conventions which would significantly shorten it. An even more powerful method of reducing the tedium of formal proofs is to derive general rules for proof construction out of the simple rules accepted as postulates. These general rules would be shown to be valid by demonstrating how every theorem proved with their assistance could equally well (if more tediously) have been proved without. Once a powerful set of supplementary rules has been developed, a "formal proof" reduces to little more than an informal indication of how a formal proof could be constructed.

4 General reservations

The axioms and rules of inference quoted in this paper have implicitly assumed the absence of side effects of the evaluation of expressions and conditions. In proving properties of programs expressed in a language permitting side effects, it would be necessary to prove their absence in each case before applying the appropriate proof technique. If the main purpose of a high level programming language is to assist in the construction and verification of correct programs, it is doubtful whether the use of functional notation to call procedures with side effects is a genuine advantage.

Another deficiency in the axioms and rules quoted above is that they give no basis for a proof that a program successfully terminates. Failure to terminate may be due to an infinite loop; or it may be due to violation of an implementation-defined limit, for example, the range of numeric operands, the size of storage, or an operating system time limit. Thus the notation "$P\{Q\}R$" should be interpreted "provided that the program successfully terminates, the properties of its results are described by R." It is fairly easy to adapt the axioms so that they cannot be used to predict the "results" of nonterminating programs; but the actual use of the axioms would now depend on knowledge of many implementation-dependent features, for example, the size and speed of the computer, the range of numbers, and the choice of overflow technique. Apart from proofs of the avoidance of infinite loops, it is probably better to prove the "conditional" correctness of a program and rely on an implementation to give a warning if it has had to abandon execution of the program as a result of violation of an implementation limit.

Finally it is necessary to list some of the areas which have not been covered: for example, real arithmetic, bit and character manipulation, complex arithmetic, fractional arithmetic, arrays, records, overlay definition, files, input/output, declarations, subroutines, parameters, recursion, and parallel execution. Even the characterization of integer arithmetic is far from complete. There does not appear to be any great difficulty in dealing with these points, provided that the programming language is kept simple. Areas which do present real difficulty are labels and jumps, pointers, and name parameters. Proofs of programs which make use of these features are likely to be elaborate, and it is not surprising that this should be reflected in the complexity of the underlying axioms.

5 Proofs of program correctness

The most important property of a program is whether it accomplishes the intentions of its user. If these intentions can be described rigorously by making assertions about the values of variables at the end (or at intermediate points) of the execution of the program, then the techniques described in this paper may be used to prove the correctness of the program, provided that the implementation of the programming language conforms to the axioms and rules which have been used in the proof. This fact itself might also be established by deductive reasoning, using an axiom set which describes the logical properties of the hardware circuits. When the correctness of a program, its compiler, and the hardware of the computer have all been established with mathematical certainty, it will be possible to place great reliance on the results of the program, and predict their properties with a confidence limited only by the reliability of the electronics.

The practice of supplying proofs for nontrivial programs will not become widespread until considerably more powerful proof techniques become available, and even then will not be easy. But the practical advantages of program proving will eventually outweigh the difficulties, in view of the increasing costs of programming error. At present, the method which a programmer uses to convince himself of the correctness of his program is to try it out in particular cases and to modify it if the results produced do not correspond to his intentions. After he has found a reasonably wide variety of example cases on which the program seems to work, he believes that it will always work. The time spent in this program testing is often more than half the time spent on the entire programming project; and with a realistic costing of machine time, two thirds (or more) of the cost of the project is involved in removing errors during this phase.

The cost of removing errors discovered after a program has gone into use is often greater, particularly in the case of items of computer manufacturer's software for which a large part of the expense is borne by the user. And finally, the cost of error in certain types of programs may be almost incalculable—a lost spacecraft, a collapsed building, a crashed aeroplane, or a world war. Thus the practice of program proving is not only a theoretical pursuit, followed in the interests of academic respectability, but a serious recommendation for the reduction of the costs associated with programming error.

The practice of proving programs is likely to alleviate some of the other problems which afflict the computing world. For example, there is the problem of program documentation, which is essential, firstly, to inform a potential user of a subroutine how to use it and what it accomplishes, and secondly, to assist in further development when it becomes necessary to update a program to meet changing circumstances or to improve it in the light of increased knowledge. The most rigorous method of formulating the purpose of a subroutine, as well as the conditions of its proper use, is to make assertions about the values of variables before and after its execution. The proof of the correctness of these assertions can then be used as a lemma in the proof of any program which calls the subroutine. Thus, in a large program, the structure of the whole can be clearly mirrored in the structure of its proof. Furthermore, when it becomes necessary to modify a program, it will always be valid to replace any subroutine by another which satisfies the same criterion of correctness. Finally, when examining the detail of the algorithm, it seems probable that the proof will be helpful in explaining not only *what* is happening but *why*.

Another problem which can be solved, insofar as it is soluble by the practice of program proofs, is that of transferring programs from one design of computer to another. Even when written in a so-called machine-independent programming language, many large programs inadvertently take advantage of some machine-dependent property of a particular implementation, and unpleasant and expensive surprises can result when attempting to transfer it to another machine. However, presence of a machine-dependent feature will always be revealed in advance by the failure of an attempt to prove the program from machine-independent axioms. The programmer will then have the choice of formulating his algorithm in a machine-independent fashion, possibly with the help of environment enquiries; or if this involves too much effort or inefficiency, he can deliberately construct a machine-dependent program, and rely for his proof on some machine-dependent axiom, for example, one of the versions of A11 (Section 2). In the latter case, the axiom must be explicitly quoted as one of the preconditions of successful use of the program. The program can still, with complete confidence, be transferred to any other machine which happens to satisfy the same machine-dependent axiom; but if it becomes necessary to transfer it to an implementation which does not, then all the places where changes are required will be clearly annotated by the fact that the proof at that point appeals to the truth of the offending machine-dependent axiom.

Thus the practice of proving programs would seem to lead to solution of three of the most pressing problems in software and programming, namely, reliability, documentation, and compatibility. However, program proving, certainly at present, will be difficult even for programmers of high caliber; and may be applicable only to quite simple program designs. As in other areas, reliability can be purchased only at the price of simplicity.

6 Formal language definition

A high level programming language, such as ALGOL, FORTRAN, or COBOL, is usually intended to be implemented on a variety of computers of differing size, configuration, and design. It has been found a serious problem to define these languages with sufficient rigour to ensure compatibility among all implementors. Since the purpose of compatibility is to facilitate interchange of programs expressed in the language, one way to achieve this would be to insist that all implementations of the language shall "satisfy" the axioms and rules of inference which underlie proofs of the properties of programs expressed in the language, so that all predictions based on these proofs will be fulfilled, except in the event of hardware failure. In effect, this is equivalent to accepting the axioms and rules of inference as the ultimately definitive specification of the meaning of the language.

Apart from giving an immediate and possibly even provable criterion for the correctness of an implementation, the axiomatic technique for the definition of programming language semantics appears to be like the formal syntax of the ALGOL 60 report, in that it is sufficiently simple to be understood both by the implementor and by the reasonably sophisticated user of the language. It is only by bridging this widening communication gap in a single document (perhaps even provably consistent) that the maximum advantage can be obtained from a formal language definition.

Another of the great advantages of using an axiomatic approach is that axioms offer a simple and flexible technique for leaving certain aspects of a language *undefined*, for example, range of integers, accuracy of floating point, and choice of overflow technique. This is absolutely essential for standardization purposes, since otherwise the language will be impossible to implement efficiently on differing hardware designs. Thus a programming language standard should consist of a set of axioms of universal applicability, together with a choice from a set of supplementary axioms describing the range of choices facing an implementor. An example of the use of axioms for this purpose was given in Section 2.

Another of the objectives of formal language definition is to assist in the design of better programming languages. The regularity, clarity, and ease of implementation of the ALGOL 60 syntax may at least in part be due to the use of an elegant formal technique for its definition. The use of axioms may lead to similar advantages in the area of "semantics," since it seems likely that a language which can be described by a few "self-evident" axioms from which proofs will be relatively easy to construct will be preferable to a language with many obscure axioms which are difficult to apply in proofs. Furthermore, axioms enable the language designer to express his general *intentions* quite simply and directly, without the mass of detail which usually accompanies algorithmic descriptions. Finally, axioms can be formulated in a manner largely independent of each other, so that the designer can work freely on one axiom or group of axioms without fear of unexpected interaction effects with other parts of the language.

Acknowledgments. Many axiomatic treatments of computer programming ([Yanov 58; Igarashi 64; de Bakker 68]) tackle the problem of proving the equivalence, rather than the correctness, of algorithms. Other approaches ([McCarthy 63; Burstall 68*]) take recursive functions rather than programs as a starting point for the theory. The suggestion to use axioms for defining the primitive operations of a computer appears in ([van Wijngaarden 66; Laski 68]). The importance of program proofs is clearly emphasized in [Naur 66*], and an informal technique for providing them is described. The suggestion that the specification of proof techniques provides an adequate formal definition of a programming language first appears in [Floyd 67]. The formal treatment of program execution presented in this paper is clearly derived from Floyd. The main contributions of the author appear to be: (1) a suggestion that axioms may provide a simple solution to the problem of leaving certain aspects of a language undefined; (2) a comprehensive evaluation of the possible benefits to be gained by adopting this approach both for program proving and for formal language definition.

However, the formal material presented here has only an expository status and represents only a minute proportion of what remains to be done. It is hoped that many of the fascinating problems involved will be taken up by others.

9
Proof of a Program: FIND[1]

C. A. R. Hoare
University of Oxford

Abstract *A proof is given of the correctness of the algorithm "Find." First, an informal description is given of the purpose of the program and the method used. A systematic technique is described for constructing the program proof during the process of coding it, in such a way as to prevent the intrusion of logical errors. The proof of termination is treated as a separate exercise. Finally, some conclusions relating to general programming methodology are drawn.*

1 Introduction

In a number of papers ([Naur 66*; Dijkstra 68e*; Hoare 69*] the desirability of proving the correctness of programs has been suggested and this has been illustrated by proofs of simple example programs. In this paper the construction of the proof of a useful, efficient, and nontrivial program, using a method based on invariants, is shown. It is suggested that if a proof is constructed as part of the coding process for an algorithm, it is hardly more laborious than the traditional practice of program testing.

2 The program "Find"

The purpose of the program Find [Hoare 61*] is to find that element of an array $A[1:N]$ whose value is fth in order of magnitude; and to rearrange the array in such a way that this element is placed in $A[f]$; and furthermore, all elements with subscripts lower than f have lesser values, and all elements with subscripts greater than f have greater values. Thus on completion of the program, the following relationship will hold:

$$A[1], A[2], \ldots, A[f-1] \leqslant A[f] \leqslant A[f+1], \ldots, A[N]$$

This relation is abbreviated as Found.

[1]Copyright © 1971, Association for Computing Machinery, Inc., reprinted by permission.

One method of achieving the desired effect would be to sort the whole array. If the array is small, this would be a good method; but if the array is large, the time taken to sort it will also be large. The Find program is designed to take advantage of the weaker requirements to save much of the time which would be involved in a full sort.

The usefulness of the Find program arises from its application to the problem of finding the median or other quantiles of a set of observations stored in a computer array. For example, if N is odd and f is set to $(N+1)/2$, the effect of the Find program will be to place an observation with value equal to the median in $A[f]$. Similarly the first quartile may be found by setting f to $(N+1)/4$, and so on.

The method used is based on the principle that the desired effect of Find is to move lower valued elements of the array to one end—the "left-hand" end—and higher valued elements of the array to the other end —the "right-hand" end. (See Table I(a)). This suggests that the array be scanned, starting at the left-hand end and moving rightward. Any element encountered which is small will remain where it is, but any element which is large should be moved up to the right-hand end of the array, in exchange for a small one. In order to find such a small element, a separate scan is made, starting at the right-hand end and moving leftward. In this scan, any large element encountered remains where it is; the first small element encountered is moved down to the left-hand end in exchange for the large element already encountered in the rightward scan. Then both scans can be resumed until the next exchange is necessary. The process is repeated until the scans meet somewhere in the middle of the array. It is then known that all elements to the left of this meeting point will be small, and all elements to the right will be large. When this condition holds, we will say that the array is *split at* the given point into two parts (see Table I(b)).

The reasoning of the previous paragraph assumes that there is some means of distinguishing small elements from large ones. Since we are interested only in their comparative values, it is sufficient to select the value of some arbitrary element before either of the scans starts; any element with lower value than the selected element is counted as small, and any element with higher value is counted as large. The fact that the discriminating value is arbitrary means that the place where the two scans will meet is also arbitrary; but it does not affect the fact that the array will be split at the meeting point, wherever that may be.

Now consider the question on which side of the split the fth element in order of value is to be found. If the split is to the right of $A[f]$, then the desired element must of necessity be to the left of the split, and all elements to the right of the split will be greater than it. In this case, all elements to the right of the split can be ignored in any future processing, since they are already in their proper place, namely to the right of $A[f]$ (see Table I(c)). Similarly, if the split is to the left of $A[f]$, the element to be found must be to the right of the split, and all elements to the left of the

Table 1

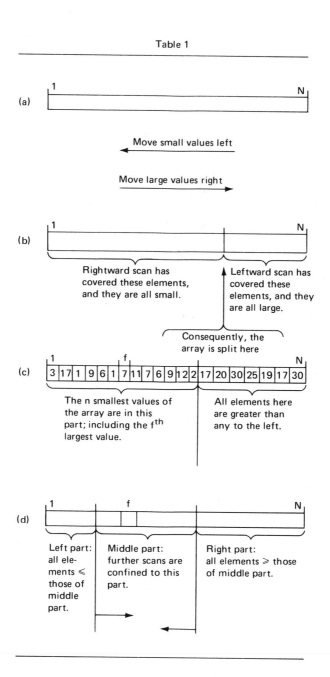

split must be equal or less than it; furthermore, these elements can be ignored in future processing.

In either case, the program proceeds by repeating the rightward and leftward scans, but this time one of the scans will start at the split rather than at the beginning of the array. When the two scans meet again, it will be known that there is a second split in the array, this time perhaps on the other side of $A[f]$. Thus again, we may proceed with the rightward and leftward scans, but we start the rightward scan at the split on the left of $A[f]$ and the leftward scan at the split on the right, thus confining attention only to that part of the array that lies between the two splits; this will be known as the *middle part* of the array (see Table I(d)).

When the third scan is complete, the middle part of the array will be split again into two parts. We take the new middle part as that part which contains $A[f]$ and repeat the double scan on this new middle part. The process is repeated until the middle part consists of only one element, namely $A[f]$. This element will now be equal to or greater than all elements to the left and equal to or less than all elements to the right; and thus the desired result of Find will be accomplished.

This has been an informal description of the method used by the program Find. Diagrams have been used to convey an understanding of how and why the method works, and they serve as an intuitive proof of its correctness. However, the method is described only in general terms, leaving many details undecided; and accordingly, the intuitive proof is far from watertight. In the next section, the details of the method will be filled in during the process of coding it in a formal programming language; and simultaneously, the details of the proof will be formalized in traditional logical notation. The end product of this activity will be a program suitable for computer execution, together with a proof of its correctness. The reader who checks the validity of the proof will thereby convince himself that the program requires no testing.

3 Coding and proof construction

The coding and proof construction may be split into several stages, each stage dealing with greater detail than the previous one. Furthermore, each stage may be systematically analyzed as a series of steps.

3.1 Stage 1: problem definition

The first stage in coding and proof construction is to obtain a rigorous formulation of what is to be accomplished, and what may be assumed to begin with. In this case we may assume:

(a) The subscript bounds of A are 1 and N.

(b) $1 \leqslant f \leqslant N$.

The required result is:

$$\forall p,q\left(1 \leqslant p \leqslant f \leqslant q \leqslant N \supset A[p] \leqslant A[f] \leqslant A[q]\right) \qquad [\text{Found}]$$

3.2 Stage 2: the general method

(1) The first step in each stage is to decide what variables will be required to hold intermediate results of the program. In the case of Find, it will be necessary to know at all times the extent of the middle part, which is currently being scanned. This indicates the introduction of variables m and n to point to the first element $A[m]$ and the last element $A[n]$ of the middle part.

(2) The second step is to attempt to describe more formally the purpose of each variable, which was informally described in the previous step. This purpose may be expressed as a formula of logic which is intended to remain true throughout the execution of the program, even when the value of the variable concerned is changed by assignment.[1] Such a formula is known as an *invariant*. As mentioned above, m is intended to point to the leftmost element of the middle part of the array; and the middle part at all times contains $A[f]$; consequently m is never greater than f. Furthermore, there is always a split just to the left of the middle part, that is between $m-1$ and m. Thus the following formula should be true for m throughout execution of the program:

$$m \leqslant f \ \& \ \forall p,q\left(1 \leqslant p < m \leqslant q \leqslant N \supset A[p] \leqslant A[q]\right)$$

$$[m\text{-invariant}]$$

Similarly, n is intended to point to the rightmost element of the middle part; it must never be less than f, and there will always be a split just to the right of it:

$$f \leqslant n \ \& \ \forall p,q\left(1 \leqslant p \leqslant n < q \leqslant N \supset A[p] \leqslant A[q]\right)$$

$$[n\text{-invariant}]$$

(3) The next step is to determine the initial values for these variables. Since the middle part of the array is intended to be the part that still requires processing, and since to begin with the whole array requires processing, the obvious choice of initial values of m and n are 1 and N, respectively, indicating the first and last elements of the whole array. The code required is:

$$m := 1; \quad n := N$$

[1] Except possibly in certain "critical regions."

(4) It is necessary next to check that these values satisfy the relevant invariants. This may be done by substituting the initial value for the corresponding variable in each invariant, and ensuring that the result follows from facts already known:

$$1 \leqslant f \leqslant N \supset 1 \leqslant f \;\&\; \forall p,q(1 \leqslant p < 1 \leqslant q \leqslant N \supset A[p] \leqslant A[q])$$

$$\text{[Lemma 1]}$$

$$1 \leqslant f \leqslant N \supset f \leqslant N \;\&\; \forall p,q(1 \leqslant p \leqslant N < q \leqslant N \supset A[p] \leqslant A[q])$$

$$\text{[Lemma 2]}$$

The quantified clause of each lemma is trivially true since the antecedents of the implications are always false.

(5) After setting the initial values, the method of the program is repeatedly to reduce the size of the middle part, until it contains only one element. This may be accomplished by an iteration of the form:

while $m < n$ **do** "reduce middle part"

(6) It remains to prove that this loop accomplishes the objectives of the program as a whole. If we write the body of the iteration properly (i.e. in such a way as to preserve the truth of all invariants) then all invariants will still be true on termination. Furthermore, termination will occur only when $m < n$ goes false. Thus it is necessary only to show that the combination of the truth of the invariants and the falsity of the while clause expression $m < n$ implies the truth of Found.

$$m \leqslant f \;\&\; \forall p,q(1 \leqslant p < m \leqslant q \leqslant N \supset A[p] \leqslant A[q])$$

$$\&\, f \leqslant n \;\&\; \forall p,q(1 \leqslant p \leqslant n < q \leqslant N \supset A[p] \leqslant A[q]) \;\&\; \neg m < n$$

$$\supset \forall p,q(1 \leqslant p \leqslant f \leqslant q \leqslant N \supset A[p] \leqslant A[f] \leqslant A[q]) \quad \text{[Lemma 3]}$$

The antecedents imply that $m = n = f$. If $1 \leqslant p \leqslant f \leqslant q \leqslant N$, then either $p = f$, in which case $A[p] \leqslant A[f]$ is obvious, or $p < f$, in which case substituting f for both m and g in the first quantified antecedent gives $A[p] \leqslant A[f]$. A similar argument shows that $A[f] \leqslant A[q]$.

At this point, the general structure of the program is as follows:

$$m := 1; \; n := N;$$

while $m < n$ **do** "reduce middle part"

Furthermore, this code has been proved to be correct, provided that the body of the contained iteration is correct.

3.3 Stage 3: reduce the middle part

(1) The process for reducing the middle part involves a scan from the left and from the right. This requires two pointers, i and j, pointing to elements $A[i]$ and $A[j]$ respectively. In addition, a variable r is required to hold the

arbitrary value which has been selected to act as a discriminator between "small" and "large" values.

(2) The i pointer is intended to pass over only those array elements with values smaller than r. Thus all array elements strictly to the left of the currently scanned element $A[i]$ will be known always to be equal to or less than r:

$$m \leqslant i \ \& \ \forall p(1 \leqslant p < i \supset A[p] \leqslant r) \qquad [\,i\text{-invariant}\,]$$

Similarly the j pointer passes over only large values, and all elements strictly to the right of the currently scanned element $A[j]$ are known always to be equal to or greater than r:

$$j \leqslant n \ \& \ \forall q(j < q \leqslant N \supset r \leqslant A[q]) \qquad [\,j\text{-invariant}\,]$$

Since the value of r does not change, there is no need for an r-invariant.

(3) The i pointer starts at the left of the middle part, i.e. at m; and the j pointer starts at the right of the middle part, i.e. at n. The initial value of r is taken from an arbitrary element of the middle part of the array. Since $A[f]$ is always in the middle part, its value is as good as any.

(4) The fact that the initial values satisfy the i- and j-invariants follows directly from the truth of the corresponding m- and n-invariants; this is stated formally in the following lemmas:

$$f \leqslant N \ \& \ m \leqslant f \ \& \ \forall p,q(1 \leqslant p < m \leqslant q \leqslant N \supset A[p] \leqslant A[q])$$
$$\supset m \leqslant m \ \& \ \forall p(1 \leqslant p < m \supset A[p] \leqslant A[f]) \qquad [\text{Lemma 4}]$$

$$1 \leqslant f \ \& \ f \leqslant n \ \& \ \forall p,q(1 \leqslant p \leqslant n < q \leqslant N \supset A[p] \leqslant A[q])$$
$$\supset n \leqslant n \ \& \ \forall q(n < q \leqslant N \supset A[f] \leqslant A[q]) \qquad [\text{Lemma 5}]$$

The first of these is proved by setting q to f and the second by setting p to f.

(5) After setting the initial values, the method is to repeatedly add one to i and subtract one from j, until they cross over. This may be achieved by an iteration of the form:

while $i \leqslant j$ **do** "increase i and decrease j"

On exit from this loop, $j < i$ and all invariants are intended to be preserved.

If j and i cross over above f, the proposed method assigns j as the new value of n; if they cross over below f, i is assigned as the new value of m.

    if $f \leqslant j$ **then** $n := j$

  else if $i \leqslant f$ **then** $m := i$

        else go to L

The destination of the jump will be determined later.

(6) The validity of these assignments is proved by showing that the new value of n or m satisfies the corresponding invariant whenever the assignment takes place. In these proofs it can be assumed that the i- and j-invariants hold; and furthermore, since the assignment immediately follows the iteration of (5), it is known that $j<i$. Thus the appropriate lemma is:

$$j<i \ \& \ \forall p(1 \leqslant p<i \supset A[p] \leqslant r) \ \& \ \forall q(j<q \leqslant N \supset r \leqslant A[q])$$

$$\supset \textbf{if } f \leqslant j \textbf{ then } f \leqslant j \ \& \ \forall p,q(1 \leqslant p \leqslant j<q \leqslant N \supset A[p] \leqslant A[q])$$

$$\textbf{else if } i \leqslant f \textbf{ then } i \leqslant f \ \& \ \forall p,q(1 \leqslant p<i \leqslant q \leqslant N \supset A[p] \leqslant A[q])$$

$$[\text{Lemma 6}]$$

The proof of this is based on the fact that if $1 \leqslant p \leqslant j<q \leqslant N$, then $p<i$ (since $j<i$), and both $A[p] \leqslant r$ and $r \leqslant A[q]$. Hence $A[p] \leqslant A[q]$. Similarly, if $1 \leqslant p<i \leqslant q \leqslant N$, then $j<q$, and the same result follows.

It remains to determine the destination of the jump **go to** L. This jump is obeyed only if $j<f<i$, and it happens that in this case it can be proved that the condition Found has already been achieved. It is therefore legitimate to jump straight to the end of the program. The lemma which justifies this is:

$$1 \leqslant f \leqslant N \ \& \ j<f<i \ \& \ \forall p(1 \leqslant p<i \supset A[p] \leqslant r) \ \& \ \forall q(j<q \leqslant N \supset r \leqslant A[q])$$

$$\supset \forall p,q(1 \leqslant p \leqslant f \leqslant q \leqslant N \supset A[p] \leqslant A[f] \leqslant A[q]) \qquad [\text{Lemma 7}]$$

This may be readily proved: if f is put for q in the antecedent, we obtain $r \leqslant A[f]$. Similarly, putting f for p in the antecedent we obtain $A[f] \leqslant r$. Hence $A[f]=r$. If $1 \leqslant p \leqslant f \leqslant q \leqslant N$, then $1 \leqslant p<i$ (since $f<i$) and $j<q \leqslant N$ (since $j<f$) and hence the i-invariant states that $A[p] \leqslant r$ and the j-invariant states that $r \leqslant A[q]$. But r has already been proved equal to $A[f]$.

This concludes the outline of the program required to reduce the middle part:

> $r := A[f]; \quad i := m; \quad j := n;$
>
> **while** $i \leqslant j$ **do** "increase i and decrease j";
>
> **if** $f \leqslant j$ **then** $n := j$
>
> **else if** $i \leqslant f$ **then** $m := i$
>
> > **else go to** L

This program has been proved to be correct, in that it preserves the truth of both the m- and n-invariants, provided that the body of the contained loop preserves these invariants as well as the i- and j-invariants.

3.4 Stage 4: increase i and decrease j

At this stage there is no need to introduce further variables and no further invariants are required. The construction of the code is not therefore split into the steps as before.

The first action of this part of the program is to use the i-pointer to scan rightward, passing over all elements with value less than r. This is accomplished by the loop:[2]

while $A[i] < r$ **do** $i := i + 1$

The fact that this loop preserves the truth of the invariant is expressed in the obvious lemma:

$$A[i] \leqslant r \,\&\, m \leqslant i \,\&\, \forall p(1 \leqslant p < i \supset A[p] \leqslant r)$$

$$\supset m \leqslant i + 1 \,\&\, \forall p(1 \leqslant p < i + 1 \supset A[p] \leqslant r) \quad [\text{Lemma } 8]^3$$

The next action is to use the j-pointer to scan leftward, passing over all elements greater than r. This is accomplished by the loop:

while $r < A[j]$ **do** $j := j - 1$

which is validated by the truth of:

$$r \leqslant A[j] \,\&\, j \leqslant n \,\&\, \forall q(j < q \leqslant N \supset r \leqslant A[q])$$

$$\supset j - 1 \leqslant n \,\&\, \forall q(j - 1 < q \leqslant N \supset r \leqslant A[q]) \quad [\text{Lemma } 9]$$

On termination of the first loop, it is known that $r \leqslant A[i]$, and on termination of the second loop $A[j] \leqslant r$. If i and j have not crossed over, an exchange of the elements they point to takes place. After the exchange, it is obvious that

$$A[i] \leqslant r \leqslant A[j],$$

and hence Lemmas 8 and 9 justify a further increase in i and decrease in j:

if $i \leqslant j$ **then**

begin "exchange $A[i]$ and $A[j]$";

$i := i + 1; \quad j := j - 1$

end

---

[2] The reason for the strict inequality is connected with termination. See Section 4.

[3] This lemma is not strictly true for some implementations of computer arithmetic. Suppose that N is the largest number representable in the integer range, that $m = i = N$, and that modulo arithmetic is used. Then $i + 1$ will be the smallest number representable, and will certainly be less than m. The easiest way to evade this problem is to impose on the user of the algorithm the insignificant restriction that $N <$ maxint, where maxint is the largest representable integer.

Thus the process of increasing i and decreasing j preserves the truth of all the invariants, provided that the exchange of $A[i]$ and $A[j]$ does so, and the program takes the form:

while $A[i] < r$ **do** $i := i+1$;

while $r < A[j]$ **do** $j := j-1$;

if $i \leqslant j$ **then**

        begin "exchange $A[i]$ and $A[j]$";

          $i := i+1; \quad j := j-1$

        end

3.5 Stage 5: exchange $A[i]$ and $A[j]$

The code for performing the exchange is:

$$w := A[i]; \quad A[i] := A[j]; \quad A[j] := w$$

Although this code uses a new variable w, there is no need to establish an invariant for it, since its value plays a purely temporary role.

The proof that the exchange preserves the invariants is not trivial, and depends critically on the fact that $i \leqslant j$. Let A' stand for the value of the array as a whole after the exchange has taken place. Then obviously:

$$A'[i] = A[j] \tag{1}$$

$$A'[j] = A[i] \tag{2}$$

$$\forall s (s \neq i \ \& \ s \neq j \supset A'[s] = A[s]) \tag{3}$$

The preservation of the i-invariant is stated in the lemma:

$$m \leqslant i \leqslant j \ \& \ \forall p (1 \leqslant p < i \supset A[p] \leqslant r)$$

$$\supset m \leqslant i \ \& \ \forall p (1 \leqslant p < i \supset A'[p] \leqslant r) \qquad [\text{Lemma 10}]$$

This is proved by observing that if $p < i \leqslant j$ then $p \neq i$ and $p \neq j$ and by (3), $A'[p] = A[p]$.

Similarly the preservation of the j-invariant is guaranteed by the lemma:

$$i \leqslant j \leqslant n \ \& \ \forall q (j < q \leqslant N \supset r \leqslant A[q])$$

$$\supset j \leqslant n \ \& \ \forall q (j < q \leqslant N \supset r \leqslant A'[q]) \qquad [\text{Lemma 11}]$$

The proof likewise proceeds by observing that $i \leqslant j < q$ implies that $q \neq i$ and $q \neq j$, and therefore by (3), $A'[q] = A[q]$.

The preservation of the m-invariant is guaranteed by the truth of the following lemma:

$$m \leqslant i \leqslant j \ \& \ \forall p,q (1 \leqslant p < m \leqslant q \leqslant N \supset A[p] \leqslant A[q])$$

$$\supset \forall p,q (1 \leqslant p < m \leqslant q \leqslant N \supset A'[p] \leqslant A'[q]) \qquad [\text{Lemma 12}]$$

Outline proof:

Assume $1 \leqslant p < m \leqslant q \leqslant N$; hence $p \neq i$ and $p \neq j$ (since $p < m \leqslant i \leqslant j$). Therefore by (3),

$$A'[p] = A[p]. \tag{4}$$

Substituting i and then j for q in the antecedent, we obtain $A[p] \leqslant A[i]$ and $A[p] \leqslant A[j]$. Consequently $A'[p] \leqslant A'[j]$ and $A'[p] \leqslant A'[i]$ (from (4), (1), and (2)). Furthermore, for all $q \neq i$ and $q \neq j$, $A'[p] = A[p] \leqslant A[q] = A'[q]$ (by (4) and (3)). Hence $A'[p] \leqslant A'[q]$ for all $q(m \leqslant q \leqslant N)$.

The preservation of the n-invariant is guaranteed by a similar lemma:

$$i \leqslant j \leqslant n \;\&\; \forall p,q\big(1 \leqslant p \leqslant n < q \leqslant N \supset A[p] \leqslant A[q]\big)$$

$$\supset \forall p,q\big(1 \leqslant p \leqslant n < q \leqslant N \supset A'[p] \leqslant A'[q]\big) \qquad [\text{Lemma 13}]$$

The proof is very similar to that of Lemma 12, and is left as an exercise.

Table II

```
begin
    comment   This program operates on an array A[1:N], and a
        value of f (1 ≤ f ≤ N). Its effect is to rearrange the elements
        of A in such a way that:
            ∀p,q(1 ≤ p ≤ f ≤ q ≤ N ⊃ A[p] ≤ A[f] ≤ A[q]);
    integer m,n;   comment
            m ≤ f & ∀p,q(1 ≤ p < m ≤ q ≤ N ⊃ A[p] ≤ A[q]),
            f ≤ n & ∀p,q(1 ≤ p ≤ n < q ≤ N ⊃ A[p] ≤ A[q]);
        m := 1;   n := N;
    while m < n do
    begin integer r,i,j,w;
        comment
                m ≤ i & ∀p(1 ≤ p < i ⊃ A[p] ≤ r),
                j ≤ n & ∀q(j < q ≤ N ⊃ r ≤ A[q]);
            r := A[f];   i := m;   j := n;
        while i ≤ j do
        begin while A[i] < r do i := i + 1;
            while r < A[j] do j := j − 1;
            comment   A[j] ≤ r ≤ A[i];
            if i ≤ j then
            begin w := A[i];   A[i] := A[j];   A[j] := w;
                comment   A[i] ≤ r ≤ A[j];
                i := i + 1;   j := j − 1
            end
        end increase i and decrease j;
        if f < j then n := j
        else if i ≤ f then m := i
            else go to L
        end reduce middle part;
    L:
end Find
```

3.6 The whole program

The gradual evolution of the program code and proof through several stages has been carried out in the previous sections. In presenting the code of the program as a whole, the essential invariants and other assertions have been preserved as comments. Thus a well-annotated version of the program appears in Table II.

4 Termination

The proof given so far has concentrated on proving the correctness of the program supposing that it terminates; and no attention has been given to the problem of proving termination. It is easier in this case to prove termination of the inner loops first.

The proof of the termination of:

while $A[i] < r$ **do** $i := i + 1$

depends on the recognition that at all times there will be an element in the middle part to the right of $A[i]$ whose value is equal to or greater than r. This element will act as a "stopper" to prevent the value of i from increasing beyond the value n. More formally, it is necessary to establish an additional invariant for i, which is true before and during the loop; i.e. throughout execution of "reduce middle part." This invariant is:

$$\exists p (i \leqslant p \leqslant n \ \& \ r \leqslant A[p]) \tag{5}$$

Obviously if this is true, the value of i is necessarily bounded by n; it cannot increase indefinitely, and the loop must therefore terminate.

The fact that (5) is an invariant for the duration of the particular loop is established by the following lemmas:

$$m \leqslant f \leqslant n \supset \exists p (m \leqslant p \leqslant n \ \& \ A[f] \leqslant A[p]) \qquad [\text{Lemma 14}]$$

PROOF. take f for p.

$$A[i] < r \ \& \ \exists p (i \leqslant p \leqslant n \ \& \ r \leqslant A[p])$$
$$\supset \exists p (i+1 \leqslant p \leqslant n \ \& \ r \leqslant A[p]) \qquad [\text{Lemma 15}]$$

PROOF. consider the p whose existence is asserted by the antecedent. Since $r \leqslant A[p] \ \& \ A[i] < r, p \neq i$. Hence $i + 1 \leqslant p$.

$$r \leqslant A[i] \ \& \ i+1 \leqslant j-1 \ \& \ j \leqslant n$$
$$\supset \exists p (i+1 \leqslant p \leqslant n \ \& \ r \leqslant A'[p]) \qquad [\text{Lemma 16}]$$

PROOF. Take j for p. Then $A'[p] = A'[j] = A[i] \geqslant r$.

Lemma 14 shows that the invariant is true after the initialization of "reduce middle part." Lemma 15 shows that the invariant is preserved by **while** $A[i] < r$ **do** $i := i+1$, and Lemma 16 shows that the invariant is preserved by the final compound statement of "reduce middle part," providing that $i \leqslant j$ after the execution of this statement. Since the body of the loop is not reentered unless this condition is satisfied, the invariant is unconditionally true at the beginning of the second and subsequent repetitions of "reduce middle part."

The termination of the loop

while $r < A[j]$ **do** $j := j-1$

is established in a very similar manner. The additional invariant is

$$\exists q(m \leqslant q \leqslant j \ \& \ A[q] \leqslant r) \tag{6}$$

and the lemmas required are Lemma 14 and

$$r < A[j] \ \& \ \exists q(m \leqslant q \leqslant j \ \& \ A[q] \leqslant r)$$
$$\supset \exists q(m \leqslant q \leqslant j-1 \ \& \ A[q] \leqslant r) \qquad [\text{Lemma 17}]$$
$$A[j] \leqslant r \ \& \ i+1 \leqslant j-1 \ \& \ m \leqslant i$$
$$\supset \exists q(m \leqslant q \leqslant j-1 \ \& \ A'[q] \leqslant r) \qquad [\text{Lemma 18}]$$

The proofs of these lemmas are very similar to those for Lemmas 15 and 16.

This proof of termination is more than usually complex; if the program were rewritten to include an extra test ($i \leqslant n$ or $m \leqslant j$) in each loop, termination would have been obvious. However, the innermost loops would have been rather less efficient.

The proof of termination of the middle loop is rather simpler. The loop for increasing i and decreasing j must terminate; since if the conditional statement it contains is not obeyed then j is already less than i, and termination is immediate; whereas if $j \geqslant i$, then i is necessarily incremented and j decremented, and they must cross over after a finite number of such operations.

Proof of the termination of the outermost loop depends on the fact that on termination of the middle loop both $m < i$ and $j < n$. Therefore whichever one of the assignments $m := i$ or $n := j$ is executed, the distance between n and m is strictly decreased. If neither assignment is made, **goto** L is executed, and terminates the loop immediately.

The proof that at the end of the middle loop both $m < i$ and $j < n$ depends on the fact that on the first execution of the loop body the conditional **if** $i \leqslant j$ **then**... is actually executed. This is because at this stage $A[f]$ is still equal to r, and therefore the rightward scan of i cannot pass over $A[f]$. Similarly the leftward scan of j cannot pass over $A[f]$. Thus on termination of both innermost loops $i \leqslant f \leqslant j$. Thus the condition $i \leqslant j$ is satisfied, and i is necessarily incremented, and j is necessarily decremented. Recall that this reasoning applies only to the first time round this loop—but once is enough to ensure $m < i$ and $j < n$, since i is a nondecreasing quantity and j is a nonincreasing quantity.

5 Reservation

In the proof of Find, one very important aspect of correctness has not been treated, namely, that the program merely rearranges the elements of the array A, without changing any of their values. If this requirement were not stated, there would be no reason why the program Find should not be written trivially:

for $i := 1$ **step** 1 **until** N **do** $A[i] := i$

since this fully satisfies all the other criteria for correctness.

The easiest way of stating this additional requirement is to forbid the programmer to change the array A in any other way than by exchanging two of its elements. This requirement is clearly met by the Find program and not by its trivial alternative.

If it is desired to formulate the requirement in terms of conditions and invariants, it is necessary to introduce the concept of a permutation; and to prove that for arbitrary A_0,

$$A \text{ is a permutation of } A_0, \qquad\qquad [\text{Perm}]$$

is an invariant of the program. Informally this may be proved in three steps:

(a) "exchange $A[i]$ and $A[j]$" is the only part of the program which changes A,
(b) exchanging is a permutation,
(c) the composition of two permutations is also a permutation.

The main disadvantages of the formal approach are illustrated by this example. It is far from obvious that the invariance of Perm expresses exactly what we want to prove about the program; when the definition of Perm is fully and formally expressed, this is even less obvious; and finally, if the proof is formulated in the manner of the proofs of the other lemmas of this paper, it is very tedious.

Another problem which remains untreated is that of proving that all subscripts of A are within the bounds 1 to N.

6 Conclusion

This paper has illustrated a methodology for systematic construction of program proofs together with the programs they prove. It uses a "top-down" method of analysis to split the process into a number of stages, each stage embodying more detail than the previous one; the proof of the correctness of the program at each stage leads to and depends upon an accurate formulation of the characteristics of the program to be developed at the next stage.

Within each stage, there are a number of steps: the decision on the nature of the data required; the formulation of the invariants for the data; the construction of the code; the formulation and proof of the lemmas. In this paper, the stages and steps have been shown as a continuous progress, and it has not been necessary to go back and change decisions made earlier. In practice, reconsideration of earlier decisions is frequently necessary, and this imposes on the programmer the need to reestablish the consistency of invariants, program, lemmas, and proofs. The motivation for taking this extra trouble during the design and coding of a program is that it is hoped to reduce or eliminate trouble at phases which traditionally come later—program testing, documentation, and maintenance.

Similar systematic methods of program construction are described in [Naur 69a*; Dijkstra 72d*]; this present paper, however, places greater emphasis on the formalization of the characteristics of the program as an aid to the avoidance of logical and coding errors. In the future, it may be possible to enlist the aid of a computer in formulating the lemmas, and perhaps even in checking the proofs [Floyd 67; King 69].

Acknowledgments. The author is grateful to the referee and to John Reynolds for his meticulous comments and general encouragement in the preparation of this paper.

10
An Approach to Correctness Proofs of Semicoroutines

Ole-Johan Dahl
University of Oslo

Abstract *The paper discusses local correctness criteria and local correctness proofs of semicoroutines subject to certain simplifying assumptions. A nontrivial worked example is given.*

1 Introduction

An important goal in programming is to construct programs that are easy to understand. A good way to achieve understanding of a program is to prove that it is correct. Since a program easily proved correct is probably easy to understand, one looks for program structuring mechanisms which admit simple and powerful proof rules. A simple correctness proof is not necessarily easy to find, unless certain key assertions about the program variables are given. Therefore such assertions should be provided with the program text as comments, and in such quantity that the construction of a correctness proof is trivial.

In the present paper we shall discuss correctness criteria and correctness proofs of coroutines. More specifically we consider so called *semicoroutines* as defined in [Dahl 71*] and expressed in a slightly modified Simula 67. A class of semicoroutines is thus defined by a class declaration, say C.

$$\textbf{class } C; \quad \langle \text{class body} \rangle;$$

A semicoroutine of the class C is a dynamic instance of the class body, and is named by a reference variable, say X.

$$X := \textbf{new } C$$

In general any number of semicoroutines of the same class (or different ones) may coexist. We assume for simplicity that each semicoroutine is named by one and only one reference variable throughout its life.

Consider a process consisting of the execution of a master program M and a single semicoroutine X (Fig. 1). It can be viewed as two separate

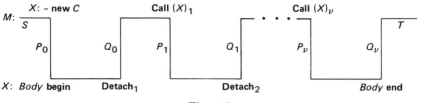

Figure 1

processes operating in parallel, but such that only one is executing at a time, while the other is waiting.

Control is transferred from M to X at the time when X is generated, i.e., when M executes the generator "**new** C", and whenever M executes "**call** (X)". Control returns to M whenever X executes a **detach** statement, and at the time of termination of X. The figure gives a pictorial representation of the sequence of events in time. There is a mapping which maps each event **call**(X) onto some occurrence of **call**(X) in the program text of M, and similarly for the other events of M and X.

Understanding the processes M and X requires a prior knowledge (except in special cases) of the interface between them. The interface consists of assertions $P_0, P_1, P_2, \ldots$ and $Q_0, Q_1, Q_2, \ldots$ characterizing the state vector at the time of transition of control from M to X and from X to M respectively (see the figure). Assuming that M calls X ν times, after which X terminates, we can formulate a proof rule for the process as a whole with a formalism similar to that of Hoare.

$$P_0\{X:-\textbf{new } C\}Q_0, \ \forall t \in [1,\nu]: P_t\{\textbf{call}(X)_t\}Q_t \vdash S\{M\}T, \tag{1}$$

$$\frac{\forall t \in [1,\nu]: Q_{t-1}\{\textbf{detach}_t\}P_t \vdash P_0\{\text{body of } C\}Q_\nu}{S\{M,C\}T}$$

The rule as it stands leaves little hope of providing a correctness proof of the semicoroutine separately from M, or any clue as to what the criterion of its correctness should be. A major difficulty is the fact that the assertions P_t and Q_t in general are predicates on the whole state vector. This reflects the fact that Simula 67 permits the entire state vector to be accessible to both the master program and the semicoroutine.

In order to simplify matters we partition the state vector s into three parts: a local to M, b local to X, and a communication area c. (In Simula 67 the locality criteria could be enforced by a compiler by outlawing references to nonlocals from within class bodies as well as remote references into class bodies; however, some additional syntax would be needed to identify the communication area. We do not wish to consider questions of syntax here.)

M. Clint, in his treatment of coroutines in [Clint 73], requires a similar partitioning of the state vector, and (1) is an elaboration and adaptation of his proof rule for cooperating routines. Clint adds the following proof rule for each detach statment in X,

$$\frac{\vdash Q\,\{\mathbf{detach}\}\,P}{\vdash Q \wedge \forall c(P \supset B)\{\mathbf{detach}\}\,B} \tag{2}$$

where P and Q are predicates on c and B is an arbitrary predicate on (b,c). The rule expresses the fact that the local quantities b are unchanged across a detach statement.

A similar rule holds for each statement $\mathbf{call}(X)$ in M, where A is an arbitrary predicate on (a,c).

$$\frac{\vdash P\,\{\mathbf{call}(X)\}\,Q}{\vdash P \wedge \forall c(Q \supset A)\{\mathbf{call}(X)\}\,A} \tag{3}$$

The rules (2) and (3) show that predicates on c alone bracketing $\mathbf{call}(X)$ or $\mathbf{detach}$ may be extended to predicates on the whole accessible part of the state vector. Consequently it is sufficient that the P_i and Q_i of (1) be predicates on the communication area alone. This is the simplification which arises from partitioning the state vector as above.

The problem of mapping (1) onto the program texts of M and X is solved in principle by introducing two "mythical" program variables: γ local to M whose value is the number of times that "$\mathbf{call}(X)$" has been performed, and δ local to X whose value is the number of times that $\mathbf{detach}$ has been performed (in X). By definition the following relations hold (see the figure above).

within M: $\gamma < \nu \supset \gamma + 1 = \delta$ (after the generation of X),

within X: $\delta = \gamma$,

and $\gamma = \delta = 0$ initially.

We may notice in passing that $\gamma = \nu$ implies $\delta = \nu$ in M, because the last return to M is through the termination of X, not by a $\mathbf{detach}$ operation. It follows that X is callable if and only if $\delta - \gamma = 1$.

Writing $P(c,t)$ for P_t and $Q(c,t)$ for Q_t rule (1) gets the following form.

$P(c,0)\{X:-\mathbf{new}\,C\}Q(c,\ 0),$

$0 \leqslant \gamma < \nu \wedge P(c,\gamma+1)\{\mathbf{call}(X)\}Q(c,\gamma) \vdash S\{M\}T$

$$\frac{0 \leqslant \delta < \nu \wedge Q(c,\delta)\{\mathbf{detach}\}\,P(c,\delta) \vdash P(c,0)\{\text{body of } C\}Q(c,\nu)}{\vdash S\{M,C\}T} \tag{1'}$$

(2) and (3) may be replaced the following slightly stronger rules.

$$\frac{\vdash Q\,\{\mathbf{detach}\}\,P}{\vdash Q \wedge \forall c(P^\delta_{\delta+1} \supset B^\delta_{\delta+1})\{\mathbf{detach}\}\,B} \tag{2'}$$

$$\frac{\vdash P\,\{\mathbf{call}(X)\}\,Q}{\vdash P \wedge \mathsf{y}c(Q^\gamma_{\gamma+1} \supset A^\gamma_{\gamma+1})\{\mathbf{call}(X)\}\,A} \tag{3'}$$

These rules, in addition to the constancy of ordinary local quantities, express the facts that **detach** increases δ by 1, and **call**(X) increases γ by 1.

Termination of X is not essential for the correct behavior of M. For instance, if M calls X μ times, $\mu < \nu$, then from the point of view of X the $(\mu + 1)$'th dynamic instance of **detach** does not terminate, and neither does X. On the other hand, if X terminates too early, i.e. $\nu < \mu$, then the $(\nu + 1)$'th dynamic instance of **call**(X) will not terminate properly. Thus it is important that a semicoroutine carries on "long enough" without terminating. In fact, from the point of view of a master program a non-terminating semicoroutine is "safer" than one which terminates. This indicates that expressions of the form

$$P \{\text{body}\} Q$$

are not necessarily useful as correctness criteria for a semicoroutine viewed separately from its master program. The requirement that it behave according to given interface specifications may be more relevant. It is certainly true that a proof using (1'), given proper termination, permits us to infer the validity of the interface assumptions. Thus an indirect proof of a given semicoroutine may be constructed by first writing a master program reflecting its intended use, and then proving the combined program. However, we investigate below some special cases when correctness criteria are easily formulated and proved locally.

2 Producer/consumer relationships

We impose a producer/consumer relationship on the pair M,X by defining the communication area c to be a set of read-only variables with respect to one of them (the consumer).

Assume that X is the producer and M the consumer. Let the states of the communication area c at successive executions of **detach** be $c_0, c_1, c_2, \ldots$. Then the interface specifications are

$$P_t : c = c_{t-1}, \qquad Q_t : c = c_t.$$

If the semicoroutine X is a selfcontained process receiving no inputs, the whole sequence c_t must be completely determined by the initial state of X. We may conclude that $c_{t+1} = f(c_t, t)$. Then by a simple formal derivation (3') reduces to

$$\vdash_i A^{\gamma,c}_{\gamma+1, f(c,\gamma)} \{\text{call}(X)\} A, \tag{3c}$$

where $\vdash_i$ means "deducible from the interface specifications."

(Assumption of (3'):

$$c = c_\gamma \{\text{call}(X)\} c = c_\gamma.$$

Conclusion of (3'):

$$c=c_\gamma \wedge \forall c(c=c_{\gamma+1}=f(c_\gamma,\gamma) \supset A_{\gamma+1}^\gamma)\{\textbf{call}(X)\}A,$$

where the precondition reduces to that of (3c).)

(3c) states the intuitively obvious fact that the effect of **call**(X) as seen from M is an assignment $c:=f(c,\gamma)$ to the communication variable(s) (disregarding the effect on the mythical γ). A motivation for using a semicoroutine, rather than a procedure f, to perform the computation is that the former may utilize local state information to reduce the work involved. In contrast a procedure would have to regenerate such information from the parameter values at each activation. This is true even if f does not depend on γ, as shown by the example of Section 3.

The proof rule (2') for the **detach** statement of X reduces to

$$\vdash_i B_{\delta+1}^\delta\{\textbf{detach}\}B$$

which is simple and intuitively obvious. But it does not contribute much to proving that the semicoroutine behaves according to specifications. What must be proved is that

$$B_{f(c,\delta-1)}^c\{E\}B$$

for any sequence E of events occurring between two successive dynamic instances of **detach**. Since such event sequences are not in general mapped onto syntactic components of the program text, proof rules derived from program structure are not immediately helpful.

As an aid for proving and annotating the semicoroutine we may introduce a mythical local variable c' whose value is the state of the communication area at the time of the last execution of **detach**. Noting that $c'=c_{\delta-1}$ holds on either side of any detach we may derive from (2') the rule

$$\vdash_i c=f(c',\delta-1) \wedge B_{\delta+1,c}^{\delta,c'}\{\textbf{detach}\}B \wedge c=c' \tag{2p}$$

which defines that a mythical assignment $c':=c$ is an implicit side effect of the **detach** operation. The assertion $c=f(c',\delta-1)$ is what must be proved for every textual occurrence of **detach** in the semicoroutine. Technically it is a hypothesis about the interface, to be inserted in front of **detach** as indicated by (2p) (and also at body **end**). The hypothesis is proved valid when it has been verified, working backwards through the program text, that $c=c'$ is true after each occurrence of **detach** (and also at body **begin**). The initial value of c' is defined equal to the initial state of the communication area c, before the first "output" c_0 has been produced. If that state is undefined, the value of $f(c',-1)$ should be independent of c'.

Consider next the case that X is the consumer and M is the producer, and let again $c_0,c_1,c_2,\ldots$ be the sequence of states produced and consumed. Frequently the purpose of a consuming semicoroutine is such that any functional relation between consecutive inputs is irrelevant, if indeed it exists at all. For instance, the purpose could be to perform certain statistical measurements on the sequence consumed, or to compute some function of the input, given that it is a character sequence with a given syntactic structure.

Clearly the behavior of the semicoroutine will depend on the inputs. Let b_t be the local state at the time of the event **detach**, (see the figure above), we may write

$$b_{t+1} = f(b_t, c_t, t), \qquad t = 0, 1, \dots.$$

However, the examples above suggest that it may be more useful to define the current local state as a function of that part of the input sequence which has so far been consumed.

$$b_{t+1} = F(\langle c_0, c_1, \dots, c_t \rangle), \qquad t = 0, 1, \dots. \tag{4}$$

Also the interface specifications may take the form of predicates on the sequence transmitted. In our case the producer M must guarantee the validity of P_t, whereas X has no other interface obligation than leaving the communication area c unchanged.

$$P_t: P(\langle c_0, c_1, \dots, c_t \rangle) \wedge c = c_t, \qquad Q_t: c = c_t. \tag{5}$$

Notice that predicate P, as well as function F of (4), are implicitly parameterized by t, since the length of the sequence parameter is by definition equal to $t+1$. In order to make sense the predicate P must be monotonic with respect to the sequence length.

$$P(\langle c_0, c_1, \dots, c_t \rangle) \supset P(\langle c_0, c_1, \dots, c_s \rangle) \quad \text{for } s < t; \text{ and } P(\langle \; \rangle) = \textit{true}. \tag{6}$$

We may map (4) and (5) onto the program text by introducing a mythical variable Hc called the *communication history*, whose value shall be the sequence of values produced by M. Hc is extended by an element equal to the current value of c as the result of an implied side effect of the **call**(X) operation. We derive the following proof rules from (2') and (3').

$$\vdash_i \forall c' \big(P(\langle Hc, c' \rangle) \supset B_{\langle Hc, c' \rangle, c}^{Hc, c} \big) \{ \textbf{detach} \} \, B \tag{2c}$$

$$\vdash_i P(\langle Hc, c \rangle) \wedge A_{\langle Hc, c \rangle}^{Hc} \{ \textbf{call}(X) \} A \tag{3p}$$

(2c) expresses that **detach** has the implied side effects of assigning new values to the communication area, and appending them to the communication history. It follows that $c = last(Hc)$ everywhere in X.

Predicate B could have the form $b = F(Hc^-) \wedge P(Hc)$, where Hc^- denotes the sequence obtained from Hc by deleting its last element, i.e., that part of the communication history which has so far been "digested" by X. Then the following rule is derived from (2c) and (6).

$$\vdash_i P(Hc) \supset b = F(Hc) \{ \textbf{detach} \} b = F(Hc^-) \wedge P(Hc) \tag{2c'}$$

The precondition of (2c') is what must be proved for every occurrence of **detach** (and body **end**). The proof is established by working backwards through the program text and proving that the postassertion of (2c') for each occurrence of **detach** implies whatever assertion has been constructed at that point. (At body **begin** $b = F(\langle \ \rangle)$ must hold).

For a terminating consumer semicoroutine a correctness criterion of the form

$$P_0\{\text{body}\}\,P(H_c) \supset b = F(Hc) \tag{7}$$

is meaningful.

The concept of communication history is useful for selfcontained producer semicoroutines as well. The mythical variable Hc may be used instead of the variables γ, δ, and c' introduced above. The rule (2p) takes the following form

$$\vdash_i c = f'(Hc) \wedge B^{Hc}_{\langle Hc, c \rangle}\{\text{detach}\}\,B, \tag{2p'}$$

where $f'(Hc) = f(last(Hc), length(Hc) - 1)$, f as in (2p).

If the semicoroutine terminates, the correctness criterion (where S is a specified sequence)

$$P_0\{\text{body}\}\,Hc = S \tag{8}$$

is adequate, because it characterizes the total behavior of the semicoroutine as seen from an external point of view.

Frequently a producer X with respect to a communication area c may be a consumer with respect to an area d. X may be a semicoroutine with respect to c and a master program with respect to d, or vice versa. In both cases, assuming that X terminates, a relevant correctness criterion is obtained as a "combination" of (7) and (8),

$$P_0\{\text{body}\}\,P(Hd) \supset Hc = F(Hd), \tag{9}$$

where $P(Hd)$ is the interface assumption on the consumed sequence. In some cases one would require of X that it behave in a predictable way for any arbitrary input sequence. In that case the interface assumption is void (excepting declared properties of the area d), and (9) might be replaced by a criterion of the following form

$$P_0\{\text{body of } X\}\,Hc = \textbf{if}\,P(Hd)\,\textbf{then}\,F(Hd)\,\textbf{else}\,E(Hd),$$

where $E(Hd)$ might contain "error messages".

3 A worked example

As a nontrivial example we choose an adaptation of a program given in [Knuth 73b] for producing all permutations of the number $1, 2, \ldots, n$ according to a method developed by Trotter.

The permutation sequence is generated by successive interchanges of neighbor elements, which makes the algorithm very efficient.

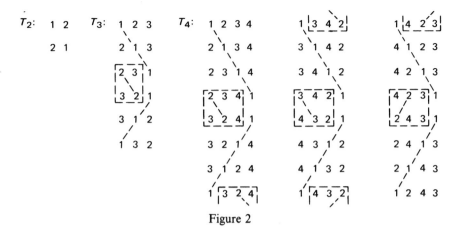

Figure 2

In order to give a rough indication of the method we list above the complete Trotter sequences T_n of the numbers $\{1,2,\ldots,n\}$ for $n=2,3,4$ (Fig. 2).

In general, T_n of $\{1,2,\ldots,n\}$ is obtained from T_{n-1} of $\{2,3,\ldots,n\}$ by expanding each element X of the latter sequence into a subsequence of T_n. The subsequence is obtained from X by inserting the digit 1 in all possible positions. Then, by induction, T_n sequences through all permutations exactly once. By inserting the 1's alternately from left to right and from right to left it turns out that successive permutations are produced by always swapping neighbor elements.

The algorithm may be structured as a cooperation of n semicoroutines, each assigned to move a certain digit back and forth within a certain substring. In the program below (Fig. 3) the semicoroutines are of the class *Gdigit*, and are called $G[1], G[2], \ldots, G[n]$. $G[k]$ is assigned to move the number $n-k+1, k=1,2,\ldots,n$.

The whole cooperation, including a master program *Main*, is defined as a producer semicoroutine of the class *Tpermuter*, which terminates after having produced the sequence T_n, where n is a parameter. The communi-

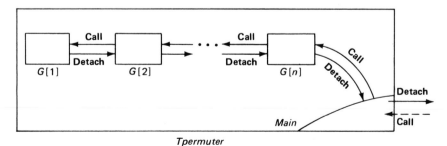

Tpermuter

Figure 3

cation area of the *Tpermuter* consists of the quantities

$$\text{\textbf{Boolean} } more; \qquad \text{\textbf{integer array} } p[1:n];$$

where p sequences through the permutations, and more is *true* until finally it is set to *false* to signal the end of the sequence. The correctness criterion with respect to p is that $Hp = T_n$ immediately before termination, provided that $n \geqslant 1$.

```
class Tpermuter(integer n);

begin Boolean more;   integer array p[1:n];
      integer t;   ref(Gdigit) array G[1:n];
      class Gdigit(integer k);
      begin integer i;
            i: = 0; p[k]: = k;
            if k = 1 then detach; more: = false
            else G[k - 1]: - new Gdigit(k - 1);
               loop: loop: detach;
                     while i < k - 1:
                           swap(p[t + i],p[t + i + 1]);
                           {0 ≤ i < k - 1}i: = i + 1;
                     repeat; {i = k - 1}
                     call(G[k - 1]);
                     loop: detach;
                     while i > 0:
                           swap(p[t + i],p[t + i - 1]);
                           {0 < i ≤ k - 1}i: = i - 1;
                     repeat;   {i = 0}
                     t: = t + 1; call(G[k - 1]);
               repeat
          fi
      end of Gdigit;
Main: more: = true; G[n]:- new Gdigit(n); {p = (1, 2, ..., n)}
      loop: detach; t: = 1; call(G[n]); while more repeat
{Hp = T_n}
end of Tpermuter;
```

One syntactic construct of the program text deserves a comment. Let SL stand for statement list and BE stand for Boolean expression. Then

$$\text{\textbf{loop}: } SL_1; \text{ \textbf{while} } BE: SL_2; \text{ \textbf{repeat}}$$

is a generalization of the **while-** and **repeat**-statements of Pascal. The **while**-clause represents the loop test and exit, which may occur anywhere in the loop. If the **while**-clause is missing, the loop is nonterminating. The following proof rule is valid for the complete construct.

$$\frac{\vdash P\, \{SL_1\}\, Q, \vdash Q \wedge BE\, \{SL_2\}\, P}{\vdash P\, \{\text{\textbf{loop}: } SL_1; \text{ \textbf{while} } BE: SL_2; \text{ \textbf{repeat}}\}\, Q \wedge {\sim} BE}$$

We may simplify the correctness proof of the *Tpermuter* class by observing that the variable i of $G[k]$ $(k=1,2,\ldots,n)$ is equal to the inversion count of the digit $n-k+1$ associated with $G[k]$:

$$i = inv(n-k+1) \tag{10}$$

An inversion count $inv(d)$ with respect to a permutation p is the number of digits greater than d which occur to the left of d in p. (10) is obviously valid initially since p is initialized to $(1,2,\ldots,n)$ and all i's to zero. We now prove informally that the operations performed by an arbitrary $G[k]$ from one **detach** to the next leave (10) unchanged. The proof is based on the assertions occurring in the program text above and two additional invariants for $G[k]$.

$$\forall j \in [t, t+k-1] : p[j] \geq n-k+1 \tag{11}$$

$$p[t+i] = n-k+1 \tag{12}$$

Assume that (10) holds for G's to the right of $G[k]$. Since $G[k]$ is operating each of those G's is at rest in one of its **call**-statements. Consequently the corresponding i's have extreme values, 0 or $k'-1$ for $G[k']$ $(k<k' \leq n)$. Furthermore t is one larger than the number of such i's equal to zero. (10) now implies that the associated digits, $1,2,\ldots,n-k$, are collected at the left and right ends of $p, t-1$ of them at the left end. We may conclude that the k largest numbers of p, $n-k+1,\ldots,n$, are collected within the segment $s = p[t:t+k-1]$, (11). By the bounds on i within the innermost loops of $G[k]$, its swap operations can only move digits of the segments, thus preserving (11). Initially the digit $n-k+1$ is positioned at the left end of s and $i=0$, which means that (12) is satisfied. It is obviously preserved by the operations on p and i in $G[k]$.

It only remains to show that the validity of (11) and (12) is preserved by the operation **call**($G[k-1]$). But by induction any $G[k']$ $(k'<k)$ can only operate on a subsegment of s which does not contain the digit $n-k+1$. (12) shows that (10) is valid for $G[k]$, since $inv(n-k+1)$ must be equal to its relative position i in s. This completes our informal proof of (10) for all G's.

There is a one–one correspondence between nth order permutations and their inversion tables

$$inv(1), inv(2), \ldots, inv(n),$$

and since $0 \leq inv(k) \leq n-k$, an inversion table read backwards is a number in the base $(1,2,\ldots,n)$ number system. It is easily seen that the sequence of such numbers which corresponds to the Trotter permutation sequence is a base $(1,2,\ldots,n)$ "reflected Gray code sequence" $S_{1,n}$, where each digit position is counted up and down alternately, and only one digit is changed at each step.

$S_{1,4}$	T_4				
0000	1234	0020	1342	0110	1423
0001	2134	0021	3142	0111	4123
0002	2314	0022	3412	0112	4213
0003	2341	0023	3421	0113	4231
0013	3241	0123	4321	0103	2431
0012	3214	0122	4312	0102	2413
0011	3124	0121	4132	0101	2143
0010	1324	0120	1432	0100	1243

By (10) the "array" $G.i$ of variables $G[1].i, G[2].i,\ldots,G[n].i$ contains the reversed inversion table of p. We may therefore prove the correctness of *Tpermuter* by regarding $G.i$ as its communication area and proving that its communication history Hi satisfies (13) immediately prior to termination (for $n \geqslant 1$).

$$Hi = S_{1,n} \tag{13}$$

In order to carry out a (more) formal proof of (13) we need a formal definition of $S_{1,n}$.

$$
\begin{aligned}
S_{n+1,n} &= \bar{S}_{n+1,n} = \langle \varepsilon \rangle \\
R_{0,k,n} &= \langle\ \rangle \\
R_{i+1,k,n} &= \langle R_{i,k,n}, i | S^{(i)}_{k+1,n} \rangle \qquad (i=0,1,\ldots,k-1) \\
S_{k,n} &= R_{k,k,n} \qquad (k=n,n-1,\ldots,1)
\end{aligned}
\tag{14}
$$

$S_{k,n}$ is a base $(k,k+1,\ldots,n)$ reflected Gray code sequence. $\bar{S}$ stands for the sequence S reversed, and $S^{(i)}$ for S reversed i times, i.e.,

$$S^{(i)} = \textbf{if } even(i) \textbf{ then } S \textbf{ else } \bar{S}$$

$i|S$ is the sequence obtained from S by extending each element of S by the digit i at the left, and ε is a digit string of length zero.

By defining $R'_{i,k,n}$ such that $\langle R'_{i,k,n}, \bar{R}_{i,k,n} \rangle = \bar{S}_{k,n}$ we derive

$$
\begin{aligned}
R'_{k,k,n} &= \langle\ \rangle \\
R'_{i,k,n} &= \langle R'_{i+1,k,n}, i | S^{(i+1)}_{k+1,n} \rangle \qquad (i=k-1,k-2,\ldots,0) \\
\bar{S}_{k,n} &= R'_{0,k,n} \qquad (k=n,n-1,\ldots,1).
\end{aligned}
\tag{15}
$$

In our correctness proof we may disregard all statements operating on the quantities p and t as being irrelevant. The proof techniques of Section 2 may be applied if we regard each *Gdigit* semicoroutine $G[k]$ as a producer–consumer with respect to its left and right neighbors (or *Main*). It turns out that the direction of information flow is formally determined by our choice of communication areas, and two different correctness proofs may thus be obtained.

The most intuitively natural choice is perhaps to define $G[1:k-1].i$ to be the communication area linking $G[k]$ to its left neighbor ($k \geq 2$). Then $G[k]$ consumes the next element of the sequence $S_{1,k-1}$ produced by $G[k-1]$ and produces a subsequence of $S_{1,k}$ by appending different i-values at the right end.

However, given the definition (14) a more direct correctness proof is constructed as follows. In order to clarify the terminology we call $G.i$ the *external* communication area linking the *Tpermuter* as a whole to its unspecified master. Hi is the corresponding external communication history. We now define the *internal* communication area connecting $G[k]$ to its right neighbor (or *Main*) to be a slice of width $[k+1:n]$ of the mythical variable Hi, i.e., the current external communication history of the variables $G[k+1].i, \ldots, G[n].i$. The slice is denoted $Hi[k+1:n]$.

Formally, $G[k]$ "consumes" from $G[k+1]$ (or *Main*) the current value of $Hi[k+1:n]$ by a **detach** operation, and it "produces" the current value of $Hi[k:n]$ by an operation **call**$(G[k-1])$ (for $k \neq 1$). Since consecutive values produced by $G[k]$ are functionally related, we may use the techniques displayed in the first half of Section 2 for a local correctness proof of $G[k]$ ($2 \leq k \leq n$). We introduce three mythical local variables for $G[k]$ (cf. Section 2), γ, δ, and H', the last one denoting the output last produced. Let Hin_δ mean the value consumed by **detach** number δ, and let $Hout_\gamma$ mean the value produced by **call** number γ. Then we state the following interface assumptions and corresponding proof rules applicable in $G[k]$.

$$Hin_\delta = \langle Hin_{\delta-1}, S_{k+1,n}^{(\delta-1)} \rangle \qquad (Hin_0 = \langle \; \rangle), \tag{16}$$

$$Hout_\gamma = \langle Hout_{\gamma-1}, S_{k,n}^{(\gamma-1)} \rangle \qquad (Hout_0 = \langle \; \rangle), \tag{17}$$

$$\vdash_i P_{\delta+1, \langle Hin, S_{k+1,n}^{(\delta)} \rangle}^{\delta, Hin} \{\textbf{detach}\} P, \tag{18}$$

$$\vdash_i Hout = \langle H', S_{k,n}^{(\gamma)} \rangle \wedge P_{\gamma+1, Hout}^{\gamma, h'} \{\textbf{call}(G[k-1])\} P \wedge H' = Hout, \tag{19}$$

where Hin means $Hi[k+1:n]$ and $Hout$ means $Hi[k:n]$.

Below is given a fully annotated version of the main loop of $G[k]$ ($k \neq 1$), irrelevant operations ommited. The program text constitutes a framework for a local correctness proof of $G[k]$. A formal proof consists in verifying that the assertions in the text are mutually related as required by the proof rules established for the various statements and constructs.

Since the outer loop is nonterminating the formal objective is to derive

$$P_0 \{\text{outer loop}\} \textit{false}$$

using the proof rule

$$\frac{\vdash P\,\{SL\}\,P}{\vdash P\,\{\textbf{loop}:\,SL;\,\textbf{repeat}\}\,false}$$

to achieve that objective.

$[2\leqslant k\leqslant n\wedge i=\gamma=\delta=0\wedge Hi[k:n]=H'=\langle\ \rangle\}$
$\textbf{loop}:\{i=0\wedge even(\gamma)\wedge even(\delta)\wedge Hi[k:n]=H'\}$
    $\textbf{loop}:\{0\leqslant i<k\wedge even(\gamma)\wedge even(\delta+i)\wedge Hi[k:n]=\langle H',R_{i,k,n}\rangle\}$
        $\textbf{detach};$
        $\{0\leqslant i<k\wedge even(\gamma)\wedge odd(\delta+i)\wedge Hi[k:n]=$
        $\langle H',R_{i,k,n},i|S_{k+1,n}^{(\delta-1)}\rangle=\langle H',R_{i,k,n},i|S_{k+1,n}^{(i)}\rangle=\langle H',R_{i+1,k,n}\rangle\}$
    $\textbf{while } i<k-1:\ i:=i+1;$
    $\textbf{repeat};$
    $\{i=k-1\wedge even(\gamma)\wedge odd(\delta+i)\wedge Hi[k:n]=\langle H',R_{k,k,n}\rangle$
    $=\langle H',S_{k,n}^{(\gamma)}\rangle\}$
    $\textbf{call}(G[k-1]);$
    $\{i=k-1\wedge odd(\gamma)\wedge odd(\delta+i)\wedge Hi[k:n]=H'\}$
    $\textbf{loop}:\ \{0\leqslant i<k\wedge odd(\gamma)\wedge odd(\delta+i)\wedge Hi[k:n]=\langle H',R_{i+1,k,n}'\rangle\}$
        $\textbf{detach};$
        $\{0\leqslant i<k\wedge odd(\gamma)\wedge even(\delta+i)\wedge Hi[k:n]=$
        $\langle H',R_{i+1,k,n}',i|S_{k+1,n}^{(\delta-1)}\rangle=\langle H',R_{i+1,k,n}',i|S_{k+1,n}^{(i-1)}\rangle=\langle H',R_{i,k,n}'\rangle\}$
    $\textbf{while } i>0:\ i:=i-1;$
    $\textbf{repeat};$
    $\{i=0\wedge odd(\gamma)\wedge even(\delta)\wedge Hi[k:n]=\langle H',R_{0,k,n}'\rangle=\langle H',S_{k,n}^{(\gamma)}\rangle\}$
    $\textbf{call}(G[k-1]);$
$\textbf{repeat}$

In applying (18) to each occurrence of **detach**, notice that Hin of (18) is the slice of width $[k+1:n]$ of the sequence mentioned in the precondition. The contents of the remaining slice $[k:k]$ is defined by the local variable i.

The local correctness proof shows the validity of the output assumption (17), given the input assumption (16). In order to prove the cooperation as a whole we have to show that (16) is valid. For $k\neq n$ we have (cf. Section 2) $G[k].\delta=G[k+1].\gamma$ whenever $G[k]$ is operating. It follows immediately that (17) applied to $G[k+1]$ implies (16) applied to $G[k]$. For $k=n$ (16) requires that the values consumed should increase by one element of length zero at a time ($S_{n+1,n}=\bar{S}_{n+1,n}=\langle\varepsilon\rangle$ by (14)). Since $G[n]$ has the input communication area $Hi[n+1:n]$ of width zero, and there is precisely one ("external") **detach** for every **call**($G[n]$) in *Main*, the values produced by *Main* are those required.

The final step in the proof of *Tpermuter* follows by considering $G[1]$. It does not enter its main loop, but performs its first and only **detach** immediately after initialization. This **detach** consumes through $Hi[2:n]$ the output produced by $G[2]$ in its first call, which according to (17) is $S_{2,n}$. Since variable i of $G[1]$ remains equal to zero, it follows that the complete external communication history Hi has the value $0|S_{2,n}=R_{1,1,n}=S_{1,n}$ at the moment when $G[1]$ emerges from its **detach**. Since variable *more* is now set to *false*, *Main* exits from its loop and terminates immediately upon regaining control.

Returning to the original *Tpermuter* communicating through the quantities *more* and p, we have established the following result for its total behavior,

$$n \geqslant 1\{\text{body}\}H=\langle \textit{true}|T_n,\textit{false}|\text{some } p\rangle$$

where H is the complete output history, and the last element of H is produced as the result of termination. The latter should be regarded as an "end of file" signal by the master program.

Acknowledgments. The author wishes to thank Arne Wang for constructive criticism and help in cleaning up formal derivations. D. E. Knuth, in addition to formulating the *Tpermuter* class, also provided the material on the Trotter algorithm and its connection to Gray codes at one of his lectures at the University of Oslo [Knuth 73b]. Thanks are also due to IFIP WG2.3 for reacting to a talk on "histories", which may have clarified the author's ideas on the subject more than those of the committee members.

11
An Axiomatic Proof Technique
for Parallel Programs[1]

Susan Owicki
Stanford University

David Gries
Cornell University

Abstract *A language for parallel programming, with a primitive construct for synchronization and mutual exclusion, is presented. Hoare's deductive system for proving partial correctness of sequential programs is extended to include the parallelism described by the language. The proof method lends insight into how one should understand and present parallel programs. Examples are given using several of the standard problems in the literature. Methods for proving termination and the absence of deadlock are also given.*

1 Introduction

The importance of correctness proofs for sequential programs has long been recognized. Advocates of structured programming have argued that a well structured program should be easy to prove correct, and that programs should be written with a correctness proof in mind. In this connection, Hoare's deductive system [Hoare 69*], using axioms, inference rules and assertions, has been the most influential. Not only has Hoare shown us how to prove programs correct, his deductive system has shown us how to understand programs in an informal manner, and has given us insight into how to write better programs.

The need for correctness proofs for parallel programs is even greater. When several processes can be executed in parallel, the results can depend on the unpredictable order in which actions from different processes are executed, resulting in a complexity too great to handle informally. Even worse, program testing will rarely uncover all mistakes since the particular interactions in which errors are visible may not occur. A proof method is required that teaches us how to handle parallelism in a simple, understandable manner.

A number of methods have been used in proofs for parallel programs. The most common is reliance on informal arguments—a risky business

[1] This research was partially supported by National Science Foundation grant GJ-42512.

given the complexity of parallel program interactions. More formal approaches have included application of Scott's mathematical semantics [Cadiou 73], the reduction method of [Lipton 74b], and the Church–Rosser approach of [Rosen 74].

This paper, based on the PhD thesis of the first author, extends the attempt of [Hoare 72g*] to include parallelism in this deductive system. We feel it is intuitive enough to be used as a basis for reliable proof outlines, and it has given us insight into how to understand parallel programs. Other approaches related to our work are contained in [Ashcroft 71, 73; Lauer 73b; Newton 75].

Any parallel programming language must contain statements for describing cooperation between processes—synchronization, mutual exclusion, and the like. We provide a flexible but primitive tool, so primitive that other methods for synchronization such as semaphores and events can be easily described using it. This means that the deductive system can be used to prove correctness of programs using other methods as well. It can also be used to prove correctness of programs of such a fine degree of interleaving that the only mutual exclusion need be the memory reference. This has been done for the [Dijkstra 76b*] on-the-fly garbage collector, with fairly good results given the complexity of this algorithm, in [Gries 77c*].

The paper is organized as follows. In Section 2 we describe Hoare's work briefly. In Section 3 we introduce the parallel language and extend his system to include it. In Section 4 we give several examples of proofs of partial correctness, while in Section 5 we show how to describe semaphores in the language and give examples. Sections 6 and 7 are devoted to discussions of proofs of other important properties of parallel programs: the absence of deadlock and termination. We summarize our work in Section 8.

Thanks go to Charles Moore for many valuable discussions about parallel processing, and also to Robert Constable and Marvin Solomon. We are grateful to the members of IFIP Working Group 2.3 on programming methodology, especially to Tony Hoare and Edsger W. Dijkstra, for the opportunity to present and discuss this material in its various stages at working group meetings. The observation that the memory reference must have "reasonable" properties, as discussed in Section 3, was made by John Reynolds.

2 Proofs of properties of sequential programs

Let P and Q be assertions about variables and S a statement. Informally, the notation

$$\{P\}S\{Q\}$$

means: if P is true before execution of S, then Q is true after execution of

S. Nothing is said of termination; Q holds *provided* S terminates. The notation

$$\frac{a}{b}$$

means: if a is true, then b is also true. Using such notation, [Hoare 69*] describes a deductive system for proving properties of sequential programs. Let P, P_i represent assertions, x a variable, E an expression, B a Boolean expression and S, S_i statements, then the axioms for the five kinds of statements allowed are:

(2.1) null $\qquad\qquad \{P\}\textbf{skip}\{P\}$

(2.2) assignment $\qquad \{P_E^x\}x := E\{P\}$ where P_E^x is the assertion formed by replacing every free occurrence of x in P by E.

(2.3) alternation $\qquad \dfrac{\{P\wedge B\}S_1\{Q\},\{P\wedge\neg B\}S_2\{Q\}}{\{P\}\textbf{ if } B \textbf{ then } S_1 \textbf{ else } S_2\{Q\}}$

(2.4) iteration $\qquad\quad \dfrac{\{P\wedge B\}S\{P\}}{\{P\}\textbf{ while } B \textbf{ do } S\{P\wedge\neg B\}}$

(2.5) composition $\qquad \dfrac{\{P_1\}S_1\{P_2\},\{P_2\}S_2\{P_3\},\ldots,\{P_n\}S_n\{P_{n+1}\}}{\{P_1\}\textbf{ begin } S_1;\ S_2;\ldots;S_n \textbf{ end}\{P_{n+1}\}}$

In addition, we have the following rule of consequence:

(2.6) consequence $\qquad \dfrac{\{P_1\}S\{Q_1\},P\vdash P_1,Q_1\vdash Q}{\{P\}S\{Q\}}$

The notation $P\vdash Q$ means it is possible to prove Q using P as an assumption. The deductive system to be used in proving Q from P is not given; it could be any system that is valid for the data types and operations used in the programming language.

Note that declarations have been omitted, purely for the sake of simplicity. Hence all variable are globally defined. We also choose not to give the syntax of expressions or assertions. In general, we use an ALGOL-like syntax for expressions, while assertions will be given in a mixture of mathematical notation and English.

Now let us briefly discuss proofs of properties of sequential programs. When we write $\{P\}S\{Q\}$, this implies the existence of a proof of $\{P\}S\{Q\}$, using axioms (2.1)–(2.6). For example, suppose we have

$$S \equiv \textbf{begin } x := a;\ \textbf{if } e \textbf{ then } S1 \textbf{ else } S2 \textbf{ end}$$

and suppose we already have proofs

$$\{P1\wedge e\}S1\{Q1\} \quad \text{and} \quad \{P1\wedge\neg e\}S2\{Q1\}.$$

Then a proof of $\{P\}S\{Q\}$ might be:

(2.7) (1) $\{P1_a^x\}x:=a\{P1\}$ assignment

    (2) $\dfrac{\{P1_a^x\}x:=a\{P1\},P\vdash P1_a^x}{\{P\}x:=a\{P1\}}$ rule of consequence

    (3) $\dfrac{\{P1\wedge e\}S1\{Q1\},\{P1\wedge\neg e\}S2\{Q1\}}{\{P1\}\textbf{ if }e\textbf{ then }S1\textbf{ else }S2\{Q1\}}$ alternation

    (4) $\dfrac{\{P1\}\textbf{ if }e\textbf{ then }S1\textbf{ else }S2\{Q1\},Q1\vdash Q}{\{P1\}\textbf{ if e then S1 else S2}\{Q\}}$ rule of consequence

    (5) $\dfrac{\{P\}x:=a\{P1\},\{P1\}\textbf{ if }e\textbf{ then }S1\textbf{ else }S2\{Q\}}{\{P\}\textbf{ begin }x:=a;\textbf{ if }e\textbf{ then }S1\textbf{ else }S2\textbf{ end }\{Q\}}$ composition

This proof is made much more understandable by giving a *proof outline*, in which the program is given with assertions interleaved at appropriate places, as in (2.8). In such a proof outline, two adjacent assertions $\{P1\}\{P2\}$ denote a use of the rule of consequence, where $P1\vdash P2$.

(2.8) $\{P\}$
    begin $\{P\}$
          $\{P1_a^x\}$
          $x:=a;$
          $\{P1\}$
          if e **then** $\{P1\wedge e\}$
                 $S1$
                 $\{Q1\}$
             else $\{P1\wedge\neg e\}$
                 $S2$
                 $\{Q1\}$
          $\{Q1\}$
          $\{Q\}$
    end
    $\{Q\}$

Most of our proofs will be presented in this style. If $P1\vdash P2$ can be understood easily, we will sometimes only write $P1$, or $P2$. Thus, we might have written

(2.9) **begin** $\{P\}x:=a;\{P1\}\ldots$

leaving out the assertion $\{P1_a^x\}$ in (2.8). However, each statement S is always preceded directly by one assertion, called its *precondition*, written $pre(S)$. In (2.8), $pre(x:=a)=P1_a^x$ while in (2.9) $pre(x:=a)=P$. This notion of a precondition of a statement is important for our work. Similarly, the *postcondition post(S)* is the assertion following statement S.

We may also leave out assertions entirely for a sequence of assignments or simple conditionals, since the necessary weakest precondition of the sequence can always be derived from the postcondition—from the result assertion of the sequence. However, as we shall see, in the parallel case this can sometimes lead to our inability to develop a proof; this situation can sometimes be remedied by explicitly stating stronger preconditions. Proofs of correctness in the face of parallelism require much more care then the simple sequential case.

We will later discuss proofs of properties of parallel programs, such as termination and the absence of deadlock. These are actually properties of the *execution* of a program, and in order to discuss them we should introduce an operational model of the language and show that the deductive system is consistent with it. This has been done for the sequential system by [Hoare 74b*; Cook 75], and for the parallel system by [Owicki 75*]. The systems have also been shown to be complete in a restricted sense by Cook and Owicki; informally this means that every program you would expect to be able to prove partially correct, can indeed be proved in this system.

We will not introduce an operational model here, but will rely on the reader's knowledge that this can be done and his knowledge about execution of programs. We should however discuss assertions somewhat.

An assertion P is a Boolean function defined over the possible values of all the variables of the program. Let the state m of the machine denote the set of values of all variables at any moment during execution. By the phrase "P is true at that moment", we mean that $P[m] = \textbf{true}$. By $P = \textbf{true}$ we mean that $P[m] = \textbf{true}$ for all possible states m.

Our informal proof outlines and proofs of properties of execution rely on the following property, which must be true if the deductive system is to be consistent with the operational model:

(2.10) *Let S be a statement in a program T, and $pre(S)$ the precondition of S in a proof outline of $\{P\}T\{Q\}$. Suppose execution of T begins with P true and reaches a point where S is about to begin execution, with the variables in state m. Then $pre(S)[m] = \textbf{true}$.*

3 Proof of correctness of parallel programs

We introduce parallelism by extending the sequential language with two new statements—one to initiate parallel processing, the other to coordinate processes to be executed in parallel.

Let $S1, S2, \dots, Sn$ be statements. Then execution of the **cobegin** statement

$$\textbf{cobegin } S1 \| S2 \| \cdots \| Sn \textbf{ coend}$$

causes the statements Si to be executed in parallel. Execution of the **cobegin** statement terminates when execution of all the processes Si have terminated. There are no restrictions on the way in which parallel execution is implemented; in particular, nothing is assumed about the relative speeds of the processes.

We do require that each assignment statement and each expression be executed or evaluated as an individual, indivisible action. However this restriction can be lifted if programs adhere to the following simple convention (which we follow in this paper):

(3.1) Each expression E may refer to at most one variable y that can be changed by another process while E is being evaluated, and E may refer to y at most once. A similar restriction holds for assignment statements $x := E$.

With this convention, the only indivisible action need be the memory reference. That is, suppose process Si references variable (location) c while a different process Sj is changing c. We require that the value received by Si for c be the value of c either before or after the assignment to c, but it may not be some spurious value caused by the fluctuation of the value of c during assignment. Thus, our parallel language can be used to model parallel execution on any reasonable machine.

The second statement has the form

await B **then** S

where B is a Boolean expression and S a statement not containing a **cobegin** or another **await** statement. When a process attempts to execute an **await**, it is delayed until the condition B is true. Then the statement S is executed as an indivisible action. Upon termination of S, parallel processing continues. If two or more processes are waiting for the same condition B, any one of them may be allowed to proceed when B becomes true, while the others continue waiting. In some applications it is necessary to specify the order in which waiting processes are scheduled, but for our purposes any scheduling rule is acceptable. Note that evaluation of B is part of the indivisible action of the **await** statement; another process may not change variables so as to make B false after B has been evaluated but before S begins execution.

The **await** statement can be used to turn any statement S into an indivisible action:

await true then S

or it may be used purely as a means of synchronization:

await "some condition" **then skip**

Note that the **await** is not proposed as a new synchronization statement to be inserted in the next programming language; it is too powerful to be implemented efficiently. Rather, it is provided as a means of representing a number of standard synchronization primitives such as semaphores. Thus to verify a program that uses semaphores, one first expresses the semaphore operations as **awaits**, and then applies the techniques given here.

We now turn to formal definitions of these statements, in (3.2) and (3.3). The definition of the **await** is straightforward, but (3.3) will require an explanation, along with a definition of "interference-free":

(3.2) **await** $\dfrac{\{P \wedge B\} S \{Q\}}{\{P\} \ \textbf{await} \ B \ \textbf{then} \ S \{Q\}}$

(3.3)   **cobegin** $\dfrac{\{P1\} S1 \{Q1\}, \ldots, \{Pn\} Sn \{Qn\} \ \text{are interference-free}}{\{P1 \wedge \cdots \wedge Pn\} \quad \textbf{cobegin} \quad S1 \| \cdots \| Sn \quad \textbf{coend} \ \{Q1 \ \wedge \cdots \wedge Qn\}}$

Definition (3.3) says that the effect of executing $S1, \ldots, Sn$ in parallel is the same as executing each one by itself, provided the processes don't "interfere" with each other. The key word is of course "interfere". One possibility to obtain non-interference is not to allow shared variables, but this is too restrictive. A more useful rule is to require that certain assertions used in the proof $\{Pi\} Si \{Qi\}$ of each process are left invariantly true under parallel execution of the other processes. For if these assertions are not falsified, then the proof $\{Pi\} Si \{Qi\}$ will still hold and consequently Qi will still be true upon termination! For example, the assertion $\{x \geqslant y\}$ remains true under execution of $x := x + 1$, while the assertion $\{x = y\}$ does not. The invariance of an assertion P under execution of a statement S is explained by the formula

$$\{P \wedge pre(S)\} S \{P\}$$

We now give the definition of "interference-free".

(3.4) **Definition.** Given a proof $\{P\} S \{Q\}$ and a statement T with precondition $pre(T)$, we say that T *does not interfere with* $\{P\} S \{Q\}$ if the following two conditions hold:

(a) $\{Q \wedge pre(T)\} T \{Q\}$.
(b) Let S' be any statement within S but not within an **await**. Then
$$\{pre(S') \wedge pre(T)\} T \{pre(S')\}.$$

(3.5) **Definition.** $\{P1\} S1 \{Q1\}, \ldots, \{Pn\} Sn \{Qn\}$ *are interference-free* if the following holds. Let T be an **await** or assignment statement (which does not appear in an **await**) of process Si. Then for all $j, j \neq i$, T does not interfere with $\{Pj\} Sj \{Qj\}$.

We will from time to time make program transformations that obviously don't affect correctness, such as replacing **begin** S **end** by S, and replacing **await true then** $x := E$ by $x := E$ provided the assignment satisfies (3.1).

One transformation that is necessary in proving correctness of parallel programs is the addition (or deletion) of assignments to so-called *auxiliary variables*. These auxiliary variables are needed only for the proof of correctness and other properties, and not in the program itself. Typically, they record the history of execution or indicate which part of a program is currently executing. The need for such variables has been independently recognized by many; the first reference we have found to them is [Clint 73]. We define:

(3.6) **Definition.** Let AV be a set of variables that appear in S only in assignments $x := E$, where x is in AV. Then AV is an *auxiliary variable set* for S.

(3.7) **Auxiliary variable transformation.** *Let AV be an auxiliary variable set for S', and P and Q assertions that do not contain free variables from AV. Let S be obtained from S' by deleting all assignments to the variables in AV. Then*

$$\frac{\{P\}S'\{Q\}}{\{P\}S\{Q\}}$$

We shall give examples of the use of the deductive system (2.1)–(2.6), (3.2), (3.3), (3.7) in the next section. But first let us discuss it. Rule (3.3) teaches us to understand parallel processes in two steps. First, understand each process Si, that is study its proof, as an independent, sequential program, disregarding parallel execution completely. *Then* show that execution of each other process does not interfere with the *proof* of Si.

The conventional way of showing non-interference has been to see whether execution of a process Sj interferes with the *execution* of Si. Thus we find phrases like "Suppose Sj does so and so, and then Si executes this and does that". This interleaving of two dynamic objects, the execution of Si and Sj, is very difficult if not impossible to understand for many parallel processes, and it is too easy to miss an argument somewhere.

By concentrating on whether Sj can affect the *proof* of Si's correctness, we turn our attention to a static object, which is easier to deal with. Showing noninterference is quite mechanical; make up a list of Si's preconditions, a second list of Sj's assignments and **awaits**, and show that each element of the second list does not disturb the truth of each assertion in the first.

If a statement T of Sj does interfere with a precondition P of Si, then either the program is incorrect or else Si's proof is inadequate. Often the proof $\{Pi\}Si\{Qi\}$ can be adjusted—assertions can be weakened, keeping the proof still valid, until Sj no longer interferes with them. In any case, the possibility of the programmer missing a particular case is quite low as long as he is careful and persists; this is not the case with earlier informal reasoning.

4 Examples of proof outlines of partial correctness

EXAMPLE 1. A proof outline for a very simple program is given in (4.1). It is obvious that the program "works," as long as $S1$ and $S2$ are interference-free. This requires verification of 4 formulas:

1. $\{pre(S1) \wedge pre(S2)\} S2 \{pre(S1)\}$:

$$\{(x=0 \vee x=2) \wedge (x=0 \vee x=1)\}$$
$$\{x=0\}$$
await true then $\{x=0\}$
$$x: = x+2$$
$$\{x=2\}$$
$$\{x=2\}$$
$$\{x=0 \vee x=2\}$$

2. $\{Q1 \wedge pre(S2)\} S2 \{Q1\}$ (verification left to the reader)
3. $\{pre(S2) \wedge pre(S1)\} S1 \{pre(S2)\}$ (left to the reader)
4. $\{Q2 \wedge pre(S1)\} S1 \{Q2\}$ (left to the reader)

(4.1) $\{x=0\}$

$\quad S:\textbf{cobegin } \{x=0\}$
$$\{x=0 \vee x=2\}$$
$$S1: \textbf{await true then } x: = x+1$$
$$\{Q1: x=1 \vee x=3\}$$

$\quad\quad \|$

$$\{x=0\}$$
$$\{x=0 \vee x=1\}$$
$$S2: \textbf{await true then } x: = x+2$$
$$\{Q2: x=2 \vee x=3\}$$

$\quad \textbf{coend}$

$$\{(x=1 \vee x=3) \wedge (x=2 \vee x=3)\}$$
$$\{x=3\}$$

Suppose we replace $S1$ by the single assignment statement $x: = x+1$. Then the program does not follow convention (3.1). Hence the proof method could not be used to prove this program correct for execution in an environment where the grain of interleaving is finer than the assignment statement. In fact, execution of the program (with this change) could result in the value 2 or 3 for x.

EXAMPLE 2. Consider the more realistic problem of finding the first component $x(k)$ of an array $x(1:M)$, if there is one, which is greater than zero. Program *Findpos* (4.2), given in [Rosen 74], does this using two parallel processes to check the even and odd subscripted array elements separately. In (4.3) we present a proof outline, except for the interference-free check. Note that *Findpos* uses no **await** statement.

(4.2)

> *Findpos*: **begin**
>   *initialize*: $i := 2; j := 1; eventop := M+1; oddtop := M+1;$
>   *search*:**cobegin**
>   *Evensearch*:**while** $i < min(oddtop, eventop)$ **do**
>   **if** $x(i) > 0$ **then** $eventop := i$
>   **else** $i := i+2$
>   ‖
>   *Oddsearch*: **while** $j < min(oddtop, eventop)$ **do**
>   **if** $x(j) > 0$ **then** $oddtop := j$
>   **else** $j := j+2$
>   **coend**;
> $k := min(eventop, oddtop)$
>   **end**

(4.3) $\{ES \wedge OS\}$
>   *search*: **cobegin** $\{ES\}$
>   *Evensearch*: **while** $i < min(oddtop, eventop)$ **do**
> $\{ES \wedge i < eventop \wedge i < M+1\}$
>   **if** $x(i) > 0$
>   **then** $\{ES \wedge i < M+1 \wedge x(i) > 0 \wedge i < eventop\}$
> $eventop := i$
> $\{ES\}$
>   **else** $\{ES \wedge i < eventop \wedge x(i) \leqslant 0\}$
> $i := i+2$
> $\{ES\}$
> $\{ES\}$
> $\{ES \wedge i \geqslant min(oddtop, eventop)\}$
>   ‖
> $\{OS\}$
>   *Oddsearch*: **while** $j < min(oddtop, eventop)$ **do**
> $\{OS \wedge i < oddtop \wedge j < M+1\}$
>   **if** $x(j) > 0$
>   **then** $\{OS \wedge j < M+1 \wedge x(j) > 0 \wedge j < oddtop\}$
> $oddtop := j$
> $\{OS\}$
>   **else** $\{OS \wedge j < oddtop \wedge x(j) \leqslant 0\}$
> $j := j+2$
> $\{OS\}$
> $\{OS\}$
> $\{OS \wedge j \geqslant min(oddtop, eventop)\}$
>   **coend**
> $\{OS \wedge ES \wedge i \geqslant min(oddtop, eventop) \wedge j \geqslant min(oddtop, eventop)\}$
> $k := min(oddtop, eventop)$
> $\{k \leqslant M+1 \wedge \forall l(0 < l < k \Rightarrow x(l) \leqslant 0) \wedge (k \leqslant M \Rightarrow x(k) > 0)\}$

where

$$ES = \left\{ \begin{array}{l} eventop \leqslant M + 1 \wedge \forall l((l\ even \wedge 0 < l < i) \Rightarrow x(l) \leqslant 0) \wedge i\ even \\ \wedge (eventop \leqslant M \Rightarrow x(eventop) > 0) \end{array} \right\}$$

$$OS = \left\{ \begin{array}{l} oddtop \leqslant M + 1 \wedge \forall l((l\ odd \wedge 0 < l < j) \Rightarrow x(l) \leqslant 0) \wedge j\ odd \\ \wedge (oddtop \leqslant M \Rightarrow x(oddtop) > 0) \end{array} \right\}$$

While studying (4.3) do not worry about interaction between *Evensearch* and *Oddsearch*; look upon them as sequential, independent programs. To verify the interference-free property, we must show that each assignment in *Oddsearch* leaves invariantly true each precondition and the final assertion of *Evensearch*. (The argument that *Evensearch* does not interfere with *Oddsearch* is symmetric.) The only assignment in *Oddsearch* that changes a variable in one of *Evensearch*'s assertions is $oddtop := j$, and the only clause in *Evensearch*'s assertions that references $oddtop$ is $i \geqslant min(eventop, oddtop)$. Thus we must show that

(4.4) $\{i \geqslant min(eventop, oddtop) \wedge pre\ (oddtop := j)\}$
        $oddtop := j$
        $\{i \geqslant min(eventop, oddtop)\}$

Since $pre(oddtop := j) \Rightarrow j < oddtop$, (4.4) is certainly true. Thus, for this program, establishing the interference-free property was quite simple.

EXAMPLE 3. We consider a standard problem from the literature of parallel programming. A producer process generates a stream of values for a consumer process. Since the producer and consumer proceed at a variable but roughly equal pace, it is profitable to interpose a buffer between the two processes, but since storage is limited, the buffer can only contain N values. The description of the buffer is:

(4.5) $buffer[0 : N - 1]$ is the shared buffer;
        $in =$ number of elements added to the buffer;
        $out =$ number of elements removed from the buffer;
        the buffer contains $in\text{-}out$ values. These are in order, in
        $buffer[out\ \mathbf{mod}\ N], \ldots, buffer[(out + in - out - 1)\ \mathbf{mod}\ N]$.

In (4.6) we show a solution to the problem in a general environment. In (4.7), we consider a program using this solution that copies an array of values $A[1 : M]$ into an array $B[1 : M]$. (4.8) gives a proof outline for the main program; (4.9) and (4.10) proof outlines for the separate processes. To show the interference-free property, first note that assertion I is invariant throughout both processes. The only assignment in the consumer that might invalidate an assertion of the producer is $out := out + 1$. The only assertion of the producer that it could possibly invalidate is $in\text{-}out < N$, but clearly increasing out leaves this true. Hence the consumer does not interfere with the producer; similar reasoning shows that the producer does not interfere with the consumer.

(4.6)   **begin comment** See (4.5) for description of buffer;
      in : =0; *out* : =0;
      cobegin *producer*:...
              await *in-out* $<N$ **then skip**;
              add : *buffer* [*in* **mod** N] : = *next value*;
              markin : *in* : = *in* + 1;

                    ...

    ||

        consumer:...
        await *in-out* >0 **then skip**;
        remove : *this value* : = buffer[*out* **mod** N];
        markout : *out* : = *out* + 1

           ...

      coend
    end

(4.7)   *fg*1 : **begin comment** See (4.5) for description of buffer;
      in : =0; *out* : =0; *i* : =1; *j* : =1;
      cobegin *producer*: **while** $i \leqslant M$ **do**
                  begin *x* : = $A[i]$;
                        await *in-out* $<N$ **then skip**;
                        add : *buffer*[*in* **mod** N] : = *x*;
                        markin : *in* : = *in* + 1;
                        i : = *i* + 1
                  end

      ||

        consumer : **while** $j \leqslant M$ **do**
                begin await *in-out* >0 **then skip**;
                    remove : *y* : = *buffer*[*out* **mod** N];
                    markout : *out* : = *out* + 1;
                    $B[j]$: = *y*;
                    j : = *j* + 1
                end
      coend
    end

(4.8)   Proof outline for *fg*1 (main program)

  $\{M \geqslant 0\}$
  *fg*1 : **begin** *in* : =0; *out* : =0; *i* : =1; *j* : =1;
    $\{I \wedge i = in + 1 = 1 \wedge j = out + 1 = 1\}$
    *fg*1′ : **cobegin**
        $\{I \wedge i = in + 1 = 1\}$ *producer* $\{I \wedge i = in + 1 = M + 1\}$
      $\| \{I \wedge j = out + 1 = 1\}$ *consumer* $\{I \wedge (B[k] = A[k], 1 \leqslant k \leqslant M)\}$
        coend
    end
  $\{B[k] = A[k], 1 \leqslant k \leqslant M\}$

$$\text{where } I = \left\{ \begin{array}{l} buffer[(k-1) \bmod N] = A[k], \ out < k \leqslant in \\ \wedge \, 0 \leqslant in\text{-}out \leqslant N \\ \wedge \, 1 \leqslant i \leqslant M+1 \\ \wedge \, 1 \leqslant j \leqslant M+1 \end{array} \right\}$$

(4.9)   Proof outline for $fg1$ (*producer*). Invariant I is as in (4.8).

$$\{ I \wedge i = in+1 \}$$
$producer :$ **while** $i \leqslant M$ **do**
    begin $\{ I \wedge i = in+1 \wedge i \leqslant M \}$
        $x := A[i];$
        $\{ I \wedge i = in+1 \wedge i \leqslant M \wedge x = A[i] \}$
        await $in\text{-}out < N$ **then skip**;
        $\{ I \wedge i = in+1 \wedge i \leqslant M \wedge x = A[i] \wedge in\text{-}out < N \}$
        $add : buffer[in \bmod N] := x;$
        $\{ I \wedge i = in+1 \wedge i \leqslant M \wedge buffer[in \bmod N] = A[i] \wedge in\text{-}out < N \}$
        $markin : in = in+1;$
        $\{ I \wedge i = in \wedge i \leqslant M \}$
        $i := i+1$
        $\{ I \wedge i = in+1 \}$
    end
$\{ I \wedge i = in+1 = M+1 \}$

(4.10)   Proof outline for $fg1$ (*consumer*). Invariant I is as in (4.8).

$$\{ I \wedge IC \wedge j = out+1 \}$$
$consumer :$ **while** $j \leqslant M$ **do**
    begin $\{ I \wedge IC \wedge j = out+1 \wedge j \leqslant M \}$
        await $in\text{-}out > 0$ **then skip**;
        $\{ I \wedge IC \wedge j = out+1 \wedge j \leqslant M \wedge in\text{-}out > 0 \}$
        $remove : y := buffer[out \bmod N];$
        $\{ I \wedge IC \wedge j = out+1 \wedge j \leqslant M \wedge in\text{-}out > 0 \wedge y = A[j] \}$
        $markout : out := out+1;$
        $\{ I \wedge IC \wedge j = out \wedge j \leqslant M \wedge y = A[j] \}$
        $B[j] := y;$
        $\{ I \wedge IC \wedge j = out \wedge j \leqslant M \wedge B[j] = A[j] \}$
        $j := j+1$
        $\{ I \wedge IC \wedge j = out+1 \wedge j \leqslant M+1 \}$
    end
$\{ I \wedge IC \wedge j = out+1 = M+1 \}$
$\{ I \wedge (B[k] = A[k], 1 \leqslant k \leqslant M) \}$
where $IC = \{ B[k] = A[k], 1 \leqslant k < j \}$

5 Implementing semaphores

A semaphore *sem* is an integer variable that can only be accessed by two operations, *P* and *V*.

$P(sem)$: if $sem > 0$, $sem := sem - 1$; otherwise suspend the process until $sem > 0$.

$V(sem)$: $sem := sem + 1$.

The *P* and *V* operations are indivisible. They can be represented by synchronization statements as follows.

$P(sem)$: **await** $sem > 0$ **then** $sem := sem - 1$;

$V(sem)$: **await true then** $sem := sem + 1$

Semaphores, as first defined by [Dijkstra 68a*] were slightly different:

$P'(sem)$: $sem := sem - 1$; if $sem < 0$ then the process is suspended on a queue associated with *sem*.

$V'(sem)$: $sem := sem + 1$; if $sem \leqslant 0$, awaken one of the processes on the semaphore's queue.

A possible implementation of these operations uses a Boolean array *waiting*, with one element for each process. Initially $waiting[i] = $ **false**, and $waiting[i] = $ **true** implies that *i* is on the queue.

```
P'(sem):  await true then
              begin sem := sem - 1;
                    if sem < 0 then waiting[this process] := true;
              end;
              await ¬ waiting[this process] then skip;
V'(sem):  await true then
              begin sem := sem + 1;
                    if sem ≤ 0 then
                        begin choose i such that waiting[i];
                              waiting[i] := false
                        end
              end
```

In some cases the effects of the operations *P* and *V* are different from those of *P'* and *V'*, but for the properties we discuss—partial correctness, absence of deadlock, and termination—these differences are irrelevant. See [Lipton 74a] for a comparison of the two kinds of semaphore operations. We leave it to the reader to define semaphores *P"* and *V"*, like *P'* and *V'*, except that the longest waiting process always gets served next.

Given a program with semaphores, the semaphore operations can be replaced by the corresponding **await**s. The result is an equivalent program which can be proved correct using the methods presented in this paper. A number of other synchronization primitives can also be modelled using **await**.

Consider a second version of the producer-consumer program, $fg2$ (5.1), which uses semaphores *full* and *empty* to synchronize access to the buffer. In (5.2) we show the translation of the semaphores into **awaits**; (5.2) also uses auxiliary variables needed for a proof of partial correctness. In (5.3) we give a proof outline for the main program; in (5.4) the proof outline for the consumer (the producer is omitted, since it is similar). The proof is essentially the same as for the earlier version $fg1$ of the program. Using inference rule (3.7), the auxiliary variables can be removed to yield a proof of $\{M \geqslant 0\}$ $fg2$ $\{B[k] = A[k], \ 1 \leqslant k \leqslant M\}$. The producer does not interfere with the proof of the consumer because the assertions in this proof include only I (which is invariantly true in both processes) and variables not changed by the producer. Likewise, the consumer does not interfere with the proof of the producer.

[Habermann 72] presents this solution to the producer-consumer problem and provides an informal proof of correctness. He uses special functions that count the number of P and V operations on each semaphore; these play the same role as our auxiliary variables.

(5.1) $fg2$: **begin comment** *buffer* $[0:N-1]$ *is the shared buffer,*
    full = number of full places in *buffer*
    (semaphore),
    empty = number of empty places (semaphore);
  $full := 0;\ empty := N;\ i := 1;\ j := 1;$
  cobegin *producer* : **while** $i \leqslant M$ **do**
        begin $x := A[i];$
          $P(empty);$
          $buffer[i \bmod N] := x;$
          $V(full);$
          $i := i+1$
        end

        $\|$

      consumer : **while** $j \leqslant M$ **do**
        begin $P(full);$
          $y := buffer[j \bmod N];$
          $V(empty);$
          $B[j] := y;$
          $j := j+1$
        end

      coend
    end

(5.2)

```
fg2' : begin comment Pempty, Vempty, Pfull, Vfull are
                      auxiliary variables;
      full : = 0; empty : = N; i : = 1; j : = 1;
      Pfull, Vfull, Pempty, Vempty : = 0, 0, 0, 0;
      cobegin producer : while i ⩽ M do
                  begin x : = A[i];
                          await empty > 0 then
                              begin empty : = empty − 1;
                                    Pempty : = Pempty + 1 end;
                          buffer[i mod N] : = x;
                          await true then
                              begin full : = full + 1; Vfull : = Vfull + 1 end;
                          i : = i + 1
                  end
          ||
              consumer : while j ⩽ M do
                  begin await full > 0 then
                              begin full : = full − 1; Pfull : = Pfull + 1 end;
                          y : = buffer[j mod N];
                          await true then
                              begin empty : = empty + 1;
                                    Vempty : = Vempty + 1 end;
                          B[j] : = y;
                          j : = j + 1
                  end
      coend
      end
```

(5.3)   Proof outline of fg2' (main program)

```
fg2' : begin
          full : = 0; empty : = N; i : = 1; j : = 1;
          Pfull, Vfull, Pempty, Vempty : = 0, 0, 0, 0;
          {I ∧ Vfull = Pempty ∧ i = Vfull + 1 ∧ Vempty = Pfull
          ∧ j = Vempty + 1}
          cobegin
                  {I ∧ Vfull = Pempty ∧ i = Vfull + 1}
                  producer
                  {I}
              ||
                  {I ∧ Vempty = Pfull ∧ j = Vempty + 1}
                  consumer
                  {I ∧ (B[k] = A[k], 1 ⩽ k ⩽ M)}
          coend
          end
      {B[k] = A[k], 1 ⩽ k ⩽ M}
```

where $I = (buffer[k \bmod N] = A[k], \ Vempty < k \leqslant Vfull)$
$\qquad \wedge full = Vfull - Pfull$
$\qquad \wedge empty = N + Vempty - Pempty$
$\qquad \wedge 1 \leqslant i \leqslant M + 1$
$\qquad \wedge 1 \leqslant j \leqslant M + 1$

(5.4)   Proof outline for $fg2'$ (*consumer*). Invariant I is given in (5.3).

$\{I \wedge IC \wedge Vempty = Pfull \wedge j = Vempty + 1\}$
consumer : **while** $j \leqslant M$ **do**
$\quad$ **begin** $\{I \wedge IC \wedge Vempty = Pfull \wedge j = Vempty + 1 \wedge j \leqslant M\}$
$\qquad$ **await** $full > 0$ **then**
$\qquad\quad$ **begin** $full : = full - 1; \ Pfull : = Pfull + 1$ **end**;
$\qquad\quad \{I \wedge IC \wedge Vempty = Pfull - 1 \wedge j = Vempty + 1 \wedge j \leqslant M\}$
$\qquad$ $y : = buffer[j \bmod N]$;
$\qquad\quad \{I \wedge IC > Vempty = Pfull - 1 \wedge j = Vempty + 1$
$\qquad\quad \wedge j \leqslant M \wedge y = A[j]\}$
$\qquad$ **await true then**
$\qquad\quad$ **begin** $empty : = empty + 1; \ Vempty : = Vempty + 1$ **end**;
$\qquad\quad \{I \wedge IC \wedge Vempty = Pfull \wedge j = Vempty \wedge j \leqslant M \wedge y = A[j]\}$
$\qquad$ $B[j] : = y$;
$\qquad\quad \{I \wedge IC \wedge Vempty = Pfull \wedge j = Vempty \wedge j \leqslant M \wedge B[j] = A[j]\}$
$\qquad$ $j : = j + 1$
$\qquad\quad \{I \wedge IC \wedge Vempty = Pfull \wedge j = Vempty + 1 \wedge j \leqslant M + 1\}$
$\quad$ **end**
$\{I \wedge IC \wedge j = M + 1\}$
$\{I \wedge (B[k] = A[k], \ 1 \leqslant k \leqslant M)\}$
where $IC = (B[k] = A[k], \ 1 \leqslant k < j)$

6 Blocking and deadlock

Because of the **await** statements, a process may be delayed, or "blocked" at an **await** until its condition B is true.

(6.1) **Definition.** Suppose a statement S is being executed. S is *blocked* if it has not terminated, but no progress in its execution is possible because it (or all of its subprocesses that have not yet terminated) are delayed at an **await**.

Blocking by itself is harmless; processes may become blocked and unblocked many times during execution. However, if the whole program becomes blocked, this is serious because it can never be unblocked and thus the program cannot terminate.

(6.2) **Definition.** Execution of a program *ends in deadlock* if it is blocked.

(6.3) **Definition.** A program S with proof $\{P\}$ S $\{Q\}$ is *free from deadlock* if no execution of S that begins with P true ends in deadlock.

We wish to derive sufficient conditions under which a program is free from deadlock. First of all, a proof of correctness of a program S includes a proof of correctness of a program S', together with several applications of the auxiliary variable rule (3.7) which reduce S' to S. Since the reduction consists of deleting assignments to auxiliary variables, we take as obvious the following theorem (a proof with respect to a particular execution model appears in [Owicki 75*]).

(6.4) **Theorem.** *Suppose program S' is free from deadlock, and suppose S is derived from S' by application of inference rule (3.7). Then S is also free from deadlock.*

We are now in a position to give sufficient conditions for freedom from deadlock.

(6.5) **Theorem.** *Let S be a statement with proof $\{P\}$ S $\{Q\}$. Let the* **await***s of S that do not occur within* **cobegin***s of S be*

$$A_j : \textbf{await } B_j \textbf{ then} \ldots$$

Let the **cobegin***s of S that do not occur within other* **cobegin***s of S be*

$$T_k : \textbf{cobegin } S_1^k \| S_2^k \| \cdots \| S_{n_k}^k \textbf{ coend}$$

Define

$$D(S) = \left[\bigvee_j \left(pre(A_j) \wedge \neg B_j \right) \right] \vee \left[\bigvee_k D_1(T_k) \right]$$
$$D_1(T_k) = \left[\bigwedge_i \left(post(S_i^k) \vee D(S_i^k) \right) \right] \wedge \left[\bigvee_i D(S_i^k) \right]$$

Then $D(S) = \textbf{false}$ implies that in no execution of S can S be blocked. Hence, if S is a program, S is free from deadlock.

PROOF. We show by induction on the level of nesting of **cobegin**s in S that S blocked in state m implies $D(S)[m] = \textbf{true}$. Hence $D(S) = \textbf{false}$ would indicate that S cannot be blocked. Suppose S has no **cobegin**s. Then it is blocked at a single **await** with label A_j. Therefore $(pre(A_j) \wedge \neg B_j)[m] = \textbf{true}$ and $D(S)[m] = \textbf{true}$.

Suppose S contains **cobegin**s, and is blocked in state m. Then either it is blocked at an **await** A_j, in which case $D(S)[m] = \textbf{true}$ as above, or one of its parallel processes T_k is blocked. Consider one of T_k's processes S_i^k. By induction, we know that if S_i^k is blocked in state m, that $D(S_i^k)[m] = \textbf{true}$. Now, since T_k is blocked, then each of its processes S_i^k has terminated or is blocked, and moreover, at least one of its processes S_i^k is blocked.

Inspection of formula $D_1(T_k)$ shows therefore that $D_1(T_k)[m]=\textbf{true}$. Hence $D(S)[m]=\textbf{true}$. Q.E.D.

Note that (6.5) provides a static check in order to prove a property of all executions of S; to show freedom from deadlock we need only manipulate the assertions in the proof of correctness. The amount of detail is directly proportional to the level of nesting of parallel statements.

If a statement S contains no parallel statements, then $\bigvee_k D_1(T_k)$ is the empty union and is false, and hence $D(S)$ reduces to

$$\bigvee_j \left(pre(A_j) \wedge \neg B_j \right).$$

If, further, S has no **awaits**, then this union is also empty and $D(S)$ is **false**. Thus, a sequential program without **awaits** is free from deadlock. It is also easy to apply the theorem to show that if a program has no **awaits**, or if all **awaits** have the form **await true then**..., then the program is free from deadlock. Finally if a parallel statement T is not supposed to terminate, i.e. $post(T)=\textbf{false}$, then $D_1(T)$ reduces to

$$D_1(T) = \bigwedge_i D(S_i) \quad \text{where the } S_i \text{ are the processes of } T.$$

Section 4 contains several examples of programs with proof outlines. Program (4.1) is free from deadlock since the conditions of the **awaits** are all **true**. *Findpos* in (4.2) is free from deadlock since it has no **await**.

To prove freedom from deadlock for the producer-consumer program (4.7), we use its proof outline given in (4.8)–(4.10). We have

$$D(producer) \quad \Rightarrow in < M \wedge in\text{-}out = N$$
$$post(producer) \quad \Rightarrow in = M$$
$$D(consumer) \quad \Rightarrow out < M \wedge in\text{-}out = 0$$
$$post(producer) \quad \Rightarrow out = M$$

Writing $D_1(fg1')=x\wedge y$, where $fg1'$ is the **cobegin** statement, we then rewrite x as the "or" of 4 terms.

$$x \Rightarrow [in < M \wedge in\text{-}out = N \wedge out < M \wedge in\text{-}out = 0]$$
$$\bigvee [in < M \wedge in\text{-}out = N \wedge out = M]$$
$$\bigvee [in = M \wedge out < M \wedge in\text{-}out = 0]$$
$$\bigvee [in = M \wedge out = M]$$
$$\Rightarrow N = 0 \bigvee N < 0 \bigvee \textbf{false} \bigvee in = out = M$$
$$\Rightarrow N \leqslant 0 \bigvee in = out = M$$
$$y = D(producer) \bigvee D(consumer) \Rightarrow in < M \bigvee out < M$$
$$D(fg1) = D_1(fg1') = x \wedge y \Rightarrow N \leqslant 0.$$

Hence, sufficient conditions for freedom from deadlock in $fg1$ is that $N > 0$—that is, the buffer has room for at least one element.

In some programs using semaphores, it is often useful to know how many processes can be blocked at a particular moment, waiting to enter a critical section. We can prove a general theorem about such programs, generalizing the idea of blocking a bit at the same time.

(6.6) **Theorem.** *Consider a program of the form (6.7). Then at any point of execution at most $n - m$ of the processes $S1, \ldots, Sn$ can be blocked at $P(s)$. Furthermore, if a process is blocked at $P(s)$, then m processes are executing the critical section or $V(s)$.*

(6.7) $s := m;$ ...
       cobegin $S1 \| \cdots \| Sn \| \cdots \| Sp$ **coend**

    where each $Si, 1 \leqslant i \leqslant n$, has the form given below, none of the processes $Si, i > n$, reference s, and the only references to s are those shown:

    $Si:$ ...
        while true do
          begin noncritical section;
             $P(s);$
             critical section;
             $V(s);$
             noncritical section
        end

PROOF. In (6.8) we show this same program written using **await**s, with auxiliary variables, and with a proof outline. The assertions that $INCi = 1$ throughout the critical section and $INCi = 0$ elsewhere are justified since the only operations on $INCi$ are those explicitly shown. Similarly, assertion I holds throughout because there are no other operations on s. The interference-free requirement is easily verified, because each assertion is a statement about $INCi$, which is not changed in $Sj, j \neq i$, and about I, which is invariant over the statements in process Sj.

Now suppose $n - m + k, k \geqslant 0$, processes are blocked at $P(s)$. Then we have $INCi = 0$ for these processes, and hence $s = m - \sum_{j=1}^{n} INCj > 0$. But the fact that the processes are blocked at $P(s)$ implies that $s = 0$, and we have a contradiction.

Secondly, suppose a process is blocked but only $m - k, k > 0$ processes are executing their critical section or the **await true** statement. Because a process is blocked we have $s \leqslant 0$. But since $m - k$ processes are executing their critical section, for each of these processes we have $INCi = 1$, and together with invariant I this yields $s > 0$. Thus we have a contradiction.

(6.8) $s: = m;\ INC1, INC2,\ldots, INCn: = 0,0,\ldots,0;\ \ldots$

$\{(INCi = 0, 1 \leqslant i \leqslant n)\}$

cobegin $S1\|\cdots\|Sn\|\cdots\|Sp$ **coend**

$\{\textbf{false}\}$

where $Si, 1 \leqslant i \leqslant n,$ *is*

$\{I \wedge INCi = 0\}$

$Si: \ldots$

    while true do
    begin $\{I \wedge INCi = 0\}$
        noncritical section;
        $\{I \wedge INCi = 0\}$
        await $s > 0$ **then begin** $s: = s - 1;\ INCi: = 1$ **end;**
        $\{I \wedge INCi = 1\}$
        critical section;
        $\{I \wedge INCi = 1\}$
        await true then begin $s: = s + 1;\ INCi: = 0$ **end;**
        $\{I \wedge INCi = 0\}$
        noncritical section
    end
  $\{\textbf{false}\}$

where $I \equiv s = m - \sum_{i=1}^{n} INCi\ \wedge\ (\forall i, 1 \leqslant i \leqslant n, 0 \leqslant INCi \leqslant 1)$

Theorem 6.6 thus confirms our understanding of the semaphore.

7 Termination

Let us suppose that all operations are defined so that they always yield a value in the expected range. Then the only way a sequential program can fail to terminate is to loop infinitely in some **while** loop. In order to include proof of termination in a useful practical manner, one can replace the iteration inference rule (2.4) with another. Let t be an integer function of the program variables. A loop **while** B **do** S with invariant P must terminate if it can be shown that when the loop is executing t is positive—i.e., $(P \wedge B) \Rightarrow t > 0$—and that each execution of the loop body S is guaranteed to decrease t by at least one. Using a new variable T the latter is established by

$$\{P \wedge B\}\ T: = t;\ S\ \{t \leqslant T - 1\}.$$

This gives us the new inference rule for iteration:

(7.1) *iteration* $$\frac{\{P\wedge B\}T:=t;\ S\ \{P\wedge t\leqslant T-1\},\ (P\wedge B)\Rightarrow t>0}{\{P\}\textbf{while}\ B\ \textbf{do}\ S\ \{P\wedge\neg B\}}$$
     with
     termination

Suppose we prove correctness of each process of a parallel program using (7.1) instead of (2.4). Proving noninterference will then automatically prove that $\{P\wedge B\}T:=t;\ S\ \{t\leqslant T-1\}$ holds in the face of parallel execution, since this is included in rule (7.1). Hence, all loops progress towards termination under parallel execution. (Note that, essentially one need only show that the integer function t for a loop is never *increased* by parallel execution, and this is the technique we will later use.)

The only way for a program *not* to terminate, then, is that deadlock occurs. To prohibit deadlock, we replace rule (3.3) for the **cobegin** statement by another rule (7.2), in which the property *deadlock-free* is defined as the sufficient conditions given in theorem (6.5) for freedom from deadlock:

(7.2) *cobegin* $\{P1\}S1\{Q1\},\ldots,\{Pn\}Sn\{Qn\}$ interference-free,
     with $\dfrac{\{P1\}S1\{Q1\},\ldots,\{Pn\}Sn\{Qn\}\ \text{deadlock-free}}{\{P1\wedge\cdots\wedge Pn\}\ \textbf{cobegin}\ S1\|\cdots\|Sn\ \textbf{coend}}$
     termination
$$\{Q1\wedge\cdots\wedge Qn\}$$

As an example, consider program *Findpos* (4.3). We have thus far shown partial correctness. To show termination of *Evensearch* using rule (7.1) instead of (2.4), we introduce the function

$$te\equiv min(oddtop,\ eventop)-i$$

Note that for the loop in *Evensearch*, $B\Rightarrow te>0$. Secondly, execution of the loop increases i and decreases te. Similarly, we use the integer function $t0\equiv min(eventop,\ oddtop)-j$ to show that *Oddtop* terminates. To show non-interference of *Evensearch* by *Oddsearch*, we show that *Oddsearch* does not increase te (the argument for *Evensearch* not interfering with *Oddsearch* is similar). The only statement in Oddsearch that changes a variable of te is $oddtop:=j$. We now show that execution of this does not increase te:

$$\{te=c\wedge pre(oddtop:=j)\}$$

$$\{min(oddtop,\ eventop)-i=c\wedge j<oddtop\}$$

$$\{min(j,\ eventop)-i\leqslant c\}$$

$$oddtop:=j$$

$$\{min(oddtop,\ eventop)-i\leqslant c\}$$

Finally, there is no deadlock since there are no **await**s in the program.

8 Conclusions

We have developed a deductive system for proving properties of parallel programs, building on work by [Hoare 69*, 72g*]. Besides partial correctness, the system lends itself to proving other properties: freedom from deadlock, and termination. Once one has a partial correctness proof, one can often prove these other properties just by manipulating in some fashion the assertions already created for the partial correctness proof. Hence the proofs of these properties of execution only require work with static objects—the assertions—instead of with the dynamic execution of the program.

A number of other properties could be considered: priority assignments, progress for each process, blocking of some subset of the processes, etc. Many of these are difficult to define in a uniform way, while others require a model with definite rules for scheduling competing processes. Hopefully, future work will broaden the range of properties that can be dealt with using axiomatic methods.

The synchronization primitive discussed is admittedly primitive; [Owicki 76a*] covers the same material using a higher level synchronization statement, Hoare's **with-when** statement. However, this primitive synchronization statement has proved useful. First, it has given us insight into how to understand parallel processes, as discussed in Section 3. Secondly, we have used it on a number of parallel programs from the literature— *Findpos*, the consumer-producer problem, etc., and we feel it will be useful in practical work with parallel programs. It gives us a method for dealing more formally with other synchronization primitives.

The "insight" gained from this work, towards understanding parallelism, may not have come across well if the reader already understood the examples beforehand. A quite complicated problem with as fine a grain of interleaving as can be imagined, the [Dijkstra 76b*] on-the fly garbage collector, has been proved correct in what we feel is a satisfactory manner [Gries 76a*], and we invite the reader to study it. The first author was also able to verify the semaphore solutions for readers and writers proposed by Courtois, Heymans and Parnas. This was fairly hard to do, because of the complexity of their solution which gives priority to the writer.

12
Programming with Transition Diagrams[1]

John C. Reynolds
Syracuse University

Abstract   *In situations where the avoidance of* **goto** *statements would be inhibiting, programs can be methodically constructed by using transition diagrams. The key requirement is that the relevant assertions must be simple enough to permit exhaustive reasoning. The method is illustrated by programs for fast exponentiation, merging, and path-finding in a directed graph.*

Introduction

The **goto** controversy has generated more heat than light, and has exaggerated the importance of control structures in programming methodology. Yet hiding behind this controversy is a serious question. It is not whether **goto**s are good or bad, nor whether some new control structure can provide a desirable balance between the flexibility of **goto**s and the intelligibility of simple iteration and conditional statements. The real question is how—in situations where their flexibility is really needed—to use **goto**s methodically, reliably, and clearly.

By means of three examples, I would like to suggest that the answer is to use transition diagrams with assertions at their nodes, and to keep these assertions simple enough that they can be reasoned about exhaustively.

Fast exponentiation

As a first example, consider computing x^n in time $\log n$. We want a program satisfying the specification

$\{n \geqslant 0\}$ "Compute x^n" $\{y = x^n\}$.

To construct this program in a top-down fashion without using **goto**s, we

[1] Work supported by National Science Foundation Grant MCS 75-22002.

begin with the invariant

$$I \equiv y \times z^k = x^n \,\&\, k \geqslant 0.$$

Since this invariant embodies the essential idea behind the algorithm, one would expect the rest of the program development to be straightforward.

The invariant can be attained by an obvious initialization, and it implies the goal of the program when $k = 0$. Thus "Compute x^n" expands into

> **begin integer** k; **real** z;
> $y := 1.0$; $z := x$; $k := n$;
> "Achieve $k = 0$ while maintaining I"
> **end**,

where "Achieve $k = 0$ while maintaining I" obviously expands into

> **while** $k \neq 0$ **do**
> > "Decrease k while maintaining I".

It would be correct to expand "Decrease k while maintaining I" into the statement

$$STEP \equiv \textbf{begin } k := k - 1; \, y := y \times z \textbf{ end},$$

which satisfies $\{I \,\&\, k \neq 0\}\ STEP\ \{I\}$. But using only $STEP$ gives a slow algorithm; for speed we must also employ the statement

$$HALVE \equiv \textbf{begin } k := k \div 2; \, z := z \times z \textbf{ end},$$

which satisfies $\{I \,\&\, even(k)\} HALVE \{I\}$.

Thus to complete the algorithm we must compose "Decrease k while maintaining I" out of the slow $STEP$, which always works, and the fast $HALVE$, which only works for even k. However, there are at least two correct compositions:

> **if** $odd(k)$ **then** $STEP$ **else** $HALVE$.   (I)
> **begin if** $odd(k)$ **then** $STEP$; $HALVE$ **end**.   (II)

Moreover, each of these versions is in some respect worse than the other.

Their limitations are more evident at the level of "Achieve $k = 0$ while maintaining I":

> **while** $k \neq 0$ **do**   (I)
> > **if** $odd(k)$ **then** $STEP$ **else** $HALVE$.

> **while** $k \neq 0$ **do**   (II)
> > **begin if** $odd(k)$ **then** $STEP$; $HALVE$ **end**.

In (I) there is redundant testing; each execution of $STEP$ will produce an even number that will be unnecessarily subjected to the test $odd(k)$. In (II) the loop will conclude with a final execution of $HALVE$, which will not affect the result but which can cause unnecessary overflow.

It is at this point that the prohibition of **gotos** seems to chafe. To avoid the limitations of (I) and (II), we shall collapse the structure of our algorithm slightly, and express "Achieve $k=0$ while maintaining I" directly in terms of *STEP* and *HALVE*, using a transition diagram.

The nodes of this transition diagram will be the possible states of knowledge about the conditions that are relevant to the program. Except for the invariant, which is always true at this level of abstraction, the only relevant conditions are $k=0$ and $even(k)$. For one of these conditions there are three states of knowledge: $k=0$, $k\neq0$, and *don't know*. For the two conditions, there would be nine states if the conditions were independent, but since $k=0$ implies $even(k)$ there are only six states, described by the assertions:

true (i.e., *don't know*)
$k=0$
$k\neq0$
even (k)
odd(k)
$k\neq0\ \&\ even(k).$

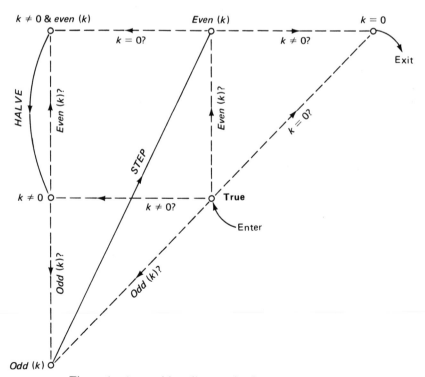

Figure 1   A transition diagram for fast exponentiation.

Two kinds of arcs will occur in the transition diagram. Tests will be represented by complementary pairs of arcs indicated by dashed lines, and operations will be represented by individual arcs indicated by solid lines. The test arcs are obvious—we simply put in all possible tests of the relevant conditions that provide increased information.

The next step is to determine the preconditions for performing the various operations. If $k = 0$, exit should occur, since the goal of the program has been achieved. If $k \neq 0 \,\&\, even(k)$, $HALVE$ can be performed. If $odd(k)$, then $STEP$ must be performed.

Finally, we must analyze $STEP$ and $HALVE$ to determine the information about $k = 0$ and $even(k)$ that will be known after execution. It is easily seen that $STEP$ and $HALVE$ satisfy

$$\{I \,\&\, odd(k)\} \; STEP \; \{I \,\&\, even(k)\}$$
$$\{I \,\&\, k \neq 0 \,\&\, even(k)\} \; HALVE \; \{I \,\&\, k \neq 0\}$$

(which are more stringent than the specifications given earlier). These specifications directly determine the placement of the operation arcs.

Thus "Achieve $k = 0$ while maintaining I" is realized by the transition diagram shown in Figure 1. Entrance occurs at the node **true** since the precondition of the program does not imply any information about $k = 0$ or $even(k)$.

The foregoing argument should convince the reader of conditional correctness. For total correctness, one must also be sure that there are no dead ends—which is obvious by inspection—and that no loops can run on forever. To clarify the latter question, the geometry of Figure 1 has been chosen so that, if **true** is taken as the origin, then increasing distance represents increasing information. As a consequence, the only arcs that do not increase distance from the origin—at least one of which must occur in evey loop—are the operations $STEP$ and $HALVE$. Thus termination is assured since, when their specified preconditions are true, both of these operations will always decrease k without making it negative.

Emanating from the entrance node are two pairs of arcs denoting distinct tests, so that the transition diagram is nondeterminate. However this is an advantage: We have shown that all possible executions of the diagram will be correct, so we are free to resolve the nondeterminacy without regard to correctness. In this case, the decision does not matter much, though a weak argument can be made that beginning with the test $odd(k)$ will usually be faster.

The result is a program that avoids the defects of both earlier versions. Moreover, the program is still essentially structured, since the nature of invariant I only affects the details of $STEP$ and $HALVE$ and plays no role in the construction of the transition diagram. In effect, the transition diagram is a program for a machine whose primitive instructions, $STEP$ and $HALVE$, are guaranteed by the machine designer to preserve the integrity of the machine (i.e., the invariant) when used in accordance with their specifications. Of course, it is precisely this suppression of the invariant that permits us to limit our attention to the conditions $k=0$ and $even(k)$, which are so simple that we can easily deal with all possible states of knowledge.

On the other hand, our program is certainly less structured than versions (I) or (II), and consequently more complicated. But the result is not chaos. There is still enough structure that the program can be constructed and understood methodically.

To represent a transition diagram in a conventional language, one can use a block in which each node appears as a label with an attached assertion, each operation is a sequence of statements beginning with a label and ending with a **goto** statement, and each test is a conditional statement containing a pair of **goto** statements. The invariant, which must hold at all labels, is stated at the beginning of the block. For example, the program for fast exponentiation is:

$$\{n \geqslant 0\}$$
begin integer k; **real** z;
$y := 1.0; z := x; k := n;$
    begin $\{$invariant: $y \times z^k = x^n \& k \geqslant 0\}$
    enter: $\{$**true**$\}$ **if** $odd(k)$ **then goto** *od* **else goto** *ev*;
    nz: $\{k \neq 0\}$ **if** $odd(k)$ **then goto** *od* **else goto** *nzev*;
    ev: $\{even(k)\}$ **if** $k=0$ **then goto** *zr* **else goto** *nzev*;
    od: $\{odd(k)\}$ $k := k-1; y := y \times z;$ **goto** *ev*;
    nzev: $\{k \neq 0 \& even(k)\}$ $k := k \div 2; z := z \times z;$ **goto** *nz*;
    zr: $\{k=0\}$
    end
end
$\{y = x^n\}.$

For clarity, we have avoided passing through a label from the preceding statement. The labels have been ordered to make termination evident: Each backward jump is preceded by a statement that decreases k.

To the author's surprise, D. Gries has found a **goto**-free program (using only ";", conditional, and **while** constructions to combine statements) that is schematically equivalent to the above. Its construction, and the question of whether it is more natural than the use of transition diagrams, is left as an exercise for the reader.

Merging

As a second example, consider merging two ordered arrays X, with subscripts from ax to bx, and Y, with subscripts from ay to by, into an array Z, with subscripts from az to bz, which is just the right size to receive

the result. A precise specification is

$$\{ax \leqslant bx+1 \,\&\, ay \leqslant by+1 \,\&\, az \leqslant bz+1$$
$$\&(bx - ax + 1) + (by - ay + 1) = (bz - az + 1)$$
$$\&\, ordered(X, ax, bx) \,\&\, ordered(Y, ay, by)\}$$
"*Merge*"
$$\{ordered(Z, az, bz) \,\&\, merged(X, ax, bx, Y, ay, by, Z, az, bz)\},$$

where

$ordered(X, a, b) \equiv (\forall i,j) a \leqslant i < j \leqslant b$ implies $X(i) \leqslant X(j)$, and *merged*(…) asserts that Z is a rearrangement of the concatenation of X and Y, i.e.,

$$merged(X, ax, bx, Y, ay, by, Z, az, bz) \equiv$$
$$(\exists P) P \in perm(\{i \,|\, az \leqslant i \leqslant bz\}) \,\&$$
$$(\forall i) az \leqslant i \leqslant bz \text{ implies } Z(P(i)) =$$
$$\text{if } i - az + ax \leqslant bx \text{ then } X(i - az + ax)$$
$$\text{else } Y(i - az - (bx - ax + 1) + ay),$$

where $perm(S)$ is the set of permutations (one-to-one functions) from the set S onto itself.

Since all three arrays will be scanned from left to right, each array will be partitioned into a processed and an unprocessed part, as shown in Figure 2.

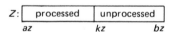

Figure 2   Arrays for merging.

The invariant describes this partitioning and asserts that the unprocessed part of Z is the right size, that the processed part of Z is ordered and is a rearrangement of the concatenation of the processed parts of X and Y, and that all processed values are smaller or equal to all unprocessed values:

$$I \equiv$$
$$ax \leqslant kx \leqslant bx+1 \,\&\, ay \leqslant ky \leqslant by+1 \,\&\, az \leqslant kz \leqslant bz+1$$
$$\&\,(bx - kx + 1) + (by - ky + 1) = (bz - kz + 1)$$
$$\&\, ordered(Z, az, kz - 1)$$
$$\&\, merged(X, ax, kx - 1, Y, ay, ky - 1, Z, az, kz - 1)$$
$$\&\, all \leqslant (Z, az, kz - 1, X, kx, bx)$$
$$\&\, all \leqslant (Z, az, kz - 1, Y, ky, by),$$

where

$$all \leq (X,a,b,Y,c,d) \equiv$$
$$(\forall i,j) a \leq i \leq b \ \& \ c \leq j \leq d \text{ implies } X(i) \leq Y(j).$$

This invariant can be attained by making the processed array parts empty, and it implies the goal of the program when the unprocessed parts of both X and Y (and therefore of Z) are empty. Thus "*Merge*" expands into:

begin integer kx, ky, kz;
$kx := ax; ky := ay; kz := az$;
"Achieve $kx > bx$ and $ky > by$ while maintaining I"
end.

The rest of the program will be built out of two operations:

$COPYX \equiv$ **begin** $Z(kz) := X(kx); kx := kx + 1; kz := kz + 1$ **end**
$COPYY \equiv$ **begin** $Z(kz) := Y(ky); ky := ky + 1; kz := kz + 1$ **end**.

Roughly speaking, either $COPYX$ or $COPYY$ will preserve the invariant, depending upon whether $X(kx)$ or $Y(ky)$ is the smallest unprocessed value. However, a precise specification must take into account the possibility that the unprocessed part of X or Y may be empty:

$$\{I \ \& \ kx \leq bx \ \& (ky > by \textbf{ or } (ky \leq by \ \& \ X(kx) \leq Y(ky)))\} \ COPYX \ \{I\}$$
$$\{I \ \& \ ky \leq by \ \& (kx > bx \textbf{ or } (kx \leq bx \ \& \ Y(ky) \leq X(kx)))\} \ COPYY \ \{I\}.$$

At this stage we may suppress the rather formidable invariant, and focus on the remaining conditions $kx \leq bx, ky \leq by$, and $X(kx) \leq Y(ky)$. The first two conditions are independent, and therefore lead to $3 \times 3 = 9$ states, but $X(kx) \leq Y(ky)$ is only meaningful when both $kx \leq bx$ and $ky \leq by$ are true (i.e., when both unprocessed array parts are nonempty), and therefore leads to only two additional states.

Exit can occur when $kx > bx \ \& \ ky > by$, and the conditions when $COPYX$ and $COPYY$ can occur are shown clearly by their specifications. Finally, if we examine the effect of $COPYX$ separately for the two nodes at which it will occur, we can deduce the more stringent specification

$$\{I \ \& \ kx \leq bx \ \& \ ky > by\} \ COPYX \ \{I \ \& \ ky > by\}$$
$$\{I \ \& \ kx \leq bx \ \& \ ky \leq by \ \& \ X(kx) \leq Y(ky)\} \ COPYX \ \{I \ \& \ ky \leq by\}$$

since $COPYX$ does not affect the emptyness of the unprocessed part of Y. Similarly,

$$\{I \ \& \ ky \leq by \ \& \ kx > bx\} \ COPYY \ \{I \ \& \ kx > bx\}$$
$$\{I \ \& \ ky \leq by \ \& \ kx \leq bx \ \& \ X(kx) \geq Y(ky)\} \ COPYY \ \{I \ \& \ kx \leq bx\}.$$

Thus "Achieve $kx > bx$ and $ky > by$ while maintaining I" can be realized by the transition diagram shown in Figure 3.

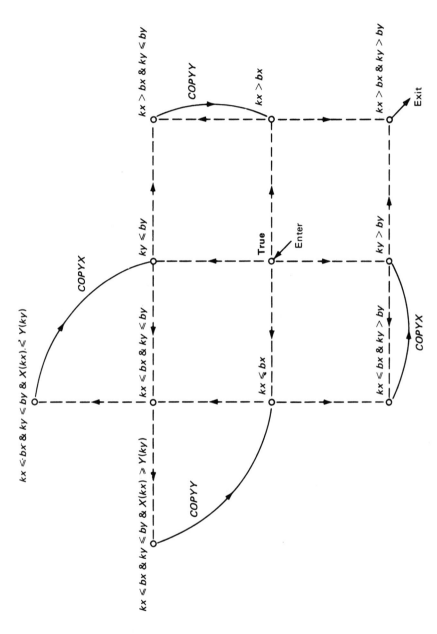

Figure 3   A transition diagram for merging.

In comparison with most merging programs, this version has the virtue of avoiding redundant testing of the emptyness of unprocessed array parts. Moreover, in the nondeterministic version, the program preserves the symmetry between X and Y that characterized the original problem. However, this symmetry must be broken to resolve the nondeterminacy (which occurs at the entrance node and also at $kx \leqslant bx \,\&\, ky \leqslant by$ when $X(kx) = Y(ky)$).

Path-finding in a directed graph

The final example shows the use of transition diagrams in an abstract rather than a concrete program, and it also illustrates the utility of jumps out of blocks and procedures. We will construct a program that, given a finite directed graph and two sets X and Y of nodes, will determine whether a path exists from some member of X to some member of Y. The program will be abstract in the sense that **node** and **nodeset** will be used as primitive data types, with appropriate primitive operations.

For a node set S, let $\Gamma(S)$ ($\Gamma^*(S), \Gamma^\dagger(S), \Gamma^{\dagger *}(S)$) stand for the set of immediate successors (successors, immediate predecessors, predecessors) of S, i.e., the nodes that can be reached in one step forward (zero or more steps forward, one step backward, zero or more steps backward) from members of S. This notation can be used to describe the existence of a path from X to Y in three equivalent ways:

$$G \equiv nonempty(\Gamma^*(X) \cap Y)$$
$$\equiv nonempty(X \cap \Gamma^{\dagger *}(Y))$$
$$\equiv nonempty(\Gamma^*(X) \cap \Gamma^{\dagger *}(Y)).$$

The program will send control to the label *success* if G is true, or to the label *failure* if G is false.

The basic method of computation is to maintain two disjoint sets: TX containing successors of X, and TY containing predecessors of Y. There will also be a subset SX of TX containing nodes whose immediate successors are known to belong to TX, and a subset SY bearing the analogous relation to TY. The situation can be described by the two invariants:

$$I1 \equiv SX \subseteq TX \subseteq \Gamma^*(X) \,\&\, SY \subseteq TY \subseteq \Gamma^{\dagger *}(Y) \,\&\, empty(TX \cap TY)$$
$$I2 \equiv X \subseteq TX \,\&\, \Gamma(SX) \subseteq TX \,\&\, Y \subseteq TY \,\&\, \Gamma^\dagger(SY) \subseteq TY.$$

The first of these invariant plays a special role. Although we will not carry the development of our program to the point of designing a concrete data representation, it is important to realize that $I1$ provides a constraint that could be used at the concrete level to permit a more efficient choice of data representation than would otherwise be possible. But to take advantage of this constraint, we must insure that $I1$ holds not just at certain points, but at all points in the abstract program.

We begin by devising operations for adding elements to the sets TX and TY while maintaining $I1$. It is easily seen that

$$\{z \notin TY \& I1 \& z \in \Gamma^*(X)\} TX := TX \cup \{z\} \{I1\}.$$

On the other hand, $z \in TY \& I1 \& z \in \Gamma^*(X)$ implies G, which permits a jump to the label *success*. Thus

$$\{I1 \& z \in \Gamma^*(X)\} \text{ if } z \in TY \text{ then goto } success \text{ else } TX := TX \cup \{z\} \{I1\}.$$

In effect, we have an operation that behaves like $TX := TX \cup \{z\}$, yet is miraculously guaranteed to keep TX and TY disjoint, since any program that performs the operation with $z \in TY$ will cease to be executed. Next, using an obvious notation for iterating over a set (in an unspecified order), we can build an operation for adding an entire set to TX:

procedure *putx*(**nodeset** W);
  for $z \in W$ **do if** $z \in TY$ **then goto** *success* **else** $TX := TX \cup \{z\}$,

which behaves like $TX := TX \cup W$, yet satisfies

$$\{I1 \& W \subseteq \Gamma^*(X)\} putx(W) \{I1\}.$$

Applying similar reasoning to TY gives

procedure *puty*(**nodeset** W);
  for $z \in W$ **do if** $z \in TX$ **then goto** *success* **else** $TY := TY \cup \{z\}$,

which behaves like $TY := TY \cup W$, yet satisfies

$$\{I1 \& W \subseteq \Gamma^{\dagger *}(Y)\} puty(W) \{I1\}.$$

Having developed these basic operations, we can return to the overall program, and proceed from the top downwards. By induction on path length, it can be shown that $I2 \& SX = TX$ implies $\Gamma^*(X) \subseteq TX$ and that $I2 \& SY = TY$ implies $\Gamma^{\dagger *}(Y) \subseteq TY$. Thus $I1 \& I2 \& (SX = TX$ or $SY = TY)$ implies that G is false. This suggests the program:

begin nodeset TX, TY, SX, SY;
"Achieve $I1$";
"Achieve $I2$ while maintaining $I1$";
"Achieve $SX = TX$ or $SY = TY$ while maintaining $I1 \& I2$";
goto *failure*
end.

It is straightforward to fill in the first two operations:

begin nodeset TX, TY, SX, SY;
$TX := TY := SX := SY := \{ \ \}$;
$putx(X); puty(Y)$;
"Achieve $SX = TX$ or $SY = TY$ while maintaining $I1 \& I2$";
goto *failure*
end.

(However, note that $TX := X$; $TY := Y$ would be an incorrect second operation, since $I1$ would not be preserved if X and Y had members in common.)

To develop the rest of the program, we construct a transition diagram using the following pair of operations:

$STEPX \equiv$ **begin node** u;
$\qquad u := choose(TX - SX); SX := SX \cup \{u\};$
$\qquad putx(\Gamma(u))$
$\qquad$ **end**;
$STEPY \equiv$ **begin node** u;
$\qquad u := choose(TY - SY); SY := SY \cup \{u\};$
$\qquad puty(\Gamma^{\dagger}(u))$
$\qquad$ **end**,

which increase SX or SY while preserving both invariants:

$$\{I1 \& I2 \& SX \neq TX\} STEPX \{I1 \& I2\}$$
$$\{I1 \& I2 \& SY \neq TY\} STEPY \{I1 \& I2\}.$$

Here $choose(S)$ is a primitive operation that accepts a nonempty set and produces an unspecified member. It is vital to leave this operation nondeterministic at the abstract level in order to provide an adequate degree of freedom for the design of a data representation. (Indeed, this is probably the most vital role of nondeterminism in programming.)

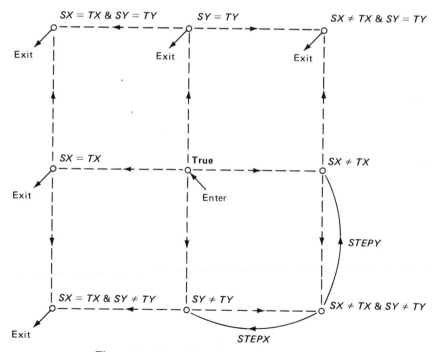

Figure 4   A transition diagram for path-finding.

The relevant conditions for the transition diagram are $SX = TX$ and $SY = TY$, which are independent and therefore lead to a transition diagram with nine states. Exit can occur in any state in which either $SX = TX$ or $SY = TY$. On the other hand, $STEPX$ and $STEPY$ should only be performed in states where there is no possibility of exiting or of performing a test that might lead to an exit. The only such state is $SX \neq TX \,\&\, SY \neq TY$, which permits either $STEPX$ or $STEPY$. Moreover, in this state $STEPX$ will maintain $SY \neq TY$, since it does not change SY or TY, and $STEPY$ will similarly maintain $SX \neq TX$. Thus we have the transition diagram shown in Figure 4.

Most of the nondeterminism can be resolved by exiting whenever possible and by arbitrarily choosing the test $SX = TX$ at the initial state.

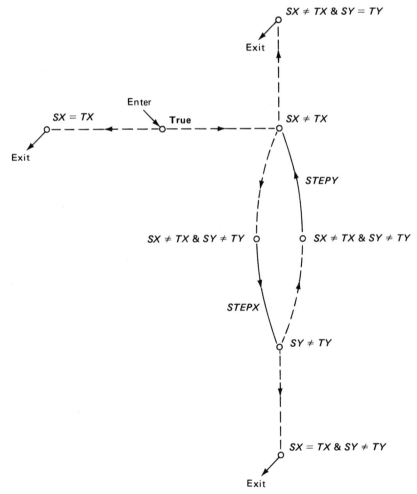

Figure 5 A determinate transition diagram for path-finding.

(As a consequence, the two states $SX = TX \& SY = TY$ and $SY = TY$ become disconnected, and vanish from the transition diagram.) However, the remaining nondeterminism is more problematical. Dropping $STEPX$ or $STEPY$ would give a correct but inefficient program that only searches forward from X or backward from Y. For most graphs, it is better to search in both directions so that, if a path exists, TX and TY will intersect at an intermediate point. The simplest way of accomplishing this is to alternate $STEPX$ and $STEPY$, which can be done by spliting the node $SX \neq TX \& SY \neq TY$ as shown in Figure 5.

Afterthoughts

After devising these ideas, I have had the experience of teaching them, and my enthusiasm has been tempered by a significant minority of students who have employed them both incorrectly and unnecessarily. Transition diagrams are a tool for constructing complicated programs systematically, but they do not justify the use of such programs when simpler ones would do the job. They are unlikely to be useful in the hands of programmers who habitually underestimate the limitations of their own intellects.

Recently, I have become aware that similar ideas have been developed independently by M. H. Van Emden [Van Emden 77].

Acknowledgments

I am indebted to the members of IFIP Working Group 2.3, who have provided motivation, inspiration, and helpful criticism. I am also grateful for the hospitality of the University of Edinburgh and the support of the Science Research Council during the period when this paper was written.

13
Guarded Commands, Nondeterminacy, and Formal Derivation of Programs[1]

Edsger W. Dijkstra
Burroughs Corporation

Abstract   *So-called "guarded commands" are introduced as a building block for alternative and repetitive constructs that allow nondeterministic program components for which at least the activity evoked, but possibly even the final state, is not necessarily uniquely determined by the initial state. For the formal derivation of programs expressed in terms of these constructs, a calculus will be shown.*

1 Introduction

In Section 2, two statements, an alternative construct and a repetitive construct, are introduced, together with an intuitive (mechanistic) definition of their semantics. The basic building block for both of them is the so-called "guarded command," a statement list prefixed by a boolean expression: only when this boolean expression is initially true is the statement list eligible for execution. The potential nondeterminacy allows us to map otherwise (trivially) different programs on the same program text, a circumstance that seems largely responsible for the fact that programs can now be derived in a manner more systematic than before.

In Section 3, after a prelude defining the notation, a formal definition of the semantics of the two constructs is given, together with two theorems for each of the constructs (without proof).

In Section 4, it is shown how, based upon the above, a formal calculus for the derivation of programs can be founded. We would like to stress that we do not present "an algorithm" for the derivation of programs: we have used the term "a calculus" for a formal discipline—a set of rules—such that, if applied successfully: (1) it will have derived a correct program; and (2) it will tell us that we have reached such a goal. (We use the term as in "integral calculus.")

2 Two statements made from guarded commands

If the reader accepts "other statements" as indicating, say, assignment statements and procedure calls, we can give the relevant syntax in BNF [Naur 60*]. In the following we have extended BNF with the convention that the braces {...} should be read as "followed by zero or more instances of the enclosed."

⟨guarded command⟩::=⟨guard⟩→⟨guarded list⟩
⟨guard⟩::=⟨boolean expression⟩
⟨guarded list⟩::=⟨statement⟩{;⟨statement⟩}
⟨guarded command set⟩::=⟨guarded command⟩{ ▯⟨guarded command⟩}
⟨alternative construct⟩::= **if** ⟨guarded command set⟩ **fi**
⟨repetitive construct⟩::= **do** ⟨guarded command set⟩ **od**
⟨statement⟩::=⟨alternative construct⟩|⟨repetitive construct⟩|
                  "other statements"

The semicolons in the guarded list have the usual meaning: when the guarded list is selected for execution its statements will be executed successively in the order from left to right; a guarded list will only be selected for execution in a state such that its guard is true. Note that a guarded command by itself is *not* a statement; it is a component of a guarded command set from which statements can be constructed. If the guarded command set consists of more than one guarded command, they are mutually separated by the separator ▯; our text is then an arbitrarily ordered enumeration of an unordered set; i.e., the order in which the guarded commands of a set appear in our text is semantically irrelevant.

Our syntax gives two ways for constructing a statement out of a guarded command set. The alternative construct is written by enclosing it by the special bracket pair **if**...**fi**. If in the initial state none of the guards is true, the program will abort; otherwise an arbitrary guarded list with a true guard will be selected for execution.

Note. If the empty guarded command set were allowed **if fi** would be semantically equivalent to "abort". (End of note.)

An example—illustrating the nondeterminacy in a very modest fashion —would be the program that for fixed x and y assigns to m the maximum value of x and y:

if $x \geqslant y \to m := x$
▯ $y \geqslant x \to m := y$
fi

The repetitive construct is written down by enclosing a guarded command set by the special bracket pair **do**...**od**. Here a state in which none of the guards is true will not lead to abortion but to proper termination; the complementary rule, however, is that it will only terminate in a state in which none of the guards is true: when initially or upon completed execution of a selected guarded list one or more guards are true, a new selection for execution of a guarded list with a true guard will take place, and so on. When the repetitive construct, has terminated properly, we know that all its guards are false.

Note. If the empty guarded command set were allowed **do od** would be semantically equivalent to "skip". (End of note.)

An example—showing the nondeterminacy in somewhat greater glory —is the program that assigns to the variables $q1$, $q2$, $q3$, and $q4$ a permutation of the values $Q1$, $Q2$, $Q3$, and $Q4$, such that $q1 \leqslant q2 \leqslant q3 \leqslant q4$. Using concurrent assignment statements for the sake of convenience, we can program

$q1, q2, q3, q4 := Q1, Q2, Q3, Q4;$
do $q1 > q2 \rightarrow q1, q2 := q2, q1$
$\square$ $q2 > q3 \rightarrow q2, q3 := q3, q2$
$\square$ $q3 > q4 \rightarrow q3, q4 := q4, q3$
od.

To conclude this section, we give a program where not only the computation but also the final state is not necessarily uniquely determined. The program should determine k such that for fixed value $n(n > 0)$ and a fixed function $f(i)$ defined for $0 \leqslant i < n$, k will eventually satisfy: $0 \leqslant k < n$ **and** $(\forall i: 0 \leqslant i < n: f(k) \geqslant f(i))$. (Eventually k should be the place of a maximum.)

$k := 0; j := 1;$

do $j \neq n \rightarrow$ **if** $f(j) \rightarrow f(k) \rightarrow j := j + 1$
$\qquad\qquad\qquad \square f(j) \geqslant f(k) \rightarrow k := j; j := j + 1$
$\qquad$ **fi**
od.

Only permissible final states are possible and each permissible final state is possible.

3 Formal definition of the semantics

3.1 Notational prelude

In the following sections we shall use the symbols P, Q, and R to denote (predicates defining) boolean functions defined on all points of the state space; alternatively we shall refer to them as "conditions," satisfied by all states for which the boolean function is true. Two special predicates that we denote by the reserved names T and F play a special role: T denotes the condition that, by definition, is satisfied by all states; F denotes, by definition, the condition that is satisfied by no state at all.

The way in which we use predicates (as a tool for defining sets of initial or final states) for the definition of the semantics of programming language constructs has been directly inspired by [Hoare 69*], the main difference being that we have tightened things up a bit: while Hoare introduces sufficient pre-conditions such that the mechanisms will not produce the wrong result (but may fail to terminate), we shall introduce necessary and sufficient—i.e. so-called "weakest"—pre-conditions such that the mechanisms are guaranteed to produce the right result.

More specifically: we shall use the notation $wp(S, R)$, where S denotes a statement list and R some condition on the state of the system, to denote the weakest precondition for the initial state of the system such that activation of S is guaranteed to lead to a properly terminating activity leaving the system in a final state satisfying the post-condition R. Such a wp—which is called "a predicate transformer" because it associates a pre-condition with any post-condition R—has, by definition, the following properties.

1. For any S, we have for all states: $wp(S, F) = F$ (the so-called Law of the Excluded Miracle).
2. For any S and any two post-conditions, such that for all states $P \Rightarrow Q$, we have for all states: $wp(S, P) \Rightarrow wp(S, Q)$.
3. For any S and any two post-conditions P and Q, we have for all states $(wp(S, P)$ **and** $wp(S, Q)) = wp(S, P$ **and** $Q)$.
4. For any deterministic S and any post-conditions P and Q, we have for all states $(wp(S, P)$ **or** $wp(S, Q)) = wp(S, P$ **or** $Q)$.

For nondeterministic mechanisms S, the equality has to be replaced by an implication; the resulting formula follows from the second property.

Together with the rules of propositional calculus and the semantic definitions to be given below, the above four properties take over the role of the "rules of inference" as introduced in [Hoare 69*].

We take the position that we know the semantics of a mechanism S sufficiently well if we know its predicate transformer, i.e. can derive $wp(S, R)$ for any post-condition R.

Note. We consider the semantics of S only defined for those initial states for which it has been established a priori that they satisfy $wp(S, T)$, i.e. for which proper termination is guaranteed (even in the face of possibly non-deterministic behavior); for other initial states we don't care. By suitably changing S, if necessary, we can always see to it that $wp(S, T)$ is decidable. (End of note.)

EXAMPLE I. The semantics of the empty statement denoted by "skip" are given by the definition that for any post-condition R, we have wp ("skip", R) = R.

EXAMPLE 2. The semantics of the assignment statement "$x := E$" are given by $wp(\text{"}x := E\text{"}, R) = R_E^x$ in which R_E^x denotes a copy of the predicate defining R in which each occurrence of the variable x is replaced by (E).

EXAMPLE 3. The semantics of the semicolon ";" as concatenation operator are given by

$$wp(\text{"}S1; S2\text{"}, R) = wp(S1, wp(S2, R)).$$

3.2 The alternative construct

In order to define the semantics of the alternative construct we define two abbreviations:

Let IF denote   if $B_1 \rightarrow SL_1 \,\square\, \ldots \,\square\, B_n \rightarrow SL_n$ fi;

let BB denote $(\exists i : 1 \leqslant i \leqslant n : B_i)$;

then, by definition

$$wp(IF, R) = (BB \text{ and } (\forall i : 1 \leqslant i \leqslant n : B_i \Rightarrow wp(SL_i, R))).$$

(The first term BB requires that the alternative construct as such will not lead to abortion on account of all guards false; the second term requires that each guarded list eligible for execution will lead to an acceptable final state.) From this definition we can derive—by simple substitutions:

Theorem 1. *From* $(\forall i : 1 \leqslant i \leqslant n : (Q \text{ and } B_i) \Rightarrow wp(SL_i, R))$ *for all states we can conclude that* $(Q \text{ and } BB) \Rightarrow wp(IF, R)$ *holds for all states.*

Let t denote some integer function defined on the state space, and let $wdec(S, t)$ denote the weakest precondition such that activation of S is guaranteed to lead to a properly terminating activity leaving the system to a final state such that the value of t is decreased by at least 1 (compared to its initial value). In terms of $wdec$ we can formulate the very similar:

Theorem 2. *From* $(\forall i : 1 \leqslant i \leqslant n : (Q \text{ and } B_i) \Rightarrow wdec(SL_i, t))$ *for all states we can conclude that* $(Q \text{ and } BB) \Rightarrow wdec(IF, t)$ *holds for all states.*

Note (which can be skipped at first reading). The relation between wp and $wdec$ is as follows. For any point X in the state space we can regard $wp(S, t \leqslant t_0)$ as an equation with t_0 as the unknown. Let its smallest solution for t_0 be $tmin(X)$. (Here we have added the explicit dependence on the state X.) Then $tmin(X)$ can be interpreted as the lowest upper bound for the final value of t if the mechanism S is activated with X as initial state. Then, by definition, $wdec(S, t) = (tmin(X) \leqslant t(X) - 1) = (tmin(X) < t(X))$. (End of note.)

3.3 The repetitive construct

As is to be expected, the definition of the repetitive construct

do $B_1 \rightarrow SL_1 \,\square\, \ldots \,\square\, B_n \rightarrow SL_n$ **od,**

which we denote by DO, is more complicated. Let

$$H_0(R) = (R \text{ and non } BB)$$

and for $k > 0$,

$$H_k(R) = (wp(IF, H_{k-1}(R)) \text{ or } H_0(R))$$

(where IF denotes the *same* guarded command set enclosed by "**if fi**"). Then, by definition

$$wp(DO, R) = (\exists k : k \geqslant 0 : H_k(R)).$$

(Intuitively, $H_k(R)$ can be interpreted as the weakest pre-condition guaranteeing proper termination after at most k selections of a guarded list, leaving the system in a final state satisfying R.) Via mathematical induction we can prove:

Theorem 3. *If we have for all states* $(P$ **and** $BB) \Rightarrow (wp(IF, P)$ **and** $wdec(IF, t)$ **and** $t \geqslant 0)$ *we can conclude that we have for all states* $P \Rightarrow wp(DO, P$ **and non** $BB)$.

Note. The antecedent of Theorem 3 is of the form of the consequents of Theorems 1 and 2. (End of note.)

Because T is the condition by definition satisfied by all states, $wp(S, T)$ is the weakest pre-condition guaranteeing proper termination for S. This allows us to formulate an alternative theorem about the repetitive construct, viz.:

Theorem 4. *From* $(P$ **and** $BB) \Rightarrow wp(IF, P)$ *for all states, we can conclude that we have for all states* $(P$ **and** $wp(DO, T)) \Rightarrow wp(DO, P$ **and non** $BB)$.

Note. In connection with the above theorems, P is called "the invariant relation" and t is called "the variant function." Theorems 3 and 4 are easily proved by mathematical induction, with k as the induction variable. (End of note.)

4 Formal derivation of programs

The formal requirement of our program performing $m := max(x, y)$—see above— is that for fixed x and y it establishes the relation

$$R : (m = x \text{ or } m = y) \text{ and } m \geqslant x \text{ and } m \geqslant y.$$

Now the Axiom of Assignment tells us that "$m:=x$" is the standard way of establishing the truth of $m=x$ for fixed x, which is a way of establishing the truth of the first term of R. Will "$m:=x$" do the job? In order to investigate this, we derive and simplify:

$$wp(\text{"}m:=x\text{"},R)=(x=x \text{ or } x=y) \text{ and } x \geqslant x \text{ and } x \geqslant y$$
$$=x \geqslant y.$$

Taking this weakest pre-condition as its guard, Theorem 1 tells us that

if $x \geqslant y \rightarrow m:=x$ **fi**

will produce the correct result if it terminates successfully. The disadvantage of this program is that $BB \neq T$; i.e. it might lead to abortion; weakening BB means looking for alternatives which might introduce new guards. The obvious alternative is the assignment "$m:=y$" with the guard $wp(\text{"}m:=y\text{"},R)=y \geqslant x$; thus we are led to our program

if $x \geqslant y \rightarrow m:=x$
◻ $y \geqslant x \rightarrow m:=y$
fi

and by this time $BB=T$, and therefore we have solved the problem. (In the meantime we have proved that the maximum of two values is always defined, viz. that R considered as equation for m always has a solution.)

As an example of the derivation of a repetitive construct we shall derive a program for the greatest common divisor of two positive numbers; i.e. for fixed, positive X and Y we have to establish the final relation $x=gcd(X,Y)$.

The formal machinery only gets in motion once we have chosen our invariant relation and our variant function. The program then gets the structure

"establish the relation P to be kept invariant";
do "decrease t as long as possible under variance of P"
od.

Suppose that we choose for the invariant relation

$$P: gcd(X,Y)=gcd(x,y) \text{ and } x>0 \text{ and } y>0,$$

a relation that has the advantage of being easily established by $x:=X$; $y:=Y$. The most general "something" to be done under invariance of P is of the form $x,y:=E1,E2$, and we are interested in a guard B such that

$$(P \text{ and } B) \Rightarrow wp(\text{"}x,y:=E1,E2\text{"},P)$$
$$=(gcd(X,Y)=gcd(E1,E2) \text{ and } E1>0 \text{ and } E2>0).$$

Because the guard must be a computable boolean expression and should not contain the computation of $gcd(X,Y)$—for that was the whole problem—we must see to it that the expressions $E1$ and $E2$ are chosen so that the first term $gcd(X,Y)=gcd(E1,E2)$ is implied by P, which is true if

$gcd(x,y) = gcd(E1,E2)$. In other words we are invited to massage the value pair (x,y) in such a fashion that their gcd is not changed. Because— and this is the place at which to mobilize our mathematical knowledge about the gcd-function—$gcd(x,y) = gcd(x-y,y)$, a possible guarded list would be $x := x-y$. Deriving $wp(\text{``}x := x-y\text{''}, P) = (gcd(X,Y) = gcd(x-y,y)$ **and** $x-y > 0$ **and** $y > 0)$ and omitting all terms of the conjunction implied by P, we find the guard $x > y$ as far as the invariance of P is concerned. Besides that we must require guaranteed decrease of the variant function t. Let us investigate the consequences of the choice $t = x+y$. From

$$wp(\text{``}x := x-y\text{''}, t \leqslant t_0) = wp(\text{``}x := x-y\text{''}, x+y \leqslant t_0) = (x \leqslant t_0),$$

we conclude that $tmin = x$; therefore $wdec(\text{``}x := x-y\text{''}, t) = (x < x+y) = (y > 0)$.

The requirement of monotonic decrease of t imposes no further restriction of the guard because $wdec(\text{``}x := x-y\text{''}, t)$ is fully implied by P, and at our first effort we come to

$x := X; y := Y;$
$\textbf{do } x > y \rightarrow x := x-y \textbf{ od}.$

Alas, this single guard is insufficient: from P **and non** BB we are not allowed to conclude $x = gcd(X,Y)$. In a completely analogous manner, the alternative $y := y-x$ will require as its guard $y > x$, and our next effort is

$x := X; y := Y;$
$\textbf{do } x > y \rightarrow x := x-y$
$\quad \fbox{} \ y > x \rightarrow y := y-x$

od.

Now the job is done, because with this last program **non** $BB = (x=y)$ and $(P$ **and** $x=y) \Rightarrow (x = gcd(X,Y))$, because $gcd(x,x) = x$.

Note. The choice of $t = x+2y$ and the knowledge of the fact that the gcd is a symmetric function could have led to the program

$x := X; y := Y;$
$\textbf{do } x > y \rightarrow x := x-y$
$\quad \fbox{} \ y > x \rightarrow x,y := y,x$
$\textbf{od}.$

The swap $x,y := y,x$ can never destroy P: the guard of the last guarded list is fully caused by the requirement that t is effectively decreased. (End of note.)

In both cases the final game has been to find a large enough set of such guarded lists that BB, the disjunction of their guards, was sufficiently weak: in the case of the alternative construct the purpose is avoiding abortion, in the case of the repetitive construct the goal is getting BB weak enough such that P **and non** BB is strong enough to imply the desired post-condition R.

It is illuminating to compare our first version of Euclid's Algorithm with what we would have written down with the traditional clauses:

$x := X; y := Y;$ (version A)
while $x \neq y$ **do if** $x > y$ **then** $x := x - y$
                                       else $y := y - x$ **fi od**

and

$x := X; y := Y;$ (version B)
while $x \neq y$ **do while** $x > y$ **do** $x := x - y$ **od;**
                           while $y > x$ **do** $y := y - x$ **od**
              od.

In the fully symmetric version with the guarded commands the algorithm has been reduced to its bare essentials, while the traditional clauses force us to choose between versions A and B (and others), a choice that can only be justified by making assumptions about the time taken for tests and about expectation values for traversal frequencies. (But even taking the time taken for tests into account, it is not clear that we have lost: the average number of necessary tests per assignment ranges with guarded commands from 1 to 2, equals 2 for version A and ranges from 1 to 2.5 for version B. If the guards of a guarded command set are evaluated concurrently—nothing in our semantics excludes that—the new version is timewise superior to all the others.) The virtues of the *case*-construction have been extended to repetition as well.

5 Concluding remarks

The research, the outcome of which is reported in this article, was triggered by the observation that Euclid's Algorithm could also be regarded as synchronizing the two cyclic processes "**do** $x := x - y$ **od**" and "**do** $y := y - x$ **od**" in such a way that the relation $x > 0$ **and** $y > 0$ would be kept invariantly true. It was only after this observation that we saw that the formal techniques we had already developed for the derivation of the synchronizing conditions that ensure the harmonious cooperation of (cyclic) sequential processes, such as can be identified in the total activity of operating systems, could be transferred lock, stock, and barrel to the development of sequential programs as shown in this article. The main difference is that while for sequential programs the situation "all guards false" is a desirable goal—for it means termination of a repetitive construct—one tries to avoid it in operating systems—for there it means deadlock.

The second reason to pursue these investigations was my personal desire to get a better appreciation, which part of the programming activity can be regarded as a formal routine and which part of it seems to require "invention." While the design of an alternative construct now seems to be a reasonably straightforward activity, that of a repetitive construct requires what I regard as "the invention" of an invariant relation and a variant function. My presentation of this calculus should, however, not be interpreted as my suggestion that all programs should be developed in this way: it just gives us another handle.

The calculus does, however, explain my preference for the axiomatic definition of programming language semantics via predicate transformers above other definition techniques: the definition via predicate transormers seems to lend itself most readily to being forged into a tool for the goal-directed activity of program composition.

Finally, I would like to add a word or two about the potential nondeterminacy. Having worked mainly with hardly self-checking hardware, with which nonreproducing behavior of user programs is a very strong indication of a machine malfunctioning, I had to overcome a considerable mental resistance before I found myself willing to consider nondeterministic programs seriously. It is, however, fair to say that I could never have discovered the calculus before having taken that hurdle: the simplicity and elegance of the above would have been destroyed by requiring the derivation of deterministic programs only. Whether nondeterminacy is eventually removed mechanically—in order not to mislead the maintenance engineer —or (perhaps only partly) by the programmer himself because, at second thought, he does care—e.g. for reasons of efficiency—which alternative is chosen is something I leave entirely to the circumstances. In any case we can appreciate the nondeterministic program as a helpful stepping stone.

Acknowledgments. In the first place my acknowledgments are due to the members of the IFIP Working Group WG2.3 on "Programming Methodology." Besides them, W. H. J. Feijen, D. E. Knuth, M. Rem, and C. S. Scholten have been directly helpful in one way or another. I should also thank the various audiences—in Albuquerque (courtesy NSF), in San Diego and Luxembourg (courtesy Burroughs Corporation)—that have played their role of critical sounding board beyond what one is entitled to hope.

14
A System which Automatically Improves Programs

J. Darlington and R. M. Burstall
University of Edinburgh

Abstract *Methods are given for mechanically converting programs that are easy to understand into more efficient ones, converting recursion equations using high level operations into lower level flowchart programs. The main transformations involved are (i) recursion removal (ii) eliminating common subexpressions and combining loops (iii) replacing procedure calls by their bodies (iv) introducing assignments which overwrite list cells no longer in use (compile-time garbage collection).*

1 Introduction

This paper is an introduction to an automatic program improving system that we have implemented and are developing further.

A programmer is able to present his algorithms to the system in a clear and abstract language. The system converts them to efficient but probably not transparent versions.

For example, here are two versions of one program which reverses lists.

(i)

$$reverse(x) = \textbf{if } null(x) \textbf{ then } nil$$
$$\textbf{else } concat(reverse\ (tl(x)),$$
$$cons(hd(x), nil))^1$$

(ii)

$$reverse(x) = \textbf{result} := nil;$$
$$\textbf{while not } null(x)$$
$$\textbf{do begin}$$
$$temp := tl(x); \quad tl(x) := \textbf{result};$$
$$\textbf{result} := x; \quad x := temp;$$
$$\textbf{end}$$

---

[1] The operations we use are based on the POP-2 language [Burstall 71*]. The main features to note are that *hd* is the LISP car, *tl* the LISP cdr and *concat* joins two lists (the LISP append).

One is clear and abstract, the other more tortuous but efficient. Given the first as a definition, a competent programmer should be able to produce the second. Our system can do this for him.

The system is built around the concept of abstract programming, and we hope to encourage a user to formulate his algorithms in abstract terms appropriate to his problem domain and leave to the system the task of implementing them efficiently.

Our work[2] was partly inspired by the homily in [Minsky 70] on form versus content in computer science in which he recommended programming as a good application area for Artificial Intelligence work. It was also influenced by Dijkstra's ideas on structured programming, differing in that we start from a functional LISP-like language.

Our investigation took as its starting point a collection of procedures appearing in [Ambler 71], which aimed to provide transparent, but quite efficient operations on finite sets. We used this example to study the transformations which are needed to implement a collection of high level procedures as efficient code. To enable one to write programs about finite sets some operations on sets, for example,

> CONSSET(x, S)—adding an element x to a set S
> CHOOSE(S)—choosing an element from a set S
> MINUS(x, S)—subtracting an element x from a set S
> UNION(X, Y)—$\{x | x \in X \quad \text{or} \quad x \in Y\}$
> INTERSECTION(X, Y)—$\{x | x \in X \quad \text{and} \quad x \in Y\}$

are implemented as structured definitions in terms of the array or list primitives available in the programming language. The user of the set system can define and run new functions, such as powerset, using these operations. However, when he looks at his definition, he notices that he could have produced a much more efficient program by writing a special procedure for powerset directly in terms of the array or list primitives. This is what our system attempts to do. A well written program in a LISP-like language expresses its structure as a hierarchy of functions. Our system eliminates higher level function calls to gain efficiency, flattening this hierarchy. Four distinct improvement processes seemed to be indicated.

1. Recursion removal.
2. Eliminating redundant computation, by merging common subexpressions and combining loops.
3. Replacing procedure calls by their bodies.
4. Causing the program to re-use data cells which are no longer needed, in order to reduce storage allocation and garbage collection at run time.

We have devised algorithms to perform these processes on programs and implemented these algorithms as POP-2 programs (Section 7 gives an

---

[2] First reported to the 1973 International Conference on Artificial Intelligence.

example of their use). These algorithms are applicable to a variety of domains and require only a collection of rules specifying potentially useful equivalences for a particular domain. We have tried our program on our original example (programs about finite sets), and we can reproduce automatically a lot of the tricks incorporated in the original handwritten programs for the sets domain.

The overall system using processes 1 to 4 takes as input programs in a nonimperative language of recursive definitions and converts them, via intermediate stages, into an imperative language. This imperative language uses **while** statements as well as recursive definitions and permits assignment to components of data structures.

In order to produce efficient programs the system must use properties such as associativity or commutativity for the operations to be performed.

The principle techniques used are (i) matching, involving functional abstraction to detect the form of a recursive definition, (ii) matching to detect common subexpressions and compound operations involving the occurrence of several functional symbols, using algebraic equivalences, (iii) symbolic running to extract meanings from programs and check that a tentatively constructed sequence of instructions produces the required result. No elaborate theorem proving techniques are used, and the programs run quite fast, even though we have not worked to code them efficiently.

2 Recursion removal

In this stage the system attempts to convert the set of recursion equations to a single iterative program in the same operations. During this process particular attention is paid to the semantics of the operations making up the recursion equations. This process is generally applicable; the only input required is the set of recursion equations and a table of rules giving algebraic laws for the operations used.

There has been considerable theoretical investigation into how to translate recursive schemas into equivalent iterative schemas, e.g. [Strong 70; Garland 71], although as far as we know only the BBN LISP compiler makes use of any of these ideas, and this only for simple recursions. These studies apply to translations of a schema that preserve its effect for all interpretations of the primitives. Our program uses translations which preserve the effect of a schema only for a class of interpretations in which the primitives obey a given set of algebraic laws; we follow [Cooper 66], which contains examples of such translations. We are only interested in translations which will improve efficiency. The results for translations of schemas to maintain equivalence under all interpretations seem to be too weak for practical purposes.

The translations that we achieve are of two types:

(i) where the computation sequence of the resulting iterative program is a rearrangement of the computation sequence of the recursive program but contains the same number of steps. In these cases we save time and storage overhead associated with the stacking mechanisms (cf. factorial function below).

(ii) where the tree grown by the recursive calls contains redundancies because the same values are calculated at separate nodes. Our system may produce an iterative program whose computation sequence is shorter as well as having fewer overheads (cf. the Fibonacci function below).

Our system for recursion removal consists of four parts:

(i) A set of translation rules. Each rule has (a) a recursive schema over certain primitives (b) an iterative schema over these primitives and (c) a set of equations over the primitives (and possibly some extra restrictions) which, if satisfied, ensure that the iterative schema produces the same result as the recursive one.

(ii) A matching algorithm. This determines whether a set of equations is an instance of the recursive schema in one of the rules, and if so finds the substitution.

(iii) A simple equality-based theorem prover. This seeks to prove that a substitution is legitimate, i.e., that the equations associated with the rule are satisfied.

(iv) A control program. This first partitions the input equations into the smallest disjoint subsets such that if the equation for f involves a call of g and *vice versa* then they are in the same subset. Then, for each subset separately, it tries to find a translation rule which applies to that subset, using the matching algorithm and the theorem prover, and effects the translation to iterative form if it finds one.

The matching algorithm is a second order one, in that it finds a substitution which takes primitive constants to expressions and also primitive functions to functions or lambda expressions. It is described in [Darlington 72]. It was coded for lucidity, not speed. Consider for example this translation rule

Recursion schema
$$f(x) = \begin{cases} a \rightarrow b \\ \textbf{not } a \rightarrow h(d, f(e)) \end{cases}$$

Iterative schema

$f(x) =$ **if** a **then result** $:= b$
    else begin result $:= d;$ $x := e;$
        while not a **do**
            begin result $:= h(\text{result}, d);$ $x := e$
            end;
        result $:= h(\text{result}, b)$
end

Equations

$$h(h(\alpha, \beta), \gamma) = h(\alpha, h(\beta, \gamma)) \quad \text{(associativity)}$$

Restriction: x does not occur free in h.

The factorial function defined by the recursion equation

$$fact(x) = \begin{cases} x = 0 \rightarrow 1 \\ x \neq 0 \rightarrow mult(x, fact(x - 1)) \end{cases}$$

is an instance of this recursive schema, with substitution $a = (x = 0)$, $b = 1$, $d = x$, $e = (x - 1)$, $h = mult$. This is legitimate since *mult* satisfies the equation for h in the rule.
    The translation is

$fact(x) =$
    if $x = 0$ **then result** $:= 1$
        else begin
            result $:= x;$ $x := x - 1;$
            while $x \neq 0$ **do**
                begin result $:= mult(\text{result}, x);$ $x := x - 1;$
                end;
            result $:= mult(\text{result}, 1)$
        end

This translation took 3.5 seconds on an ICL 4130 where the time for a CONS is 400 microseconds, and for HD and TL 50 microseconds. The same system took approximately 0.6 seconds to calculate factorial (30) using the recursive definition and 0.06 seconds using the iterative. The reverse function defined by the recursion equation

$$reverse(x) = \begin{cases} null(x) \rightarrow nil \\ \text{not } null(x) \rightarrow concat(reverse(tl(x)), cons(hd(x), nil)) \end{cases}$$

is also an instance of this recursive schema, with substitution $a = null(x)$, $b = nil$, $d = cons(hd(x), nil)$, $e = tl(x)$, $h = \lambda x1\, x2;\ concat(x2, x1)$. This is a legitimate substitution. Notice the abstracted function that matches with h.

The translation is

$reverse(x) =$
  if $null(x)$ **then** **result** $: = nil$
        else begin
            result $: = cons(hd(x), nil);$ $x : = tl(x);$
            while not $null(x)$ **do**
                begin result $: = concat(cons(hd(x), nil), $ **result**$);$
                    $x : = tl(x)$
            end;
            result $: = concat(nil, $ **result**$)$
            end

This translation took 52.7 seconds. To reverse a list of length 40 took approximately 1.8 seconds using the recursive definition and .06 seconds using the iterative.

This section of our system shows the influence of programs written at M.I.T., e.g. by Moses and Winograd, which incorporate knowledge about certain problem domains. New knowledge in the form of translation rules can easily be added to the system. The system currently uses five schemas which we give below.

2.1 *Table 1. Schemas used*

Schema 1

  Recursion schema

$$f(x) = \begin{cases} a \rightarrow b \\ \textbf{not } a \rightarrow h(d, f(e)) \end{cases}$$

  Iterative schema (i)

    if a **then result** $: = b$
        else begin
            result $: = d;$ $x : = e;$
            while not a **do**
                begin result $: = h($**result**$, d);$ $x : = e$ **end**;
            result $: = h($**result**$, b)$
            end

  Equation (i)

    $h(h(\alpha, \beta), \gamma) = h(\alpha, h(\beta, \gamma))$ (associativity)
    Restriction: x does not occur free in h.

Iterative schema (ii)

> **result** : = b;
> **while not** a **do**
>   **begin result** : = $h(d, \text{result})$; $x := e$ **end**

Equation (ii)

$$h(\alpha, h(\beta, \gamma)) = h(\beta, h(\alpha, \gamma))$$
Restriction: x does not occur free in h or b.

Iterative schema (iii)

> **result** : = b; $xsave := x$; $x := $ "*unique x such that a*";[3]
> **while not** $x = xsave$ **do**
>   **begin** $x := $ "*inverse of e*" (x);   **result** : = $h(d, \text{result})$ **end**

Equation (iii)

None.
Restrictions: the unique x such that a is true and the inverse of e
             both exist.
             x does not occur free in b or h.

Schema 2

Recursion schema

$$f(x1, x2) = \begin{cases} a \rightarrow b \\ \textbf{not } a \rightarrow h(d, f(e1, e2)) \end{cases}$$

Iterative schema

> **result** : = b;
> **while not** a **do**
>   **begin result** : = $h(d, \text{result})$; $xsave := e1$; $x2 := e2$; $x1 := xsave$
>   **end**

Equation

$$h(\alpha, h(\beta, \gamma)) = h(\beta, h(\alpha, \gamma));$$
Restrictions: $x1$ does not occur free in h or b,
             $x2$ does not occur free in h or b.

---

[3] To be able to use this and some later translations the system has to know whether there is a unique value that makes true the piece of program text associated with a and whether the piece of program text matched with e has a known inverse. The system accomplishes this by interrogating the user and if this is so asking him to input values to meet these requirements.

Schema 3

Recursion schema

$$f(x)= \begin{cases} a \to b \\ \textbf{not } a \to h(f(d1), f(d2)) \end{cases}$$

Iterative schema (i)

result $:= b$; $xsave := x$; $x :=$ "*unique x such that a*";
while not $x = xsave$ **do**
    begin $x :=$ "*inverse of d1*"(x);   **result** $:= h(\textbf{result}, \textbf{result})$ **end**

Equation (i)

$d1 = d2$

Restrictions: x does not occur free in h or b; the unique x such that
                a, and the inverse of $d1$ both exist.

Iterative schema (ii)

$y1 := b$; $y2 := b$;   **result** $:= b$;
while not a **do**
    begin result $:= h(y1, y2)$; $y1 := y2$;
                $y2 :=$ **result**; $x := d1$ **end**

Equations (ii)

$h(\alpha, h(\beta, \gamma)) = h(\beta, h(\alpha, \gamma))$; $d2 = d1\{d1|x\}^4$
Restriction: x does not occur free in h or b. a implies $a\{d1/x\}$.

Iterative schema (iii)

result $:= b$;
while not a **do**
    begin result $:= h(\textbf{result}, \textbf{result})$; $x := d1$ **end**

Equation (iii)

$d1 = d2$;
Restriction: x does not occur free in h or b.

Schema 4

Recursion schema

$$f(x)= \begin{cases} a \to b \\ \textbf{not } a \to h(f(d)) \end{cases}$$

[4] $A\{B|v\}$ means A with every occurrence of v replaced by B.

Iterative schema (i)

> **while not** a **do** $x := d$;
> **result** $:= b$

Equation (i)

> $h = \lambda x;\ x$

Iterative schema (ii)

> **result** $:= b$; $xsave := x$; $x := $ "*unique x such that a*";
> **while not** $x = xsave$ **do**
>   **begin** $x := $ "*inverse of d*" (x);   **result** $:= h(\text{result})$ **end**

Equation (ii)

> None.
> Restrictions: x does not occur free in h or b. The unique x such
> that a and the inverse of d both exist.

Schema 5

> *Recursion schema*
>
> $$f(x,y) = \begin{cases} a \to b \\ \textbf{not } a \to h(f(d1,d2)) \end{cases}$$
>
> *Iterative schema*
>
> > **while not** a **do**
> >   **begin** $xsave := d1$; $y := d2$; $x := xsave$ **end**;
> > **result** $:= b$
>
> *Equation*
>
> $h = \lambda x;\ x$

2.2 Practical use

With these schemas the system managed to translate a fair proportion of
examples which we invented or took from actual programs; some of these
are given below. How adequate the system would be in a wider context we
have not determined, although we feel that the empirical adequacy of the
system, as opposed to its theoretical completeness, is the important question.

Current work splits the recursion translation into two parts. The first
attempts to translate recursive programs to more efficient recursive pro-

grams and the second translates these programs to iterative programs if possible. This two stage process means that more translations are available than earlier.

2.3 Examples

(i)

$$factorial(n) = \begin{cases} n=0 \rightarrow 1 \\ \textbf{not } n=0 \rightarrow mult(n, factorial(n-1)) \end{cases}$$

can be translated in 3 ways by Schema 1. We saw a translation using iterative schema (i) above. Another translation using iterative schema (ii) is

result : = 1;
while not $n=0$ **do**
   begin result : = $mult(n, \textbf{result})$; $n := n-1$ **end**

This translation took 2.5 seconds.

(ii)

$$Fibonacci(n) = \begin{cases} n=0 \quad \textbf{or} \quad n=1 \rightarrow 1 \\ \textbf{not}(n=0 \quad \textbf{or} \quad n=1) \rightarrow plus(Fibonacci(n-1) \\ \qquad\qquad\qquad\qquad\qquad (Fibonacci(n-2)) \end{cases}$$

goes to

$y1 := 1$; $y2 := 1$;   **result** : = 1;
while not $(n=0 \quad \textbf{or} \quad n=1)$ **do**
   begin result : = $plus(y1,y2)$; $y1 := y2$;
         $y2 :=$ **result**; $x := n-1$
   end

by Schema 3, iterative schema (ii). This translation took 48.25 seconds to calculate. Fibonacci (20) took 12.8 seconds using the recursive definition and .125 using the iterative definition.

(iii) A function to compute the union of two sets in terms of *consset*, *choose* and *minus*.

$$union(x,y) = \begin{cases} nullset(x) \rightarrow y \\ \textbf{not } nullset(x) \rightarrow consset(choose\ (x), \\ \qquad\qquad\qquad\qquad union(minus(choose(x),x),y)) \end{cases}$$

goes to

result : = y;
while not $nullset(x)$ **do**
     begin result : = $connset(choose(x), \textbf{result})$;
         $x := minus(choose(x),x)$
     end

by Schema 2.

(iv) A function to compute the Boolean (powerset) of a set is

$$bool(s) = \begin{cases} nullset(s) \rightarrow \{nilset\} \\ \textbf{not } nullset(s) \rightarrow union\ (bool(minus(choose(s)),s)), \\ \qquad\qquad\qquad\qquad g(bool(minus(choose(s),s),s)) \end{cases}$$

$$g(s,x) = \begin{cases} nullset(s) \rightarrow nilset \\ \textbf{not } nullset(s) \rightarrow consset(consset(x, \{choose(s)\})), \\ \qquad\qquad\qquad\qquad g(minus(choose(s),s),x) \end{cases}$$

This splits into two separate tasks corresponding to the two separate equations. The first equation matches with Schema 3 but as the *s* occurs outside the recursive calls no translation is achieved although the two recursive calls are identical.

The second equation matches with Schema 2 and the translation produced is

> **result** : = *nilset*;
> **while not** *nullset(s)* **do**
>   **begin result** : = *consset(consset(x, {choose(s)}),* **result**);
>   *xsave* : = *minus(choose(s),s)*;
>   *x* : = *x*;
>   *s* : = *xsave*
>   **end**

The system later reduces the last 3 assignments to 1.

(v) If we write the member function as

$$member(x,y) = \begin{cases} null(y) \rightarrow false \\ \textbf{not } null(y) \textbf{ and } x = hd(y) \rightarrow true \\ \textbf{not } null(y) \textbf{ and not } x = hd(y) \rightarrow member(x,tl(y)) \end{cases}$$

the system preprocesses this into a form that matches with Schema 5 and produces a translation

> **while not** *null(y)* **and not** $x = hd(y)$ **do**
>   **begin** *xsave* : = *x*;   *y* : = *tl(y)*;   *x* : = *xsave*   **end**;
> **if** *null(y)* **then** *false*;
> **if not** *null(y) and* $x = hd(y)$ **then** *true*

Again the system is able later to improve the sequence of assignments and final conditionals.

3 Eliminating redundant computation

3.1 Compound operations

After removing as much recursion as possible the flattening is continued by removing procedure calls. This proceeds top down, a layer at a time, rewriting each program into another one. However, we do not proceed by the normal method of first replacing the calls of each procedure by its definition (in-line code introduction) and then optimising. Before replacing procedure calls we manipulate the program to eliminate as much redundant computation as possible and make the program more amenable to efficient implementation (see Section 4). This we do by examining the semantic content of the given program. At present we are unable to do this for whole progams and we modify them in portions consisting of sequences of tests and assignments within a loop. Consider the following sequence of assignments

$S := union(intersection(T, U), V)$;
$W := union(intersection(T, U), W)$

Clearly we can eliminate repeated computation of $intersection(T, U)$, rewriting the sequence as

$X := intersection(T, U)$;
$S := union(X, V)$;
$W := union(X, W)$

Suppose now that *intersection* and *union* are to be implemented in terms of list processing. The procedure body for $union(X, Y)$ might be

result $:= Y$;
while not $null(X)$ **do begin**
    if not $member(hd(X), Y)$
    then result $:= cons(hd(X),$ **result**$)$;
    $X := tl(X)$
   end

By replacing each call of *union* by this code we would obtain a program which has two loops on X. But this is unnecessary; the two can be combined into a single loop on X which builds up two result lists simultaneously. We could let the system replace each call of *union* separately and then try to combine the loops, but this would be quite difficult. Instead we let the system do as much manipulation as possible at the higher level, before replacing procedure calls by their bodies. Thus it would first synthesize a *compound operation*, which we will call *doubleunion*, with definition

$doubleunion(X, Y, Z) = \langle union(X, Y), union(X, Z) \rangle$

It would then rewrite the assignment as

$X := intersection(T, U);$
$\langle S, W \rangle := doubleunion(X, V, W)$

The system is able to produce a body of code for $doubleunion \ (X, Y, Z)$, viz.

result1 $:= Y;$ **result2** $:= Z;$
while not $null(X)$ **do**
   begin if not $member(hd(X), Y)$
        then result1 $:= cons(hd(X),$ **result1**$);$
      if not $member(hd(X), Z)$
        then result2 $:= cons(hd(X),$ **result2**$);$
      $X := tl(X)$
  end

and this body will be used to replace the call of *doubleunion* in the next stage (see Section 4).

Notice that if we had started instead with the program

$S := union(intersection(U, T), V);$
$W := union(W, intersection(T, U))$

we could have made the same economies, given the fact that intersection and union are both commutative.

3.2 Origin of compound operations

To be able to spot opportunities for forming compound operations and produce the appropriate code bodies, the system preprocesses the definitions to produce

(i) A list showing which combinations of higher level operations can be formed into useful compound operations. This is used during the manipulation of the higher level program.

(ii) A schematic table that enables any synthesised compound operation to be expanded into code which is already in an optimised form. This table is used in the next stage to replace procedure calls by their bodies (see Section 4).

This list and table are then used in the transformations of all programs written using these operations. To produce them the program uses a rewrite rule showing how certain combinations of loops can be condensed.

Suppose for example that it is given these definitions:

$union(X, Y) = \textbf{result} := Y;$
$\quad\quad\quad\quad$ **while not** $null(X)$ **do**
$\quad\quad\quad\quad\quad\quad$ **begin if not** $member(hd(X), Y)$ **then**
$\quad\quad\quad\quad\quad\quad\quad\quad\quad$ **result** $:= cons(hd(X),$ **result**$)$;
$\quad\quad\quad\quad\quad\quad\quad$ $X := tl(X)$
$\quad\quad\quad\quad\quad\quad$ **end**

$subtract(X, Y) = \textbf{result} := nil;$
$\quad\quad\quad\quad\quad$ **while not** $null(X)$ **do begin**
$\quad\quad\quad\quad\quad\quad\quad$ **if not** $member(hd(X), Y)$ **then**
$\quad\quad\quad\quad\quad\quad\quad$ **result** $:= cons(hd(X),$ **result**$)$;
$\quad\quad\quad\quad\quad\quad\quad$ $X := tl(X)$
$\quad\quad\quad\quad\quad\quad$ **end**
$intersection(X, Y) = \textbf{result} := nil;$
$\quad\quad\quad\quad\quad\quad$ **while not** $null(X)$ **do**
$\quad\quad\quad\quad\quad\quad$ **begin**
$\quad\quad\quad\quad\quad\quad$ **if** $member(hd(X), Y)$ **then**
$\quad\quad\quad\quad\quad\quad\quad\quad$ **result** $:= cons(hd(X),$ **result**$)$;
$\quad\quad\quad\quad\quad\quad\quad$ $X := tl(X)$
$\quad\quad\quad\quad\quad\quad$ **end**

All these definitions can be condensed using a rewrite rule

$f1(x,y) = y := a(x);$
$\quad\quad\quad$ **while** $p(x)$ **do**
$\quad\quad\quad\quad$ **begin** $y := g(x,y);$ $\quad x := f(x)$ $\quad$ **end**

and

$f2(x,y) = z := b(x);$
$\quad\quad\quad$ **while** $p(x)$ **do**
$\quad\quad\quad\quad$ **begin** $z := h(x,z);$ $\quad x := f(x)$ $\quad$ **end**

rewrites to

$f12(x,y,z) = y := a(x);$ $\quad z := b(x);$
$\quad\quad\quad\quad$ **while** $p(x)$ **do**
$\quad\quad\quad\quad\quad$ **begin** $z := h(x,z);$ $\quad y := g(x,y);$
$\quad\quad\quad\quad\quad\quad\quad$ $x := f(x)$
$\quad\quad\quad\quad$ **end**

so that $f12(x,y,z) = \langle f1(x,y), f2(x,z) \rangle$

Here x,y,z may each represent several variables, not just one, and a,b,f,g,h are arbitrary functions.

The system uses this to preprocess the definitions and produces

(i) a list ((union, subtract, intersection)) showing that all these operations can be combined into compound operations, provided that when they occur in programs the variables they iterate on (in this case the first variable) have the same value, and

(ii) a table from which code can be produced to realise any synthesised compound operator of this type, namely

$$\langle body \rangle ::= \langle part\ 1 \rangle;$$
$$\textbf{while not } null(var1)\ \textbf{do}$$
$$\textbf{begin}$$
$$\langle part\ 2 \rangle;$$
$$var1 := tl(var1)$$
$$\textbf{end}$$

$\langle part\ 1 \rangle$ *for union* :: =   **result**$_i$:= $var2$
      for subtract :: =   **result**$_i$:= nil
      for intersection :: =   **result**$_i$:= nil

$\langle part\ 2 \rangle$ *for union* :: =   **if not** $member(hd(var1), var2)$
                            then result$_i$:= $cons(hd(var1),$ **result**$_i 2)$
      for subtract :: =   **if not** $member(hd(var1), var2)$
                            then result$_i$:= $cons(hd(var1),$ **result**$_i)$
      for intersection :: = **if** $member(hd(var1), var2)$
                            then result$_i$:= $cons(hd(var1),$ **result**$_i)$

3.3 Program manipulation

If we work on assignment sequences directly it is not easy to recognise common subexpressions and to detect opportunities for introducing compound operations. So the system executes the given sequence of assignments *symbolically* and finds what *state transformation* it produces, that is, it computes the final value for each identifier as an expression in terms of the initial values. In the above example, given initial symbolic values S_0, T_0, U_0, V_0, and W_0, for variables S, T, U, V and W the final state vector is

$$\langle S = union(intersection(T_0, U_0), V_0),\ T = T_0,\ U = U_0,\ V = V_0,$$
$$W = union(intersection(T_0, U_0), W_0)\rangle$$

The search for common subexpressions and compound operations is performed on the 5-tuple of expressions constituting the values of S, T, U, V and W. This state 5-tuple is rewritten, introducing subsidiary variables in **where** clauses (in fact the internal representation uses pointers to list structures), thus

$$\langle S, T, U, V, W \rangle = \langle y, T_0, U_0, V_0, z \rangle$$
$$\textbf{where } \langle y, z \rangle = doubleunion(x, V_0, W_0)$$
$$\textbf{where } x = intersection(T_0, U_0)$$

This new 5-tuple of expressions must now be converted back to assignments.

To summarize, there are three steps: (1) convert from assignments to state transformation, (2) rewrite the state transformations, and (3) convert back to assignments. We will make a few more remarks about each.

Step 1. From the sequence of commands the transformation induced is extracted by running the sequence on symbolic data. From this state transformation a set of equivalent transformations are produced by applying all the appropriate algebraic equations (commutativity etc.), to a given degree of effort.

Step 2. In each of these state transformations the program seeks common subexpressions and compound operations.

The improvements made in this step can be represented as rewriting rules on *n*-tuples of expressions. They introduce '**where** clauses' using new identifiers, to show the sharing. Let E, F and G be meta-variables denoting expressions and v be a meta-variable denoting a (suitably distinct) identifier. We use $E(E_1,\ldots,E_n)$ to denote an expression with sub-expressions $E_1,\ldots,E_n$.

The rewriting rule for extracting common subexpressions is:

Rewrite '$\langle E_1(E),\ldots,E_n(E)\rangle$' *as* '$\langle E_1(v),\ldots,E_n(v)\rangle$ **where** $v=E$'

The rewriting rule for introducing a compound operation f, defined by $f(x_1,\ldots,x_k)=\langle F_1(x_1,\ldots,x_k),\ldots,F_m(x_1,\ldots,x_k)\rangle$ is:

Rewrite '$\langle E_1(F_1(G_1,\ldots,G_k),\ldots,F_m(G_1,\ldots,G_k)),\ldots,$

$$E_n(F_1(G_1,\ldots,G_k),\ldots,F_m(G_1,\ldots,G_k))\rangle'$$

as '$\langle E_1(v_1,\ldots,v_k),\ldots,E_n(v_1,\ldots,v_k)\rangle$
     where $\langle v_1,\ldots,v_k\rangle=f(G_1,\ldots,G_k)$'

A quite elaborate matching process is used to determine where these rules are applicable (see [Darlington 72]). For each of the variant state transformations produced by using the equations, the system finds all subexpressions occurring in it and matches the F_i against them for each compound f. At this stage only the most promising one as judged by a rough efficiency estimate is retained. This is rewritten in terms of the compound operations.

Step 3. The system converts the rewritten state transformation to a sequence of assignments. It calculates a set of differences between the final expressions for the identifiers and their initial values, and then performs a G.P.S.-like search ([Ernst 67; Simon 72]). For example, trying to achieve the transformation $\langle X=consset(X_0,Y_0),\ Y=X_0,\ Z=X_0\rangle$ the system notices three differences between initial and final values. It tries to remove these in all possible sequences until it succeeds. It would first try '$X:=consset(X,Y)$', but Y still differs from its final value and X_0 is lost. So it tries successively '$Y:=X;\ Z:=X$', which loses Y too soon, and '$Z:=X;$

$X := consset(X, Y)$; $Y := Z$'. If necessary it introduces extra identifiers.

It seems crucial that the manipulation is done on the higher level program, before replacing procedure calls, for two reasons.

(a) The higher level programs are often much simpler and easier to understand, since usually a single operation expands into a body of code.

(b) We are able to make full use of the algebraic laws appropriate to this higher level. For example, once calls to set operations have been replaced by their list processing bodies many possibilities for rearrangement and optimisation will have been lost. Thus $union(X, Y) = union(Y, X)$ but if union is represented by list concatenation, $\otimes$, the results $X \otimes Y$ and $Y \otimes X$ are two different lists although they represent the same set. So no list optimiser would commute the arguments however great the gains in efficiency.

4 Replacing procedure calls by their bodies

Here the system replaces calls of basic operations by their procedure bodies and replaces compound operations by code bodies produced using the compound operator table described earlier.

In our example above the program

$X := intersection(T, U)$;
$\langle S, W \rangle := doubleunion(X, V, W)$

expands into a list program

```
result := nil;
while not null(T)
   do begin if member(hd(T), U)
               then result := cons(hd(T), result);
          T := tl(T)
      end;
X := result; result1 := V; result2 := W;
while not null(X)
   do begin if not member(hd(X), V)
               then result1 := cons(hd(X), result1);
            if not member(hd(X), W)
               then result2 := cons(hd(X), result2);
          X := tl(X)
      end;
S := result1;   W := result2
```

At present the system has definitions to provide a choice of two representations for sets: lists or bit strings. These involve different sets of compound operations. The user chooses one of the representations.

5 Re-using discarded list cells

In any program that contains lists as data structures our system is able to take the improvement further. It attempts to transform constructive list programs, which allow assignment only to identifiers, into destructive ones, which allow assignment to parts of structures, for example '$hd(Y):=X$'. In LISP terms it eliminates CONS in favour of REPLACA and REPLACD. Programs written 'destructively' are efficient in store usage, but they are recognised as being difficult to understand or debug since side effects of destructive assignments are often far from obvious.

The process involved in this transformation follows the same pattern as described in Section 3. It is regarded as a rewriting between two levels of language, a 'constructive' list language and a 'destructive' list language. Again the system operates by finding the state transformation and reinterpreting it as efficiently as possible.

The optimisation attempted is to avoid store usage by re-using any list cells that will have been discarded. This process can be thought of as a compile time garbage collection.

The system takes a sequence of assignments and works out the symbolic state transformation they induce. Usually information is available to make the starting state more detailed than before. Thus before $X:=tl(X)$ we know that X should have as value a list of at least one element. To examine store usage we explicitly name list cells and define a starting state in terms of identifiers I, Atoms A, list cells C, and variables V. Thus a state is a triple of finite functions.

$$val: I \to A \cup C \cup V$$
$$hd: C \to A \cup C \cup V$$
$$tl: C \to A \cup C \cup V$$

The variables, V, stand for unspecified list cells or atoms (compare the variables X_0, Y_0, Z_0 used previously).

For example before the program

$$Y:=cons(hd(X), Y);$$
$$X:=tl(X)$$

the system creates a symbolic state

$$val(X)=c_1, \; val(Y)=c_3, \; hd(c_1)=a_1, \; tl(c_1)=c_2,$$
$$hd(c_3)=v_1, \; tl(c_3)=v_2, \; hd(c_2)=v_3, \; tl(c_2)=v_4$$

and after executing the above program on this symbolic state it would have a final state

$$val(X)=c_2, \; val(Y)=c_4, \; hd(c_1)=a_1, \; tl(c_1)=c_2, \; hd(c_4)=a_1,$$
$$tl(c_4)=c_3, \; hd(c_3)=v_1, \; tl(c_3)=v_2, \; hd(c_2)=v_3, \; tl(c_2)=v_4$$

The system now performs a 'symbolic garbage collection' on this state description to see if any cells have been discarded, and attempts to re-use these to avoid the introduction of new cells. In the example it finds that it can use the discarded cell c_1 instead of introducing the new cell c_4, and it rewrites the final state thus

$$val(X) = c_2,\ val(Y) = c_1,\ hd(c_1) = a_1,\ tl(c_1) = c_3,$$
$$hd(c_2) = v_3,\ tl(c_2) = v_4,\ hd(c_3) = v_1,\ tl(c_3) = v_2$$

The system now tries various sequences of assignments (exhaustively, but with a G.P.S.-like difference-operator table) to achieve a sequence of instructions to implement the new transformation but avoiding *cons*'s. In our example the sequence produced is

$$NEWVAR1 := tl(X);\ tl(X) := Y;\ Y := X;\ X := NEWVAR1$$

Thus the list reverse program

```
result: = nil;
while not null(X) do
   begin result: = cons(hd(X), result);   X:= tl(X)   end
```

is automatically converted to a reverse program which uses no new store:

```
result: = nil;
while not null(X) do
   begin NEWVAR1:= tl(X);
      tl(X): = result; result:= X; X:= NEWVAR1
   end
```

This translation took 2.125 seconds.

6 Use of the system, and recent developments

The first implementation of the system was completed in January 1973. This enables a user to experiment with the system using simple interactive facilities; a sample dialogue is given below. The user can invoke any of the three processes; recursion removal (Stage 1 above), eliminating redundant computation with code introduction (Stage 2 and 3), and destructive list processing (Stage 4).

The system can be applied to a new domain of discourse just by giving it new rules and definitions. The table of recursive schemas and iterative equivalents and the table of iterative compounds are independent of domain; they may of course be extended. To apply the system to the finite sets domain, so that it translates recursion equations in basic set operations (*consset, choose, nullset*, etc.) to destructive list processing programs or to bit string processing programs, we have provided the following.

 (i) Equations about the basic set operations, commutativity etc. (used in Stages 1 and 2)
(ii) Procedure bodies to implement the basic set operations by list operations (used in Stage 3)
(ii') As (ii) for bit strings instead of lists.

For the finite set application the system has a few extra tricks built into it as program.

Since 1973, helped by ideas in the Boyer-Moore LISP theorem prover [Boyer 75], we have developed a method that unifies and extends the separate improvement processes described here. In this new work all the optimising processes are performed on the programs in recursion equation form. We find that this makes manipulation much easier. The basis for this new improvement system is six transformation rules on recursion equations. With these we can repeat all the improvements mentioned here and achieve many more besides (with the exception of re-using discarded list cells which we have not looked at yet). This system can be extended smoothly to program synthesis; that is the transformation of non-executable definitions of algorithms into efficient executable forms. At present (July 1975) we have implemented a basic version of this new system. The simple formal nature of this system makes it easy to implement. What is lacking at present is the sort of programming knowledge that is present in the earlier work. We are looking at ways of adding this knowledge to the new system. This recent work is reported in [Burstall 77*; Darlington 75].

The idea of symbolic execution of parts of a program has proved fruitful. It has also been used at Edinburgh ([Topor 75; Boyer 75]) in their LISP theorem prover. Our expression optimising techniques seem to go beyond those used in current compilers (see for example [Rohl 72]; [Hopgood 69] gives further references).

7 Example of use

```
: STARTSYSTEM;                    (user commences dialogue)
START OF OPTIMISATION.INPUT PROGRAM
TO BE OPTIMISED                   (system's response)
```

```
: union(x,y)=                     (user inputs program)
nullset(x)→y,
not nullset(x)→consset(choose(x), union(minus(choose(x),x),y))
WHICH OPTIMISATION WOULD YOU LIKE PERFORMED
: REC                             (user requests recursion removal stage)
```

RESULTING PROGRAM IS
result := *y*;   (system outputs result)
while not *nullset*(*x*) **do**
begin result := *consset*(*choose*(*x*), **result**);
   xsave := *minus*(*choose*(*x*), *x*);
   y := *y*;
   x := *xsave*
end
WHICH OPTIMISATION WOULD YOU LIKE PERFORMED
: CODEINTRO (user wishes to continue optimising this program)
DO YOU WISH TO IMPLEMENT IN LISTS OR BIT STRINGS
: BIT STRINGS
RESULTING PROGRAM IS
l := *length*(*x*); *n* := 1; **result** := *y*;
while *n* ⩽ *l* **do**
begin if *x*[*n*] = 1 **then**
                begin result [*n*] := 1; *x*[*n*] := 0;
                     xsave := *x*
                end;
       n := *n* − 1
end
WHICH OPTIMISATION WOULD YOU LIKE PERFORMED
: FINISHED   (user has finished with this program)
DO YOU WISH TO PERFORM ANOTHER OPTIMISATION
: YES   (user continues with another program)
INPUT PROGRAM TO BE OPTIMISED
:   *doneshuffle* := *true*;   (user inputs sorting program)
      while *doneshuffle* **do**
       begin *doneshuffle* := *false*;
             result := *nil*; *last* := *hd*(*xl*);
          while not *null*(*tl*(*xl*)) **do**
           begin if *last* ⩽ *hd*(*tl*(*xl*))
                then
                begin result := *cons*(*last*, **result**);
                     xl := *tl*(*xl*); *last* := *hd*(*xl*)
                end
                else
                begin *xl* := *tl*(*xl*);
                     result := *cons*(*hd*(*xl*), **result**);
                     doneshuffle := *true*
                end
         end;
        result := *cons*(*last*, **result**);
        xl := *reverse*(**result**)
        end;
        result := *xl*

WHICH OPTIMISATION WOULD YOU LIKE PERFORMED
: MAKEDEST   (stage 4 store overwriting)
RESULTING PROGRAM IS

```
      doneshuffle : = true;
      while doneshuffle do
       begin doneshuffle : = false;
            result : = nil;  last : = hd(xl);
         while not null(tl(xl)) do
         begin if last ≤ hd(tl(xl))
           then begin
                   hd(xl) : = last;  last : = hd(tl(xl));
                   newvar1 : = tl(xl);  tl(xl) : = result;
                   result : = xl;  xl : = newvar1
               end
           else begin
                   newvar1 : = tl(xl);
                   hd(xl) : = hd(tl(xl));
                   tl(xl) : = result;  result : = xl;
                   xl : = newvar1;  doneshuffle : = true
               end
         end
      result : = cons(last, result);
       xl : = reverse(result)
      end;
     result : = xl
```

Acknowledgments. We would like to thank our colleagues in the School of Artificial Intelligence for many helpful conversations, Bernard Lang for correcting omissions in the schemata conditions, Brian Randell for valuable criticism, Eleanor Kerse for speedy and accurate typing, and the Science Research Council for financial support.

PART III

HARNESSING PARALLELISM

The primary impetus behind the study of parallel programming, or concurrent programming as some would call it, was the necessity to write operating systems. While the first computers were simple enough to be considered sequential in nature, the advent of faster central processing units and the accompanying discrepancy in speed between the central processor and peripheral devices forced the consideration of possible concurrent activity of these mechanisms. The operating system was asked to control concurrent activity, and to control it in such a way that concurrent activity was maximized.

This desire for concurrent activity resulted in machine features such as the channel and the interrupt—the mechanism by which termination of an I/O activity is signaled. The main problem with the interrupt, as far as the operating system designer was concerned, was its inherent unpredictability. Not knowing exactly when an interrupt could occur, the operating system had to be designed to expect an interrupt at any *time.*

With the advent of multiprogramming and interactive, on-line processing, it became clear that the original motivation for parallelism—the control and exploitation of concurrent I/O—was only a special case, and some fundamental concepts began to emerge for study and use in more general parallel programming situations. Thus emerged the general idea of a set of processes *executing concurrently, with the need for* synchronization *and mutual* exclusion *(with respect to time) of some of their activities. The past 10–15 years have seen an enormous amount of activity in studying the general problem, a very small part of which is presented here.*

Now, the article An axiomatic proof technique for parallel programs *in Part II presents a theory of parallel programming that can be quite useful in dealing with certain kinds of parallelism. However, for many tasks it is far too general. In effect, using it is an attempt to ride the parallel programming horse bareback, relying on theory and skill but without any physical aids. Most riders need equipment, in the form of programming language constructs, to facilitate riding the horse.*

As early as 1964–1965 PL/1 did furnish such equipment: tasks, event names, on-conditions, and so forth. But, this equipment did not sell well, partly because it was not based on a good theory or methodology for understanding parallelism, and partly because of the odd way it was attached to the sequential part of the language. (For example, the procedure is confused with the task; the on-unit is a bewildering mixture of executable statement and declaration.)

So let us see what other equipment has been developed.

An important step was the invention of the semaphore by Edsger W. Dijkstra, which took place around 1965 [Dijkstra 68c*]. A semaphore s can be operated on by the operators V(s) and P(s), which the reader may know as signal(s) *and* wait(s). *Semaphores were used in the "bottom layer" of the T.H.E. Multiprogramming System [Dijkstra 68d*, 71d*] in order to hide the uglier primitive of the hardware, the interrupt. The monograph [Dijkstra 68c*] gave the field a firm foundation by introducing and analyzing critical sec-tions, mutual exclusion, semaphores, message buffers, and deadlock. The article [Dijkstra 71d*] provides more analysis, and also argues against earlier synchronization mechanisms, such as* wait *and* cause *operating on* event *variables.*

The semaphore was recognized early as a rather primitive construct, and attempts were made to develop other synchronization and exclusion mechanisms. The critical region *construct,* **region** r **do** S *is generally attri-buted to Tony (C.A.R.) Hoare and Per Brinch Hansen. Here, resource r is a group of shared variables. Any references to them must be within a* **region** r **do** S *statement, and only one process can execute a critical region for r at a time (others must wait their turn). And now we see what such equipment can do for us: the problem of insuring that at most one process at a time can reference a particular shared variable is reduced to a syntactic, almost trivial exercise!*

To provide synchronization, Hoare extended the construct to the condi-tional *critical region* **with** r **when** B **do** S; *in addition to waiting its turn to use the resource r, a process had to wait until its guard B was true before executing S. Brinch Hansen, on the other hand, added* queuing variables *to provide for synchronization.*

Their articles on this topic, Towards a theory of parallel programming *and* Structured multiprogramming *are reproduced in Part III. Besides reading two interesting viewpoints on synchronization, the reader will find good discussions of objectives for and difficulties with theories of parallel program-ming. Hoare's article also contains initial investigations into providing an axiomatic definition for the conditional critical region; this work was extended by Susan Owicki in her Ph.D. thesis (see [Owicki 75*, 76a*]).*

The next tool to be developed in this line was the monitor. *In [Dijkstra 71d*], Dijkstra proposed taking out from N processes the critical sections that refer to a set of common variables and combining them to form a new (N + 1)st process, called a* secretary. *Thus, all references to the shared variables were to be made in a single process, the* secretary. *The term* monitor *and a language notation for it (based on the SIMULA 67 class concept) are due to Brinch Hansen, while the concept was then also developed by Hoare.*

The last two articles in Part III allow for further comparison of their ideas; we present Hoare's 1974 article, Monitors: an operating system structuring concept *and Brinch Hansen's 1975 article,* The programming language Concurrent Pascal. *Again, both articles are worthwhile not only for their discussion of the construct—in this case the monitor—but also for their expression of a general philosophy and methodology for parallel programming.*

After reading these articles, the reader may wish to turn to Brinch Hansen's new book [Brinch Hansen 77*], *which gives the complete Solo operating system written in* Concurrent Pascal.

Thus far, I have outlined the history of one line of equipment for riding the parallel programming horse. While this is the only line presented in detail in Part III, the reader might wish to at least know what else is available from other manufacturers.

Petri nets, *developed by Carl A. Petri in his 1962 thesis, have long been used by some as a tool in reasoning about parallel programming. The reader is referred to the Computing Surveys article* [Peterson 77], *which contains 93 further references to the literature.*

Message passing *offers another viable approach to harnessing parallelism, and may very well be better suited for distributed networks. In fact, message passing was used in the time sharing operating system for the CDC 6600, which, with its ten peripheral processors, can be considered to be a distributed network* [Harrison 67]. *A better explanation of the message passing concept can be found in* [Brinch Hansen 70*].

With respect to semaphores, A. Nico Habermann gave one of the first formalizations, using "auxiliary variables", in [Habermann 72]. *Others have extended the semaphore concept to make it more flexible, but it remains too primitive.*

*Habermann is also responsible, along with Roy H. Campbell, for introduc-*ing path expressions *as a means of expressing synchronization requirements* [Campbell 74]. *By means of a regular expression over the names of procedures or statements, one describes all allowed execution sequences of those procedures or statements, and it is up to the implementation to assure that this requirement is met.*

Finally, Niklaus Wirth's new language MODULA should be mentioned [Wirth 77a*, 77b*]. *MODULA, which uses the* monitor *concept, has been designed with so-called* real-time *programming in mind. The article* [Wirth 77b*] *begins the development of a methodology for real-time programming.*

15
Towards a Theory of Parallel Programming

C. A. Hoare
University of Oxford

Abstract *The objectives for a theory of parallel programming are discussed. Programming constructs for parallelism, including means for expressing resource constraints and synchorinzation, are discussed and formally defined.*

Objectives

The objectives in the construction of a theory of parallel programming as a basis for a high-level programming language feature are:

1. Security from error. In many of the applications of parallel programming the cost of programming error is very high, often inhibiting the use of computers in environments for which they would otherwise be highly suitable. Parallel programs are particularly prone to time-dependent errors, which cannot be detected by either program testing or run-time checks. It is therefore very important that a high-level language designed for this purpose should provide complete security against time-dependent errors by means of a *compile-time* check.

2. Efficiency. The spread of real-time computer applications is severely limited by computing costs; and in particular by the cost of main store. If a feature to assist in parallel programming is to be added to a language used for this purpose, it must not entail any noticeable extra run-time overhead in space or speed, neither on programs which use the feature heavily, nor on programs which do not; efficient implementation should be possible on a variety of hardware designs, both simple and complex; and there should be no need for bulky or slow compilers.

3. Conceptual simplicity. A good high-level language feature should provide a simple conceptual framework within which the programmer can formulate his problems and proceed in an orderly fashion to their solution. In particular, it should give guidance on how to structure a program in a perspicuous fashion, and verify that each component of the structure contributes reliably to a clearly defined overall goal.

4. Breadth of application. The purposes for which parallel programming have been found useful are:

(a) To take advantage of genuine multi-processing hardware.
(b) To achieve overlap of lengthy input or output operations with computing.
(c) Operating system implementation.
(d) Real-time applications.
(e) Simulation studies.
(f) Combinatorial or Heuristic Programming.

Ideally, a language feature for parallel programming suitable for inclusion in a general-purpose programming language should cater adequately for all these highly disparate purposes.

The design of high-level programming languages which simultaneously satisfy these four objectives is one of the major challenges to the invention, imagination and intellect of Computer Scientists of the present day. The solutions proposed in this paper cannot claim to be final, but it is believed that they form a sound basis for further advance.

Parallel processes

The concept of two or more processes occurring simultaneously in the real world is a familiar one; however, it has proved exceptionally difficult to apply the concept to programs acting in parallel in a computer. The usual definition of the effect of parallel actions is in terms of "an arbitrary interleaving of units of action from each program." This presents three difficulties:

1. That of defining a "unit of action".
2. That of implementing the interleaving on genuinely parallel hardware.
3. That of designing programs to control the fantastic number of combinations involved in arbitrary interleaving.

Our approach to the solution of these problems is based on the observation that in the real world simultaneous processes generally occur in different parts of physical space (it is difficult to give any explanation of what it would mean for two processes to be occurring in the same place). Thus our normal concept of simultaneity is closely bound up with that of spatial separation. The concept of spatial separation has an analogue in computer programs that are operating on entirely disjoint sets of variables, and interacting with their environment through entirely disjoint sets of peripheral equipment. Obvious examples are programs being run on separate computers, or on the same computer under the control of a conventional multiprogramming system.

In such cases, where there is no possibility of communication or interaction between the programs, the question whether a given action of one program preceded, followed, or was simultaneous with a given action of the other program is wholly without significance. On a "Newtonian" view, the question must have a definite answer, even if we can neither know nor care what it is. For practical purposes, it is equally acceptable to take an "Einsteinian" view that there is *no* relative ordering between events occurring in disjoint programs being executed in parallel; and that *each* action of one program is simultaneous with *all* the actions of the other programs.

We introduce the notation

$$\{Q_1 // Q_2 // \cdots // Q_n\}$$

to indicate that the program statements $Q_1, Q_2, \ldots, Q_n$ are disjoint processes to be executed in parallel. It is expected that the compiler will check the disjointness of the processes by ensuring that no variable subject to change in any of the Q_i is referred to at all in any Q_j for $i \neq j$. Thus it can be guaranteed by a compile-time check that no time-dependent errors could ever occur at run time. It is assumed that the high-level language in use has the decent property that it is possible to tell by inspection which variables and array names appear to the left of an assignment which might be executed in any given statement of a program.

The desired effect of the parallel statement described above is to initiate execution of each of the Q_i in parallel; and when they are *all* terminated, execution of the parallel statement is also complete. Each Q_i may contain any of the normal program features—assignments, conditionals, iterations, blocks, declarations, subroutine calls—of the base language; but if recursion or dynamic storage allocation is used, this will involve replacing the simple stack by a "cactus" stack. It would be wise to ban the use of jumps out of a parallel statement, since these would be not only difficult to define and to use correctly, but can also cause considerable implementation problems. In a language designed for parallel programming there is an even stronger case for the abolition of jumps than in more conventional high-level languages.

Some languages (e.g. PL/1) give the programmer the ability to specify and even to change the priorities of the parallel processes. For most applications this appears to be an unnecessary complexity, whose effective use will depend on many detailed machine and implementation oriented considerations. In practice it has been found that the general-purpose scheduling method of giving control to the process which has used the least computer time in the recent past achieves acceptably high efficiency in most circumstances. The programmer can therefore safely be encouraged to "abstract from" the relative speeds and priorities of his processes, and allow the implementor of his programming language to decide on his behalf.

The way in which parallel programs can be proved to achieve some desired objective is simple. Suppose each Q_i is designed to ensure that R_i is true when it finishes, on the assumption that P_i is true before it starts. Then on completion of

$$\{Q_1//Q_2//\cdots//Q_n\}$$

all the R_i will be true, provided that all the P_i were true beforehand. Thus each Q_i makes its contribution to the common goal. But one caution is necessary: none of the P_i or R_i may mention any variable which is subject to change in any of the Q_j for $j \neq i$. A formal statement of this and following program proving principles will be found in the Appendix.

The facility for specifying parallelism of disjoint programs appears to be adequate for use of genuine multiprocessing hardware, and for the overlap of input and output operations with computing. But of course the more interesting problems require some form of interaction between the parallel programs; and this will be the topic of the following sections.

Example: input/output overlap.

A simple program inputs an array, processes it, and outputs it. In order to achieve overlap of input, output and processing, it adopts a simple buffering scheme.

```
input (lastone);
{process (lastone)//input (thisone)};
while some remain do
begin {input (nextone)//process (thisone)//output (lastone)};
      lastone: = thisone; thisone: = nextone
end;
{process(thisone)//output(lastone)};
output(thisone).
```

Resource constraints

One of the reasons why parallel programs need to interact with each other is because they need to share some limited resource. For example, several parallel programs may need to communicate with a single operator through a single console; or to present a series of lines for output on a single line printer. In such cases it is usually important that no other process be permitted to access the resource while a given process is using it; for example, one process must be permitted to complete its conversation with the operator without interruption from other processes; and an "arbitrary interleaving" of lines from files output by different parallel processes would be wholly unacceptable.

We may thus envisage the action of each parallel process as follows: for part of the time it operates freely in parallel with all the other processes, but occasionally it enters a so-called *critical region* C; and while it is executing C, it must have exclusive use of some resource r. On completion of C, the resource is freed, and may be allocated to any other process (or the same one again) which wishes to enter a critical region with respect to the same resource. Thus the effect of a critical region is to re-establish the necessary degree of serialism into the parallel execution, so that only one of the processes may enter its critical region at any time. Thus critical regions from different processes are executed strictly serially, in an arbitrarily interleaved order.

This reintroduction of "arbitrary interleaving" does not suffer from the disadvantages mentioned earlier, since:

1. The unit of action (=critical region) is defined by the programmer.
2. The necessary synchronization will be relatively infrequent, so that software-assisted implementation is acceptable.
3. The user has no desire or need to control the "interleaving" involved in the use of common resources, since these make no difference whatsoever to the results of his program.

If a parallel statement is to include critical regions with respect to a resource constraint, I suggest the following notation

$$\{\textbf{resource } r; Q_1//Q_2//...//Q_n\}$$

where r is the name of the non-local quantity (e.g. lineprinter, console, etc.) which constitutes the resource.

Then inside the processes $Q_1, Q_2, ..., Q_n$, a critical region C is signalled by the notation

with r do C

The compiler is expected to check that no resource is used or referred to outside its critical regions.

The run-time implementation of this feature will depend on the nature of the basic synchronization facility provided by the hardware of the computer. If we assume that a Boolean semaphore mechanism is "built-in", the implementation is trivial. A resource declaration causes a Boolean semaphore to be created; each critical region in the object code is preceded by seizing this semaphore (the P-operation) and followed by releasing it (the V-operation).

This method of dealing with resource constraints encourages the programmer to ignore the question of which of several outstanding requests for a resource should be granted. In general, the density of utilization of a resource should be sufficiently low that the chance of two requests arriving during the critical period of a third process should be relatively infrequent; for if the resource is a serious bottleneck, it is hardly worth setting up parallelism at all. Thus the relatively simple strategy of granting the resource to the one that has waited longest would seem to be perfectly adequate. Where it is not adequate, the facilities described in the next section can be used to program a more subtle strategy.

Another problem which arises from resource constraints is that of the deadly embrace. Fortunately, a simple compile-time check can guarantee against this danger, if the programmer is willing to observe a simple discipline; when one critical region is nested inside another, the resource involved in the outer region should always have been declared as such *before* that declared in the inner region. This will mean that sometimes resources are acquired rather *before* they are actually needed, just as the nested nature of critical regions may mean that resources are kept longer than needed. Even when this occurs, it may be preferable to the alternatives, which include run-time checks and the generalized banker's algorithm.

The proof of programs which share resources will be virtually identical to that of non-sharing processes. However, the non-local variables which constitute the resource must be regarded for proof purposes as though they were local to each of their regions; since their initial values must be regarded as arbitrary, and their final values are "lost" to the program on exit from the critical region. This shows that from an abstract point of view, the seizure of a common resource could have been replaced simply by a local declaration of the variable required; and the only reason for introducing the constraint is because limitations of hardware availability make it unwise or impossible to provide enough "local" quantities to enable two processes to enter their critical regions together.

Cooperating processes

In order for processes to cooperate on a common task, it is necessary that they communicate or interact through some common item of data. Within each process, any updating of this item must be regarded as a critical region, not interruptable by similar updatings in another processes. However, on exit from a critical region, this data item *retains* its value, which can then be examined and updated by other processes. Thus with the understanding of the retention of the value of the "resource," it appears that no new language feature is required to permit the construction of programs involving cooperating processes.

In order to see how such a facility might be used, it is helpful to draw an analogy. The resource r may be a potentially large structure (building) which starts off in some null condition (empty site), and which is built up to some desired state by performance of a number of operations of different types; $C_1, C_2, \ldots, C_m$ (laying a brick, fitting a window). It does not matter much in what order these operations are performed, so their execution may be delegated to a set of parallel processes (builders), each of which will on occasion invoke one of the permissible operations. Since an operation will update the common resource r, it must be invoked as a critical region. When each process detects that it has fulfilled its task, it terminates. When the tasks of all processes are complete, the structure r will also be complete.

In many cases it will not be permissible to perform the updating operations on r in a wholly random order; for example, the windows cannot be inserted in a building until the frames are installed. In general, a process must be allowed to test the state of r before entering a critical region, to see whether the corresponding operation is permissible or not; and if not, to wait until other processes have brought r into a state in which the operation can be carried out. Let B be a Boolean expression which tests the permissibility of an operation carried out by a critical region C. Then I suggest the notation:

with r **when** B **do** C

to specify that C is not to be carried out until B is true.

Some care must be exercised in the implementation of this new feature. The first action (as before) is to seize the semaphore associated with r. Then the condition B is tested. If it is *false*, then the given process will hang itself up on a queue of processes waiting for r, and must then *release* the semaphore. If B is *true*, the critical region C is executed normally; and on completion the queue of waiting processes (if any) will be inspected, in the order of longest wait.

Then the waiting condition B for each waiting process is re-evaluated. If it is still *false*, the process remains on the queue. If *true*, it executes its critical region C, and then repeats the scan of the queue. Thus it is guaranteed that B will be true on entry to a critical region prefixed by **when** B; it is also guaranteed at all times (outside critical regions) that no process is waiting when its B is *true*; for B can only *become* true as a result of some critical operation by another process, and it is retested after each such operation. The programmer must be encouraged to ensure that this retesting is not too time-consuming.

In order to verify the correctness of a system of cooperating processes, it is necessary to define what is meant by a permissible operation on the resource r. This may usually be accomplished by giving some propositional formula I, specifying some property of r, which must remain true at all times (outside critical regions); such a proposition is known as an *invariant* for the resource. Obviously I must not mention any variable subject to change in any of the parallel processes. Now the condition for harmonious cooperation of the processes is that each process after updating the resource in a critical region must leave the resource in a state which satisfies I; and in return the process may assume that I is true before each entry to one of its own critical regions. Also, each process may assume that its condition B for entry of a critical region will be true before execution of the critical region starts. If all processes of a parallel program cooperate harmoniously, and if I is true before entering the program, then it is known that on completion of the program I will still be true.

EXAMPLE (Bounded Buffer). A process Q_1 produces a stream of values which are consumed by a parallel process Q_2. Since the production and consumption of values proceed at a variable but roughly equal pace, it is profitable to interpose a buffer between the two processes; but since storage is limited the buffer can only contain N values. Our program takes the form (using PASCAL notations):

> B: **record** *inpointer, outpointer, count* : *Integer*;
>   *buffer*:**array** $0..N-1$ **of** T **end**;
> {**resource** B; $Q_1//Q_2$}

We maintain the following variables:

count: the number of values in the buffer.
inpointer: if count $<N$, this is the first empty place in the buffer;
            otherwise it equals outpointer.
outpointer: if count >0 this is the place where the next consumed value
            will be taken from; otherwise it equals inpointer.

The initial values of these variables are all zero.
The critical region inside the producer is as follows:

> **with** B **when** *count* $<N$ **do**
>   **begin** *buffer* [*inpointer*]: $=$ *next value*;
>   *inpointer*: $=$ (*inpointer* $+1$) **mod** N;
>   *count*: $=$ *count* $+1$
>   **end**

The critical region inside the consumer is

> **with** B **when** *count* >0 **do**
>   **begin** *this value*: $=$ *buffer* [*outpointer*];
>   *outpointer*: $=$ (*outpointer* $+1$) **mod** N;
>   *count*: $=$ *count* -1
>   **end**

EXAMPLE (Spaghetti Eaters). Five Benthamite philosophers spend their lives between eating and thinking. To provide them sustenance, a wealthy benefactor has given each of them his own place at a round table, and in the middle is a large and continually replenished bowl of spaghetti, from which they can help themselves when they are seated. The spaghetti is so long and tangled that it requires *two* forks to be conveyed to the mouth; but unfortunately the wealthy benefactor has provided only five forks in all, one between each philosopher's place. The only forks that a philosopher can pick up are those on his immediate right and his immediate left.

It can be seen that no two neighbors can be eating at a time. The problem is to write a program for each philosopher which will ensure that he contributes at all times to the greatest good of the greatest number.

When a philosopher is hungry, he must go to his own place and pick up two forks. Supposing each philosopher adopts the practice of picking up his left fork first. Then there is a grave danger that all philosophers will get hungry simultaneously, and all pick up their left forks; then they would slowly but inexorably starve to death. If the philosophers all put their left forks down on finding the right fork unobtainable, there is still a danger that they will continue to starve while repeatedly picking up and putting down their left forks in perfect unison.

One solution to this vicious circle is to arrange that one of the philosophers always picks up his *right* fork first. Then either he or the philosopher on his left must always have the opportunity of eating. This is basically the solution suggested earlier, of establishing a linear sequence of resources, and ensuring that all claims of more than one resource observe the standard sequence. The period of eating for each philosopher may be regarded as critical a region with respect to his right fork, nested immediately within the critical region for his left fork, for example:

with *fork A* **do with** *fork B* **do** *eat spaghetti*;

but for the last philosopher the nesting is reversed:

with *fork A* **do with** *fork E* **do** *eat spaghetti*.

This solution is a great improvement, and certainly prevents universal starvation; but it still does not ensure optimum utilization of resources, since it is possible for three adjacent philosophers to remain holding one fork each while one of their colleagues is eating; and one would hope that a slightly more intelligent strategy could be devised in such a case to enable the middle one to eat.

The correct solution requires the use of synchronization facilities to guarantee that each philosopher either picks up *no* forks or he picks up *both* his forks. Picking up a single fork must be avoided. Thus we introduce an array:

integer **array** *possforks*$[0:4]$;

possforks$[i]$ takes values 0, 1 or 2 (with initial value 2), and indicates the number of forks available to philosopher i. This array itself is a resource, which can be inspected or updated by any philosopher. Each philosopher on feeling hungry first waits until two forks are available to him, and then reduces the number of forks available to his immediate neighbors, seizes the forks, and eats. On completion, he increases the number of forks available to his neighbors. Thus three successive critical regions are required in philosopher i:

with *possforks* **when** *possforks* $[i] = 2$ **do**
           begin *possforks*$[(i-1)$**mod**$5]: = possforks[(i-1)$**mod**$5] - 1;$
                     possforks$[(i+1)$**mod**$5]: = possforks[(i+1)$**mod**$5] - 1$
          end;
with *fork A* **do with** *fork B* **do** eat spaghetti;
with *possforks* **do**
           begin *possforks*$[(i-1)$**mod**$5]: = possforks[(i-1)$**mod**$5] + 1;$
                     possforks$[(i+1)$**mod**$5]: = possforks[(i+1)$**mod**$5] + 1$
          end.

Additional points

It is hoped that the basic concepts and facilities introduced in the previous sections will be found adequate for most purposes. However, it seems that a few additional simple notations and features may increase their convenience and range of application.

Array remapping

This paper proposes that the introduction of parallelism is meaningful only when no process refers to variables changed by another process (excluding critical regions). However, a compile time check on the observance of this discipline is sometimes too restrictive, since it would prevent two processes operating in parallel on different elements of the same array. A proposal to mitigate this problem is to permit the programmer to declare a local *remapping* of an array, within a block; this splits the array down into disjoint parts, each with its own name; and these separate names can now be updated in separate processes. A notation for expressing the remapping might be:

begin map $a[1:12], b, c \ [0:i]$**on** $X; \dots$ **end,**

which declares a as a local name for an array consisting of the first 12 elements of X, b as the thirteenth element, and c as the next $i+1$ elements. Array X should not be referred to within the block.

EXAMPLE (Quicksort). Using this facility it is possible, if sufficient parallel hardware is available, to sort an array of size N in time proportional to N.

```
procedure Quicksort(A,m,n);
    begin integer i,j,
            partition(A,i,j,m,n);
            begin map B[m:j], X[j+1:i-1], c[i:n] on A;
                {Quicksort(B,m,j)//Quicksort(c,i,n)}
            end
    end Quicksort
```

Resource arrays

The facility for remapping storage gives a simple method by which parallel processes can operate simultaneously on different parts of a data structure. However, it can be used only when it is known in advance which parts are going to be used by each process. Sometimes, the choice of which element or elements of an array are to be seized for a particular critical region can only be made on entry to that region; this means that each element of the array must be regarded as a *separate* resource, which can be allocated and deallocated independently of its neighbors. Such an array may be declared

resource array R,

and the critical regions may take the form:

with $r = R[i]$ do Q,

where r is used within Q as a local name for $R[i]$ and R itself must not be mentioned in Q.

One obvious application of resource arrays is in the real time maintenance of a table of information; and if a random access file is regarded as a form of sparse array, this gives the facility of the PL/1 EXCLUSIVE attribute. Another application is in dealing with a set of homogeneous resources, such as disc handlers, where the programmer does not care *which* handler(s) he is allocated in a particular critical region. As an example of the use of the feature, we suppose that the number of handlers required in each critical region is different, and that as before we wish to avoid the possibility that more than one process should have a partially fulfilled request.

To achieve this, we use a resource *request*, which is allocated to a process during the time that its request is being fulfilled. There is also a *set* resource *free* which contains the numbers of all free handlers; *mine* is a local *set* variable containing the numbers of the handlers allocated to me. A critical region requiring two handlers would be surrounded by small critical regions that carry out the administration, thus:

with *request* **do** {**with** *free* **when** *size (free)* $\geqslant 2$ **do**
                  { *mine*: = *first two of (free)*; *free*: = *free* & ¬ *mine*}};
with *a* = *handler*[*first(mine)*] **do**{**with** *b* = *handler*[*second(mine)*] **do**
               use a and b} ;
with *free* **do** *free*: = *free* v *mine*.

Acknowledgments. It will be obvious to all how much this paper owes to the thought and writings of Professor E. W. Dijkstra, to whom I owe the concepts of the critical region, the semaphore, the deadly embrace and the simple method of its avoidance, and the examples of the bounded buffer and the spaghetti eaters. Less obvious but equally invaluable has been his constant encouragement in the search for a concept to "replace" the semaphore in a high-level programming language, and my ambition of meeting his high standards of rigour and programming style.

I am also deeply indebted to many friends and colleagues who have kindly followed me in many a wild goose chase, and in particular to Maurice Clint, whose advice and experience have been especially valuable.

Appendix

Formal definition

It has been suggested that a specification of proof procedures for proving correctness of programs would be a useful method of defining languages with a certain desired degree of indeterminacy. This appendix applies the formal language definition technique to parallel programming.

Let V_i be the set of variables subject to change in Q_i. Then it is assured:

1. no variable of $V_i - \{r\}$ occurs free in I or in P_j, Q_j, or R_j for $j \neq i$.
2. r is not free in P, R, P_i, Q_i, R_i, except in a critical region with respect to r.

Then letting $r\,inv\,I$ state that I is the invariant for r, we can formulate the following two rules

$$r\ inv\ I$$
$$\frac{B\,\&\,I\,\&\,P\,\{\,C\,\}\,R\,\&\,I}{P\,\{\text{with }r\text{ when }B\text{ do }C\,\}\,R} \qquad\qquad \text{criticality}$$

$$\frac{r\,inv\,I, P_1\{Q_1\}R_1, P_2\{Q_2\}R_2, \ldots, P_n\{Q_n\}R_n}{I\,\&\,P_1\,\&\ldots\&\,P_n\,\{\text{resource }r; Q_1//Q_2//\ldots//Q_n\}\,I\,\&\,R_1\,\&\ldots R_n}$$

$$\text{simultaneity}$$

These two rules cover all cases if we adopt the conventions:

1. **when** *true* can be omitted.
2. If there are no critical regions with respect to r, "**resource** r" can be omitted; and I may then be taken as *true*.

16
Structured Multiprogramming[1]

Per Brinch Hansen
University of Southern California

Abstract   *This paper presents a proposal for structured representation of multiprogramming in a high level language. The notation used explicitly associates a data structure shared by concurrent processes with operations defined on it. This clarifies the meaning of programs and permits a large class of time-dependent errors to be caught at compile time. A combination of critical regions and event variables enables the programmer to control scheduling of resources among competing processes to any degree desired. These concepts are sufficiently safe to use not only within operating systems but also within user programs.*

1 Introduction

The failure of operating systems to provide reliable long-term service can often be explained by excessive emphasis on functional capabilities at the expense of efficient resource utilization, and by inadequate methods of program construction.

In this paper, I examine the latter cause of failure and propose a language notation for structured multiprogramming. The basic idea is to associate data shared by concurrent processes explicitly with operations defined on them. This clarifies the meaning of programs and permits a large class of time-dependent errors to be caught at compile time.

The notation is presented as an extension to the sequential programming language Pascal [Wirth 71c*]. It is used in a textbook to explain operating system principles concisely by algorithms [Brinch Hansen 73a*]. Similar ideas have been explored independently by Hoare. The conditional critical regions proposed in [Hoare 72g*] are a special case of the ones introduced here.

[1]Copyright©1972, Association for Computing Machinery, Inc., reprinted by permission.

2 Disjoint processes

Our starting point is the *concurrent statement*

cobegin $S1; S2; \ldots; Sn$ **coend**

introduced in [Dijkstra 68c*]. This notation indicates that statements $S1, S2, \ldots, Sn$ can be executed concurrently; when all of them are terminated, the following statement in the program (not shown here) is executed.

This restricted form of concurrency simplifies the understanding and verification of programs considerably, compared to unstructured *fork* and *join* primitives.

Algorithm 1 illustrates the use of the concurrent statement to copy records from one sequential file to another.

The variables here are two sequential files, f and g, with records of type T; two buffers, s and t, holding one record each; and a Boolean, *eof*, indicating whether or not the end of the input file has been reached.

ALGORITHM 1. Copying of a sequential file.

```
var f, g; file of T;   s, t: T;   eof: Boolean;
begin
    input(f,s,eof);
    while not eof do
    begin t: = x;
        cobegin
            output(g,t);
            input(f,s,eof)
        coend
    end
end
```

Input and output of single records are handled by two standard procedures. The algorithm inputs a record, copies it from one buffer to another, outputs it, and at the same time, inputs the next record. The copying, output, and input are repeated until the input file is empty.

Now suppose the programmer by mistake expresses the repetition as follows:

```
while not eof do
cobegin
    t: = s;
    output(g,t);
    input(f,s,eof)
coend
```

The copying, output, and input of a record can now be executed concurrently. To simplify the argument, we will only consider cases in which these processes are arbitrarily *interleaved* but *not overlapped* in time. The erroneous concurrent statement can then be executed in six different ways with three possible results: (1) if copying is completed before input and output are initiated, the *correct* record will be output; (2) if output is completed before copying is initiated, the *previous* record will be output again; and (3) if input is completed before copying is initiated, and this in turn completed before output is initiated, the *next* record will be output instead.

This is just for a single record of the output file. If we copy a file of 10,000 records, the program can give of the order of $3^{10,000}$ different results!

The actual sequence of operations in time will depend on the presence of other (unrelated) computations and the (possibly time-dependent) scheduling policy of the installation. It is therefore very unlikely that the programmer will ever observe the same result twice. The only hope of locating the error is to study the program text. This can be very frustrating (if not impossible) when it consists of thousands of lines and one has no clues about where to look.

Multiprogramming is an order of magnitude more hazardous than sequential programming unless we ensure that the results of our computations are *reproducible in spite of errors*. In the previous example, this can easily be checked at compile time.

In the correct version of Algorithm 1, the output and input processes operate on disjoint sets of variables (g,t) and (f,s,eof). They are called *disjoint or noninteracting processes*.

In the erroneous version of the algorithm, the processes are not disjoint: the output process refers to a variable t changed by the copying process; and the latter refers to a variable s changed by the input process.

This can be detected at compile time if the following rule is adopted: a concurrent statement defines disjoint processes $S1, S2, \ldots, Sn$ which can be executed concurrently. This means that a variable vi changed by statement Si cannot be referenced by another statement Sj (where $j \neq i$). In other words, we insist that a variable subject to change by a process must be strictly *private* to that process; but disjoint processes can refer to *shared* variables not changed by any of them.

Throughout this paper, I tacitly assume that sequential statements and assertions made about them only refer to variables which are *accessible* to the statements according to the rules of disjointness and mutual exclusion. The latter rule will be defined in Section 3.

Violations of these rules must be detected at compile time and prevent execution. To enable a compiler to check the disjointness of processes the language must have the following property: it must be possible by simple inspection of a statement to distinguish between its constant and variable parameters. I will not discuss the influence of this requirement on language design beyond mentioning that it makes unrestricted use of *pointers* and *side-effects* unacceptable.

The rule of disjointness is due to Hoare [Hoare 72g*]. It makes the *axiomatic property* of a concurrent statement S very simple: if each component statement Si terminates with a result Ri provided a predicate Pi holds before its execution then the combined effect of S is the following:

$$\{P\}S\{R\}$$

where

$$P \equiv P1 \& P2 \& \ldots \& Pn$$
$$R \equiv R1 \& R2 \& \ldots \& Rn$$

As Hoare puts it: "Each Si makes its contribution to the common goal."

3 Mutual exclusion

The usefulness of disjoint processes has its limits. We will now consider *interacting processes*—concurrent processes which access shared variables.

A *shared variable* v of type T is declared as follows:

var v: **shared** T

Concurrent processes can only refer to and change a shared variable inside a structured statement called a *critical region*

region v **do** S.

This notation associates a statement S with a shared variable v.

Critical regions referring to the same variable exclude each other in time. They can be arbitarily interleaved in time. The idea of progressing towards a final result (as in a concurrent statement) is therefore meaningless. All one can expect is that each critical region leaves certain relationships among the components of a shared variable v unchanged. These relationships can be defined by an assertion I about v which must be true after initialization of v and before and after each subsequent critical region associated with v. Such an assertion is called an *invariant*.

When a process enters a critical region to execute a statement S, a predicate P holds for the variables accessible to the process outside the critical region and an invariant I holds for the shared variable v accessible inside the critical region. After the completion of S, a result R holds for the former variables and invariant I has been maintained. So a critical region has the following axiomatic property:

$\{P\}$
region v **do** $\{P\&I\}S\{R\&I\}$
$\{R\}$

4 Process communication

Mutual exclusion of operations on shared variables makes it possible to make meaningful statements about the effect of concurrent computations. But when processes cooperate on a common task they must also be able to wait until certain conditions have been satisfied by other processes.

For this purpose I introduce a synchronizing primitive, **await**, which delays a process until the components of a shared variable v satisfy a condition B:

region v **do**
begin...**await** B; ...**end**

The await primitive must be textually enclosed by a critical region. If critical regions are nested, the synchronizing condition B is associated with the innermost enclosing region.

The await primitive can be used to define *conditional critical regions* of the type proposed in [Hoare 72g*]:

"*Consumer*"   "*Producer*"
region v **do**   **region** v **do** $S2$
begin await B; $S1$ **end**

The implementation of critical regions and await primitives is illustrated in Figure 1. When a process, such as the consumer above, wishes to enter a critical region, it enters a *main queue* Qv associated with a shared variable v. After entering its critical region, the consumer inspects the shared variable to determine whether it satisfies a condition B. In that case, the consumer completes its critical region by executing a statement $S1$;

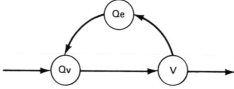

Figure 1   Scheduling of conditional critical regions V by means of process queues Qv and Qe.

otherwise, the process leaves its critical region *temporarily* and joins an *event queue Qe* associated with the shared variable.

All processes waiting for one condition or another on variable v enter the same event queue. When another process (here called the producer) changes v by a statement $S2$ inside a critical region, it is possible that one or more of the conditions expected by processes in the event queue will be satisfied. So, after completion of a critical region, all processes in the event queue Qe are transferred to the main queue Qv to enable them to reenter their critical regions and inspect the shared variable v again.

It is possible that a *consumer* will be transferered in vain between Qv and Qe several times before its condition B holds. But this can only occur as frequently as *producers* change the shared variable. This controlled amount of *busy waiting* is the price we pay for the conceptual simplicity achieved by using arbitrary Boolean expressions as synchronizing conditions.

The desired *invariant I* for the shared variable v must be satisfied before an **await** primitive is executed. When the waiting cycle terminates, the *assertion B & I* holds.

As an example, consider the following resource allocation problem: two kinds of concurrent processes, called readers and writers, share a single resource. The readers can use the resource simultaneously, but the writers must have exclusive access to it. When a writer is ready to use the resource, it should be enabled to do so as soon as possible.

This problem is solved by Algorithm 2. Here variable v is a record consisting of two integer components defining the number of *readers* currently using the resource and the number of *writers* currently waiting for or using the resource. Both *readers* and *writers* are initialized to zero.

ALGORITHM 2. Resource sharing by readers and writers.

```
var v: shared record readers, writers: integer end;
    w: shared Boolean;
"Reader"                        "Writer"
region v do                     region v do
begin                           begin
  await writers = 0;              writers: = writers + 1;
  readers: = readers + 1          await readers = 0
end;                            end;
read;                           region w do write;
region v do                     region v do
readers: = readers - 1          writers: = writers - 1
```

Mutual exclusion of readers and writers is achieved by letting readers wait until the number of writers is zero, and vice versa. Mutual exclusion of individual writers is ensured by the critical region on the Boolean w.

The priority rule is obeyed by increasing the number of writers by one as soon as one of them wishes to use the resource. This will delay subsequent reader requests until all pending writer requests are satisfied.

A correctness proof of Algorithm 2 is outlined in [Brinch Hansen 72b*]. In this paper I also point out the superiority of conditional critical regions over *semaphores* [Dijkstra 68c*]. Compared to the original solution to the problem [Parnas 71a*], Algorithm 2 demonstrates the conceptual advantage of a structured notation.[1]

The conceptual simplicity of critical regions is achieved by ignoring details of scheduling: the programmer is unaware of the sequence in which waiting processes enter critical regions and access shared resources. This assumption is justified for processes which are so *loosely connected* that simultaneous requests for the same resources rarely occur.

But in most computer installations *resources* are *heavily used* by a large group of users. In this situation, an operating system must be able to *control the scheduling of resources explicitly* among competing processes.

To do this a programmer must be able to associate an arbitrary number of event queues with a shared variable and control the transfers of processes to and from them. In general, I would therefore replace the previous proposal for conditional delays with the following one:

The declaration

var e: **event** v

associates an event queue e with a shared variable v.

A process can leave a critical region associated with v and join the event queue e by executing the standard procedure

await(e)

Another process can enable all processes in the event queue e to reenter their critical regions by executing the standard procedure

cause(e)

A consumer/producer relationship must now be expressed as follows:

"*Consumer*"	"*Producer*"
region v **do**	**region** v **do**
begin	**begin**
while not B **do** *await*(e);	*S2*;
S1	*cause*(e)
end	**end**

[1] The original solution includes the following refinement: when a writer decides to make a request at most one more reader can complete a request ahead of it. This can be ensured by surrounding the reader request in Algorithm 2 with an additional critical region associated with a shared Boolean r.

Although less elegant than the previous notation, the present one still clearly shows that the consumer is waiting for condition *B* to hold. And we can now control process scheduling to any degree desired.

To simplify explicit scheduling, I suggest that processes reentering their critical regions from event queues take priority over processes entering critical regions directly through a main queue (see Figure 1). If the scheduling rule is completely unknown to the programmer as before, additional variables are required to ensure that resources granted to waiting processes remain available to them until they reenter their critical regions.

Algorithm 3 is a simple example of completely controlled resource allocation. A number of processes share a pool of equivalent resources. Processes and resources are identified by indices of type *P* and *R* respectively. When resources are *available*, a process can *acquire* one immediately; otherwise, it must enter a request in a data structure of type **set of** *P* and wait until a resource is *granted* to it. It is assumed that the program controls the entry and removal of set elements completely.

ALGORITHM 3. Scheduling of heavily used resources.

```
var v: shared record
              available: set of R;
                     requests: set of P;
                     grant: array P of event v
              end;
procedure reserve(process: P; var resource: R);
region v do
begin while empty(available) do
   begin enter(process, requests);
     await(grant[process])
   end;
   remove(resource, available)
end;
procedure release(resource: R);
var process: P;
region v do
begin enter(resource, available);
   if not empty(requests) then
   begin remove(process, requests);
     cause(grant[process])
   end
end.
```

5 Conclusion

I have presented structured multiprogramming concepts that have simple axiomatic properties and permit extensive compile time checking and generation of efficient machine code.

The essential properties of these concepts are:

1. A distinction between disjoint and interacting processes;
2. An association of shared data with operations defined on them;
3. Mutual exclusion of these operations in time;
4. Synchronizing primitives which permit partial or complete control of process scheduling.

These are precisely the concepts needed to implement *monitor procedures* such as the ones described in [Brinch Hansen 70*]. They appear to be sufficiently safe to use not only within operating systems but also within user programs to control local resources.

17
Monitors: An Operating System Structuring Concept[1]

C. A. R. Hoare
University of Oxford

Abstract *This paper develops Brinch Hansen's concept of a monitor as a method of structuring an operating system. It introduces a form of synchronization, describes a possible method of implementation in terms of semaphores and gives a suitable proof rule. Illustrative examples include a single resource scheduler, a bounded buffer, an alarm clock, a buffer pool, a disk head optimizer, and a version of the problem of readers and writers.*

1 Introduction

A primary aim of an operating system is to share a computer installation among many programs making unpredictable demands upon its resources. A primary task of its designer is therefore to construct resource allocation (or scheduling) algorithms for resources of various kinds (main store, drum store, magnetic tape handlers, consoles, etc.). In order to simplify his task, he should try to construct separate schedulers for each class of resource. Each scheduler will consist of a certain amount of local administrative data, together with some procedures and functions which are called by programs wishing to acquire and release resources. Such a collection of associated data and procedures is known as a *monitor*; and a suitable notation can be based on the *class* notation of SIMULA67 [Dahl 72b*]:

> *monitorname*: **monitor**
>   **begin**...declarations of data local to the monitor;
>   **procedure** *procname* (...formal parameters...);
>   **begin**...procedure body...**end**;
>   ...declarations of other procedures local to the monitor;
>   ...initialization of local data of the monitor...
>   **end**

Note that the procedure bodies may have local data, in the normal way.

In order to call a procedure of a monitor, it is necessary to give the name of the monitor as well as the name of the desired procedure, separating them by a dot:

monitorname.procname(...actual parameters...)

In an operating system it is sometimes desirable to declare several monitors with identical structure and behavior, for example to schedule two similar resources. In such cases, the declaration shown above will be preceded by the word **class**, and the separate monitors will be declared to belong to this class:

monitor 1, *monitor* 2: *classname.*

Thus the structure of a class of monitors is identical to that described for a data representation in [Hoare 72f*], except for the addition of the basic word *monitor*. The word *shared* is used for the same purpose in [Brinch Hansen 73a*].

The procedures of a monitor are common to all running programs, in the sense that any program may at any time attempt to call such a procedure. However, it is essential that only one program at a time actually succeed in entering a monitor procedure, and any subsequent call must be held up until the previous call has been completed. Otherwise, if two procedure bodies were in simultaneous execution, the effects on the local variables of the monitor could be chaotic. The procedures local to a monitor should not access any nonlocal variables other than those local to the same monitor, and these variables of the monitor should be inaccessible from outside the monitor. If these restrictions are imposed, it is possible to guarantee against certain of the more obscure forms of time-dependent coding error; and this guarantee could be underwritten by a visual scan of the text of the program, which could readily be automated in a compiler.

Any dynamic resource allocator will sometimes need to delay a program wishing to acquire a resource which is not currently available, and to resume that program after some other program has released the resource required. We therefore need: a "wait" operation, issued from inside a procedure of the monitor, which causes the calling program to be delayed; and a "signal" operation, also issued from inside a procedure of the same monitor, which causes exactly one of the waiting programs to be resumed immediately. If there are no waiting programs, the signal has no effect. In order to enable other programs to release resources during a wait, a wait operation must relinquish the exclusion which would otherwise prevent entry to the releasing procedure. However, we decree that a signal operation be followed immediately by resumption of a waiting program, without possibility of an intervening procedure call from yet a third program. It is only in this way that a waiting program has an absolute guarantee that it can acquire the resource just released by the signalling program without any danger that a third program will interpose a monitor entry and seize the resource instead.

In many cases, there may be more than one reason for waiting, and these need to be distinguished by both the waiting and the signalling operation. We therefore introduce a new type of "variable" known as a "condition"; and the writer of a monitor should declare a variable of type condition for each reason why a program might have to wait. Then the wait and signal operations should be preceded by the name of the relevant condition variable, separated from it by a dot:

condvariable.wait;
condvariable.signal

Note that a condition "variable" is neither true nor false; indeed, it does not have any stored value accessible to the program. In practice, a condition variable will be represented by an (initially empty) queue of processes which are currently waiting on the condition; but this queue is invisible both to waiters and signallers. This design of the condition variable has been deliberately kept as primitive and rudimentary as possible, so that it may be implemented efficiently and used flexibly to achieve a wide variety of effects. There is a great temptation to introduce a more complex synchronization primitive, which may be easier to use for many purposes. We shall resist this temptation for a while.

As the simplest example of a monitor, we will design a scheduling algorithm for a single resource, which is dynamically acquired and released by an unknown number of customer processes by calls on procedures

procedure *acquire*;
procedure *release*

A variable[1]

busy : *Boolean*

determines whether or not the resource is in use. If an attempt is made to acquire the resource when it is busy, the attempting program must be delayed by waiting on a variable

nonbusy : *condition*

which is signalled by the next subsequent release. The initial value of busy is false. These design decisions lead to the following code for the monitor:

single resource : **monitor**
begin *busy* : *Boolean*;
   nonbusy : *condition*;
  procedure *acquire*;
  begin if *busy* **then** *nonbusy.wait*;
     busy : = *true*
  end;

---

[1]As in Pascal, a variable declaration is of the form: ⟨*variable identifier*⟩ : ⟨*type*⟩;

procedure *release*;
  begin *busy* : = *false*;
      nonbusy.signal
  end;
  busy : = *false*; **comment** *initial value*;
end *single resource*Notes

Notes

1. In designing a monitor, it seems natural to design the procedure headings, the data, the conditions, and the procedure bodies, in that order. All subsequent examples will be designed in this way.

2. The acquire procedure does not have to retest that busy has gone false when it resumes after its wait, since the release procedure has guaranteed that this is so; and as mentioned before, no other program can intervene between the signal and the continuation of exactly one waiting program.

3. If more than one program is waiting on a condition, we postulate that the signal operation will reactivate the longest waiting program. This gives a simple neutral queuing discipline which ensures that every waiting program will eventually get its turn.

4. The single resource monitor simulates a Boolean semaphore [Dijkstra 68c*] with *acquire* and *release* used for *P* and *V* respectively. This is a simple proof that the monitor/condition concepts are not in principle less powerful than semaphores, and that they can be used for all the same purposes.

2 Interpretation

Having proved that semaphores can be implemented by a monitor, the next task is to prove that monitors can be implemented by semaphores.

Obviously, we shall require for each monitor a Boolean semaphore *mutex* to ensure that the bodies of the local procedures exclude each other. The semaphore is initialized to 1; a *P(mutex)* must be executed on entry to each local procedure, and a *V(mutex)* must usually be executed on exit from it.

When a process signals a condition on which another process is waiting, the signalling process must wait until the resumed process permits it to proceed. We therefore introduce for each monitor a second semaphore *urgent* (initialized to 0), on which signalling processes suspend themselves by the operation *P(urgent)*. Before releasing exclusion, each process must test whether any other process is waiting on *urgent*, and if so, must release it instead by a *V(urgent)* instruction. We therefore need to count the number of processes waiting on *urgent*, in an integer *urgentcount* (initially zero). Thus each exit from a procedure of a monitor should be coded:

if *urgentcount* > 0 **then** $V(urgent)$ **else** $V(mutex)$

Finally, for each condition local to the monitor, we introduce a semaphore *condsem* (initialized to 0), on which a process desiring to wait suspends itself by a $P(condsem)$ operation. Since a process signalling this condition needs to know whether anybody is waiting, we also need a count of the number of waiting processes held in an integer variable *condcount* (initially 0). The operation *cond.wait* may now be implemented as follows (recall that a waiting program must release exclusion before suspending itself):

condcount : = *condcount* + 1;
if *urgentcount* > 0 **then** $V(urgent)$ **else** $V(mutex)$;
$P(condsem)$;
comment This will always wait;
condcount : = *condcount* − 1

The signal operation may be coded:

urgentcount : = *urgentcount* + 1;
if *condcount* > 0 **then** $\{ V(condsem); P(urgent) \}$;
urgentcount : = *urgentcount* − 1

In this implementation, possession of the monitor is regarded as a privilege which is explicitly passed from one process to another. Only when no one further wants the privilege is *mutex* finally released.

This solution is not intended to correspond to recommended "style" in the use of semaphores. The concept of a condition-variable is intended as a substitute for semaphores, and has its own style of usage, in the same way that while-loops or coroutines are intended as a substitute for jumps.

In many cases, the generality of this solution is unnecessary, and a significant improvement in efficiency is possible.

1.   When a procedure body in a monitor contains no wait or signal, exit from the body can be coded by a simple $V(mutex)$, since *urgentcount* cannot have changed during the execution of the body.

2.   If a *cond.signal* is the last operation of a procedure body, it can be combined with monitor exit as follows:

if *condcount* > 0 **then** $V(condsem)$
else if *urgentcount* > 0 **then** V(urgent)
          else $V(mutex)$

3.   If there is no other wait or signal in the procedure body, the second line shown above can also be omitted.

4.   If *every* signal occurs as the last operation of its procedure body, the variables *urgentcount* and *urgent* can be omitted, together with all operations upon them. This is such a simplification that O-J. Dahl suggests that signals should always be the last operation of a monitor procedure; in fact, this restriction is a very natural one, which has been unwittingly observed in all examples of this paper.

Significant improvements in efficiency may also be obtained by avoiding the use of semaphores, and by implementing conditions directly in hardware, or at the lowest and most uninterruptible level of software (e.g. supervisor mode). In this case, the following optimizations are possible.

1.   *urgentcount* and *condcount* can be abolished, since the fact that someone is waiting can be established by examining the representation of the semaphore, which cannot change surreptitiously within noninterruptible mode.

2.   Many monitors are very short and contain no calls to other monitors. Such monitors can be executed wholly in noninterruptible mode, using, as it were, the common exclusion mechanism provided by hardware. This will often involve *less* time in noninterruptible mode than the establishment of separate exclusion for each monitor.

I am grateful to J. Bezivin, J. Horning, and R. M. McKeag for assisting in the discovery of this algorithm.

3 Proof rules

The analogy between a monitor and a data representation has been noted in the introduction. The mutual exclusion on the code of a monitor ensures that procedure calls follow each other in time, just as they do in sequential programming; and the same restrictions are placed on access to nonlocal data. These are the reasons why the same proof rules can be applied to monitors as to data representations.

As with a data representation, the programmer may associate an invariant $\mathcal{I}$ with the local data of a monitor, to describe some condition which will be true of this data before and after every procedure call. $\mathcal{I}$ must also be made true after initialization of the data, and before *every* wait instruction; otherwise the next following procedure call will not find the local data in a state which it expects.

With each condition variable b the programmer may associate an assertion B which describes the condition under which a program waiting on b wishes to be resumed. Since other programs may invoke a monitor procedure during a wait, a waiting program must ensure that the invariant

$\mathcal{I}$ for the monitor is true beforehand. This gives the proof rule for waits:

$$\mathcal{I}\{b.wait\}\ \mathcal{I}\&B$$

Since a signal can cause immediate resumption of a waiting program, the conditions $\mathcal{I}\&B$ which are expected by that program must be made true before the signal; and since B may be made false again by the resumed program, only $\mathcal{I}$ may be assumed true afterwards. Thus the proof rule for a signal is:

$$\mathcal{I}\&B\{b.signal\}\mathcal{I}$$

This exhibits a pleasing symmetry with the rule for waiting.

The introduction of condition variables makes it possible to write monitors subject to the risk of deadly embrace [Dijkstra 68c*]. It is the responsibility of the programmer to avoid this risk and other scheduling disasters (thrashing, indefinitely repeated overtaking, etc. [Dijkstra 72a*]). Assertion-oriented proof methods cannot prove absence of such risks; perhaps it is better to use less formal methods for such proofs.

Finally, in many cases an operating system monitor constructs some "virtual" resource which is used in place of actual resources by its "customer" programs. This virtual resource is an abstraction from the set of local variables of the monitor. The program prover should therefore define this abstraction in terms of its concrete representation, and then express the intended effect of each of the procedure bodies in terms of the abstraction. This proof method is described in detail in [Hoare 72f*].

4 Example: bounded buffer

A bounded buffer is a concrete representation of the abstract idea of a sequence of portions. The sequence is accessible to two programs running in parallel: the first of these (the producer) updates the sequence by appending a new portion x at the end; and the second (the consumer) updates it by removing the first portion. The initial value of the sequence is empty. We thus require two operations. Operation

$$append(x:portion)$$

should be equivalent to the abstract operation

$$sequence := sequence \cap \langle x \rangle$$

where $\langle x \rangle$ is the sequence whose only item is x and $\cap$ denotes concatenation of two sequences. Operation

$$remove(\textbf{result } x:portion)$$

should be equivalent to the abstract operations

$$x := first(sequence); \ sequence := rest(sequence)$$

where *first* selects the first item of a sequence and *rest* denotes the sequence with its first item removed. Obviously, if the sequence is empty, *first* is undefined; and in this case we want to ensure that the consumer waits until the producer has made the sequence nonempty.

We shall assume that the amount of time taken to produce a portion or consume it is large in comparison with the time taken to append or remove it from the sequence. We may therefore be justified in making a design in which producer and consumer can both update the sequence, but not simultaneously.

The sequence is represented by an array:

$$buffer : \textbf{array } 0..N-1 \textbf{ of } portion$$

and two variables:

$$lastpointer : 0..N-1 \tag{1}$$

which points to the buffer position into which the next append operation will put a new item, and

$$count : 0..N \tag{2}$$

which always holds the length of the sequence (initially 0).

We define the function

$$seq \ (b,l,c) =_{df} \textbf{if } c=0 \textbf{ then } empty$$
$$\textbf{else } seq(b,l\ominus 1,c-1)\cap\langle b[l\ominus 1]\rangle$$

where the circled operations are taken modulo N. Note that if $c\neq 0$,

$$first(seq(b,l,c))=b[l\ominus c]$$

and

$$rest(seq(b,l,c))=seq(b,l,c-1)$$

The definition of the abstract sequence in terms of its concrete representation may now be given:

$$sequence =_{df} seq(buffer, \ lastpointer, \ count)$$

Less formally, this may be written

$$sequence =_{df} \langle buffer[lastpointer\ominus count],$$
$$buffer[lastpointer\ominus count\oplus 1],$$
$$...,$$
$$buffer[lastpointer\ominus 1]\rangle$$

Another way of conveying this information would be by an example and a picture, which would be even less formal.

The invariant for the monitor is:

$$0 \leqslant count \leqslant N \ \& \ 0 \leqslant lastpointer \leqslant N - 1$$

There are two reasons for waiting, which must be represented by condition variables:

$$nonempty : condition$$

means that the count is greater than 0, and

$$nonfull : condition$$

means that the count is less than N.

With this constructive approach to the design [Dijkstra 68e*], it is relatively easy to code the monitor without error.

```
bounded buffer : monitor
  begin buffer : array 0..N − 1 of portion;
        lastpointer : 0..N − 1;
        count : 0..N;
        nonempty, nonfull : condition;
    procedure append(x : portion);
      begin if count = N then nonfull.wait;
            note 0 ⩽ count < N;
            buffer[lastpointer] : = x;
            lastpointer : = lastpointer ⊕ 1;
            count : = count + 1;
            nonempty.signal
      end append;
    procedure remove(result x : portion);
      begin if count = 0 then nonempty.wait;
            note 0 < count ⩽ N;
            x : = buffer[lastpointer ⊖ count];
            nonfull.signal
      end remove;
        count : = 0; lastpointer : = 0
  end bounded buffer
```

A formal proof of the correctness of this monitor with respect to the stated abstraction and invariant can be given if desired by techniques described in [Hoare 72f*]. However, these techniques seem not capable of dealing with subsequent examples of this paper.

Single-buffered input and output may be regarded as a special case of the bounded buffer with $N = 1$. In this case, the array can be replaced by a single variable, the *lastpointer* is redundant, and we get:

```
iostream : monitor
begin buffer : portion;
      count : 0..1;
      nonempty, nonfull : condition;
   procedure append(x : portion);
      begin if count = 1 then nonfull.wait;
      buffer : = x;
      count : = 1;
      nonempty.signal
      end append;
   procedure remove(result x : portion);
      begin if count = 0 then nonempty.wait;
      x : = buffer;
      count : = 0;
      nonfull.signal
      end remove;
   count : = 0
end iostream
```

If physical output is carried out by a separate special purpose channel, then the interrupt from the channel should simulate a call of *iostream. remove(x)*; and similarly for physical input, simulating a call of *iostream. append(x)*.

5 Scheduled waits

Up to this point, we have assumed that when more than one program is waiting for the same condition, a signal will cause the longest waiting program to be resumed. This is a good simple scheduling strategy, which precludes indefinite overtaking of a waiting process.

However, in the design of an operating system, there are many cases when such simple scheduling on the basis of first-come-first-served is not adequate. In order to give a closer control over scheduling strategy, we introduce a further feature of a conditional wait, which makes it possible to specify as a parameter of the wait some indication of the priority of the waiting program, e.g.:

$$busy.wait(p)$$

When the condition is signalled, it is the program that specified the lowest value of p that is resumed. In using this facility, the designer of a monitor must take care to avoid the risk of indefinite overtaking; and often it is advisable to make priority a nondecreasing function of the time at which the wait commences.

This introduction of a "scheduled wait" concedes to the temptation to make the condition concept more elaborate. The main justifications are:

1. It has no effect whatsoever on the *logic* of a program, or on the formal proof rules. Any program which works without a scheduled wait will work with it, but possibly with better timing characteristics.

2. The automatic ordering of the queue of waiting processes is a simple fast scheduling technique, except when the queue is exceptionally long—and when it is, central processor time is not the major bottleneck.

3. The maximum amount of storage required is one word per process. Without such a built-in scheduling method, each monitor may have to allocate storage proportional to the number of its customers; the alternative of dynamic storage allocation in small chunks is unattractive at the low level of an operating system where monitors are found.

I shall yield to one further temptation, to introduce a Boolean function of conditions:

$$condname.queue$$

which yields the value true if anyone is waiting on *condname* and false otherwise. This can obviously be easily implemented by a couple of instructions, and affords valuable information which could otherwise be obtained only at the expense of extra storage, time, and trouble.

A trivially simple example is an *alarmclock* monitor, which enables a calling program to delay itself for a stated number n of time-units, or *ticks*. There are two entries:

procedure *wakeme*(n : *integer*);

procedure *tick*

The second of these is invoked by hardware (e.g. an interrupt) at regular intervals, say ten times per second. Local variables are

$$now : integer$$

which records the current time (initially zero) and

$$wakeup : condition$$

on which sleeping programs wait. But the *alarmsetting* at which these programs will be aroused is known at the time when they start the wait; and this can be used to determine the correct sequence of waking up.

alarmclock : **monitor**
begin *now* : *integer*;
   wakeup : *condition*;
  procedure *wakeme*(n : *integer*);
    begin *alarmsetting* : *integer*;
     alarmsetting : = *now* + n;
     while *now* < *alarmsetting* **do** *wakeup.wait*(*alarmsetting*);
     wakeup.signal;
     comment In case the next process is due to wake up at the
     same time;
    end;

```
procedure tick;
    begin now : = now + 1;
      wakeup.signal
    end;
  now : = 0
end alarmclock
```

In the program given above, the next candidate for wakening is actually woken at every tick of the clock. This will not matter if the frequency of ticking is low enough, and the overhead of an accepted signal is not too high.

I am grateful to A. Ballard and J. Horning for posing this problem.

6 Further examples

In proposing a new feature for a high level language it is very difficult to make a convincing case that the feature will be both easy to use efficiently and easy to implement efficiently. Quality of implementation can be proved by a single good example, but ease and efficiency of use require a great number of realistic examples; otherwise it can appear that the new feature has been specially designed to suit the examples, or vice versa. This section contains a number of additional examples of solutions of familiar problems. Further examples may be found in [Hoare 73c*].

6.1 Buffer allocation

The bounded buffer described in Section 4 was designed to be suitable only for sequences with small portions, for example, message queues. If the buffers contain high volume information (for example, files for pseudo offline input and output), the bounded buffer may still be used to store the *addresses* of the buffers which are being used to hold the information. In this way, the producer can be filling one buffer while the consumer is emptying another buffer of the same sequence. But this requires an allocator for dynamic acquisition and relinquishment of *buffer addresses*. These may be declared as a type

$$\textbf{type } bufferaddress = 1..B;$$

where B is the number of buffers available for allocation.

The buffer allocator has two entries:

$$\textbf{procedure } acquire \ (\textbf{result } b : bufferaddress)$$

which delivers a free *bufferaddress* b; and

$$\textbf{procedure } release(b : bufferaddress)$$

which returns a *bufferaddress* when it is no longer required. In order to keep a record of free buffer addresses the monitor will need:

$$freepool : \textbf{powerset } bufferaddress$$

which uses the Pascal powerset facility to define a variable whose values range over all sets of *buffer addresses*, from the empty set to the set containing all *buffer addresses*. It should be implemented as a *bitmap* of *B* consecutive bits, where the *i*th bit is 1 if and only if *i* is in the set. There is only one condition variable needed:

$$nonempty : condition$$

which means that *freepool* $\neq$ *empty*. The code for the allocator is:

```
buffer allocator : monitor
begin freepool : powerset bufferaddress;
    nonempty : condition;
  procedure acquire (result b : bufferaddress);
    begin if freepool = empty then nonempty.wait;
      b : = first(freepool);
      comment Any one would do;
      freepool : = freepool − {b};
      comment Set subtraction;
    end acquire;
  procedure release(b : bufferaddress);
    begin freepool : = freepool − {b};
      nonempty.signal
    end release;
  freepool : = all buffer addresses
end buffer allocator
```

The action of a producer and consumer may be summarized:

```
producer: begin b : bufferaddress; ...
            while not finished do
              begin bufferallocator.acquire(b);
                ...fill buffer b ...;
                bounded buffer.append(b)
              end; ...
          end producer;


consumer: begin b : bufferaddress; ...
            while not finished do
              begin bounded buffer.remove(b);
                ...empty buffer b ...;
                buffer allocator.release(b)
              end; ...
          end consumer
```

This buffer allocator would appear to be usable to share the buffers among several streams, each with its own producer and its own consumer, and its own instance of a bounded buffer monitor. Unfortunately, when the streams operate at widely varying speeds, and when the freepool is empty, the scheduling algorithm can exhibit persistent undesirable behavior. If two producers are competing for each buffer as it becomes free, a first-come-first-served discipline of allocation will ensure (apparently · fairly) that each gets alternate buffers; and they will consequently begin to produce at equal speeds. But if one consumer is a 1000 lines/min printer and the other is a 10 lines/min teletype, the faster consumer will be eventually reduced to the speed of the slower, since it cannot forever go faster than its producer. At this stage nearly all buffers will belong to the slower stream, so the situation could take a long time to clear.

A solution to this is to use a scheduled wait, to ensure that in heavy load conditions the available buffers will be shared reasonably fairly between the streams that are competing for them. Of course, inactive streams need not be considered, and streams for which the consumer is currently faster than the producer will never ask for more than two buffers anyway. In order to achieve fairness in allocation, it is sufficient to allocate a newly freed buffer to that one among the competing producers whose stream currently owns fewest buffers. Thus the system will seek a point as far away from the undesirable extreme as possible.

For this reason, the entries to the allocator should indicate for what stream the buffer is to be (or has been) used, and the allocator must keep a count of the current allocation to each stream in an array:

$$count : \textbf{array } stream \textbf{ of } integer$$

The new version of the allocator is:

```
bufferallocator : monitor
    begin freepool : powerset bufferaddress;
        nonempty : condition;
        count : array stream of integer;
    procedure acquire(result b : bufferaddress; s : stream);
        begin if freepool = empty then nonempty.wait(count[s]);
        count[s] : = count[s] + 1;
        b : = first(freepool);
        freepool : = freepool − {b}
        end acquire;
    procedure release(b : bufferaddress; s : stream)
        begin count[s] : = count[s] − 1;
        freepool : = freepool − {b};
        nonempty.signal
        end;
    freepool : = all buffer addresses;
    for s : stream do count[s] : = 0
    end bufferallocator
```

Of course, if a consumer stops altogether, perhaps owing to mechanical failure, the producer must also be halted before it has acquired too many buffers, even if no one else currently wants them. This can perhaps be most easily accomplished by appropriately fixing the size of the bounded buffer for that stream and/or by ensuring that at least two buffers are reserved for each stream, even when inactive. It is an interesting comment on dynamic resource allocation that, as soon as resources are heavily loaded, the system must be designed to fall back toward a more static regime.

I am grateful to E. W. Dijkstra for pointing out this problem and its solution [Dijkstra 72e*].

6.2 Disk head scheduler

On a moving head disk, the time taken to move the heads increases monotonically with the distance traveled. If several programs wish to move the heads, the average waiting time can be reduced by selecting first, the program which wishes to move them the shortest distance. But unfortunately this policy is subject to an instability, since a program wishing to access a cylinder at one edge of the disk can be indefinitely overtaken by programs operating at the other edge or the middle.

A solution to this is to minimize the frequency of change of direction of movement of the heads. At any time, the heads are kept moving in a given direction, and they service the program requesting the nearest cylinder in that direction. If there is no such request, the direction changes, and the heads make another sweep across the surface of the disk. This may be called the "elevator" algorithm, since it simulates the behavior of a lift in a multi-story building.

There are two entries to a disk head scheduler:

$$request(dest : cylinder)$$

where

type $cylinder = 0..cylmax$

which is entered by a program just *before* issuing the instruction to move the heads to cylinder *dest*, and

release

which is entered by a program when it has made all the transfers it needs on the current cylinder.

The local data of the monitor must include a record of the current headposition, *headpos*, the current direction of *sweep*, and whether the disk is *busy*:

headpos : *cylinder*;
direction : (*up, down*);
busy : *Boolean*

We need two conditions, one for requests waiting for an *upsweep* and the other for requests waiting for a *downsweep*:

$$upsweep, downsweep : condition$$

```
dischead : monitor
begin headpos : cylinder;
    direction : (up, down);
    busy : Boolean;
    upsweep,downsweep : condition;
  procedure request(dest : cylinder);
    begin if busy then
      if headpos < dest ∨ headpos = dest & direction = up
        then upsweep.wait(dest)
        else downsweep.wait(cylmax-dest)};
      busy : = true; headpos : = dest
    end request;
  procedure release;
    begin busy : = false;
      if direction = up then
        {if upsweep.queue then upsweep.signal
                          else {direction : = down;
                                downsweep.signal}}
        else if downsweep.queue then downsweep.signal
                          else {direction : = up;
                                upsweep.signal}
    end release;
    headpos : = 0; direction : = up; busy : = false
end dischead
```

6.3 Readers and writers

As a more significant example, we take a problem which arises in on-line real-time applications such as airspace control. Suppose that each aircraft is represented by a record, and that this record is kept up to date by a number of "writer" processes and accessed by a number of "reader" processes. Any number of "reader" processes may simultaneously access the same record, but obviously any process which is updating (writing) the individual components of the record must have exclusive access to it, or chaos will ensue. Thus we need a class of monitors; an instance of this class local to each individual aircraft record will enforce the required discipline for that record. If there are many aircraft, there is a strong motivation for minimizing local data of the monitor; and if each read or write operation is brief, we should also minimize the time taken by each monitor entry.

When many readers are interested in a single aircraft record, there is a danger that a writer will be indefinitely prevented from keeping that record up to date. We therefore decide that a new reader should not be permitted to start if there is a writer waiting. Similarly, to avoid the danger of indefinite exclusion of readers, all readers waiting at the end of a write should have priority over the next writer. Note that this is a very different scheduling rule from that propounded in [Parnas 71a*], and does not seem to require such subtlety in implementation. Nevertheless, it may be more suited to this kind of application, where it is better to read stale information than to wait indefinitely!

The monitor obviously requires four local procedures:

startread	entered by reader who wishes to read.
endread	entered by reader who has finished reading.
startwrite	entered by writer who wishes to write.
endwrite	entered by writer who has finished writing.

We need to keep a count of the number of users who are reading, so that the last reader to finish will know this fact:

$$readercount : integer$$

We also need a *Boolean* to indicate that someone is actually writing:

$$busy : Boolean$$

We introduce separate conditions for readers and writers to wait on:

$$OKtoread, OKtowrite : condition$$

The following annotation is relevant:

$OKtoread \equiv \neg busy$
$OKtowrite \equiv \neg busy \ \& \ readercount = 0$
$invariant: \ busy \Rightarrow readercount = 0$

```
class readers and writers : monitor
  begin readercount : integer;
        busy : Boolean;
        OKtoread, OKtowrite : condition;
  procedure startread;
    begin if busy \/ OKtowrite.queue then OKtoread.wait;
      readercount : = readercount + 1;
      OKtoread.signal;
      comment Once one reader can start, they all can;
    end startread;
  procedure endread;
    begin readercount : = readercount - 1;
      if readercount = 0 then OKtowrite.signal
    end endread;
```

```
procedure startwrite;
  begin
    if readercount ≠ 0 ∨ busy then OKtowrite.wait;
    busy : = true
  end startwrite;
procedure endwrite;
  begin busy : = false;
    if OKtoread.queue then OKtoread.signal
                      else OKtowrite.signal
  end endwrite;
  readercount : = 0;
  busy : = false
end readers and writers
```

I am grateful to Dave Gorman for assisting in the discovery of this solution.

7 Conclusion

This paper suggests that an appropriate structure for a module of an operating system, which schedules resources for parallel user processes, is very similar to that of a data representation used by a sequential program. However, in the case of monitors, the bodies of the procedures must be protected against re-entrance by being implemented as critical regions. The textual grouping of critical regions together with the data which they update seems much superior to critical regions scattered through the user program, as described in [Dijkstra 68c*; Hoare 72g*]. It also corresponds to the traditional practice of the writers of operating system supervisors. It can be recommended without reservation.

However, it is much more difficult to be confident about the condition concept as a synchronizing primitive. The synchronizing facility which is easiest to use is probably the conditional *wait* ([Brinch Hansen 72b*; Hoare 72g*]):

$$wait(B),$$

where B is a general Boolean expression (it causes the given process to wait until B becomes true); but this may be too inefficient for general use in operating systems, because its implementation requires re-evaluation of the expression B after every exit from a procedure of the monitor. The condition variable gives the programmer better control over efficiency and over scheduling; it was designed to be very primitive, and to have a simple proof rule. But perhaps some other compromise between convenience and efficiency might be better. The question whether the signal should always be the last operation of a monitor procedure is still open. These problems will be studied in the design and implementation of a pilot project operating system, currently enjoying the support of the Science Research Council of Great Britain.

Another question which will be studied will be that of the disjointness of monitors: Is it possible to design a separate isolated monitor for each kind of resource, so that it will make sensible scheduling decisions for that resource, using only the minimal information about the utilization of that resource, and using no information about the utilization of any resource administered by other monitors? In principle, it would seem that, when more knowledge of the status of the entire system is available, it should be easier to take decisions nearer to optimality. Furthermore, in principle, independent scheduling of different kinds of resource can lead to deadly embrace. These considerations would lead to the design of a traditional "monolithic" monitor, maintaining large system tables, all of which can be accessed and updated by any of the procedures of the monitor.

There is no a priori reason why the attempt to split the functions of an operating system into a number of isolated disjoint monitors should succeed. It can be made to succeed only by discovering and implementing good scheduling algorithms in each monitor. In order to avoid undesirable interactions between the separate scheduling algorithms, it appears necessary to observe the following principles:

1. Never seek to make an optimal decision; merely seek to avoid persistently pessimal decisions.
2. Do not seek to present the user with a virtual machine which is better than the actual hardware; merely seek to pass on the speed, size, and flat unopiniated structure of a simple hardware design.
3. Use preemptive techniques in preference to non-preemptive ones where possible.
4. Use "grain of time" [Dijkstra 71d*] methods to secure independence of scheduling strategies.
5. Keep a low variance (as well as a low mean) on waiting times.
6. Avoid fixed priorities; instead, try to ensure that every program in the system makes reasonably steady progress. In particular, avoid indefinite overtaking.
7. Ensure that when demand for resources outstrips the supply (i.e. in overload conditions), the behavior of the scheduler is satisfactory (i.e. thrashing is avoided).
8. Make rules for the correct and sensible use of monitor calls, and assume that user programs will obey them. Any checking which is necessary should be done not by a central shared monitor, but rather by an algorithm (called "user envelope") which is local to each process executing a user program. This algorithm should be implemented at least partially in the hardware (e.g. base and range registers, address translation mechanisms, capabilities, etc.).

It is the possibility of constructing separate monitors for different purposes, and of separating the scheduling decisions embodied in monitors from the checking embodied in user envelopes, that may justify a hope that monitors are an appropriate concept for the structuring of an operating system.

Acknowledgments. The development of the monitor concept is due to frequent discussions and communications with E. W. Dijkstra and P. Brinch Hansen. A monitor corresponds to the "secretary" described in [Dijkstra 71d*], and is also described in [Brinch Hansen 72a*, 73a*].

Acknowledgment is also due to the support of IFIP WG.2.3., which provides a meeting place at which these and many other ideas have been germinated, fostered, and tested.

18
The Programming Language Concurrent Pascal

Per Brinch Hansen
University of Southern California

Abstract *The paper describes a new programming language for structured programming of computer operating systems. It extends the sequential programming language Pascal with concurrent programming tools called processes and monitors. Section I explains these concepts informally by means of pictures illustrating a hierarchical design of a simple spooling system. Section II uses the same example to introduce the language notation. The main contribution of* Concurrent Pascal *is to extend the monitor concept with an explicit hierarchy of access rights to shared data structures that can be stated in the program text and checked by a compiler.*

I The purpose of Concurrent Pascal

A Background

Since 1972 I have been working on a new programming language for structured programming of computer operating systems. This language is called Concurrent Pascal. It extends the sequential programming language Pascal with concurrent programming tools called processes and monitors ([Brinch Hansen 73a*; Wirth 71c*; Hoare 74a*]).

This is an informal description of Concurrent Pascal. It uses examples, pictures, and words to bring out the creative aspects of new programming concepts without getting into their finer details. I plan to define these concepts precisely and introduce a notation for them in later papers. This form of presentation may be imprecise from a formal point of view, but is perhaps more effective from a human point of view.

B Processes

We will study concurrent processes inside an operating system and look at one small problem only: how can large amounts of data be transmitted from one process to another by means of a buffer stored on a disk?

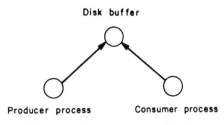

Figure 1   Process communication.

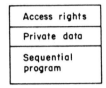

Figure 2   Process.

Fig. 1 shows this little system and its three components: a process that produces data, a process that consumes data, and a disk buffer that connects them.

The circles are *system components* and the arrows are the *access rights* of these components. They show that both processes can use the buffer (but they do now show that data flows from the producer to the consumer). This kind of picture is an *access graph*.

The next picture shows a process component in more detail (Fig. 2).

A *process* consists of a *private data* structure and a *sequential program* that can operate on the data. One process cannot operate on the private data of another process. But concurrent processes can share certain data structures (such as a disk buffer). The *access rights* of a process mention the shared data it can operate on.

C Monitors

A disk buffer is a data structure shared by two concurrent processes. The details of how such a buffer is constructed are irrelevant to its users. All the processes need to know is that they can *send* and *receive* data through it. If they try to operate on the buffer in any other way it is probably either a programming mistake or an example of tricky programming. In both cases, one would like a compiler to detect such misuse of a shared data structure.

To make this possible, we must introduce a language construct that will enable a programmer to tell a compiler how a shared data structure can be used by processes. This kind of system component is called a monitor. A monitor can synchronize concurrent processes and transmit data between

| Access rights |
| Shared data |
| Synchronizing operations |
| Initial operation |

Figure 3   Monitor.

them. It can also control the order in which competing processes use shared, physical resources. Fig. 3 shows a monitor in detail.

A *monitor* defines a *shared data* structure and all the operations processes can perform on it. These synchronizing operations are called *monitor procedures*. A monitor also defines an *initial operation* that will be executed when its data structure is created.

We can define a *disk buffer* as a monitor. Within this monitor there will be shared variables that define the location and length of the buffer on the disk. There will also be two monitor procedures, *send* and *receive*. The initial operation will make sure that the buffer starts as an empty one.

Processes cannot operate directly on shared data. They can only call monitor procedures that have access to shared data. A monitor procedure is executed as part of a calling process (just like any other procedure).

If concurrent processes simultaneously call monitor procedures that operate on the same shared data these procedures must be executed strictly one at a time. Otherwise, the results of monitor calls will be unpredictable. This means that the machine must be able to delay processes for short periods of time until it is their turn to execute monitor procedures. We will not be concerned about how this is done, but will just notice that a monitor procedure has *exclusive access* to shared data while it is being executed.

So the (virtual) machine on which concurrent programs run will handle *short-term scheduling* of simultaneous monitor calls. But the programmer must also be able to delay processes for longer periods of time if their requests for data and other resources cannot be satisfied immediately. If, for example, a process tries to receive data from an empty disk buffer it must be delayed until another process sends more data.

Concurrent Pascal includes a simple data type, called a *queue*, that can be used by monitor procedures to control *medium-term scheduling* of processes. A monitor can either *delay* a calling process in a queue or *continue* another process that is waiting in a queue. It is not important here to understand how these queues work except for the following essential rule: a process only has exclusive access to shared data as long as it continues to execute statements within a monitor procedure. As soon as a process is delayed in a queue it loses its exclusive access until another process calls the same monitor and wakes it up again. (Without this rule, it would be impossible for other processes to enter a monitor and let waiting processes continue their execution.)

Although the disk buffer example does not show this yet, monitor procedures should also be able to call procedures defined within other monitors. Otherwise, the language will not be very useful for hierarchical design. In the case of a disk buffer, one of these other monitors could perhaps define simple input/output operations on the disk. So a monitor can also have *access rights* to other system components (see Fig. 3).

D System Design

A process executes a sequential program—it is an active component. A monitor is just a collection of procedures that do nothing until they are called by processes—it is a passive component. But there are strong similarities between a process and a monitor: both define a data structure (private or shared) and the meaningful operations on it. The main difference between processes and monitors is the way they are scheduled for execution.

It seems natural therefore to regard processes and monitors as *abstract data types* defined in terms of the operations one can perform on them. If a compiler can check that these operations are the only ones carried out on the data structures, then we may be able to build very reliable, concurrent programs in which *controlled access* to data and physical resources is guaranteed before these programs are put into operation. We have then to some extent solved the *resource protection* problem in the cheapest possible manner (without hardware mechanisms and run time overhead).

So we will define processes and monitors as data types and make it possible to use several instances of the same component type in a system. We can, for example, use two disk buffers to build a *spooling system* with an input process, a job process, and an output process (Fig. 4). I will distinguish between definitions and instances of components by calling them *system types* and *system components*. Access graphs (such as Fig. 4) will always show system components (not system types).

Peripheral devices are considered to be monitors implemented in hardware. They can only be accessed by a single procedure *io* that delays the

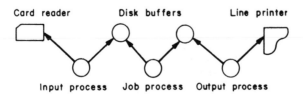

Figure 4   Spooling system.

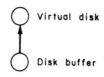

Figure 5   Buffer refinement.

calling process until an input/output operation is completed. Interrupts are handled by the virtual machine on which processes run.

To make the programming language useful for stepwise system design it should permit the division of a system type, such as a disk buffer, into smaller system types. One of these other system types should give a disk buffer access to the disk. We will call this system type a *virtual disk*. It gives a disk buffer the illusion that it has its own private disk. A virtual disk hides the details of disk input/output from the rest of the system and makes the disk look like a data structure (an array of disk pages). The only operations on this data structure are *read* and *write* a page.

Each virtual disk is only used by a single disk buffer (Fig. 5). A system component that cannot be called simultaneously by several other components will be called a *class*. A class defines a data structure and the possible operations on it (just like a monitor). The exclusive access of class procedures to class variables can be guaranteed completely at compile time. The virtual machine does not have to schedule simultaneous calls of class procedures at run time, because such calls cannot occur. This makes class calls considerably faster than monitor calls.

The spooling system includes two virtual disks but only one real disk. So we need a single *disk resource* monitor to control the order in which competing processes use the disk (Fig. 6). This monitor defines two procedures, *request* and *release* access, to be called by a virtual disk before and after each disk transfer.

It would seem simpler to replace the virtual disks and the disk resource by a single monitor that has exclusive access to the disk and does the input/output. This would certainly guarantee that processes use the disk one at a time. But this would be done according to the built-in short-term scheduling policy of monitor calls.

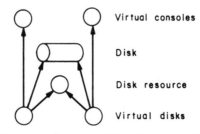

Figure 6   Decomposition of virtual disks.

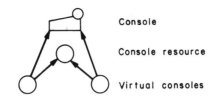

Figure 7   Decomposition of virtual consoles.

Now to make a virtual machine efficient, one must use a very simple short-term scheduling rule (such as first come, first served) ([Brinch Hansen 73a*]). If the disk has a moving access head this is about the worst possible algorithm one can use for disk transfers. It is vital that the language make it possible for the programmer to write a medium-term scheduling algorithm that will minimize disk head movements ([Hoare 74a*]). The data type *queue* mentioned earlier makes it possible to implement arbitrary scheduling rules within a monitor.

The difficulty is that while a monitor is performing an input/output operation it is impossible for other processes to enter the same monitor and join the disk queue. They will automatically be delayed by the short-term scheduler and only allowed to enter the monitor one at a time after each disk transfer. This will, of course, make the attempt to control disk scheduling within the monitor illusory. To give the programmer complete control of disk scheduling, processes should be able to enter the disk queue during disk transfers. Since *arrival* and *service* in the disk

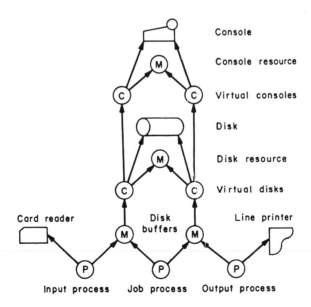

Figure 8   Hierarchical system structure.

queueing system potentially are simultaneous operations they must be handled by different system components, as shown in Fig. 6.

If the disk fails persistently during input/output this should be reported on an operator's console. Fig. 6 shows two instances of a class type, called a *virtual console*. They give the virtual disks the illusion that they have their own private consoles.

The virtual consoles get exclusive access to a single, real console by calling a *console resource* monitor (Fig. 7). Notice that we now have a standard technique for dealing with virtual devices.

If we put all these system components together, we get a complete picture of a simple spooling system (Fig. 8). Classes, monitors, and processes are marked C, M, and P.

E Scope rules

Some years ago I was part of a team that built a multi-programming system in which processes can appear and disappear dynamically ([Brinch Hansen 70*]). In practice, this system was used mostly to set up a fixed configuration of processes. Dynamic process deletion will certainly complicate the semantics and implementation of a programming language considerably. And since it appears to be unnecessary for a large class of real-time applications, it seems wise to exclude it altogether. So an operating system written in Concurrent Pascal will consist of a fixed number of processes, monitors, and classes. These components and their data structures will exist forever after system initialization. An operating system can, however, be extended by recompilation. It remains to be seen whether this restriction will simplify or complicate operating system design. But the poor quality of most existing operating systems clearly demonstrates an urgent need for simpler approaches.

In existing programming languages the data structures of processes, monitors, and classes would be called "global data." This term would be misleading in Concurrent Pascal where each data structure can be accessed by a single component only. It seems more appropriate to call them *permanent data structures*.

I have argued elsewhere that the most dangerous aspect of concurrent programming is the possibility of *time-dependent programming errors* that are impossible to locate by program testing ("lurking bugs") ([Brinch Hansen 73a*, 72a*, 73c*]). If we are going to depend on real-time programming systems in our daily lives, we must be able to find such obscure errors before the systems are put into operation.

Fortunately, a compiler can detect many of these errors if processes and monitors are represented by a structured notation in a high-level programming language. In addition, we must exclude low-level machine features (registers, addresses, and interrupts) from the language and let a virtual machine control them. If we want real-time systems to be highly reliable, we must stop programming them in assembly language. (The use of hardware protection mechanisms is merely an expensive, inadequate way of making arbitrary machine language programs behave almost as predictably as compiled programs.)

A Concurrent Pascal compiler will check that the private data of a process only are accessed by that process. It will also check that the data structure of a class or monitor only is accessed by its procedures.

Fig. 8 shows that *access rights* within an operating system normally are not tree structured. Instead they form a directed graph. This partly explains why the traditional scope rules of block-structured languages are inconvenient for concurrent programming (and for sequential programming as well). In Concurrent Pascal one can state the access rights of components in the program text and have them checked by a compiler.

Since the execution of a monitor procedure will delay the execution of further calls of the same monitor, we must prevent a monitor from calling itself recursively. Otherwise, processes can become *deadlocked*. So the compiler will check that the access rights of system components are hierarchically ordered (or, if you like, that there are no cycles in the access graph).

The *hierarchical ordering* of system components has vital consequences for system design and testing ([Brinch Hansen 74*]).

A hierarchical operating system will be tested component by component, bottom up (but could, of course, be conceived top down or by iteration). When an incomplete operating system has been shown to work correctly (by proof or testing), a compiler can ensure that this part of the system will continue to work correctly when new untested program components are added on top of it. Programming errors within new components cannot cause old components to fail because old components do not call new components, and new components only call old components through well-defined procedures that have already been tested.

(Strictly speaking, a compiler can only check that single monitor calls are made correctly; it cannot check sequences of monitor calls, for example whether a resource is always reserved before it is released. So one can only hope for compile time assurance of *partial correctness*.)

Several other reasons besides program correctness make a hierarchical structure attractive:

(1) a hierarchical operating system can be studied in a stepwise manner as a sequence of *abstract machines* simulated by programs ([Dijkstra 71d*]).

(2) a partial ordering of process interactions permits one to use *mathematical induction* to prove certain overall properties of the system (such as the absence of deadlocks) ([Brinch Hansen 73a*]).

(3) *efficient resource utilization* can be achieved by ordering the program components according to the speed of the physical resources they control (with the fastest resources being controlled at the bottom of the system) ([Dijkstra 71d*]);

(4) a hierarchical system designed according to the previous criteria is often *nearly decomposable* from an analytical point of view. This means that one can develop stochastic models of its dynamic behavior in a stepwise manner ([Simon 62]).

F Final remarks

It seems most natural to represent a hierarchical system structure, such as Fig. 8, by a two-dimensional picture. But when we write a concurrent program we must somehow represent these access rules by linear text. This limitation of written language tends to obscure the simplicity of the original structure. That is why I have tried to explain the purpose of Concurrent Pascal by means of pictures instead of language notation.

The class concept is a restricted form of the class concept of SIMULA 67 [Dahl 72b*]. [Dijkstra 71d*] suggested the idea of monitors. The first structured language notation for monitors was proposed in [Brinch Hansen 73a*] and illustrated by examples in [Hoare 74a*]. The queue variables needed by monitors for process scheduling were suggested and modified in [Brinch Hansen 72*, 73a*].

The main contribution of Concurrent Pascal is to extend monitors with explicit access rights that can be checked at compile time. Concurrent Pascal has been implemented at Caltech for the PDP 11/45 computer. Our system uses sequential Pascal as a job control and user programming language.

II The use of Concurrent Pascal

A Introduction

In Section I the concepts of Concurrent Pascal were explained informally by means of pictures of a hierarchical spooling system. I will now use the same example to introduce the language notation of Concurrent Pascal. The presentation is still informal. I am trying neither to define the language precisely nor to develop a working system. This will be done in other papers. I am just trying to show the flavor of the language.

B Processes

We will now program the system components in Fig. 8 one at a time from top to bottom (but we could just as well do it bottom up).

Although we only need one *input process*, we may as well define it as a general system type of which several copies may exist:

```
type inputprocess =
process (buffer : diskbuffer);
var block : page;
cycle
   readcards(block);
   buffer.send(block)
end
```

An input process has access to a *buffer* of type *diskbuffer* (to be defined later). The process has a private variable *block* of type *page*. The data type *page* is declared elsewhere as an array of characters:

$$\textbf{type } page = \textbf{array } (.1..512.) \textbf{ of } char$$

A process type defines a *sequential program*—in this case, an endless cycle that inputs a block from a card reader and sends it through the buffer to another process. We will ignore the details of card reader input.

The *send* operation on the buffer is called as follows (using *block* as a parameter):

$$buffer.send(block)$$

The next component type we will define is a *job process*:

```
type jobprocess =
process(input, output : diskbuffer);
var block : page;
cycle
   input.receive(block);
   update(block);
   output.send(block)
end
```

A job process has access to two disk buffers called *input* and *output*. It receives blocks from one buffer, updates them, and sends them through the other buffer. The details of updating can be ignored here.

Finally, we need an *output process* that can receive data from a disk buffer and output them on a line printer:

```
type outputprocess =
process(buffer : diskbuffer);
var block : page;
cycle
   buffer.receive(block);
   printlines(block)
end
```

The following shows a declaration of the main system components:

var *buffer1, buffer2* : *diskbuffer*;
   reader : *inputprocess*;
   master : *jobprocess*;
   writer : *outputprocess*

There is an input process, called the *reader*, a job process, called the *master*, and an output process, called the *writer*. Then there are two disk buffers, *buffer1* and *buffer2*, that connect them.

Later I will explain how a disk buffer is defined and initialized. If we assume that the disk buffers already have been initialized, we can initialize the input process as follows:

init reader(buffer1)

The **init** statement allocates space for the *private variables* of the reader process and starts its execution as a sequential process with access to *buffer1*.

The *access rights* of a process to other system components, such as *buffer1*, are also called its *parameters*. A process can only be initialized once. After initialization, the parameters and private variables of a process exist forever. They are called *permanent variables*.

The **init** statement can be used to start concurrent execution of several processes and define their access rights. As an example, the statement

init reader(buffer1), master(buffer1, buffer2), writer(buffer2)

starts concurrent execution of the reader process (with access to *buffer1*), the master process (with access to both buffers), and the writer process (with access to *buffer2*).

A process can only access its own parameters and private variables. The latter are not accessible to other system components. Compare this with the more liberal scope rules of block-structured languages in which a program block can access not only its own parameters and local variables, but also those declared in outer blocks. In Concurrent Pascal, all variables accessible to a system component are declared within its type definition. This access rule and the **init** statement make it possible for a programmer to state access rights explicitly and have them checked by a compiler. They also make it possible to study a system type as a self-contained program unit.

Although the programming examples do not show this, one can also define constants, data types, and procedures within a process. These objects can only be used within the process type.

C Monitors

The *disk buffer* is a monitor type:

```
type diskbuffer =
monitor(consoleaccess, diskaccess : resource;
    base, limit : integer);
var disk : virtualdisk; sender, receiver : queue;
    head, tail, length : integer;

procedure entry send(block : page);
begin
    if length = limit then delay(sender);
    disk.write(base + tail, block);
    tail : = (tail + 1) mod limit;
    length : = length + 1;
    continue(receiver)
end

procedure entry receive(var block : page);
begin
    if length = 0 then delay(receiver);
    disk.read(base + head, block);
    head : = (head + 1) mod limit;
    length : = length - 1;
    continue(sender)
end;

begin "initial statement";
    init disk(consoleaccess, diskaccess);
    head : = 0; tail : = 0; length : = 0
end
```

A disk buffer has access to two other components, *consoleaccess* and *diskaccess*, of type resource (to be defined later). It also has access to two integer constants defining the *base* address and *limit* of the buffer on the disk.

The monitor declares a set of *shared variables*: the *disk* is declared as a variable of type *virtualdisk*. Two variables of type *queue* are used to delay the *sender* and *receiver* processes until the buffer becomes nonfull and nonempty. Three integers define the relative addresses of the *head* and *tail* elements of the buffer and its current *length*.

The monitor defines two *monitor procedures, send* and *receive*. They are marked with the word **entry** to distinguish them from local procedures used within the monitor (there are none of these in this example).

Receive returns a *page* to the calling process. If the buffer is empty, the calling process is *delayed* in the receiver queue until another process sends a page through the buffer. The *receive* procedure will then read and remove a *page* from the head of the disk buffer by calling a *read* operation defined within the virtual disk type:

$$disk.read(base + head, block)$$

Finally, the *receive* procedure will *continue* the execution of a sending process (if the latter is waiting in the sender queue).

Send is similar to *receive*.

The queuing mechanism will be explained in detail in the next section.

The *initial statement* of a disk buffer initializes its virtual disk with access to the console and disk resources. It also sets the buffer length to zero. (Notice that a disk buffer does not use its access rights to the console and disk, but only passes them on to a virtual disk declared within it.)

The following shows a declaration of two system components of type *resource* and two *integers* defining the base and limit of a disk buffer:

var *consoleaccess, diskaccess* : *resource*;
   base, limit : *integer*;
   buffer : *diskbuffer*

If we assume that these variables already have been initialized, we can initialize a disk buffer as follows:

init *buffer*(*consoleaccess, diskaccess, base, limit*)

The **init** statement allocates storage for the parameters and shared variables of the disk buffer and executes its initial statement.

A monitor can only be initialized once. After initialization, the parameters and shared variables of a monitor exist forever. They are called *permanent variables*. The parameters and local variables of a monitor procedure, however, exist only while it is being executed. They are called *temporary variables*.

A monitor procedure can only access its own temporary and permanent variables. These variables are not accessible to other system components. Other components can, however, call procedure entries within a monitor. While a monitor procedure is being executed, it has *exclusive access* to the permanent variables of the monitor. If concurrent processes try to call procedures within the same monitor simultaneously, these procedures will be executed strictly one at a time.

Only monitors and constants can be permanent parameters of processes and monitors. This rule ensures that processes only communicate by means of monitors.

It is possible to define constants, data types, and local procedures within monitors (and processes). The local procedures of a system type can only be called within the system type. To prevent *deadlock* of monitor calls and ensure that access rights are hierarchical the following rules are enforced: a procedure must be declared before it can be called; procedure definitions cannot be nested and cannot call themselves; a system type cannot call its own procedure entries.

The absence of recursion makes it possible for a compiler to determine the store requirements of all system components. This and the use of permanent components make it possible to use *fixed store allocation* on a computer that does not support paging.

Since system components are permanent they must be declared as permanent variables of other components.

D Queues

A monitor procedure can delay a calling process for any length of time by executing a *delay* operation on a queue variable. Only one process at a time can wait in a queue. When a calling process is delayed by a monitor procedure it loses its exclusive access to the monitor variables until another process calls the same monitor and executes a *continue* operation on the queue in which the process is waiting.

The *continue* operation makes the calling process return from its monitor call. If any process is waiting in the selected queue, it will immediately resume the execution of the monitor procedure that delayed it. After being resumed, the process again has exclusive access to the permanent variables of the monitor.

Other variants of process queues (called "events" and "conditions") are proposed in [Brinch Hansen 72a*; Hoare 74a*]. They are multi-process queues that use different (but fixed) scheduling rules. We do not yet know from experience which kind of queue will be the most convenient one for operating system design. A single-process queue is the simplest tool that gives the programmer complete control of the scheduling of individual process. Later, I will show how multi-process queues can be built from single-process queues.

A queue must be declared as a permanent variable within a monitor type.

E Classes

Every disk buffer has its own virtual disk. A virtual disk is defined as a class type:

```
type virtualdisk =
class(consoleaccess, diskaccess : resource);
var terminal : virtualconsole; peripheral : disk;

procedure entry read(pageno : integer; var block : page);
var error : boolean;
```

```
begin
  repeat
    diskaccess.request;
    peripheral.read(pageno, block, error);
    diskaccess.release;
    if error then terminal.write('disk failure')
  until not error
end;

procedure entry write(pageno : integer; block : page);
begin "similar to read" end;

begin "initial statement";
  init terminal(consoleaccess), peripheral
end
```

A virtual disk has access to a console resource and a disk resource. Its permanent variables define a virtual console and a disk. A process can access its virtual disk by means of *read* and *write* procedures. These procedure entries *request* and *release* exclusive access to the real disk before and after each block transfer. If the real disk fails, the virtual disk calls its virtual console to report the error.

The *initial statement* of a virtual disk initializes its virtual console and the real disk.

Section II-C shows an example of how a virtual disk is declared and initialized (within a disk buffer).

A class can only be initialized once. After initialization, its parameters and private variables exist forever. A class procedure can only access its own temporary and permanent variables. These cannot be accessed by other components.

A class is a system component that cannot be called simultaneously by several other components. This is guaranteed by the following rule: a class must be declared as a permanent variable within a system type; a class can be passed as a permanent parameter to another class (but not to a process or monitor). So a chain of nested class calls can only be started by a single process or monitor. Consequently, it is not necessary to schedule simultaneous class calls at run time—they cannot occur.

F Input/Output

The real *disk* is controlled by a class

$$\text{type } disk = \text{class}$$

with two procedure entries

$$read(pageno, block, error);$$
$$write(pageno, block, error)$$

The class uses a standard procedure

$$io(block, param, device)$$

to transfer a block to or from the disk device. The *io* parameter is a record

```
var param : record
            operation : iooperation;
            result : ioresult;
            pageno : integer
        end
```

that defines an input/output operation, its result, and a page number on the disk. The calling process is delayed until an *io* operation has been completed.

A *virtual console* is also defined as a class

```
type virtualconsole =
class(access : resource);
var terminal : console
```

It can be accessed by *read* and *write* operations that are similar to each other:

```
procedure entry read(var text : line);
begin
    access.request;
    terminal.read(text);
    access.release
end
```

The real *console* is controlled by a class that is similar to the disk class.

G Multiprocess scheduling

Access to the console and disk is controlled by two monitors of type *resource*. To simplify the presentation, I will assume that competing processes are served in first-come, first-served order. (A much better disk scheduling algorithm is defined in [Hoare 74a*]. It can be programmed in Concurrent Pascal as well, but involves more details than the present one.)

We will define a multiprocess queue as an array of single-process queues

```
type multiqueue = array (.0..qlength-1.) of queue
```

where *qlength* is an upper bound on the number of concurrent processes in the system.

A first-come, first-served scheduler is now straight-forward to program:

```
type resource =
monitor

var free : Boolean;  q : multiqueue;
  head, tail, length : integer;

procedure entry request;
var arrival : integer;
begin
  if free then free : = false else
  begin
    arrival : = tail;
    tail : = (tail + 1) mod qlength;
    length : = length + 1;
    delay(q(.arrival.))
  end
end;

procedure entry release;
var departure : integer;
begin
  if length = 0 then free : = true else
  begin
    departure : = head;
    head : = (head + 1) mod qlength;
    length : = length − 1;
    continue (q(.departure.))
  end
end;

begin "initial statement";
  free : = true;  length : = 0;
  head : = 0;  tail : = 0
end
```

H Initial Process

Finally, we will put all these components together into a concurrent program. A Concurrent Pascal program consists of nested definitions of system types. The outermost system type is an anonymous process, called the initial process. An instance of this process is created during system loading. It initializes the other system components.

The initial process defines system types and instances of them. It executes statements that initialize these system components. In our example, the initial process can be sketched as follows (ignoring the problem of how base addresses and limits of disk buffers are defined):

```
type
    resource = monitor · · · end;
    console = class · · · end;
    virtualconsole =
        class(access : resource); · · · end;
    disk = class · · · end;
    virtualdisk =
        class(consoleaccess, diskaccess : resource); · · · end;
    diskbuffer =
        monitor(consoleaccess, diskaccess : resource;
            base, limit : integer); · · · end;
    inputprocess =
        process(buffer : diskbuffer); · · · end;
    jobprocess =
        process (input, output : diskbuffer); · · · end;
    outputprocess =
        process(buffer : diskbuffer); · · · end;
var
    consoleaccess, diskaccess : resource;
    buffer1, buffer2 : diskbuffer;
    reader : inputprocess;
    master : jobprocess;
    writer : outputprocess;
begin
    init consoleaccess, diskaccess,
        buffer1(consoleaccess, diskaccess, base1, limit1),
        buffer2(consoleaccess, diskaccess, base2, limit2),
        reader(buffer1),
        master(buffer1, buffer2),
        writer(buffer2)
end.
```

When execution of a process (such as the initial process) terminates, its private variables continue to exist. This is necessary because these variables may have been passed as permanent parameters to other system components.

Acknowledgments. It is a pleasure to acknowledge the immense value of a continuous exchange of ideas with C. A. R. Hoare on structured multiprogramming. I also thank my students L. Medina and R. Varela for their helpful comments on this paper.

PART IV

DATA TYPES

What is a data type?

A precise definition of type *(or* data type*) would be suitable in an introduction to articles on the subject. Perusal of the literature, however, led to the discovery that few have tried to define the term, and some have even explicitly shied away from doing so! Rather,* type *has been used as a vague, intuitive concept. The term does not mean the same to all, and its meaning has been changing as our understanding of programming languages has increased over the past 25 years.*

This is an odd situation, for the concept of type seems to be of central importance in programming languages. Typically, each variable, constant and expression of a program has a type associated with it, and this type information is helpful to both the human and the compiler. It is used in determining the representation of values, and it enables a compiler to reject some programs that would invoke meaningless operations.

Moreover, not everyone feels the same about types. Some feel that the type of a variable should always be specified in a declaration; others like defaults. Implicit type conversion is eschewed by some and welcomed by others. Some languages are "strongly typed," some "weakly typed," and some "typeless."

In a simple language with a fixed number of types (e.g., ALGOL 60, with types **integer, real,** *and* **Boolean***), one can survive with just an intuitive feeling for type. However, if the language is to provide a notation for "programmer-defined types," then more precision is necessary. The notation must appear so natural that it does not get in the programmer's way, and for this the language designer must be able to justify his answers to the following kinds of questions:*

1. *Must a value belong to exactly one type, or can one type be a subtype of another? (Part of the controversy over Pascal—see [Habermann 73; Lecarme 75]—was caused by confusion over this.)*
2. *If two types t1 and t2 are identically declared—"t1 = a"; "t2 = a"—are t1 and t2 names for the same type?*

3. *Should the programmer be allowed to say that two types t1 and t2 are identical but have different implementations (e.g., polar and rectangular coordinates)?*
4. *Does a constant have a type, or is it to be considered as a denotation for values in several different types?*
5. *Should implicit conversion between two programmer-defined types be definable by the programmer?*
6. *Is the type-checking system absolutely foolproof?*

These questions can only be answered systematically if one has a sound idea of what a type is. Or, one might say that attempting to answer these kinds of questions will lead to a refinement and elucidation of the concept of type.

An exact definition of type *as used in programming languages is beyond the scope of this introduction; however, the following survey of the use of* type *may prove interesting.*

A Survey of the use of type

The term type *does have a precise definition in some branches of mathematics. For example, in abstract algebra it is used to describe the number of arguments of each operation in an algebra. Secondly, a "theory of types" was developed by Bertrand Russell in order to avoid paradoxes—arguments that lead to unexplainable contradictions. The most famous paradox is due to Russell [Russell 08]:*

> *Let s be the set of all sets that are not members of themselves. Is s a member of itself or not?*

Whether you answer yes or no, you can immediately be proved wrong, so this question simply cannot be dealt with in the conventional "untyped" logic.

Russell considers a type to be "the range of significance of a propositional function, i.e. the collection of arguments for which the said function has values." Whenever a variable occurs as an argument to a function, the range of values of that variable is a type which is determined by that function. Russell then imposes restrictions on types in order to prohibit self-referencing, which is the source of all paradoxes.

The first use of type *in connection with programming languages, in the ALGOL 60 report [Naur 60*], seems to be similar in nature:*

> *The various "types" (**integer**, **real**, **Boolean**) basically denote properties of values. The types associated with syntactic units refer to the values of these units.*

Thus each variable, constant, and expression has one of the types **integer, real** *or* **Boolean**, *meaning that its value is integral, real, or Boolean. Although it was noticed that* type *had a mathematical definition, Alan Perlis, one of the authors of ALGOL 60, has informed me that* type *was used in ALGOL 60 in a nontechnical sense—it was simply a word, roughly equivalent to* kind, *used to aid in distinguishing different classes of objects.*

Note that in ALGOL 60 an array identifier does not *name a variable, and its value has no type. Instead, an ALGOL 60 identifier b (say) declared as* integer array *[1:10] is viewed simply as a convenient notational device for manipulating individuals in the collection of* subscripted variables *b[1],...,b[10]. The concept* array *allowed the use of* one *name for representing many variables, but it did not allow an array to be considered as a value in itself, to be referred to as a whole. This view was carried over to extensions of ALGOL—for example, in the Perlis–Ituriaga–Standish definition of FORMULA-ALGOL in 1966.*

The designers of FORTRAN also used type *in a nontechnical sense. For example, one early text (McCracken's* Guide to FORTRAN Programming), *considers "two kinds of numbers that can be used in FORTRAN" but discusses "four types of functions...". COBOL did not and does not use the mathematical term* variable; *instead,* data *is associated with* data names.

The use of type *as a formal programming language term is perhaps due (more than to anything else) to the fact that the syntax of ALGOL 60 was defined rigorously in a formal (BNF) grammar; the use of the rule*

$$\langle\text{type}\rangle ::= \textbf{real} \mid \textbf{integer} \mid \textbf{Boolean}$$

simply gave type *a more formal stature in programming languages than it previously had.*

Hierarchical structuring of data was a common topic of interest in the 1960s, and in fact both COBOL and PL/1 contained notations for it. However, the notion of programmer-defined types *that defined structured values seems to have come from the "Algolists." For example, in 1966 Niklaus Wirth and C.A.R. (Tony) Hoare published the design of a new ALGOL-like language [Wirth 66*], which contained the notion of "structured types." (A version of this language was implemented as ALGOL W.) Thus one had the structured values*

array: *the value is an ordered set of values, all of identical type and subscript bounds, and*

record: *the value is an ordered set of simple values of fixed, but not necessarily identical, types.*

By declaring (say)

record person (string name; integer age; Boolean male)

one defined a type (also called a record class) person *that consisted of values that were "tuples" (string, integer, Boolean). One could then declare variables with this type, e.g.,* **var** *A:* person.

Problems with programmer-defined types introduced the need for defining the term type *more precisely. The first notion seems to have been that a type simply is, or defines, a set of values, and this view corresponded closely with Russell's. Thus, in [Wirth 66*] we find:*

> *Every value is said to be of a certain* type. *The types of simple values are:* integer: *the value is an integer; ...;* bits; *the value is a linear sequence of bits.*

The Pascal report [Wirth 71c*] says that "the data type essentially defines the set of values which may be assumed...." ALGOL 68 also seems to consider "modes," i.e., generalizations of the concept "type," as sets of structured values. Indeed, the paper [Lewis 73], which extends and formalizes the ALGOL 68 approach to data types, says that "a data type in this system is any of certain sets of values." In the same Proceedings [Fischer 73] says that "abstractly, a data type T can be characterized as a set of objects,...,all identifiable as members of T."

But note how almost all these quotes secure their position by using a word (basically, essentially, abstractly) to indicate that there may be more to a type than a set, but that the exact meaning of type *is not of interest.*

The monograph [Hoare 72d*] contains a good description of the salient characteristics of type *as used in a programming language, which we quote here:*

> *(1) A type determines the class of values which may be assumed by a variable or expression.*
>
> *(2) Every value belongs to one and only one type. [This is open to debate. An early text with two of the ALGOL 60 authors as coauthors [Baumann 64] states that "type real, in accordance with standard mathematical usage, includes type integer." One also has problems in this regard with subrange types in Pascal.]*
>
> *(3) The type of a value denoted by any constant, variable, or expression may be deduced from its form or context, without any knowledge of its value as computed at runtime.*
>
> *(4) Each operator expects operands of some fixed type, and delivers a result of some fixed type... Where the same symbol is applied to several different types... this symbol may be regarded as ambiguous, denoting several different actual operators. The resolution of such systematic ambiguity can always be made at compile time.*
>
> *(5) The properties of the values of a type and of the primitive operations defined over them are specified by means of a set of axioms.*
>
> *(6) Type information is used in a high-level language both to prevent or detect meaningless construction in a program, and to determine the method of representing and manipulating data on a computer.*
>
> *(7) The types in which we are interested are those already familiar to mathematicians; namely Cartesian Products, Discriminated Union, Sets, Functions, Sequences, and Recursive Structures.*

While not providing us with a precise definition of type that can be used in developing type-defining mechanisms, Hoare has explained very well what we would like to gain from having types in a language. Note that Hoare does not say that a type is a class of values, or that a class of values determines a type, but that a type determines a class of values. This leaves open the possibility that the type may determine other things as well, such as the primitive operations on those values (as implied by characteristic (5) above).

Jim Morris, in a paper entitled Types are not sets *[Morris 73], provides an interesting viewpoint. He says that there must be more to a type than a set, but instead of defining type he focuses on the role of type checking. After discussing two purposes of type checking—authentication and secrecy—he says that whether a value belongs to a type should not turn on* what *the value is, but rather* where *it came from and* who *created it!*

Currently, one finds at least the following interpretations of type, with interpretation (3) being the prevalent informal one. The interpretation one chooses for a language will have a marked effect on the language.

1. Type *is a syntactic concept associated with constants, variables, and expressions, but not with values.*
2. A type *is a set of values.*
3. A type *is a set of values together with a set of primitive operations.*
4. A type *is defined by the* definition *of a set of operators, but there may be many models (implementations, in terms of set of values and operators) consistent with the definition.*
5. A type *is determined by the representation of its values in terms of more primitive types.*
6. A type *is determined by the representation of its values and a set of procedures operating on the representation.*
7. Types *are defined as equivalence classes of variables and constants.*

It is interesting to speculate when and where primitive operations became part of a type. The earliest reference I could find of this view is [Laski 68]. In it, John Laski says:

Briefly, the type of an object is defined by describing the operators that may be applied to it. An operator may be applied to object(s) of appropriate types. It may produce as a result an object of specified type, and it may alter values of the objects to which it is applied... Finally, and most importantly, equivalences exist between various sequences of operator application, and these may be expressed by axioms.

And Laski gives the necessary axioms for the types integer and set.

Laski's view of types does appear implicitly in a 1968-vintage language: SIMULA 67. The SIMULA class declaration can be used to define a set of values and primitive operations on them, and the first article in this section uses the class notation with a minimum of changes for precisely this purpose.

The SIMULA 67 designers were not concerned with the issue of type, *and this is why the class declaration is not described in terms of programmer-defined types. Instead, they concentrated on power and flexibility, and wanted to be able to describe "patterns of data and actions" with the class declaration. In designing SIMULA 67, little attention was paid to a topic that was on few people's minds at the time: the need for protection from many types (kinds) of errors that a programming language should provide.*

The Articles in Part IV

The three articles contained here discuss different aspects of types. The first is by C.A.R. (Tony) Hoare. Using the notation of the SIMULA 67 class *to specify the association between an abstract type and its concrete representation, Hoare discusses proof of correctness of data representations in terms of the axiomatic semantics developed in Part II. This article contributes fundamental ideas that are used in current research in programming language design, e.g., ALPHARD [Wulf 77], CLU [Liskov 76], and EUCLID [Horning 77c*].*

The second article, by John Guttag and Jim Horning, develops an approach to the specification *of abstract data types. Instead of describing each primitive operation by a "proof rule," they suggest giving a set of axioms that specifies the interrelationship between the primitive operations (in much the same way as [Laski 68] does.) The paper, based on formal work dealing with heterogeneous algebras, shows how abstract theory can be applied to yield insight into the solution of practical problems.*

John Reynold's article looks at two complementary approaches to data abstraction: the conventional programmer-defined type mechanism and "procedural data abstraction". Through an example, the advantages and disadvantages of both methods are discussed and compared. This paper appeared in the Proceedings of the IFIP WG2.3 meeting held in Munich, Germany, in September 1975; it has not been formally published.

19
Proof of Correctness of Data Representations

C. A. R. Hoare
University of Oxford

Abstract *A powerful method of simplifying the proofs of program correctness is suggested; and some new light is shed on the problem of functions with side-effects.*

1 Introduction

In the development of programs by stepwise refinement [Wirth 71a*; Dahl 72a*], the programmer is encouraged to postpone the decision on the representation of his data until after he has designed his algorithm and has expressed it as an "abstract" program operating on "abstract" data. He then chooses for the abstract data some convenient and efficient concrete representation in the store of a computer; and finally programs the primitive operations required by his abstract program in terms of this concrete representation. This paper suggests an automatic method of accomplishing the transition between an abstract and a concrete program, and also a method of proving its correctness; that is, of proving that the concrete representation exhibits all the properties expected of it by the "abstract" program. A similar suggestion was made more formally in algebraic terms in [Milner 71], which gives a general definition of simulation. However, a more restricted definition may prove to be more useful in practical program proofs.

If the data representation is proved correct, the correctness of the final oncrete program depends only on the correctness of the original abstract program. Since abstract programs are usually very much shorter and easier to prove correct, the total task of proof has been considerably lightened by factorizing it in this way. Furthermore, the two parts of the proof correspond to the successive stages in program development, thereby contributing to a constructive approach to the correctness of programs [Dijkstra 68e*]. Finally, it must be recalled that in the case of larger and more complex programs the description given above in terms of two stages readily generalizes to multiple stages.

2 Concepts and notations

Suppose in an abstract program there is some abstract variable t which is regarded as being of type T (say a small set of integers). A concrete representation of t will usually consist of several variables $c_1, c_2, \ldots, c_n$ whose types are directly (or more directly) represented in the computer store. The primitive operations on the variable t are represented by procedures $p_1, p_2, \ldots, p_m$, whose bodies carry out on the variables $c_1, c_2, \ldots, c_n$ a series of operations directly (or more directly) performed by computer hardware, and which correspond to meaningful operations on the abstract variable t. The entire concrete representation of the type T can be expressed by declarations of these variables and procedures. For this we adopt the notation of the SIMULA 67 [Dahl 70*] class declaration, which specifies the association between an abstract type T and its concrete representation:

> **class** T;
> > **begin** ... declarations of $c_1, c_2, \ldots, c_n$ ... ;
> > > **procedure** p_1 ⟨formal parameter part⟩; Q_1;
> > > **procedure** p_2 ⟨formal parameter part⟩; Q_2;
> > > ....
> > > **procedure** p_m ⟨formal parameter part⟩; Q_m;
> > > Q
> > **end**

where Q is a piece of program which assigns initial values (if desired) to the variables $c_1, c_2, \ldots, c_n$. As in ALGOL 60, any of the p's may be functions; this is signified by preceding the procedure declaration by the type of the procedure.

Having declared a representation for a type T, it will be required to use this in the abstract program to declare all variables which are to be represented in that way. For this purpose we use the notation:

> **var**(T) t;

or for multiple declarations:

> **var**(T) $t_1, t_2, \ldots$;

The same notation may be used for specifying the types of arrays, functions, and parameters. Within the block in which these declarations are made, it will be required to operate upon the variables $t, t_1, \ldots$, in the manner defined by the bodies of the procedures $p_1, p_2, \ldots, p_m$. This is accomplished by introducing a compound notation for a procedure call:

$$t_i.p_j \text{ ⟨actual parameter part⟩}$$

where t_i names the variable to be operated upon and p_j names the operation to be performed.

If P_j is a function, the notation displayed above is a function designator; otherwise it is a procedure statement. The form $t_i \cdot P_j$ is known as a *compound identifier*.

These concepts and notations have been closely modelled on those of SIMULA 67. The only difference is the use of **var**(T) instead of **ref**(T). This reflects the fact that in the current treatment, objects of declared classes are not expected to be addressed by reference; usually they will occupy storage space contiguously in the local workspace of the block in which they are declared, and will be addressed by offset in the same way as normal integer and real variables of the block.

3 Example

As an example of the use of these concepts, consider an abstract program which operates on several small sets of integers. It is known that none of these sets ever has more than a hundred members. Furthermore, the only operations actually used in the abstract program are the initial clearing of the set, and the insertion and removal of individual members of the set. These are denoted by procedure statements

$$s.insert(i)$$

and

$$s.remove(i).$$

There is also a function "$s.has(i)$," which tests whether i is a member of s.

It is decided to represent each set as an array A of 100 integer elements, together with a pointer m to the last member of the set; m is zero when the set is empty. This representation can be declared:

```
class smallintset;
begin integer m; integer array A [1 : 100];
            procedure insert(i); integer i;
                begin integer j;
                for j := 1 step 1 until m do
                    if A[j] = i then go to end insert;
                m := m + 1;
                A[m] := i;

                end insert: end insert;

            procedure remove(i); integer i;
                begin integer j, k;
                    for j := 1 step 1 until m do
                        if A[j] = i then
```

> **begin for** $k := j + 1$ **step** 1 **until** m **do**
> $$A[k-1] := A[k];$$
> **comment** close the gap over the removed member;
> $m := m - 1;$
> **go to** *end remove*
> **end**;

end remove: **end** *remove*;

Boolean procedure *has* (i); **integer** i;
begin integer j;
   has : = **false**;
   for $j := 1$ **step** 1 **until** m **do**
   if $A[j] = i$ **then**
      begin *has* : = **true**; **go to** *end contains* **end**;

end contains: **end** *has*;

$m := 0$; **comment** initialise set to empty;

end *smallintset*

Note. As in SIMULA 67, simple variable parameters are presumed to be called by value.

4 Semantics and implementation

The meaning of class declarations and calls on their constituent procedures may be readily explained by textual substitution; this also gives a useful clue to a practical and efficient method of implementation. A declaration:

$$\textbf{var}(T)t$$

is regarded as equivalent to the unbracketed body of the class declaration with **begin**...**end** brackets removed, after every occurrence of an identifier c_i or p_i declared in it has been prefixed by "t.". If there are any initialising statements in the class declaration these are removed and inserted just in front of the compound tail of the block in which the declaration is made. Thus if T has the form displayed in (1), $\textbf{var}(T)t$ is equivalent to:

> ...declarations for $t.c_1, t.c_2, \ldots, t.c_n \ldots$;
> **procedure** $t.p_1(\ldots)$; Q_1';
> **procedure** $t.p_2(\ldots)$; Q_2';
> . . . .
> **procedure** $t.p_m(\ldots)$; Q_m';

where $Q_1', Q_2', \ldots, Q_m', Q'$ are obtained from $Q_1, Q_2, \ldots, Q_m, Q$ by prefixing every occurrence of $c_1, c_2, \ldots, c_n$, $p_1, p_2, \ldots, p_m$ by "t.". Furthermore, the initialising statement Q' will have been inserted just ahead of the statements of the block body.

If there are several variables of class T declared in the same block, the method described above can be applied to each of them. But in a practical implementation, only one copy of the procedure bodies will be translated. This would contain as an extra parameter an address to the block of $c_1, c_2, \ldots, c_n$ on which a particular call is to operate.

5 Criterion of correctness

In an abstract program, an operation of the form

$$t_i.p_j(a_1, a_2, \ldots, a_{nj}) \tag{2}$$

will be expected to carry out some transformation on the variable t_i, in such a way that its resulting value is $f_j(t_i, a_1, a_2, \ldots, a_{nj})$, where f_j is some primitive operation required by the abstract program. In other words the procedure statement is expected to be equivalent to the assignment

$$t_i := f_j(t_i, a_1, a_2, \ldots, a_{nj});$$

When this equivalence holds, we say that p_j *models* f_j. A similar concept of modelling applies to functions. It is desired that the proof of the abstract program may be based on the equivalence, using the rule of assignment [Hoave 69a*], so that for any propositional formula S, the abstract programmer may assume:

$$S^{t_i}_{fj(t_i, a_1, a_2, \ldots, a_{nj})} \{t_i.p_j(a_1, a_2, \ldots, a_{nj})\} S.^1$$

In addition, the abstract programmer will wish to assume that all declared variables are initialised to some designated value d_0 of the abstract space.

The criterion of correctness of a data representation is that every p_j models the intended f_j and that the initialisation statement "models" the desired initial value; and consequently, a program operating on abstract variables may validly be replaced by one carrying out equivalent operations on the concrete representation.

---

[1] S_y^x stands for the result of replacing all free occurrences of x in S by y: if any free variables of y would become bound in S by this substitution, this is avoided by preliminary systematic alteration of bound variables in S.

Thus in the case of smallintset, we require to prove that:

$$\mathbf{var}(i)t \text{ initialises } t \text{ to } \{ \ \} \text{ (the empty set)}$$

$$t.\text{insert } (i) \equiv t := t \cup \{i\}$$

$$t.\text{remove}(i) \equiv t := t \cap \neg \{i\} \tag{3}$$

$$t.\text{has}(i) \equiv i \in t.$$

6 Proof method

The first requirement for the proof is to define the relationship between the abstract space in which the abstract program is written, and the space of the concrete representation. This can be accomplished by giving a function $\mathcal{C}(c_1, c_2, \ldots, c_n)$ which maps the concrete variables into the abstract object which they represent. For example, in the case of smallintset, the representation function can be defined as

$$\mathcal{C}(m, A) = \{i : \text{integer} | \exists k(1 \leqslant k \leqslant m \ \& \ A[k] = i)\} \tag{4}$$

or in words, "(m, A) represents the set of values of the first m elements of A". Note that in this and in many other cases $\mathcal{C}$ will be a many-one function. Thus there is no unique concrete value representing any abstract one.

Let t stand for the value of $\mathcal{C}(c_1, c_2, \ldots, c_m)$ before execution of the body Q_j of procedure p_j. Then what we must prove is that after execution of Q_j the following relation holds:

$$A(c_1, c_2, \ldots, c_n) = f_j(t, v_1, v_2, \ldots, v_{nj})$$

where $v_1, v_2, \ldots, v_{nj}$ are the formal parameters of p_j.

Using the notations of [Hoare 69a*], the requirement for proof may be expressed:

$$t = \mathcal{C}(c_1, c_2, \ldots, c_n)\{Q_j\}\mathcal{C}(c_1, c_2, \ldots, c_n) = f_j(t, v_1, v_2, \ldots, v_{nj})$$

where t is a variable which does not occur in Q_j. On the basis of this we may say: $t.p_j(a_1, a_2, \ldots, a_n) \equiv t := f_j(t, a_1, a_2, \ldots, a_n)$ with respect to $\mathcal{C}$. This deduction depends on the fact that no Q_j alters or accesses any variables other than $c_1, c_2, \ldots, c_n$; we shall in future assume that this constraint has been observed.

In fact for practical proofs we need a slightly stronger rule, which enables the programmer to give an invariant condition $I(c_1, c_2, \ldots, c_n)$, defining some relationship between the constituent concrete variables, and thus placing a constraint on the possible combinations of values which they may take. Each operation (except initialisation) may assume that I is true when it is first entered; and each operation must in return ensure that it is true on completion.

In the case of smallintset, the correctness of all operations depends on the fact that m remains within the bounds of A, and the correctness of the remove operation is dependent on the fact that the values of $A[1]$, $A[2], \ldots, A[m]$ are all different; a simple expression of this invariant is:

$$\text{size } (\mathcal{C}(m, A)) = m \leqslant 100. \tag{I}$$

One additional complexity will often be required; in general, a procedure body is not prepared to accept arbitrary combinations of values for its parameters, and its correctness therefore depends on satisfaction of some precondition $P(t, a_1, a_2, \ldots, a_n)$ before the procedure is entered. For example, the correctness of the insert procedure depends on the fact that the size of the resulting set is not greater than 100, that is

$$\text{size } (t \cup \{i\}) \leqslant 100$$

This precondition (with t replaced by $\mathcal{C}$) may be assumed in the proof of the body of the procedure; but it must accordingly be proved to hold before every call of the procedure.

It is interesting to note that any of the p's that are functions may be permitted to change the values of the c's, on condition that it preserve the truth of the invariant, and also that it preserve unchanged the value of the abstract object $\mathcal{C}$. For example, the function *has* could reorder the elements of A; this might be an advantage if it is expected that membership of some of the members of the set will be tested much more frequently than others. The existence of such a concrete side-effect is wholly invisible to the abstract program. This seems to be a convincing explanation of the phenomenon of "benevolent side-effects", whose existence I was not prepared to admit in [Hoare 69*].

7 Proof of smallintset

The proof may be split into four parts, corresponding to the four parts of the class declaration:

7.1 Initialisation

What we must prove is that after initialisation the abstract set is empty and that the invariant I is true:

$$\textbf{true}\{m := 0\}\{i | \exists k(1 \leqslant k \leqslant m \ \& \ A[k] = i)\} = \{ \ \}$$

$$\& \, \text{size } (\mathcal{C}(m, a)) = m \leqslant 100$$

Using the rule of assignment, this depends on the obvious truth of the lemma

$$\{i|\exists k(1 \leqslant k \leqslant 0 \,\&\, A[k]=i)\}=\{\ \}\,\&\, size(\{\ \})=0 \leqslant 100$$

7.2 Has

What we must prove is

$$\mathcal{Q}(m,A)=k \,\&\, I \,\{Q_{\text{has}}\}\, \mathcal{Q}(m,A)=k \,\&\, I \,\&\, has=i \in \mathcal{Q}(m,A)$$

where Q_{has} is the body of *has*. Since Q_{has} does not change the value of m or A, the truth of the first two assertions on the right hand side follows directly from their truth beforehand. The invariant of the loop inside Q_{has} is:

$$j \leqslant m \,\&\, has = i \in \mathcal{Q}(j,A)$$

as may be verified by a proof of the lemma:

$$j < m \,\&\, j \leqslant m \,\&\, has = i \in \mathcal{Q}(j,A)$$
$$\supset \textbf{if}\ A[j+1]=i\ \textbf{then}\ (\textbf{true}=i \in \mathcal{Q}(m,A))$$
$$\textbf{else}\ has = i \in \mathcal{Q}(j+1,A).$$

Since the final value of j is m, the truth of the desired result follows directly from the invariant; and since the "initial" value of j is zero, we only need the obvious lemma

$$\textbf{false} = i \in \mathcal{Q}(0,A)$$

7.3 Insert

What we must prove is:

$$P \,\&\, \mathcal{Q}(m,A)=k \,\&\, I \,\{Q_{\text{insert}}\}\, \mathcal{Q}(m,A)=(k \cup \{i\}) \,\&\, I,$$

where $P \equiv_{\text{df}} size\ (\mathcal{Q}(m,A) \cup \{i\}) \leqslant 100$.
  The invariant of the loop is:

$$P \,\&\, \mathcal{Q}(m,A)=k \,\&\, I \,\&\, i \in \mathcal{Q}(j,A) \,\&\, 0 \leqslant j \leqslant m \qquad (6)$$

as may be verified by the proof of the lemma

$$\mathcal{Q}(m,A)=k \,\&\, i \in \mathcal{Q}(j,A) \,\&\, 0 \leqslant j \leqslant m \,\&\, j < m \supset$$
$$\textbf{if}\ A[j+1]=i\ \textbf{then}\ \mathcal{Q}(m,A)=(k \cup \{i\})$$
$$\textbf{else}\ 0 \leqslant j+1 \leqslant m \,\&\, i \in \mathcal{Q}(j+1,A)$$

(The invariance of $P \,\&\, \mathcal{Q}(m,A)=k \,\&\, I$ follows from the fact that the loop does not change the values of m or A). That (6) is true before the loop follows from $i \in \mathcal{Q}(0,A)$.

We must now prove that the truth of (6), together with $j = m$ at the end of the loop, is adequate to ensure the required final condition. This depends on proof of the lemma

$$j = m \ \& \ (6) \cup A(m+1,A') = (k \cup \{i\}) \ \& \ size \ (\mathcal{Q}(m+1,A')) = m+1 \leqslant 100$$

where $A' = (A, m+1 : i)$ is the new value of A after assignment of i to $A[m+1]$.

7.4 Remove

What we must prove is

$$\mathcal{Q}(m,A) = k \ \& \ I \ \{Q_{\text{remove}}\} \mathcal{Q}(m,A) = (k \cap \neg \{i\}) \ \& \ I.$$

The details of the proof are complex. Since they add nothing more to the purpose of this paper, they will be omitted.

8 Formalities

Let T be a class declared as shown in Section 2, and let $\mathcal{Q}$, I, P_j, f_j be formulae as explained in Section 6 (free variable lists are omitted where convenient). Suppose also that the following $m+1$ theorems have been proved:

$$\textbf{true} \ \{Q\}I \ \& \ \mathcal{Q} = d_0 \tag{7}$$

$$\mathcal{Q} = t \ \& \ I \ \& \ P_j(t)\{Q_j\}I \ \& \ \mathcal{Q} = f_j(t)$$
$$\text{for procedure bodies } Q_j \tag{8}$$

$$\mathcal{Q} = t \ \& \ I \ \& \ P_j(t)\{Q_j\}I \ \& \ \mathcal{Q} = t \ \& \ p_j = f_j(t)$$
$$\text{for function bodies } Q_j. \tag{9}$$

In this section we show that the proof of these theorems is a sufficient condition for the correctness of the data representation, in the sense explained in Section 5.

Let X be a program beginning with a declaration of a variable t of an abstract type, and initialising it to d_0. The subsequent operations on this variable are of the form

(1) $t := f_j(t, a_1, a_2, \ldots, a_{nj})$ if Q_j is a procedure

(2) $f_j(t, a_1, a_2, \ldots, a_{nj})$ if Q_j is a function.

Suppose also that $P_j(t, a_1, a_2, \ldots, a_{nj})$ has been proved true before each such operation.

Let X' be a program formed from X by replacements described in Section 4, as well as the following (see Section 5):

(1) initialisation $t := d_0$ replaced by Q'

(2) $t := f_j(t, a_1, a_2, \ldots, a_{nj})$ replaced by $t.p_j(a_1, a_2, \ldots, a_{nj})$

(3) $f_j(t, a_1, a_2, \ldots, a_{nj})$ by $t.p_j(a_1, a_2, \ldots, a_{nj})$.

Theorem. *Under conditions described above, if X and X' both terminate, the value of t on termination of X will be $\mathcal{C}(c_1, c_2, \ldots, c_n)$, where $c_1, c_2, \ldots, c_n$ are the values of these variables on termination of X'.*

Corollary. *If $R(t)$ has been proved true on termination of X, $R(\mathcal{C})$ will be true on termination of X'.*

PROOF. Consider the sequence S of operations on t executed during the computation of X, and let S' be the sequence of subcomputations of X' arising from execution of the procedure calls which have replaced the corresponding operations on t in X. We will prove that there is a close elementwise correspondence between the two sequences, and that

(a) each item of S' is the very procedure statement which replaced the corresponding operation in S,
(b) the values of all variables (and hence also the actual parameters) which are common to both "programs" are the same after each operation,
(c) the invariant I is true between successive items of S',
(d) if the operations are function calls, their results in both sequences are the same,
(e) and if they are procedure calls (or the initialisation) the value of t immediately after the operation in S is given by $\mathcal{C}$, as applied to the values of $c_1, c_2, \ldots, c_n$ after the corresponding operation S'.

It is this last fact, applied to the last item of the two sequences, that establishes the truth of the theorem.

The proof is by induction on the position of an item in S.

(1) *Basis.* Consider its first item of S, $t := d_0$. Since X and X' are identical up to this point, the first item of S' must be the subcomputation of the procedure Q which replaced it, proving (a). By (7), I is true after Q in S', and also $\mathcal{C} = d_0$, proving (c) and (e). (d) is not relevant. Q is not allowed to change any non-local variable, proving (b).

(2) *Induction step.* We may assume that conditions (a) to (e) hold immediately after the $(n-1)$-th item of S and S', and we establish that they are true after the n-th. Since the value of all other variables (and the result, if a function) were the same after the previous operation in both sequences, the subsequent course of the computation must also be the same until the very next point at which X' differs from X. This establishes (a) and (b). Since the only permitted changes to the values of

$t.c_1, t.c_2, \ldots, t.c_n$ occur in the subcomputations of S', and I contains no other variables, the truth of I after the previous subcomputation proves that it is true before the next. Since S contains *all* operations on t, the value of t is the same before the n-th as it was after the $(n-1)$-th operation, and it is still equal to $\mathcal{C}$. It is given as proved that the appropriate $P_j(t)$ is true before each call of f_j in S. Thus we have established that $\mathcal{C} = t \& I \& P_j(t)$ is true before the operation in S'. From (8) or (9) the truth of (c), (d), (e) follows immediately. (b) follows from the fact that the assignment in S changes the value of no other variable besides t; and similarly, Q_j is not permitted to change the value of any variable other than $t.c_1, t.c_2, \ldots, t.c_n$.

This proof has been an informal demonstration of a fairly obvious theorem. Its main interest has been to show the necessity for certain restrictive conditions placed on class declarations. Fortunately these restrictions are formulated as scope rules, which can be rigorously checked at compile time.

9 Extensions

The exposition of the previous sections deals only with the simplest cases of the SIMULA 67 class concept; nevertheless, it would seem adequate to cover a wide range of practical data representations. In this section we consider the possibility of further extensions, roughly in order of sophistication.

9.1 Class Parameters

It is often useful to permit a class to have formal parameters which can be replaced by different actual parameters whenever the class is used in a declaration. These parameters may influence the method of representation, or the identity of the initial value, or both. In the case of smallintset, the usefulness of the definition could be enhanced if the maximum size of the set is a parameter, rather than being fixed at 100.

9.2 Dynamic object generation

In SIMULA 67, the value of a variable c of class C may be reinitialised by an assignment:

$$c := \textbf{new } C\langle\text{actual parameter part}\rangle$$

This presents no extra difficulty for proofs.

9.3 Remote identification

In many cases, a local concrete variable of a class has a meaningful interpretation in the abstract space. For example, the variable *m* of smallintset always stands for the size of the set. If the main program needs to test the size of the set, it would be possible to make this accessible by writing a function

$$\textbf{integer procedure } size;\ size := m$$

But it would be simpler and more convenient to make the variable more directly accessible by a compound identifier, perhaps by declaring it

$$\textbf{public integer } m$$

The proof technique would specify that

$$m = size\ (\mathcal{Q}(m, A))$$

is part of the invariant of the class.

9.4 Class concatenation

The basic mechanism for representing sets by arrays can be applied to sets with members of type or class other than just integers. It would therefore be useful to have a method of defining a class "smallset", which can then be used to construct other classes such as "smallrealset" or smallcarset", where "car" is another class. In SIMULA 67, this effect can be achieved by the class/subclass and virtual mechanisms.

9.5 Recursive class declaration

In SIMULA 67, the parameters of a class, or of a local procedure of the class, and even the local variables of a class, may be declared as belonging to that very same class. This permits the construction of lists and trees, and their processing by recursive procedure activation. In proving the correctness of such a class, it will be necessary to assume the correctness of all "recursive" operations in the proofs of the bodies of the procedures. In the implementation of recursive classes, it will be necessary to represent variables by a null pointer (**none**) or by the *address* of their value, rather than by direct inclusion of space for their values in block workspace of the block to which they are local. The reason for this is that the amount of space occupied by a value of recursively defined type cannot be determined at compile time.

It is worthy of note that the proof technique recommended above is valid only if the data structure is "well-grounded" in the sense that it is a pure tree, without cycles and without convergence of branches. The restrictions suggested in this paper make it impossible for local variables of a class to be updated except by the body of a procedure local to that very same activation of the class; and I believe that this will effectively prevent the construction of structures which are not well-grounded, provided that assignment is implemented by copying the complete value, not just the address.

Acknowledgments. I am deeply indebted to Doug Ross and to all authors of referenced works. Indeed, the material of this paper represents little more than my belated understanding and formalisation of their original work.

20
The Algebraic Specification of Abstract Data Types

J. V. Guttag[1]
University of Southern California

J. J. Horning
Xerox Parc

Abstract *There have been many recent proposals for embedding abstract data types in programming languages. In order to reason about programs using abstract data types, it is desirable to specify their properties at an abstract level, independent of any particular implementation. This paper presents an algebraic technique for such specifications, develops some of the formal properties of the technique, and shows that these provide useful guidelines for the construction of adequate specifications.*

1. Introduction

The class construct of SIMULA 67 [Dahl 70*] has been used as the starting point for much of the more recent work on embedding abstract types in programming languages, [e.g. Liskov 74, Morris 73]. While each of these offers a mechanism for binding together the operations and storage structures representing a type, they offer no representation-independent means for specifying the behaviour of the operations. The only representation-independent information that one can supply are the domains and ranges of the various operations. One could, for example, define a type *Queue* (of Integers) with the operations

NEW:	$\rightarrow Queue$
ADD:	$Queue \times Integer \rightarrow Queue$
FRONT:	$Queue \rightarrow Integer$
REMOVE:	$Queue \rightarrow Queue$
EMPTY?:	$Queue \rightarrow Boolean$

[1]Supported in part by the National Science Foundation under grant MCS-76-06089 and the Joint Services Electronics Program monitored by the Air Force Office of the Scientific Research under contract F44620-76C-0061.

Unfortunately, short of supplying a representation, the only mechanism for denoting what these operations "mean" is a judicious choice of names. Except for intuitions about the meaning of such words as *Queue* and *FRONT*, the operations might just as easily be defining type *Stack* as type *Queue*. The domain and range specifications for these two types are isomorphic. To rely on one's intuition about the meaning of names can be dangerous even when dealing with familiar types [Palme 73, Henderson 72]. When dealing with unfamiliar types, it is almost impossible. What is needed, therefore, is a mechanism for specifying the semantics of the operations of the type.

In this paper we shall use the algebraic axiomatic technique developed in [Guttag 75*]. This approach owes much to the work of Hoare [Hoare 72f*] and is closely related to the work in [Zilles 75, 76, Goguen 75, Spitzen 75]. Its formal basis stems from the heterogeneous algebras in [Birkhoff 70].

An algebraic specification of an abstract type consists of two parts: a syntactic specification and a set of axioms. The syntactic specification provides the syntactic and type checking information that many programming languages already require: the names, domains, and ranges of the operations associated with the type. The set of axioms defines (in a sense to be discussed later) the meaning of the operations by stating their relationships to one another.

[Spitzen 75] cites three attributes of this approach to the specification of data types:

> First, they are declarative and hence avoid programming details and language dependencies. Second, they are intuitively reasonable descriptions of the behaviour of various structures. Finally, they are sufficiently rigorous to permit a proof that a particular realization of the data structures is faithful to the specifications.

To these three attributes we should like to add a fourth advantage we feel applies particularly strongly to our specifications: they are easy to read and comprehend, thus facilitating informal verification of the fact that they do indeed conform to the intent of their creator.

2. A Short Example

Consider type *Bag* (of *Integers*) with the operations:

EMPTY_BAG:	→*Bag*
INSERT:	*Bag* × *Integer*→*Bag*
DELETE:	*Bag* × *Integer*→*Bag*
MEMBER_OF?:	*Bag* × *Integer*→*Boolean*

There are, of course, many ways to implement a *bag*. Some imply an ordering of the elements (e.g., a linked list representation), some don't (e.g., a hash table implementation). These details are not relevant to the basic notion of a *bag*. A *bag* is nothing more than a counted set. A good axiomatic definition of type *Bag* must, therefore, assert that and only that characteristic. The axioms below comprise just such a definition. The axioms should prove relatively easy to read. ("=" has its standard meaning; *s*, *i* and *i'* are typed free variables, and ?=? is an equality relation defined on type *Integer*.)

$$MEMBER\_OF?\ (EMPTY\_BAG, i) = false \qquad\qquad 1)$$

$$MEMBER\_OF?\ (INSERT(b, i), i') = \textbf{if}\ \ ? = ?(i, i') \qquad\qquad 2)$$
$$\textbf{then}\ true$$
$$\textbf{else}\ MEMBER\_OF?(b, i')$$

$$DELETE\ (EMPTY\ BAG, i) = EMPTY\_BAG \qquad\qquad 3)$$

$$DELETE\ (INSERT(b, i), i') = \textbf{if}\ ? = ?(i, i') \qquad\qquad 4)$$
$$\textbf{then}\ b$$
$$\textbf{else}\ INSERT\ (DELETE(b, i'), i)$$

As an interesting comparison, consider the following specification of type *Set*:

$$EMPTY\_SET: \qquad \rightarrow\ \ Set$$
$$INSERT: \qquad\quad Set \times Integer \rightarrow Set$$
$$DELETE: \qquad\quad Set \times Integer \rightarrow Set$$
$$MEMBER\_OF?: \quad Set \times Integer \rightarrow Boolean$$

$$MEMBER\_OF?\ (EMPTY\_SET, i) = false \qquad\qquad 5)$$

$$MEMBER\_OF?\ (INSERT(s, i), i') = \textbf{if}\ \ ? = ?(i, i') \qquad\qquad 6)$$
$$\textbf{then}\ true$$
$$\textbf{else}\ MEMBER\_OF?(s, i')$$

$$DELETE\ (EMPTY\_SET, i) = EMPTY\_SET \qquad\qquad 7)$$

$$DELETE\ (INSERT(s, i), i') = \textbf{if}\ ? = ?(i, i') \qquad\qquad 8)$$
$$\textbf{then}\ DELETE(s, i')$$
$$\textbf{else}\ INSERT\ (DELETE(s, i'), i)$$

Except for the difference in the **then** clauses of axioms 4 and 8, this specification is, for all intents and purposes, the same as that for type *Bag*. The specifications thus serve to point out the similarities and isolate the one crucial difference between these two types.

With some practice, one can become quite adept at reading algebraic axiomatizations. Practice also enhances the ability to construct such specifications, but doesn't make it trivial. The major difficulty lies in deciding how to attack the problem. Fortunately, our experience in writing algebraic specifications has led us to develop some heuristics that have proven extremely valuable in attacking this problem. A discussion of these heuristics constitutes a major portion of this paper.

Once one has constructed a specification, one must address the question of whether or not one has supplied a sufficient number of consistent axioms. The partial semantics of the type is supplied by a set of individual statements of fact. If any pair of these is contradictory, the axiomatization is inconsistent. If, for example, one were to add the axiom:

$$MEMBER\_OF?\ (DELETE(b,i),i') = \textbf{if } ?=?(i,i')$$
$$\textbf{then } false$$
$$\textbf{else } MEMBER\_OF?(b,i')$$

to the specification of type *Bag*, one would have created an inconsistent specification. There would exist values of type *Bag* for which it would be possible to prove both $MEMBER\_OF?(b,i)$ and **not** $MEMBER\_OF?(b,i)$, depending upon which axioms one chose to use. $MEMBER\_OF?\ (DELETE\ (INSERT\ (INSERT\ (EMPTY\_BAG,3),3),3),3)$ is an example of an expression for which such a contradiction could be derived.

If the combination of axioms does not convey all the vital information regarding the meaning of the operations of the type, the axiomatization is not sufficiently-complete. If the specification of an abstract type is not sufficiently-complete, it is not always possible to predict the behaviour of the programs that use the operations of the type. Experience with our methodology indicates that completeness is, in a practical sense, a more severe problem than consistency. If one has an intuitive understanding of the type being specified, one is unlikely to supply contradictory axioms. It is, on the other hand, extremely easy to overlook one or more cases. Boundary conditions, e.g., $DELETE\ (EMPTY\_BAG,i)$ are particularly likely to be overlooked. The heuristics mentioned above have been devised to ameliorate this problem. We have also designed a system that can mechanically verify the sufficient-completeness of certain specifications. This system will be discussed later in this paper. We shall also discuss another approach to algebraic specification in which consistency seems to be the primary problem.

3. A Formal look at abstract data types and their algebraic specification

Sections 1 and 2 presented informally a technique for the specification of abstract data types. This section takes a more formal look at it. This formalization is a necessary prelude to both a discussion of the inherent power of the technique and the construction of conditions sufficient to insure sufficient-completeness.

3.1. A definition of abstract type

An abstract type is basically a collection of values and operations. For this reason it is quite natural to view it as an algebraic system. A type *Natural Number*, for example, might be defined as the values $0, 1, 2\ldots$ and such operations as

$SUCC$:   *Natural Number→Natural Number*
$PSUB$:   *Natural Number × Natural Number→Natural Number*
$EQUAL?$:   *Natural Number × Natural Number→Boolean*
ABS: *Integer→Natural Number*

Note that though we have defined the values of the type to be exactly the set $\{0, 1, 2\ldots\}$, both the domains and ranges of the operations of the type may include values from outside that set. For this reason, the language of conventional homogeneous algebras is not well-suited to a discussion of abstract data types. The language of heterogeneous algebras, on the other hand, is quite well-suited.

A homogenous algebra A is a pair $[C, F]$, where C, the carrier, is a non-empty set of values, and F is a finite set of finitary operations $Fj.n$. Each $Fj.n$ is a mapping:

$$Fj.n: C^n \to C$$

[Birkhoff 70] generalized this to a heterogeneous algebra $[V, F]$, where V is a set of non-empty sets Vi, called *phyla*, and F is a finite set of finitary mappings $Fj.n$:

$$Fj.n: Vi1 \times Vi2 \times \cdots \times Vin \to Vk, \quad \text{where } \forall 1 \leqslant h \leqslant n \left[Vih \in V \right] \text{ and } Vk \in V.$$

This can be restricted to a **type algebra** $[V, F]$ where V is a set of phyla Vi, $1 \leqslant i \leqslant m$, which includes a distinguished phylum called TOI (type of interest), and F is a finite set of finitary mappings:

$$Fj.n: Vi1 \times Vi2 \times \cdots \times Vin \to Vk$$

where $\forall 1 \leqslant h \leqslant n[Vih \in V]$, $Vk \in V$, and at least one member of the set $\{Vi1, \ldots, Vin, Vk\}$ is the distinguished phylum TOI.

Thus, a type *Natural Number* may be defined as the algebra $[V, F]$ where $V = \{\{true, false\}, \{\ldots -2, -1, 0, 1, 2 \ldots\}, \{1, 2 \ldots\}\}$ and $F = \{SUCC, PSUB, EQUAL?, ABS\}$ and where the domains and ranges of the mappings are as above. The crucial difference between a general heterogeneous algebra and a type algebra is that the latter defines one phylum (TOI) in terms of the others, whereas the former defines a set of phyla by mutual recursion. The specification technique presented in this paper presupposes the existence of only one type: *Boolean*. (The existence of this type, or at least of some type with two distinct values, is necessary to define the meaning of axioms that contain conditionals.) In applying the specification technique, however, it is frequently useful to presuppose the existence of other types. The specification of type *Bag* in section 2, for example, assumes the existence of an independently-defined type *Integer*. Theoretically, it would be possible to define several types at once via mutual recursion. It seems, however, that in general a clean separation of types leads to clearer specifications.

It is hardly surprising that heterogeneous algebras are well suited to describing an algebraic system containing such common (in mathematics) domains as natural numbers, integers, and Booleans. Let us, therefore, consider a somewhat less "mathematical" example: type *Queue* (of *Integers*), with the operations:

NEW:	→*Queue*
ADD:	*Queue* × *Integer*→*Queue*
FRONT:	*Queue*→*Integer*
REMOVE:	*Queue*→*Queue*
?*EMPTY*?:	*Queue*→*Boolean*

F, of course, is the set $\{NEW, ADD, FRONT, REMOVE, ?EMPTY?\}$. It is clear that V must contain $\{\ldots -2, -1, 0, 1, 2 \ldots\}$ and $\{true, false\}$ and that $m = 3$. It is not immediately clear how to represent set *TOI*. This is not because of any intrinsic difference in the algebraic structure of queues and natural numbers, but is rather a function of the fact that a familiar notation for denoting values of type *Queue* is not available.

This common problem in specifying algebras is easily circumvented by defining the algebra in terms of a generator, rather than a carrier, set. In axiomatic set theory, for example, it is quite normal to define all sets in terms of the single generator { }, the empty set. Consider $Cl(G, F)$, the algebraic closure of F over the set G, as defined by the construction:

1) $x \in G$ implies $x \in Cl(G, F)$.
2) $Fj.n \in F$ and $x1, x2, \ldots, xn \in Cl(G)$, implies that $Fj.n(x1, x2, \ldots, xn) \in Cl(G, F)$.
3) These are the only members of $Cl(G, F)$.

Given homogeneous algebras $A = [C, F]$ and $A' = [Cl(G, F), F]$, if A' is the least subalgebra of A that included G, and $A' = A$, then G is a generator set for A. The situation with respect to heterogeneous algebras is analogous. One has family Gi of generators, and a family Ci of carriers such that:

1) $x \in Gi$ implies that $x \in Ci$
2) $Fj.n$: $Vi1 \times Vi2 \times \ldots \times Vin \rightarrow Vk$ contained in F, and $x1, x2, \ldots, xn$ contained in $Ci1 \times Ci2 \times \ldots \times Cin$ implies that $Fj.n(x1, x2, \ldots, xn)$ is contained in Ck.
3) These are the only members of the carriers Ci.

Now, returning to the *Queue* (of *Integers*) example, G may be defined as $\{\{\ldots -2, -1, 0, 1, 2 \ldots\}, \{true, false\}, \{ \}\}$, or, more succinctly, $\{Z, Boolean, \{ \}\}$. There are two crucial things to note about this definition. First, for the phyla representing integer and Boolean values, the generator and carrier sets are identical. This is necessary because, given an interpretation that doesn't stray too far from what one might expect, the operations of the algebra will not generate new values of any phylum other than *TOI*. This is something we want to be true of type algebras in general, and it is what distinguished *TOI* from the other phyla. The second thing to note about *V* is that the generator set for *TOI* is empty. This is a consequence of having chosen to treat the constant value *NEW* as a nullary "operation," rather than as a "value" (a convention we shall continue to follow). Thus one of the operations serves, in effect, as the generator for the phylum. It is essential that there be at least one operator,

$$fn: Vi1 \times Vi2 \times \ldots \times Vin \rightarrow TOI$$

where each *Vi* is contained in *V*-{*TOI*}, for in a heterogeneous algebra each carrier phylum must be non-empty. We shall follow the convention of treating such nullary (with respect to the type of interest) functions as operations throughout this development.

3.2. The semantics of abstract types

The discussion above furnishes a method for the presentation of the components that form an abstract type. To say that type *Queue* (of *Integers*) is an algebra,

$$[Cl(\{ Z, Boolean, \{ \ \} \}), \{ NEW, ADD, FRONT, REMOVE, ?EMPTY? \}]$$

however, is not enough. Such a specification gives no more information about the type than do the domain and range specifications that such languages as SIMULA 67 permit (see Section 1). The operations of the type still have to be given meanings.

This could be done by supplying an interpretation for each operation. To adopt this approach, however, is to ignore the primary reason for viewing a data type as an algebra, i.e., to provide a representation-free specification of the type. For this reason we have chosen to define the semantics of the operations of a type by supplying a set of axioms stating various properties that the algebra must possess. This is, of course, a conventional algebraic approach. The relation "=", for example, is most often defined merely by stating that it is reflexive, transitive, symmetric, and $a = b$ implies $f(a) = f(b)$. When defining familiar algebraic structures, e.g., the natural numbers, providing an axiomatization often presents no real problem. This is not, in general, the case for abstract data types.

The selection of appropriate axioms depends largely on the type being defined. It is therefore impossible to give any general procedure for constructing axiomatizations for type algebras. It is, however, possible to characterize the sort of information that must be conveyed by any axiomatization. That is to say, it is possible to give a generalization of the form that such an axiomatization should take.

A slightly different notation for abstract types will prove convenient in this discussion. Since the generator set of *TOI* is by convention always empty, it need not be explicitly included in the specification of the algebra. The set of phyla V is thus replaced by the set $I = V - \{TOI\}$. Also, for reasons that will become clear later in this discussion, the set of operations F is partitioned into disjoint sets S and O such that S contains exactly those operations whose range is *TOI*. Intuitively, S contains the operations that can be used to generate values of the type being defined and O the operations that map values of the type into other types. The need for operations to generate values of the type is clear, thus S will always be non-empty.

In principle, one could define a type for which O is empty. Such a type, however, would be uninteresting. With no way to partition the set *TOI* (O empty implies no predicates) or to relate members of the set to members of other phyla, no member of *TOI* could be distinguished from any other. That is to say, for all one could observe, every value of the type would be equivalent to every other value of the type. For all intents and purposes, there would be only one value of that type. The ability to distinguish between the values contained in *TOI* thus rests solely upon the effect that these values have when they appear in the argument lists of the operations contained in O.

A type may now be characterized as an algebra $T = [Cl(I), S + O]$ and, in light of the above discussion, it is apparent that to define the semantics of the operations contained in O is to define the semantics of the type. Recall that all functions $Fj.n$ in O are of the form

$$Fj.n\colon \ Vi1 \times Vi2 \times \ldots \times Vin \to Vk$$

where for $1 \leqslant h \leqslant n\ \ Vih \in I + \{TOI\}$ and $Vk \in I$.

Thus, the semantics of the type may be defined as a set of mappings

$$Me\colon \ O \times (I + \{TOI\})^p \to \{error\} + Vi \in I$$

where p is the maximum arity of the functions in O and for all $f \in O$ and $w \in (I + \{TOI\})^p$, $Me(f,w) = error$ (a distinguished error element) if w is not contained in the domain of f: and $Me(f,w) = y$ where $y \in Vi \in I$ if w is in the domain of f.

An example may help to clarify matters. Consider type *Queue* (of *Integers*) $= [Cl(\{Z, Boolean\}), \ \{NEW, ADD, REMOVE\} + \{FRONT, ?EMPTY?\}]$. To supply the semantics of this type one need only define the function

$$Me\colon \ \{FRONT, ?EMPTY?\} \times \{Z, Boolean, Queue\} \to \{Z, Boolean\}$$

The problem is how to present an axiomatization of such a function. The definition of *Me* implies one axiom that must be present in the axiomatization of any type:

$$\forall F_j.n, x1, \ldots, xn [(x1, \ldots, xn) \quad \text{not in the domain of} \quad Fj.n \quad \text{implies that}$$

$$Me(Fj.n, x1, \ldots, xn) = error\,]$$

Note that in an algebraic specification of an abstract type the domain of each $Fj.n$ is formally supplied by the syntactic specification. Note also that if none of the domains of the operations of the type contains *error*, and this will normally be the case, this axiom implies that

$$\forall Fj.n, x1, \ldots, xn[xi = error, 1 \leqslant i \leqslant n, \text{ implies that } Me(Fj.n, x1, \ldots, xn) = error].$$

Thus the distinguished value *error* has the property that the value of any operation applied to an argument list containing *error* is *error*. Since this axiom is a part of every type specification, it will be included implicitly in all subsequent specifications: it will be referred to as the *implicit axiom*. The question now is: how should such an axiomatization be completed?

3.3. The axiomatization of type algebras

The first point to address is what it means to "complete" an axiomatization. The notion of a complete axiom set is a familiar one to logicians. The form of definition used depends on the environment in which one is working. The statements that a complete axiom set is "one to which an independent axiom cannot be added," or "one with which every well-formed formula or its negation can be proved as a theorem," or "one for which all models are isomorphic (i.e., the axioms are categorical)," are all common. Our notion of completeness conforms to none of these statements. We have, therefore, introduced the qualifier "sufficiently" to try to differentiate our notion of completeness from these others. Above, sufficiently-complete was defined informally by saying that all one had to do was to provide a semantics for the function Me. We now define it more rigorously.

The sets I and $S + O$ of the algebra for a type T may be used to define a word algebra [Boon 59], The set of words, $L(T)$ contained in this algebra are defined inductively as follows:

1) All elements of $Vi \in I$ are contained in $L(T)$.
2) If $Fj.n$ is contained in $S + O$, and $(x1, \ldots, xn)$ is contained in the domain of $Fj.n$ and each xi, $1 \leqslant i \leqslant n$, is contained in $L(T)$, then $Fj.n(x1, \ldots, xn)$ is contained in $L(T)$.
3) These are the only terms contained in $L(T)$.

Intuitively, $L(T)$ is the language defined by the abstract type. It is the union of all the carrier phyla of the type and specifies a set of terms that may appear in the body of any program in which the type has been defined. For an axiomatization of a type to be sufficiently-complete, it must assign meaning to each of the terms in this language.

At first glance, this seems formidable. Fortunately, however, one need explicitly consider only a subset of $L(T)$. Recall that the actual goal is to define

$$Me: O \times (I + \{TOI\})^p \rightarrow Vi \in I$$

Thus, one need consider only those words contained in $L(T)$ whose outermost operation is contained in O. With this in mind, the term sufficiently-complete can now be precisely defined:

Definition. For any abstract type $T = [Cl(I), S + O]$, and any axiom set A, A is a **sufficiently-complete axiomatization** of T if and only if for every word of the form $Fj.n(x1, \ldots, xn)$ contained in $L(T)$ where $Fj.n \in O$, there exists a theorem derivable from A of the form $Fj.n(x1, \ldots, xn) = u$, where $u \in Vi \in I$. A is **consistent** if for each $Fj.n(x1, \ldots, xn)$ u is unique.

It can be shown (see Section 3.5) that the problem of establishing whether or not a set of axioms is sufficiently-complete is in general undecidable. Thus, one cannot be provided with necessary and sufficient guidelines to the construction of sufficiently-complete axiomatizations of type algebras. If, however, one is willing to accept limitations on the kinds of algebras that may be defined and on the language used to specify the axioms, it is possible to state sufficient conditions to ensure sufficient-completeness. A more complete discussion of this is contained in the next three sections.

3.4. A schema for presenting axiomatizations

An axiom set A for specifying an abstract type T will consist of the implicit axiom mentioned in Section 3.2 plus a finite set of axioms, each of which is of the form:

$$\forall x1, \ldots, xn [\, lhs = rhs \,]$$

$\forall$ and $=$ have their usual meanings. $\forall$ is the universal quantifier "for all." $=$ is reflexive, transitive, symmetric, and $P \& x = y$ implies $P(x/y)$. ($P(x/y)$ means P with y substituted for all free occurrences of x.)

For an axiomatization of a type T the number of possible axioms will be constrained by limiting the possible left hand sides to a finite set, LHS. This bounding of the left hand sides is based upon the assumption (discussed in Section 3.2.) that the significance of the values of TOI is embedded solely in the effect that these values have when they appear in the argument lists of operations contained in O. Thus, any axiom set in which all such effects were defined would be sufficiently-complete. This train of thought led to the belief that one could limit the set LHS to those terms generated by assigning free variables to the arguments of each $s \in S$ and permuting these through the appropriate positions in the argument list of each $o \in O$. Though a set of left hand sides derived via this algorithm should, in all cases, prove sufficient, it may often also prove to be inconvenient. It is sometimes convenient to generate left hand sides in which operations contained in S occur at the outermost level. (This will be discussed in Section 3.6.) The level of nesting in the left hand side, however, may still be limited to two. The set LHS is defined formally as:

$$LHS = \{ Fj.n(v1,\ldots,vn) | Fj.n \in S + O, \ \forall i \leqslant n[vi \text{ is a free}$$
$$\text{variable or } vi = Fk.m(x1,\ldots,xm)$$
$$\text{and } Fk.m \in S + O \text{ and } \forall 1 \leqslant l \leqslant m \ xl$$
$$\text{is a free variable]} \}$$

The definition of the set RHS, in which rhs must be contained, is somewhat more complex. Informally, a right hand side may be any valid expression all of whose free variables are free in the corresponding left hand side. More formally, the set of potential right hand sides for the ith axiom $RHSi$ is defined inductively as:

1) If xj is a constant or appears as a free variable in $LHSi$, then xj is contained in $RHSi$.
2) If $r1,\ldots,rm$ are contained in $RHSi$ and $Fj.m$ is an operation (not necessarily contained in $S + O$, i.e., it may be an operation from some V_i other than the TOI) whose range is any of the phyla in V, then $Fj.m(r1\ldots rm)$ is contained in $RHSi$.
3) If b,y,z are contained in $RHSi$ and b is of the form $Fj.m(r1,\ldots,rm)$ where the range of $Fj.m$ is *Boolean* then **if** b **then** y **else** z is contained in $RHSi$.
4) These are the only members of $RHSi$.

The meaning of the **if then else** construct is, as one might expect, **if** b **then** y **else** $z = [y$ if b is *true*, z if b is *false*, and undefined otherwise]. It is interesting to note that it is not essential to include the conditional expression as a primitive. Given any two distinct values, call them *TRUE* and *FALSE*, we can define an abstract type *Boolean* with an *IFTHENELSE* operation defined by the axiom:

$$IFTHENELSE \ (TRUE,x,y) = x$$
$$IFTHENELSE \ (FALSE,x,y) = y$$

Note that the mapping *Me*, which the axioms purport to define, does not appear explicitly in the axiomatization of a type. Nevertheless, the axioms can be used to define *Me*. Consider, as an example, a type *Posint* (positive integer):

$$T = [\ Cl(\{ Boolean \}), \{ ONE, SUCC, ADD \} + \{ ?ONE? \} \ ]$$

where the domains and ranges of the operations are:

ONE:	$\rightarrow Posint$
$SUCC$:	$Posint \rightarrow Posint$
ADD:	$Posint \times Posint \rightarrow Posint$
$?ONE?$:	$Posint \rightarrow Boolean$

A suitable axiomatization might include the implicit axiom plus:

1) $\forall x1 \in Posint, x2 \in Posint[ADD(x1,x2)=ADD(x2,x1)]$
2) $\forall x \in Posint[ADD(ONE,x)=SUCC(x)$
3) $\forall x1 \in Posint, x2 \in Posint[ADD(SUCC(x1),x2)=SUCC(ADD(x1,x2))]$
4) $?ONE?(ONE)=true$
5) $\forall x \in Posint[?ONE?(SUCC(x))=false]$

For this type, $O=\{?ONE?\}$ and $I=Boolean$; the domain of Me is $[\{?ONE?\} \times Posint]$ and the range $Boolean$. A simple induction on the length of words can be used to show that for all $x \in Posint$, axioms 1-3 can be used to reduce x to ONE or $SUCC^*(ONE)$. (Here, the * is the "Kleene star.") Thus, for any $x \in Posint$, $?ONE?(x)$ can be reduced to either *true* or *false*. Thus the mapping

$$Me:\{?ONE?\} \times Posint \rightarrow Boolean$$

is fully defined.

As a notational convenience, because all free variables are universally quantified over the correct type, the quantifiers that start each axiom may be dropped. Hence the notation used in section 2.

3.5. The power of the schema and the decidability of sufficiently-complete

Having restricted the manner in which type definitions may be supplied, it becomes necessary to address the question of whether or not the schema provided is sufficiently "powerful" to specify any type that one might wish to define: does the class of algebras definable via the provided mechanisms include all those algebras that might prove useful to a programmer? The answer is almost. While we cannot always specify exactly the intended algebra, we can specify a containing algebra; we can always specify an algebra that, by the forgetting of some operations, can be restricted to the intended algebra. The necessity of allowing forgetting, i.e. the use of hidden functions, is discussed in [Majster 77] and proved in [Standish 73].

Theorem 1. *Any algebraic system* $[Cl(I), S+O]$ *such that all the phyla of* I *are recursively enumerable sets and all operations contained in* $S+O$ *are partial computable functions, is contained in an algebra that may be axiomatically defined using only the primitives (as defined above)* $\forall$ *(implicitly),* $=$, *and* **if then else.**

PROOF. The proof of this theorem follows directly from Kleene's proof that every (general) recursive function can be expressed equationally [Kleene 1936]. See [Hermes 65] for a comprehensive discussion of this and closely related issues.

Thus, the schema provided for type specifications will in all instances prove to be sufficiently powerful—probably too powerful. While it is true that on rare occasions one may wish to write a non-terminating program (e.g., an operating system), in most cases non-termination is indicative of an error. In particular, it is hard to imagine a useful type, $T=[C1(I), S+O]$, where O contains a potentially non-terminating operation. It therefore seems useful to devise restrictions on the schema for building axioms that ensure that only total functions are specified as members of O. This is not to say that any input to an operation must be deemed acceptable, e.g., *NEW* as an argument to *FRONT* of type *Queue*, but merely that the operation should never fail to terminate. In the case of an unacceptable input it could, for example, return the distinguished value *error*. It is impossible to derive a set of necessary and sufficient restrictions, so we investigate sufficient conditions.

Theorem 2. *Any conditions that are sufficient to ensure sufficient-completeness will ensure that all operations contained in O are total.*

PROOF OF THEOREM 2

1) If $(x1,...,xn)$ is not contained in the domain of Fn, then, by the implicit axiom, $Fn(x1,...,xn)=error$. Thus $\forall Fn \in S+O, x1,..., xn[Fn(x1,...,xn)$ not contained in $L(T)$ implies that $Fn(x1,...,xn)$ converges to a value].

2) If $Fn(x1,...,xn)\in L(T)$ and $Fn\in O$, then, by the definition of sufficiently-complete, there exists a $u\in((Vi\in I)+\{error\})$ such that $F(x1,...,xn)=u$. Thus for all $Fn(x1,...,xn)\in L(T)$, $Fn\in O$ implies that $Fn(x1,...,xn)$ has a definite value.   □

It is important that sufficiently-complete implies that all operations contained in O are total. From the user's point of view, it means that if his axiomatization is sufficiently-complete, he not only learns something about the axiomatization but he also learns (or is reassured about) something about the operations that have been axiomatized. More importantly, theorem 2 also serves to highlight the difficulty involved in checking the sufficient-completeness of an axiomatization.

Ideally, one would like to be able to construct a total function

$$R: \quad \text{Axiom set} \times \text{syntactic specifications} \rightarrow Boolean$$

such that $R(A,ss)=true$ if A is a sufficiently-complete axiomatization of ss, and *false* otherwise. However, since, as implied above, such a function could be used to solve the halting problem, it is clear that no such function exists. Thus, one is led to consider a slightly less informative function and a somewhat different notion of completeness.

Definition. Given a total function R such that $R(A,ss) = true$ implies that A is a sufficiently-complete axiomatization of ss, A is **recognizably sufficiently-complete** with respect to R $(r.s.c.(R))$, if and only if $R(A,ss) = true$.

Unfortunately, this problem cannot be solved completely satisfactorily either.

Theorem 3. *There does not exist a function R for determining sufficient-completeness such that for all types $T = [Cl(I), S+O]$, where $F \in O$ implies that F is total, there exist $r.s.c.(R)$ axiomatizations.*

About the Proof. It is shown that if the theorem were not true the set of all total functions would be recursively enumerable. Since this is known to not be the case, the theorem must be true.

PROOF OF THEOREM 3

1) Assume that theorem 3 is not true, i.e., that there exists a function $R1$ such that for all $T = [Cl(I), S+O]$, if all $F \in O$ are total, then there exists a sufficiently-complete axiomatization, A, of T such that $R1(A, ss(T)) = true$, and further for all axiomatizations A', A' not sufficiently-complete implies that $R1(A', ss(T)) = false$.

2) Theorem 2 has an obvious corollary: that for any function R, any type $T = [Cl(I), S+O]$, and any axiom set A; if A is a $r.s.c(R)$ axiomatization of the syntactic specification of T $(ss(T))$, then all operations contained in O are total.

3) The set of all function names is known to be recursively enumerable (r.e.).

4) Therefore, the set of all finite sets of function names is r.e.

5) Thus the set of all syntactic specifications is r.e.

6) For any syntactic specification, the set of axiomatizations (according to the schema we have presented) is r.e.

7) From 5 and 6 the set of all pairs $(A, ss(T))$ is r.e.

8) From 7 and 1, $B = \{T = [Cl(I), S+O]$ or there exists an $r.s.c.(R1)$ axiomatization of $T\}$ is r.e.

9) Thus the set $BO = \{o|\text{there exists } T = [Cl(I), S+O] \text{ and } T \in B \text{ and } o \in O\}$ is r.e.

10) Thus the set $FO = \{F|F \in BO\}$ is r.e.

11) From 2, $F \in FO$ implies that F is total.

12) From 1, all total functions are contained in FO.

13) 11 and 12 imply that FO is the set of all total functions, 10 that this set is r.e.

14) But this is known not to be the case. Hence the assumption of 1 must be false.   □

The ramifications of this are not so unfortunate as they at first appear to be. In programming, the occasions when one has need of a non-primitive recursive function seem to be very rare indeed. It thus seems that if one were to construct a decision procedure $R2$ such that for all types where all operations are primitive recursive there exist $r.s.c.(R2)$ axiomatizations, one would have a procedure that would be useful for a wide range of applications. A set of restrictions on the schema for supplying axiomatizations of types around which such a decision procedure can be built is presented in the next section.

3.6. Sufficient conditions for establishing sufficient-completeness

In the introduction we argued that one of the main difficulties in supplying axiomatic specifications of abstract data types is knowing when one has "fully specified" the type. We also suggested ameliorating this problem by using a system that could check the completeness of an axiomatization and suggest ways of completing an incomplete specification. Section 3.3, however, demonstrated that in the general case the sufficient-completeness problem is unsolvable, i.e., there cannot exist a decision procedure for recognizing sufficient-completeness. Section 3.5 proved an even stronger result: there does not exist a semi-decision procedure R such that for all type algebras there exists an axiomatization that is recognizably sufficiently-complete with respect to R. Thus, the scope of any system such as that suggested in the introduction must necessarily be somewhat limited.

In this section, we present a set of conditions that are sufficient to guarantee that an axiom set is sufficiently-complete. We also prove that for any type $[Cl(I), S+O]$ if all members of $S+O$ are primitive recursive, there exists an axiomatization of that type that fulfills these conditions. These conditions can thus serve as the basis of a semi-decision procedure that can be used to show the sufficient-completeness of a large number of axiomatizations.

Convention. For notational convenience it will be assumed that for all operations contained in $S+O$, all arguments contained in TOI precede all arguments contained in other phyla in the operation's domain specification. This implies that each operation is of the form $f(y^*)$ or $f(x,y^*)$ (the y^* indicates a list, possibly empty, of arguments) where x is contained in TOI.

Definition. Consider an axiomatization A of a type $T=[Cl(I), S+O]$ and an arbitrary predicate P. A term of the form $f(x^*)$, where x^* is free, is **P-safe** if for all legal assignments to x^* there exists a theorem derivable from A of the form $f(x^*)=z$, and $P(z)$.

Definition. An axiomatization A is a **P-safe axiomatization** of a type $T=[Cl(I), S+O]$ if $\forall f \in S+O, f(x^*)$ is P-safe.

Now, consider the predicate $ATOMIC(y)$, which is true if y contains no operations contained in $S+O$ or y is of the form $s(x^*)$ where $s \in S$. It should be clear that the notion of **atomically-safe** is closely related to that of sufficiently-complete. It implies that all terms of the form $o(x^*), o \in O$, can be reduced to terms that we assume are already well-defined. The atomic-safety problem, like the sufficient-completeness problem, is unsolvable in the general case. It is, however, possible to develop conditions that are sufficient to guarantee the atomic safety of all terms of the form $o(x, y^*)$.

Consider a simplified schema for the axiomatization of abstract data types: one in which the **if then else** has been eliminated. (It will be reintroduced later.) Given this restriction, we derive some lemmas about our axiom systems in general.

Definition. For any computable measuring function M, M: *free terms→ Natural numbers*, an equation $lhs = rhs$ is **monotone in M** ($m(M)$) if and only if $M(lhs) > M(rhs)$.

Lemma A. *Consider any measuring function M, and any predicate P such that $(M(f(x^*)) = 0)$ implies $P(f(x^*))$, and any set of axioms, A. If for all terms of the form $f(x^*), f \in F$, we can derive a monotone theorem of the form $f(x^*) = z$, then A is P-safe. That is to say for all assignments to x^* there exists a theorem derivable from A of the form $f(x^*) = z$ where $P(z) = true$.*

Lemma A establishes a monotone induction principle that we shall invoke several times in the course of this paper. Its most obvious (and first) application will be to the atomic safety problem, where the predicate P is represented by the predicate *IS ATOMICALLY SAFE*. Before proceeding to apply this principle let us prove its soundness.

About the Proof. The lemma is shown to be true by induction on $M(f(x^*))$.

PROOF OF LEMMA A:
1) From the statement of the lemma, for any ground term (i.e., one with no variables of the *TOI*) $f(x^*), M(f(x^*)) = 0$ implies that there exists a theorem of the form $f(x^*) = z$ (i.e., $f(x^*) = f(x^*)$) such that $P(z)$. This forms the basis of our induction.
2) Assume that for any ground term $f(x^*)$ such that $M(f(x^*)) \leqslant n$ it is possible to derive a theorem of the form $f(x^*) = z$ where $P(z)$.
3) Consider any ground term $f(x^*)$ such that $M(f(x^*)) = n+1$. The statement of the lemma assures us that it will be possible to derive a theorem of the form $f(x^*) = w$ where $M(w) < M(f(x^*))$. That is to say

$M(w) \leqslant n$. By the induction hypotheses of step 2, it is possible to derive a theorem of the form $w = z$ such that $P(z)$. ☐

Now, let us consider a particular measuring function.

Definition. Nest(x) = the greatest depth to which operations contained in $S + O$ are nested in the term x. $NEST(o(s(j)))$ where $o \in O$, $s \in S$, and $j \in Vi \in I$, for example, equals two.

Lemma B. *A is an atomically safe axiomatization of* $T = [Cl(I), S + O]$ *if* $\forall o \in O$ *and* $\forall s \in S$ *there exists an axiom of the form* $o(s(x, y^*), w^*) = z$, *where either*

I) *the axiom is* $m(NEST)$
II) *there exist axioms* $z = z1, z1 = z2, \ldots, zn = zn + 1$ *and the theorem* $z = zn$
   $+ 1$ *is* $m(NEST)$.

PROOF OF LEMMA B
   1) Clearly, $NEST(x) = 0$ implies that x is atomic, i.e., $NEST(x) = 0$ implies $ATOMIC(x)$. Therefore, $NEST$ is a measuring function as per lemma A. ☐

Recall that the above discussion deals with axioms in which the right hand side contains no conditionals. This deficiency is remedied by lemma C.

Definition. An axiom that meets either condition I or condition II as stated in lemma B is said to be **Bsafe**.

Lemma C. *A is an atomically safe axiomatization of* $T = [Cl(I), S + O]$ *if* $\forall o \in O$ *and* $\forall s \in S$ *there exists an axiom of the form* $o(s(x, y^*), w^*) = z$ *where either*

I) z *contains no conditionals and the axiom is Bsafe.*
II) z *is of the form* **if** b **then** $z1$ **else** $z2$ *where* b *is Boolean,* $o(s(x, y^*), w^*) =$
   $z1$ *and* $o(s(x, y^*), w^*) = z2$ *are Bsafe, and* $NEST(b) <$
   $NEST(o(s(x, y^*), w^*))$ *or the range of* o *is Boolean and* $o(s(x, y^*), w^*) =$
   b *is Bsafe.*

PROOF OF LEMMA C
   1) The conditions placed on b guarantee that for any ground instance of b it is possible to derive a theorem of the form $b = $ true or a theorem of the form $b = $ false.
   2) Thus, for any ground instance of $o(s(x, y^*), w^*)$ it will be possible to derive either $o(s(x, y^*), w^*) = z1$ or $o(s(x, y^*), w^*) = z2$.
   3) The last stipulation in II above and lemma B guarantee that these will be reducible to atomic terms. ☐

Note that lemma C still does not provide for nested conditionals. Theorem 4, which concludes our development of sufficient conditions to ensure safety, remedies this.

Definition. An axiom that meets either condition I or condition II as stated in lemma C is said to be **Csafe**.

Definition. An axiom that meets either condition I or condition II of theorem 4 (below) is said to be **4safe**.

Theorem 4. *A is a safe axiomatization of* $T=[Cl(I), S+O]$ *if* $\forall o \in O$ *and* $\forall s \in S$ *there exists an axiom of the form* $o(s(x,y^*), w^*)=z$ *where either*

I) The axiom is Csafe, or
II) z is of the form **if** b **then** $z1$ **else** $z2$ where b is *Boolean*, $o(s(x,y^*), w^*)=$ $z1$ and $o(s(x,y^*), w^*)=z2$ are 4safe, and $NEST(b) < NEST$ $(o(s(x,y^*), w^*))$ or the range of o is *Boolean* and $o(s(x,y^*), w^*)=b$ is 4safe.

PROOF OF THEOREM 4:
1) Consider an axiom $o(s(x,y^*), w^*)=z$. If there is no nesting of conditionals in z, then by lemma C the theorem holds. This forms the basis of an induction.

2) Assume that the theorem holds if the level of nesting of conditionals in z is $\leq n$.

3) Consider the case where conditionals are nested to a depth of $n+1$ in z.

4) Consider the outermost conditional. It must be of the form **if** b **then** $z1$ **else** $z2$. The conditions placed on b guarantee that for any ground instance of b it is possible to derive a theorem of the form $b=$ true or $b=$ false.

5) Thus, for any ground instance of $o(s(x,y^*), w^*)$ it will be possible to derive either $o(s(x,y^*), w^*)=z1$ or $o(s(x,y^*), w^*)=z2$.

6) The depth to which conditionals are nested in $z1$ or $z2$ must be $\leq n$. Thus, by the induction hypothesis, the theorem holds.   ☐

As suggested earlier, this theorem leads directly to a set of conditions $R2$ that are sufficient to ensure sufficient-completeness. To wit, if an axiomatization of an abstract data type meets the conditions outlined in theorem 4, then the axiomatization is sufficiently-complete. At first glance, this may not seem to be a significant improvement over earlier formulations of sufficient-completeness. It does, however, have several advantages. Both the number of terms that have to be checked and the size of the axiom set A are finite. Thus, there is a reasonable bound on the time required to algorithmically determine whether or not a set of axioms is an *r.s.c.* (*R*2) axiomatization of any given type. The algorithm is a simple one:

1) Generate the set $STERMS = \{s(x^*)|s \in S$ and all members of x^* are free variables$\}$.
2) Generate the set $CTERMS = \{o(x^*)|o \in O; \; x1,...,xm \in STERMS; \; xm + 1,...,xn$ are free variables; and o is an n-ary function whose first m arguments are of type $TOI\}$
3) Do for each $x \in CTERMS$

> *notsafe*: = *true*;
> Do for each $a \in A$ while (*notsafe*)
>> If (1hs of $a = x$) & (a meets condition I or
>>> a meets condition II of theorem 4)
>> then *notsafe*: = *false*
> end;
> If *notsafe*
>> then Return (not *r.s.c.* (*R*2))
> end;
> Return (is *r.s.c.* (*R*2))

In addition to providing a procedure for checking sufficient-completeness, *R*2 provides some heuristics for constructing sufficiently-complete axiomatizations. Unfortunately, the obvious approach (i.e., beginning with the set *CTERMS* as the set of left hand sides for which right hand sides must be constructed) is often inconvenient. If some of the operations contained in *O* have several arguments of type *TOI*, *CTERMS* can be quite large. Consider, for example, type *Natural Number* $= [Cl(\{Boolean\})$, $\{ZERO, SUCC, PRED, ADD, MULTIPLY\} + \{?ZERO?,?EQUAL?\}]$. Thirty left hand sides would be generated. By providing axioms that relate values in *TOI* to one another, e.g., $ADD(SUCC(x), ZERO) = SUCC(x)$, however, the number of terms to be considered can be substantially reduced. Hence the notion of convertibility. Informally, if the values "generated" by an operation f can always be expressed in terms of other operations, then f is said to be convertible. In type *Natural Number*, for example, all terms of the form $PRED(x)$ are convertible to either *ZERO*, *error*, or $SUCC(y)$; where y does not contain *PRED*. Comvertible operations are essentially "functional extensions" that do not extend the set of values of *TOI*. More formally:

Definition. Given an axiom set A and a type $[Cl(I), S + 0 + \{f\}]$ where $f: TOI \times Vi1 \times ... \times Vin \rightarrow TOI$ is not contained in S, if for each ground term of the form $f(u, v^*)$ there exists a theorem derivable from A of the form $f(u, v^*) = z$ where z contains no instances of f, then f is said to be **convertible to S**.

Now, consider a type $T=[Cl(I),S+O]$ with a sufficiently-complete axiomatization A. Lemma D presents conditions sufficient to ensure that given an axiomatization $A+A'$ of type $T'=[Cl(I),S+O+\{f\}]$, f is convertible to S.

Definition. For any term x and any operation f, $Mf(x)$ is equal to the number of instances of f that appear in x.

Lemma D. *Consider types $T=[Cl(I),S+O]$ with axiomatization A, and $T'=[Cl(I),S+O+\{f\}]$ with axiomatization $A+A'$. f is convertible to S if for each term of the form $f(s(x^*),y^*)$ where $s\in S$ and all members of x^* and y^* are free variables, there exists in A' an axiom of the form $f(s(x^*),y^*)=z$ where either*

I) $Mf(z)=0$, or
II) *s is not a constant (i.e., it is not nullary with respect to TOI), and for every subterm w of z (including z itself), if w is of the form $f(u,v^*)$, then u is a free variable contained in x^* and all members of v^* are free variables contained in y^*.*

About the proof. It is shown by induction on depth of nesting (in steps 2–5) that for any ground term of the form $f(s(a^*),b^*)$ where $s\in S$, it is possible to derive a theorem of the form $f(s(a^*),b^*)=z$ where $Mf(f(s(a^*),b^*))>Mf(z)$. Step 1 is then invoked to show that this is a sufficient condition to guarantee the convertibility of f.

PROOF OF LEMMA D:

1) It follows directly from lemma A that if for each ground term of the form $f(s(a^*),b^*)$ where $s\in S$, it is possible to derive a theorem of the form $f(s(a^*),b^*)=z$ where $Mf(f(s(a^*),b^*))>Mf(z)$, then f is convertible to S.

2) Consider any ground term $f(s(a^*),b^*)$ such that $NEST(s(a^*))=1$. s must be a constant, thus case II of lemma D is not applicable. Hence, there must exist an applicable axiom of the form $f(s(x^*),y^*)=z$ where $Mf(z)=0$. Thus, we may directly derive a theorem of the form $f(s(a^*),b^*)=z1$ where $Mf(f(s(a^*),b^*)>Mf(z1)$.

3) Assume that if $NEST(s(a^*))\leqslant n$ then for any ground term of the form $f(s(a^*),b^*)$ it is possible to derive a theorem of the form $f(s(a^*),b^*)=z1$ where $Mf(f(s(a^*),b^*))>Mf(z1)$.

4) Consider any ground term $f(s(a^*),b^*)$ such that $NEST(s(a^*))=n+1$. The lemma asserts there must be an applicable axiom $f(s(x^*),y^*)=z$ such that either

a) $Mf(z)=0$. In this case it is possible to directly derive a theorem of the form $f(s(a^*),b^*)=z1$ where $Mf(f(s(a^*),b^*))>Mf(z)$.
b) It is possible to directly derive a theorem of the form $f(s(a^*),b^*)=z1$ where for all subterms of $z1$ of the form $f(u,v^*)$, u must be a member of a^*. $NEST(u)$ must, therefore, be less than $NEST(s(a^*))$, i.e., $NEST(u)$

$\leqslant n$. Therefore, by the assumption of step 4, it is possible to derive a theorem of the form $f(u,v^*)=z1$ where $Mf(f(u,v^*))>Mf(z1)$.

5) By induction, it is therefore possible to derive, for any ground term of the form $f(s(a^*),b^*)$, a theorem of the form $f(s(a^*),b^*)=z$ where $Mf(f(s(a^*),b^*))>Mf(z)$.

6) Therefore, by step 1, f is convertible to S.   □

Like lemma A, lemma D makes no provision for conditionals. This is rectified in theorem 5.

Definition. An axiom that meets either condition I or condition II of lemma D is said to be *Dok*.

Theorem 5. *All free terms of the form $f(x,y^*)$ are convertible to S if $\forall s \in S$ there exists a 5-ok axiom, i.e., an axiom of the form $f(s(x^*),y^*)=z$ where either*

I) z contains no conditionals and the axiom is Dok.
II) z is of the form **if** b **then** $z1$ **else** $z2$ where b is Boolean and atomic, or Boolean and 4safe, and $f(s(x^*),y^*)=z1$ and $f(s(x^*),y^*)=z2$ are 5-ok.

PROOF OF THEOREM 5:
1) The conditions placed on b guarantee that for any ground instance of $f(s(x^*),y^*)$ it is possible to derive a theorem of the form $b=$ true or of the form $b=$ false.

2) Thus, for any ground instance of $f(s(x^*),y^*)$ it will be possible to (eventually) derive a Dok theorem of the form $f(s(x^*),y^*)=z$.

3) Lemma D asserts that this is a sufficient condition to guarantee that all terms of the form $f(s(x^*),y^*)$ are convertible.   □

The concept of convertibility combined with that of safety leads to a second set of conditions $R3$ that is sufficient to guarantee sufficient-completeness. Informally, if every term of the form $o(x,y^*)$, where $o \in O$, is either safe or convertible to something that is safe, then the axiomatization is sufficiently-complete. More formally:

Theorem 6. *An axiom set A for a type $T=[C1(I),S+O]$ is sufficiently-complete if there exists a partitioning of S into disjoint sets C (constructors) and E (extensions) such that all constants are contained in C and*

1) For all $c \in C$ and all $o \in O$, the term $o(c(x^*),y^*)$, where the members of x^* and y^* are free, is 4-safe, and
2) There exists an ordering, $e1,e2,...,em$, of the functions in E, such that $e1$ is convertible to C, $e2$ is convertible to $C+\{e1\}$, etc.

About the proof. It is first shown (steps 1–3) that it is sufficient to prove that for all ground terms of the form $o(c(x^*),y^*)$, $o \in O$ and $c \in C$, there exists a theorem of the form $o(c(x^*),y^*)=z$, where z is atomic or safe. That this is true follows immediately from the definition of safe and the initial conditions specified in the theorem.

PROOF OF THEOREM 6:

1) Recall that an axiom set A is sufficiently-complete if and only if for each $w=Fj.n(x1,\ldots,xn)\in L(T)$ where $Fj.n\in O$, there exists a theorem derivable from A such that the theorem is of the form $w=u$ where u is contained in $Vi\in I$. Recall also that $u\in Vi\in I$ implies that u is atomic with respect to TOI.

2) $Fj.n\in O$ implies that at least one of $x1,\ldots,xn$ is contained in TOI, thus (by our convention) $x1\in TOI$. $x1\in TOI$ implies that $x1$ is either a constant or of the form $s(u,v^*)$, $s\in S$.

3) Because all terms of the form $e(x,y^*)$ where $e\in E$ are convertible, we need only consider those terms w where $x1$ is a constant or of the form $c(u,v^*)$ and $c\in C$.

4) Thus we need only show that for any assignment to the free variables of all terms of the form $o(c(x^*),y^*)$ where $o\in O$ and $c\in C$, there exists a theorem of the form $o(c(x^*),y^*)=z$, where z is atomic with respect to TOI.

5) That is to say all free terms of the form $o(c(x^*),y^*)$ must be safe. This is guaranteed by the first condition of the theorem.   □

Thus, the notions of safety and convertibility lead to a set of purely syntactic conditions that can be used to verify sufficient-completeness. They can, therefore, be used to build a procedure, $R3$,

$$R3: \text{axiom set}\times\text{Syntactic specification}\rightarrow Boolean$$

such that $R3(A,ss(T))=\text{true}$ only if A is a sufficiently-complete axiomatization of T. Note, however, that theorem 6 deals only with the soundness of such an $R3$. To know that $R3$ is sound is not enough. $R4=[F(A,ss(T))=false]$ is, after all, a perfectly sound procedure in that it never returns true if A is not a sufficiently-complete axiomatization of T. A useful procedure R for verifying sufficient-completeness must not only be guaranteed against returning spurious values, it also must be capable of recognizing a large class of sufficiently-complete axiomatizations. Almost all the algebraic specifications of abstract types that we have constructed were either "naturally" r.s.c. ($R3$) or not sufficiently-complete. (In the latter cases the application of $R3$ often served to indicate how the axiomatization could be successfully completed.) This "experiment" to determine the utility of $R3$ has been supplemented by the following more formal statement of its applicability:

Theorem 7. *For any type $T=[Cl(I),S+O]$ all of whose operations are primitive recursive, there exists an axiomatization A of a containing algebra (see theorem 1), such that A is r.s.c. ($R3$). I.e., there exists a partitioning of S into disjoint sets C and E such that*

I) For all $c \in C$ and all $o \in O$, the term $o(c(x^*), y^*)$ where x^* and y^* are free is safe, and

II) There exists an ordering of the functions in $E, e1, \ldots, em$, such that $e1$ is convertible to C, $e2$ is convertible to $C + \{e1\}$, etc.

About the proof. It is first shown that it is possible to construct an *r.s.c.*($R3$) specification for the set of basic primitive recursive functions. Call the type with these basic functions and the single output function $?EQUAL?$, $Prf = [Cl \ (Boolean), S + \{?EQUAL?\}]$. This will form the basis of an induction. We know, by definition, that any primitive recursive function can be generated from the members of S by a finite number of applications of composition and primitive recursion. We will assume that for any $fm \in Fm$ where Fm is the set of primitive recursive functions that can be constructed using m applications of composition and primitive recursion, there exists a set of axioms such that Fm is convertible to $S + F1 + \ldots + Fm - 1$. Finally, using this assumption, it is shown that any $fm + 1 \in FM + 1$ is convertible to $S + F1 + \ldots + Fm - 1 + Fm$.

PROOF OF THEOREM 7

1) The basic primitive recursive functions consist of one nullary function (call it $ZERO$), one unary function (call it $SUCC$), and an infinite number of projection (or "pick out") functions. Since every primitive recursive function can be constructed using only a finite subset of these projection functions, however, we need only show that any (rather than all) projection function can be specified. This is indeed the case, since any axiom of the form $f(x1, \ldots, xn) = xm$, $1 \leqslant m \leqslant n$, is safe if $f \in O$, or obeys constraint I of lemma D if $f \in S$. The basic type, Prf, for the primitive recursive functions, with $?EQUAL?$ as the output function, may be *r.s.c.* ($R3$) specified as follows:

Operations:

$ZERO:$	$\rightarrow Prf$
$SUCC:$	$Prf \rightarrow$
$?EQUAL?:$	$Prf \times Prf \rightarrow Boolean$

Axioms:

$?EQUAL?(ZERO, ZERO) = true$
$?EQUAL?(ZERO, SUCC(x)) = false$
$?EQUAL?(SUCC(x), ZERO) = false$
$?EQUAL?(SUCC(x), SUCC(y)) = ?EQUAL?(x, y)$

2) Now, assume that any fm-FM is convertible to $S + F1 + \ldots + Fm - 1$.

3) Consider $fm + 1 \in Fm + 1$. $fm + 1$ must be defined by either

a) $fm + 1(x0, x1, \ldots, xn) = h(g0(x0, \ldots, xn), \ldots, gk(x0, \ldots, xn))$, where $h, g0, \ldots, gk$ are all contained in $S + F1 + \ldots + Fm$, or

b) $fm + 1(ZERO, x1, \ldots, xn) = g(x1, \ldots, xn)$; $\quad fm + 1(SUCC(x), x1, \ldots, xn) =$

$h(fm+1(x,x1,\ldots,xn),x,x1,\ldots,xn)$ where g and h are contained in $S+F1+\ldots+Fm$.

Note that axioms that conform to either of these forms obey the restrictions outlined in lemma D. Thus $fm+1$ must be convertible to $S+F1+\ldots+Fm$. □

There are, therefore, a large number of abstract types for which r.s.c. ($R3$) axiomatizations exist. The fact that the conditions outlined above are purely syntactic means that $R3$ can be quite simple. It also means that a large number of sufficiently-complete axiomatizations will not be recognized as such. In practice, one would almost certainly wish to add some primitive rules of inference to any procedure designed to check for sufficient-completeness. One would, for example, like to be able to infer the safety of the term $?EQUAL?(ZERO,SUCC(x))$ from the axioms $?EQUAL?(x,y)=?EQUAL?(y,x)$ and $?EQUAL?(SUCC(x),ZERO)=$ *false*. A detailed discussion of inference techniques is, however, outside the scope of this paper.

An examination of the conditions comprising $R3$ leads to an informal heuristic "procedure" that has proven to be useful in constructing sufficiently-complete axiomatizations of abstract data types:

1) Partition the operations of the type, $T=[I,S+O]$ into the sets O, C, and E as defined above. (Note that there may be several such partitionings.)
2) Build the set $CTERMS=\{c(x1,\ldots,xn)|c$ is an n-ary function $\in C$ and $\forall 1\leqslant i\leqslant n[xi$ is a free variable]\}.
3) Build the set $OTERMS=\{o(x1,\ldots,xn)|o$ is an n-ary function $\in O$ and $\forall 1\leqslant i\leqslant n[$if the ith argument in the domain of o is $\in I$ then xi is a free variable, otherwise $xi\in CTERMS]\}$.
4) Build the set $ETERMS=\{e(x1,\ldots,xn)|e$ is an n-ary function contained in E and $\forall 1\leqslant i\leqslant n[$if the ith argument in the domain of o is $\in I$ then xi is a free variable, otherwise $xi\in CTERMS]\}$.
5) Consider a type $T'=[I,C+O]$. The set $OTERMS$ may be used as a set of left hand sides in constructing a safe axiomatization of T'. Construct, using the conditions of theorem 4 for guidance, such an axiomatization.
6) Complete the axiomatization of T by adding axioms that demonstrate the convertibility of all members of E. The members of $ETERMS$ form a sufficient set of left hand sides. Theorem 5 may be used for guidance in supplying the right hand sides.

Programmers tend to regard this procedure as strange and somewhat intimidating when first presented; however, we have found that they can usually master it after working a few examples, and move on with little difficulty to data types that appear in their applications. The most common types of problems are the following:

1) Although the partitioning of the operations into the sets S and O can be done purely on the basis of their ranges, the partitioning of S into C and E requires some consideration of their semantics and is not always done correctly. It is not always easy to apply the informal rule that constructors produce new values of the type while extensions merely produce values that could have been produced in other ways. In practice, the symptom of an incorrect partitioning is generally a left hand side for which a "simpler" right hand side cannot be supplied. E.g., within type *Stack*, if *POP* were classified as a constructor rather than as an extension, *OTERMS* would contain $TOP(POP(s))$; if *PUSH* were classified as an extension rather than a constructor, *ETERMS* would contain $PUSH(NEW, i)$.

2) There is a strong temptation to put too much in a single type. As a rule of thumb, we have found that types with two to four constructors are quite manageable, but that types with more than four constructors are generally more easily (and more clearly) specified by decomposing them into simpler types. (An exception to this rule of thumb is a type with a large number of constants, e.g., type *character*.)

3) Sometimes the operations of a type are most naturally specified by introducing additional "private" functions that are both defined and used within the specification, but that never explicitly appear in programs that use the type. Frequently these private functions will be output functions that indicate the "history" of a value; the symptom indicating the need for them is the inability to construct a right hand side without more information about the structure of the left hand side than is provided by our restricted definition of LHS. Note that if "private" functions are flagged as such, they need not be included in implementations of the type.

4) When constructing right hand sides, it is easy to overlook an acceptable one (in terms of theorem 7) because it doesn't seem any "simpler" than the left hand side. E.g., in defining a queue, the essential observation is that if q is non-empty, $REMOVE\ (ADD(q, i))$ can be reduced to $ADD(REMOVE(q), i)$.

Despite these problems, the discipline imposed by our restricted form of axioms seems to simplify the problem of producing axioms for any well-understood type. We will discuss both these guidelines and their application in greater detail in a future paper.

3.7. Some remarks on consistency

The consistency of an arbitrary set of axioms is, like completeness, an unsolvable problem. There are, however, many techniques that are sufficient to guarantee consistency. Two seem particularly germane in the current context.

The construction of a model is perhaps the most widely used technique for establishing the consistency of axiom sets. To show that an axiomatization of an abstract type is consistent, it is sufficient to construct a provably "correct" implementation of the type. (What it means and how to go about proving the "correctness" of implementations of abstract types is discussed in [Guttag 75*, 77a*].) From a practical point of view, this is often the best way to demonstrate consistency. If the abstract type is to be used, an implementation must eventually be provided. Hopefully, a proof of the "correctness" of this implementation will also be provided as a matter of course. If this is the case, the proof of consistency comes "free" as a side-effect. The danger in adopting this approach is that if the specification is inconsistent, it is possible to waste considerable time trying to build a model that cannot be built. This problem can be avoided by proving the consistency of a specification before trying to implement it. One way to do this is to demonstrate that the axiomatization has the Church-Rosser property [Church 36].

The conditions for establishing sufficient-completeness presented in Section 3.6 were based upon the monotonicity of the axioms, i.e., "=" was not treated as a symmetric relation. What was actually shown was that the conditions presented are sufficient to guarantee that for any term $o(x,y^*)$, $o \in O$, there exists a series of reductions,

$$o(x,y^*) \rightarrow z1 \rightarrow z3 \rightarrow \ldots \rightarrow z, \quad \text{where } z \in Vi \in I.$$

Any $r.s.c.$ ($R3$) axiomatization may, therefore, be viewed as a set of replacement rules. Thus, for any such axiomatization, consistency may be demonstrated by proving that the set of replacement rules exhibits the Church-Rosser property. Informally, a set of replacement rules is Church-Rosser if whenever one applies a replacement rule to reduce a term, and then a rule to reduce the resulting term, etc., until there is no longer an applicable rule, the final result does not depend upon the order in which the rules were applied. More formally:

Definition. If a term t can be reduced to another term t' by a single application of a replacement rule, then $t \rightarrow t'$.

Definition. $\rightarrow^*$ is the reflexive transitive closure of $\rightarrow$.

Definition. A set of replacement rules is **Church-Rosser** if and only if

$$\forall t1, t2, t3 \in L(T)[(t1 \rightarrow^* t2 \ \& \ t1 \rightarrow^* t3)$$

implies that there exists $t \in L(T)$ such that $(t2 \rightarrow^* t \ \& \ t3 \rightarrow^* t)].$

There are many ways in which replacement systems may be shown to be Church-Rosser; [Rosen 73] provides a useful survey.

4.1. Related work

The work which most closely resembles that described in this paper is that of [Zilles 78] and [Goguen 75]. We will discuss one fundamental distinction between our approach and the other two; there are also definite differences in emphasis and numerous technical differences that we will not pursue here.

Recall our assertion that the significance of values contained in *TOI* rests solely in the effect that those values have when they occur as arguments to functions contained in *O*. This assumption led us to the conclusion that values contained in *TOI* may be assumed to be the same unless provably different. [Zilles 78, Goguen 75] make the opposite assumption, i.e., that values must be considered different unless they are demonstrably equal.

This difference in viewpoint is formally expressed in terms of the congruence relations defined over *TOI* by the axioms of the type. Zilles says that, "the congruence relations used are the smallest congruence relations which contain all of the defining relations (axioms). This means that two expressions are equivalent if and only if there is a sequence of expressions such that the first and last expressions are the expressions in question and every adjacent pair of expressions can be shown to be equivalent using some defining relation." We, on the other hand, permit any congruence relation that satisfies the axioms. An example may help to clarify this distinction.

Consider the abstract type *Set* defined in section 2. Consider also two values of type *Set*, x and y, such that x is defined by the expression *INSERT(INSERT(EMPTY_SET,2),3)* and y by the expression *INSERT(INSERT(EMPTY_SET,3),2)*. It can be readily seen that the theorem $x = y$ cannot be derived from the axioms for type *Set*. It is also clear that one cannot derive the theorem $\neg(MEMBER\_OF?(DELETE(x,z),z1) = MEMBER\_OF?(DELETE(y,z),z1))$ for any $z, z1 \in Integer$. Therefore, while the smallest congruence viewpoint leads one to place x and y in different equivalence classes, our viewpoint allows us to place them in the same equivalence class.

Acknowledgments. We would like to thank John Lipson for his help with the research described in this paper and Jim Thatcher, Hans-Josef Jeanrond and the referee for suggestions that led to material improvements over the version of this paper first submitted in 1976. We would also like to thank Wlad Turski for his helpful advice and encouragement.

21

User-Defined Types and Procedural Data Structures as Complementary Approaches to Data Abstraction

John C. Reynolds[1]
Syracuse University

Abstract *User-defined types (or modes) and procedural (or functional) data structures are complementary methods for data abstraction, each providing a capability lacked by the other. With user-defined types, all information about the representation of a particular kind of data is centralized in a type definition and hidden from the rest of the program. With procedural data structures, each part of the program which creates data can specify its own representation, independently of any representations used elsewhere for the same kind of data. However, this decentralization of the description of data is achieved at the cost of prohibiting primitive operations from accessing the representations of more than one data item. The contrast between these approaches is illustrated by a simple example.*

Introduction

User-defined types and procedural data structures have both been proposed as methods for data abstraction, i.e., for limiting and segregating the portion of a program which depends upon the representation used for some kind of data. In this paper we suggest, by means of a simple example, that these methods are complementary, each providing a capability lacked by the other.

The idea of user-defined types has been developed [Morris 73, 74; Liskov 74; Fischer 73; Wulf 77] and has its roots in earlier work [Dahl 72b*]. In this approach, each particular conceptual kind of data is called a *type*, and for each type used in a program, the program is divided into two parts: a type definition and an "outer" or "abstract" program. The type definition specifies the representation to be used for the data type and a set of primitive operations (and perhaps constants), each defined in terms of

[1] Work supported by National Science Foundation Grant GJ-41540.

the representation. The choice of representation is hidden from the outer program by requiring all manipulations of the data type in the outer program to be expressed in terms of the primitive operations. The heart of the matter is that any consistent change in the data representation can be effected by altering the type definition without changing the outer program.

Various notions of procedural (or functional) data structures have been developed [Reynolds 70*; Landin 65; Balzer 67*]. In this approach, the abstract form of data is characterized by the primitive operations which can be performed upon it, and an item of data is simply a procedure or collection of procedures for performing these operations. The essence of the idea is seen most clearly in its implementation: an item of procedural data is a kind of record called a *closure* which contains both an internal representation of the data and a pointer (or flag field) to code for procedures for manipulating this representation. A program with access to a closure record is only permitted to examine or access the internal representation by executing the code indicated by the pointer, so that this code serves to close off or protect the internal representation.

In comparison with user-defined types, procedural data structures provide a decentralized form of data abstraction. Each part of the program which creates procedural data will specify its own form of representation, independently of the representations used elsewhere for the same kind of data, and will provide versions of the primitive operations (the components of the procedural data item) suitable for this representation. There need be no part of the program, corresponding to a type definition, in which all forms of representation for the same kind of data are known. But a price must be paid for this decentralization: a primitive operation can have access to the representation of only a single data item, namely the item of which the operation is a component.

Apparently this price is inevitable. If an operation is to have access to the representation of more than one item of data, each of which may have several possible representations, then its definition cannot be "decentralized" into one part for each representation, since one must provide for every possible *combination* of representations. Presumably this requires the definition to occur at a point in the program where all possible representations of the operands are known.

Linguistic preliminaries

Before illustrating these ideas, we must digress to explain (informally) the language we will use. It is an applicative language, similar to pure LISP [McCarthy 60] or the applicative subsets of GEDANKEN [Reynolds 70*], PAL [Evans 68], or ISWIM [Landin 66], but with a complete type structure somewhat like ALGOL 68 [Van Wijngaarden 75]. Types will be indicated by writing $\in \tau$, where τ is a type expression, after binding occurrences of identifiers (except where the type is obvious from context). Type expressions are constructed with the operators $\rightarrow$ denoting functional procedures, $\times$ denoting a Cartesian product, and $+$ denoting a named disjoint union.

The named disjoint union is sufficiently novel to require a more detailed explanation. If $\tau_1,\ldots,\tau_n$ are type expressions denoting the sets $S_1,\ldots,S_n$ and $i_1,\ldots,i_n$ are distinct identifiers, then

$$i_1 : \tau_1 + \cdots + i_n : \tau_n$$

is a type expression denoting the set of pairs

$$\{\langle i_k, x \rangle \mid 1 \leqslant k \leqslant n \text{ and } x \in S_k\}.$$

If e is an expression of type τ_k with value x, then

$$\textbf{inject } i_k \; e$$

is an expression of type $i_1 : \tau_1 + \cdots + i_n : \tau_n$ with value $\langle i_k, x \rangle$.

Let e be an expression of type $i_1 : \tau_1 + \cdots + i_n : \tau_n$ with value $\langle i, x \rangle$, let $i_{k_1},\ldots,i_{k_m}$ be distinct members of the set of identifiers $\{i_1,\ldots,i_n\}$, for $1 \leqslant j \leqslant m$ let l_j be an expression of type $\tau_{k_j} \rightarrow \tau'$ with value f_j, and let e' be an expression of type τ' with value x'. Then

$$\textbf{unioncase } e \textbf{ of } \left(i_{k_1} : l_1, \ldots, i_{k_m} : l_m, \textbf{other} : e' \right)$$

is an expression of type τ' with the value

$$\textbf{if} \begin{bmatrix} i = i_{k_1} \\ \vdots \\ i = i_{k_m} \\ \text{otherwise} \end{bmatrix} \textbf{then} \begin{bmatrix} f_1(x) \\ \vdots \\ f_m(x) \\ x' \end{bmatrix}$$

When $m = n$, the **other** clause will be omitted.

We use the type expression *nilset* to denote a standard one-element set, whose unique member is denoted by $\{ \; \}$.

Integer sets as a user-defined type

Our example is an implementation of the abstract concept of sets of integers. Using the approach of user-defined types, we wish to define a type *set* and primitive constants and functions

$$none \in set$$

$$all \in set$$

$$limit \in \textbf{integer} \times \textbf{integer} \times set \rightarrow set$$

$$union \in set \times set \rightarrow set$$

$$exists \in \textbf{integer} \times \textbf{integer} \times set \rightarrow \textbf{Boolean}$$

satisfying the specifications

$$none = \{\ \}$$

$all =$ The set of all (machine-representable) integers

$$limit(m,n,s) = s \cap \{k \mid m \leqslant k \leqslant n\}$$

$$union(s1,s2) = s1 \cup s2$$

when $m \leqslant n$, $exists(m,n,s) = (\exists k)m \leqslant k \leqslant n$ **and** $k \in s$

To make our solution seem more realistic, we require that the execution of *limit* and *union* should require time and space bounded by constants which are independent of their arguments. Of course this will exact a price in the speed of *exists*.

An appropriate and simple solution is to represent a set by a list structure which records the way in which the set is constructed via primitive operations. Thus the representation of a set is a disjoint union, over the four set-valued primitive functions (including constants), of sets of possible arguments for these functions. More precisely, this representation is defined by the recursive type declaration:

$$set = nonef : \textbf{nilset} + allf : \textbf{nilset} + limitf : \textbf{integer} \times \textbf{integer} \times set$$
$$+ unionf : set \times set$$

and the effect of *none, all, limit,* or *union* is to imbed its arguments into the appropriate kind of list element:

$$none = \textbf{inject } nonef\ (\ )$$

$$all = \textbf{inject } allf\ (\ )$$

$$limit(m,n,s) = \textbf{inject } limitf(m,n,s)$$

$$union(s1,s2) = \textbf{inject } unionf(s1,s2)$$

(Roughly speaking, we are representing sets by a free algebra with constants *none* and *all*, and operators *limit* and *union*.) The entire computational burden of interpreting this representation falls upon the function *exists*:

$exists(m,n,s) = \textbf{unioncase } s \textbf{ of}$
      $(nonef : \lambda(\ ). \textbf{ false},$
      $allf : \lambda(\ ). \textbf{ true},$
      $limitf : \lambda(m1,n1,s1). \ max(m,m1) \leqslant min(n,n1)$
      $\textbf{and } exists(max(m,m1), min(n,n1), s1),$
      $unionf : \lambda(s1,s2). \ exists(m,n,s1) \textbf{ or } exists(m,n,s2))$

(We assume that the operations **and** and **or** do not evaluate their second operand when the first operand is sufficient to determine their result.)

Although the above is a definition of the type *set* which meets our specifications, it can be easily improved, even within the time and space constraints imposed upon *limit* and *union*. For example, both *limit* and *union* can be optimized by taking advantage of some obvious properties of sets—the result of *limit* can be simplified when its last argument is *none* or another application of *limit*, and the result of *union* can be simplified when either argument is *none* or *all*:

limit (m,n,s) = **unioncase** s **of**
    $(nonef: \lambda( ). none,$
    $limitf: \lambda(m1,n1,s1).$ **if** $max(m,m1) \leqslant min(n,n1)$
          then inject $limitf(max(m,m1), min(n,n1), s1)$ **else** *none*,
    other : **inject** $limitf (m,n,s))$

union $(s1,s2)$ = **unioncase** $s1$ **of**
    $(nonef: \lambda( ). s2,$
    $allf: \lambda( ). all,$
    other :**unioncase** $s2$ **of**
        $(nonef: \lambda( ). s1, allf: \lambda( ). all,$
        other : **inject** $unionf (s1,s2)))$

In conclusion, we show how our specification of integer sets might be "packaged" in a language permitting user-defined types:

newtype *set* = *nonef* : **nilset** + *allf* : **nilset** + *limitf* : **integer** × **integer** × *set*
    + *unionf* : *set* × *set*
with *none* ∈ *set* = **inject** *nonef* ( ),
    all ∈ *set* = **inject** *allf* ( ),
    limit ∈ **integer** × **integer** × *set* → *set* =
        $\lambda(m,n,s).$ **unioncase** s **of**
        $(nonef: \lambda( ). none,$
        $limitf: \lambda(m1,n1,s1).$ **if** $max(m,m1) \leqslant min(n,n1)$
            then inject $limitf (max(m,m1), min(n,n1), s1)$ **else** *none*,
        other : **inject** $limitf (m,n,s)),$
    union ∈ *set* × *set* → *set* =
        $\lambda(s1,s2).$ **unioncase** $s1$ **of**
        $(nonef: \lambda( ). s2, allf: \lambda( ). all,$
        other : **unioncase** $s2$ **of**
            $(nonef: \lambda( ). s1, allf: \lambda( ). all,$
            other : **inject** $unionf (s1,s2))),$
    exists ∈ **integer** × **integer** × *set* → **Boolean** =
        $\lambda(m,n,s).$ **unioncase** s **of**
        $(nonef: \lambda( ).$ **false**,
        $allf: \lambda( ).$ **true**,
        $limitf: \lambda(m1,n1,s1). max(m,m1) \leqslant min(n,n1)$
            and $exists(max(m,m1),min(n,n1),s1),$
        $unionf: \lambda(s1,s2). exists(m,n,s1)$ **or** $exists(m,n,s2))$
in ⟨*outer program*⟩

The language used here is an outgrowth of the ideas discussed in [Reynolds 74*]. A complete exposition of this language is beyond the scope of this paper, but the following salient points should be noted.

(1) The type declaration between **newtype** and **with** binds all occurrences of the type identifier *set* throughout the above expression (including occurrences in ⟨*outer program*⟩). The ordinary declarations between **with** and **in** bind all occurrences of the ordinary identifiers *none, all, limit, union,* and *exists* throughout the expression.

(2) With regard to occurrences of *set* between **with** and **in**, the type declaration behaves like a mode definition in ALGOL 68, i.e., *set* is equivalent to the type expression on the right side of the type declaration, and the type-correctness of the text in **with…in** depends upon this type expression.

(3) In ⟨*outer program*⟩, occurrences of *set* behave like a primitive type, e.g., **integer** or **Boolean**. In other words, ⟨*outer program*⟩ must be a correctly typed expression regardless of what type expression might be equivalent to *set*. This insures that all manipulations of the user-defined type in ⟨*outer program*⟩ must be expressed in terms of the primitives declared in **with…in**.

(4) Although it is not illustrated by our example, it should be possible to declare simultaneously several related user-defined types between **newtype** and **with**. This ability is needed to permit the definition of multiargument primitive functions which act upon more than one user-defined type. An example might be the use of the types *point* and *line* in a program for performing geometrical calculations.

Integer sets as procedural data structures

We now develop integer sets as procedural data structures. The starting point is the realization that all we ever want to do to a set s, aside from using it to construct other sets, is to evaluate the Boolean expression $exists(m,n,s)$. This suggests that we can simply equate the set s with the Boolean function $\lambda(m,n). exists(m,n,s)$ that characterizes the only information we want to extract from the set.

Thus we define

$$set = \textbf{integer} \times \textbf{integer} \rightarrow \textbf{Boolean}$$

and specify that if $s \in set$ represents the "mathematical" set s_0, then for $m \leqslant n$,

$$s(m,n) = (\exists k) m \leqslant k \leqslant n \text{ and } k \in s_0.$$

The need for defining the primitive function *exists* has vanished since this function has been *internalized*—its value for a particular *set* is simply the (only component of the) *set* itself. The remaining primitive constants and functions are easily defined by:

$none = \lambda(m,n).$ **false**
$all = \lambda(m,n).$ **true**
$limit(m,n,s) = \lambda(m1,n1).$
$\quad max(m,m1) \leqslant min(n,n1)$ **and** $s(max(m,m1), min(n,n1))$
$union(s1,s2) = \lambda(m,n).$ $s1(m,n)$ **or** $s2(m,n)$

In this approach, there is no ⟨*outer program*⟩ from which the definition $set = $ **integer** $\times$ **integer** $\rightarrow$ **Boolean** is hidden. Any part of the program can create a *set* by giving an appropriate function whose internal representation (the collection of values of global variables which form the fields of the closure record) can be arbitrary. For example, in augmenting an existing program, one might write

$$\lambda(m,n).\ even(m)\ \textbf{or}\ (m < n)$$

to denote the set of even integers, or

$$\textbf{letrec}\ s = \lambda(m,n).\ (m \leqslant n)\ \textbf{and}\ (p(m)\ \textbf{or}\ s(m+1,n))\ \textbf{in}\ s$$

to denote the set of integers satisfying the predicate p. The procedural approach insures that these definitions will mesh correctly with the rest of the program, even though they introduce novel representations.

This kind of extensional capability, which is the main advantage of the procedural approach, is offset by two limitations. In the first place, although (ignoring computability considerations) every set can be represented by a function in **integer** $\times$ **integer** $\rightarrow$ **Boolean**, the converse is false. To represent a set, a function s must satisfy

$$s(m,n) = \bigvee_{k=m}^{n} s(k,k)$$

for all m and n such that $m \leqslant n$. This kind of condition, which cannot be checked syntactically, must be satisfied by all parts of the program which create sets.

A more important limitation is that only the function *exists*, which has been internalized as (the only component of) a procedural data item, is truly primitive in the sense of having access to the internal representation of a set. Essentially, we have been forced to express the functions *limit* and *union* in terms of the internalized *exists*. We are fortunate that our example permits us to do this at all. Even so, we are prevented from optimizing *limit* and *union* as we did in the user-defined-type development. There is no practically effective way that $limit(m,n,s)$ can "see" whether s has the form *none* or $limit(m1,n1,s1)$, or that $union(s1,s2)$ can "see" whether $s1$ or $s2$ has the form *none* or *all*.

In fact, this difficulty can be surmounted for *limit* but not for *union*. The solution is to internalize *limit* as well as *exists*, so that both functions have access to internal representations. Thus we represent sets by pairs of functions:

$$set = (\textbf{integer} \times \textbf{integer} \rightarrow \textbf{Boolean}) \times (\textbf{integer} \times \textbf{integer} \rightarrow set)$$

and specify that if s represents the mathematical set s_0 then for $m \leqslant n$,

$$s.1(m,n) = (\exists k)m \leqslant k \leqslant n \text{ and } k \in s_0,$$

and for all m and n, $s.2(m,n)$ represents the mathematical set

$$s_0 \cap \{k | m \leqslant k \leqslant n\}$$

(Here $s.1$ and $s.2$ denote the components of the pair s.)

In this approach, we may define *none* by:

$$none = (\lambda(m,n). \textbf{ false}, \lambda(m,n). \ none)$$

Note the peculiar kind of recursion which is characteristic of this style of programming: the second component of *none* is a function which does not call itself but rather returns itself as a component of its result.

To define *all* and *union* we first define an "external" $limit \in \textbf{integer} \times$ **integer** $\times set \rightarrow set$ which will be called upon by the internal limiting functions (i.e., the second components) of *all* and *union*:

$limit(m,n,s) =$
  $(\lambda(m1,n1).max(m,m1) \leqslant min(n,n1) \textbf{ and } s.1(max(m,m1),$
      $min(n,n1))),$
  $\lambda(m1,n1).\textbf{if } max(m,m1) \leqslant min(n,n1) \textbf{ then}$
      $limit(max(m,m1), min(n,n1), s) \textbf{ else } none)$

Then

  $all = (\lambda(m,n). \textbf{ true}, \lambda(m,n). \ limit(m,n,all))$
  $union(s1,s2) = (\lambda(m,n). \ s1.1(m,n) \textbf{ or } s2.1(m,n),$
      $\lambda(m,n). \ limit(m,n,union(s1,s2))).$

With these definitions, the internal limiting functions perform simplifications analogous to those performed by *limit* in the user-defined-type approach. Indeed, if one examines the behavior of the closures which would represent sets in an implementation of this definition, one finds that they mimic the list structures of the type approach almost exactly (except for the simplifications performed by union).

But even to someone who is experienced with procedural data structures, the internalization of *limit* is more a tour de force than a specimen of clear programming. Moreover, internalization cannot be applied to give a function such as *union* access to the internal representation of more than one argument, i.e., we could convert $union(s1,s2)$ to a component of $s1$ or of $s2$ but not both.

Conclusions

In comparison with user-defined types, procedural data structures offer a more decentralized method of data abstraction which precludes any interaction between different representations of the same kind of data. This offers the advantage of easier extensibility at the price of prohibiting primitive operations from accessing the representations of more than one data item.

Of course, the two approaches can be combined. For example, we can augment our user-defined-type definition to include an additional primitive *functset* ∈ (**integer** × **integer**→**Boolean**)→*set* which accepts a functional set (in the sense of the first part of the previous section) and produces an equivalent value of type *set*. It is sufficient to add one more kind of record to the disjoint union defining *set* and one more alternative to the branches defining *exists*:

newtype *set* = · · · + *functsetf* : (**integer** × **integer**→**Boolean**)
with ...
    functset ∈ (**integer** × **integer**→**Boolean**)→*set* = λ*f*. **inject** *functsetf f*,
    exists ∈ **integer** × **integer** × *set*→**Boolean** =
        λ(*m*,*n*,*s*). **unioncase** *s* **of**
        (...*functsetf* : λ*f*. *f*(*m*,*n*))
in ⟨*outer program*⟩

However, this kind of combination is hardly a unification. To some extent, the data-representation structuring approach of [Dahl 72b*] unifies the concepts of user-defined types and procedural data structures, but only at the expense of combining their limitations. It appears that this is inevitable, that the two concepts are inherently distinct and complementary.

The reader should be cautioned that this is a working paper describing ongoing research. In particular, the linguistic constructs we have used are tentative and will require considerable study and evolution before they can be integrated into a complete programming language. The extension of these constructs to languages with imperative features is a particularly murky area.

PART V

SOFTWARE DEVELOPMENT

Parts II–IV dealt with specific, isolated problems in programming: correctness concerns, parallelism, and "programmer-defined" data types. Part V is concerned with software development: the more general task of developing and maintaining large programs and systems of programs.

Because the problem area is so large, we can only touch upon some aspects of software development. Indeed, all the articles concern some aspect of "programming by deduction" or stepwise refinement or top-down programming (or whatever you wish to call it). Missing are articles on tool building, on designing using programs "off the shelf" the way one designs using electrical or mechanical components, on verification of correctness (commonly called debugging), on management techniques—the list could go on and on. It is not that WG2.3 as a whole considers these topics unimportant; there have been discussions on some of these topics. Nevertheless, the main emphasis in the past ten years has been on the topics presented in this volume. In any field, one tackles those problems that at the time seem most pressing, most able to provide needed insight, and most capable of being solved.

We begin with Niklaus Wirth's article, Program development by stepwise refinement, *which considers the creative activity of programming as a sequence of design decisions concerning the decomposition of tasks into subtasks and of data into data structures. Stepwise refinement, which is applicable to both small and large programming tasks, is commonly known as* top-down programming. *Appearing in 1971, this was one of the first well-publicized articles to call attention to the need for teaching systematic methods of design and construction of programs.*

David Parnas' first article discusses the use of the "buzzword" hierarchical structure. Parnas explains that there are different meanings for this term, and that a proper understanding of these different meanings is essential for work in software design and development. The point is well made and can be generalized to other terms as well; paying lip service to terms like structured programming, hierarchical structure, *and* modularize, *without understanding and mastering the principles and intent behind them, is useless.*

Parnas' second article, On the design and development of program families, *discusses an idea appearing in [Dijkstra 72d*] which is also men-*

tioned in the previous article by Wirth. Given a task X, there exists a family of solutions (refinements) X1, X2, ... Each Xi is a solution for X, but each may make restrictions on further refinements—on the algorithms or on the data structures that can be used. The thesis is that conscious attention to the family of solutions at each refinement in a program development (rather than just to a single solution) can help reduce the overall cost of development and maintenance of the programs. This paper examines and compares various programming techniques in terms of their suitability for designing such families of programs.

I cannot refrain from bringing to the fore a comment made by Parnas in this second article. He responds to the question, "When should we teach structured programming or stepwise refinement to our students?," by asking another question: "When should we teach unstructured programming?"

Brian Randell's article describes a method of system structuring that is intended to facilitate the inclusion of means for tolerating faults whose exact location and consequences have not been anticipated, such as those arising from residual design errors in large software systems. The method enables the problems of system roll-back and state restoration to be treated separately from those of ensuring continued system operation. Techniques are described for dealing with faults in sequential and in concurrent processes, using what could be described as a form of "standby sparing." Thus the work can be regarded as an attempt to extend some of the techniques of hardware fault tolerance to make them applicable in the realm of software.

Douglas Ross' article describes Structured Analysis (SA), a language for communicating ideas. One of the major problems in developing systems of programs is the problem of documentation. Documentation is needed in order to specify the task completely and concisely enough so that both the customer and the analyst can understand and agree upon it. Documentation is needed to describe the overall architecture of the design. Documentation is needed to describe to each programmer his detailed task. Ross claims that SA (whose function is "to bind up, structure, and communicate units of thought" expressed in any language) together with his structured analysis and design methodology can help solve the problems of designing and documenting such large systems.

22
Program Development by Stepwise Refinement[1]

Niklaus Wirth
Eidgenössische Technische Hochschule

Abstract *The creative activity of programming—to be distinguished from coding—is usually taught by examples serving to exhibit certain techniques. It is here considered as a sequence of design decisions concerning the decomposition of tasks into subtasks and of data into data structures. The process of successive refinement of specifications is illustrated by a short but nontrivial example, from which a number of conclusions are drawn regarding the art and the instruction of programming.*

1 Introduction

Programming is usually taught by examples. Experience shows that the success of a programming course critically depends on the choice of these examples. Unfortunately, they are too often selected with the prime intent to demonstrate what a computer can do. Instead, a main criterion for selection should be their suitability to exhibit certain widely applicable *techniques*. Furthermore, examples of programs are commonly presented as finished "products" followed by explanations of their purpose and their linguistic details. But active programming consists of the design of *new* programs, rather than contemplation of old programs. As a consequence of these teaching methods, the student obtains the impression that programming consists mainly of mastering a language (with all the peculiarities and intricacies so abundant in modern PL's) and relying on one's intuition to somehow transform ideas into finished programs. Clearly, programming courses should teach methods of design and construction, and the selected examples should be such that a gradual *development* can be nicely demonstrated.

This paper deals with a single example chosen with these two purposes in mind. Some well-known techniques are briefly demonstrated and motivated (strategy of preselection, stepwise construction of trial solutions, introduction of auxiliary data, recursion), and the program is gradually developed in a sequence of *refinement steps*.

In each step, one or several instructions of the given program are decomposed into more detailed instructions. This successive decomposition or refinement of specifications terminates when all instructions are expressed in terms of an underlying computer or programming language, and must therefore be guided by the facilities available on that computer or language. The result of the execution of a program is expressed in terms of data, and it may be necessary to introduce further data for communication between the obtained subtasks or instructions. As tasks are refined, so the data may have to be refined, decomposed, or structured, and it is natural to *refine program and data specifications in parallel*.

Every refinement step implies some design decisions. It is important that these decisions be made explicit, and that the programmer be aware of the underlying criteria and of the existence of alternative solutions. The possible solutions to a given problem emerge as the leaves of a tree, each node representing a point of deliberation and decision. Subtrees may be considered as *families of solutions* with certain common characteristics and structures. The notion of such a tree may be particularly helpful in the situation of changing purpose and environment to which a program may sometime have to be adapted.

A guideline in the process of stepwise refinement should be the principle to decompose decisions as much as possible, to untangle aspects which are only seemingly interdependent, and to defer those decisions which concern details of representation as long as possible. This will result in programs which are easier to adapt to different environments (languages and computers), where different representations may be required.

The chosen sample problem is formulated at the beginning of Section 3. The reader is strongly urged to try to find a solution by himself before embarking on the paper which—of course—presents only one of many possible solutions.

2 Notation

For the description of programs, a slightly augmented ALGOL 60 notation will be used. In order to express repetition of statements in a more lucid way than by use of labels and jumps, a statement of the form

    repeat ⟨statement sequence⟩
    until ⟨Boolean expression⟩

is introduced, meaning that the statement sequence is to be repeated until the Boolean expression has obtained the value **true**.

3 The 8-queens problem and an approach to its solution[1]

> Given are an 8×8 chessboard and 8 queens which are hostile to each other. Find a position for each queen (a configuration) such that no queen may be taken by any other queen (i.e., such that every row, column, and diagonal contains at most one queen).

This problem is characteristic for the rather frequent situation where an analytical solution is not known, and where one has to resort to the method of trial and error. Typically, there exists a set A of candidates for solutions, among which one is to be selected which satisfies a certain condition p. Thus a solution is characterized as an x such that $(x \in A) \wedge p(x)$.

A straightforward program to find a solution is:

repeat Generate the next element of A and call it x
until $p(x) \vee$ (no more elements in A);
if $p(x)$ **then** $x =$ solution

The difficulty with this sort of problem usually is the sheer size of A, which forbids an exhaustive generation of candidates on the grounds of efficiency considerations. In the present example, A consists of $64!/(56! \times 8!) \doteq 2^{32}$ elements (board configurations). Under the assumption that generation and test of each configuration consumes $100 \ \mu s$, it would roughly take 7 hours to find a solution. It is obviously necessary to invent a "shortcut," a method which eliminates a large number of "obviously" disqualified contenders. This *strategy of preselection* is characterized as follows: Find a representation of p in the form $p = q \wedge r$. Then let $B_r = \{x | (x \in A) \wedge r(x)\}$. Obviously $B_r \subseteq A$. Instead of generating elements of A, only elements of B_r are produced and tested on condition q instead of p. Suitable candidates for a condition r are those which satisfy the following requirements:

1. B_r is much smaller than A.
2. Elements of B_r are easily generated.
3. Condition q is easier to test than condition p.

The corresponding program then is:

repeat Generate the next element of B_r and call it x
until $q(x) \vee$ (no more elements in B_r);
if $q(x)$ **then** $x =$ solution

A suitable condition r in the 8-queens problem is the rule that in every column of the board there must be exactly one queen. Condition q then

---

[1] This problem was investigated by C. F. Gauss in 1850.

merely specifies that there be at most one queen in every row and in every diagonal, which is evidently somewhat easier to test than p. The set B_r (configurations with one queen in every column) contains "only" $8^8 = 2^{24}$ elements. They are generated by restricting the movement of queens to columns. Thus all of the above conditions are satisfied.

Assuming again a time of 100 μs for the generation and test of a potential solution, finding a solution would now consume only 100 seconds. Having a powerful computer at one's disposal, one might easily be content with this gain in performance. If one is less fortunate and is forced to, say, solve the problem by hand, it would take 280 hours of generating and testing configurations at the rate of one per second. In this case it might pay to spend some time finding further shortcuts. Instead of applying the same method as before, another one is advocated here which is characterized as follows: Find a representation of trial solutions x of the form $[x_1, x_2, \ldots, x_n]$, such that every trial solution can be generated in steps which produce $[x_1], [x_1, x_2], \ldots, [x_1, x_2, \ldots, x_n]$ respectively. The decomposition must be such that:

1. Every step (generating x_j) must be considerably simpler to compute than the entire candidate x.
2. $q(x) \supset q(x_1 \ldots x_j)$ for all $j \leqslant n$.

Thus a full solution can never be obtained by extending a partial trial solution which does not satisfy the predicate q. On the other hand, however, a partial trial solution satisfying q may not be extensible into a complete solution. This method of *stepwise construction of trial solutions* therefore requires that trial solutions failing at step j may have to be "shortened" again in order to try different extensions. This technique is called *backtracking* and may generally be characterized by the program:

```
j: = 1;
repeat trystep j;
    if successful then advance else regress
until (j < 1)∨(j > n)
```

In the 8-queens example, a solution can be constructed by positioning queens in successive columns starting with column 1 and adding a queen in the next column in each step. Obviously, a partial configuration not satisfying the mutual nonaggression condition may never be extended by this method into a full solution. Also, since during the jth step only j queens have to be considered and tested for mutual nonaggression, finding a partial solution at step j requires less effort of inspection than finding a complete solution under the condition that all 8 queens are on the board all the time. Both stated criteria are therefore satisfied by the decomposition in which step j consists of finding a safe position for the queen in the jth column.

The program subsequently to be developed is based on this method; it generates and tests 876 partial configurations before finding a complete solution. Assuming again that each generation and test (which is now more easily accomplished than before) consumes one second, the solution is found in 15 minutes, and with the computer taking 100 μs per step, in 0.09 seconds.

4 Development of the program

We now formulate the stepwise generation of partial solutions to the 8-queens problem by the following first version of a program:

variable *board,pointer,safe*;
considerfirstcolumn;
repeat *trycolumn*;
   if *safe* **then**
      begin *setqueen*; *considernextcolumn* **end**
      else *regress*
until *lastcoldone* $\bigvee$ *regressoutoffirstcol*

This program is composed of a set of more primitive instructions (or procedures) whose actions may be described as follows:

> *considerfirstcolumn*. The problem essentially consists of inspecting the safety of squares. A pointer variable designates the currently inspected square. The column in which this square lies is called the currently inspected column. This procedure initializes the pointer to denote the first column.
> *trycolumn*. Starting at the current square of inspection in the currently considered column, move down the column either until a safe square is found, in which case the Boolean variable *safe* is set to **true**, or until the last square is reached and is also unsafe, in which case the variable *safe* is set to **false**.
> *setqueen*. A queen is positioned onto the last inspected square.
> *considernextcolumn*. Advance to the next column and initialize its pointer of inspection.
> *regress*. Regress to a column where it is possible to move the positioned queen further down, and remove the queens positioned in the columns over which regression takes place. (Note that we may have to regress over at most two columns. Why?)

The next step of program development chosen was to refine the descriptions of the instructions *trycolumn* and *regress* as follows:

procedure *trycolumn*;
repeat *advancepointer*: *testsquare*
until *safe* $\bigvee$ *lastsquare*

```
procedure regress;
  begin reconsiderpriorcolumn;
    if ¬ regressoutoffirstcol then
    begin removequeen;
      if lastsquare then
        begin reconsiderpriorcolumn;
          if ¬ regressoutoffirstcol then removequeen
        end
    end
  end
```

The program is expressed in terms of the instructions:

considerfirstcolumn
considernextcolumn
reconsiderpriorcolumn
advancepointer
testsquare (sets the variable *safe*)
setqueen
removequeen

and of the predicates:

lastsquare
lastcoldone
regressoutoffirstcol

In order to refine these instructions and predicates further in the direction of instructions and predicates available in common programming languages, it becomes necessary to express them in terms of data representable in those languages. A decision on how to represent the relevant facts in terms of data can therefore no longer be postponed. First priority in decision making is given to the problem of how to represent the positions of the queens and of the square being currently inspected.

The most straightforward solution (i.e. the one most closely reflecting a wooden chessboard occupied by marble pieces) is to introduce a Boolean square matrix with $B[i,j] = $ **true** denoting that square (i,j) is occupied. The success of an algorithm, however, depends almost always on a suitable choice of its data representation in the light of the ease in which this representation allows the necessary operations to be expressed. Apart from this, consideration regarding storage requirements may be of prime importance (although hardly in this case). A common difficulty in program design lies in the unfortunate fact that at the stage where decisions about data representations have to be made, it often is still difficult to foresee the details of the necessary instructions operating on the data, and often quite impossible to estimate the advantages of one possible representation over another. In general, it is therefore advisable to delay decisions about data representation as long as possible (but not until it becomes obvious that no realizable solution will suit the chosen algorithm).

In the problem presented here, it is fairly evident even at this stage that the following choice is more suitable than a Boolean matrix in terms of simplicity of later instructions as well as of storage economy.

j is the index of the currently inspected column; (x_j, j) is the coordinate of the last inspected square; and the position of the queen in column $k < j$ is given by the coordinate pair (x_k, k) of the board. Now the variable declarations for pointer and board are refined into:

integer j $(0 \leqslant j \leqslant 9)$
integer array $x[1:8]$ $(0 \leqslant x_i \leqslant 8)$

and the further refinements of some of the above instructions and predicates are expressed as:

procedure *considerfirstcolumn*;
   begin $j := 1$; $x[1] := 0$ **end**;
procedure *considernextcolumn*;
   begin $j := j + 1$; $x[j] := 0$ **end**;
procedure *reconsiderpriorcolumn*; $j := j - 1$;
procedure *advancepointer*;
   $x[j] := x[j] + 1$;
Boolean procedure *lastsquare*;
   $lastsquare := x[j] = 8$;
Boolean procedure *lastcoldone*;
   $lastcoldone := j > 8$;
Boolean procedure *regressoutoffirstcol*;
   $regressoutoffirstcol := j < 1$

At this stage, the program is expressed in terms of the instructions:

testsquare
setqueen
removequeen

As a matter of fact, the instructions *setqueen* and *removequeen* may be regarded as vacuous, if we decide that the procedure *testsquare* is to determine the value of the variable *safe* solely on the grounds of the values $x_1 \ldots x_{j-1}$ which completely represent the positions of the $j-1$ queens so far on the board. But unfortunately the instruction *testsquare* is the one most frequently executed, and it is therefore the one instruction where considerations of efficiency are not only justified but essential for a good solution of the problem. Evidently a version of *testsquare* expressed only in terms of $x_1 \ldots x_{j-1}$ is inefficient at best. It should be obvious that *testsquare* is executed far more often than *setqueen* and *removequeen*. The latter procedures are executed whenever the column (j) is changed (say m times), the former whenever a move to the next square is undertaken (i.e. x_j is changed, say n times). However, *setqueen* and *removequeen* are the only procedures which affect the chessboard. Efficiency may therefore be gained by the method of *introducing auxiliary variables* $V(x_1 \ldots x_j)$ such that:

1. Whether a square is safe can be computed more easily from $V(x)$ than from x directly (say in u units of computation instead of ku units of computation).
2. The computation of $V(x)$ from x (whenever x changes) is not too complicated (say of v units of computation).

The introduction of V is advantageous (apart from considerations of storage economy), if

$$n(k-1)u > mu \quad \text{or} \quad \frac{n}{m}(k-1) > \frac{v}{u},$$

i.e. if the gain is greater than the loss in computation units.

A most straightforward solution to obtain a simple version of *testsquare* is to introduce a Boolean matrix B such that $B[i,j] = \textbf{true}$ signifies that square (i,j) is not taken by another queen. But unfortunately, its recomputation whenever a new queen is removed (v) is prohibitive (why?) and will more than outweigh the gain.

The realization that the relevant condition for safety of a square is that the square must lie neither in a row nor in a diagonal already occupied by another queen, leads to a much more economic choice of V. We introduce Boolean arrays a, b, c with the meanings:

$a_k = \textbf{true}$: no queen is positioned in row k

$b_k = \textbf{true}$: no queen is positioned in the /-diagonal k

$c_k = \textbf{true}$: no queen is positioned in the \-diagonal k

The choice of the index ranges of these arrays is made in view of the fact that squares with equal sum of their coordinates lie on the same /-diagonal, and those with equal difference lie on the same \-diagonal. With row and column indices from 1 to 8, we obtain:

Boolean array $a[1:8], b[2:16], c[-7:7]$

Upon every introduction of auxiliary data, care has to be taken of their *correct initialization*. Since our algorithm starts with an empty chessboard, this fact must be represented by initially assigning the value **true** to all components of the arrays a, b, and c. We can now write:

procedure *testsquare*;
    $safe := a[x[j]] \wedge b[j + x[j]] \wedge c[j - x[j]]$;
procedure *setqueen*;
    $a[x[j]] := b[j + x[j]] := c[j - x[j]] := \textbf{false}$;
procedure *removequeen*;
    $a[x[j]] := b[j + x[j]] := c[j - x[j]] := \textbf{true}$.

The correctness of the latter procedure is based on the fact that each queen currently on the board had been positioned on a safe square, and that all queens positioned after the one to be removed now had already been removed. Thus the square to be vacated becomes safe again.

A critical examination of the program obtained so far reveals that the variable $x[j]$ occurs very often, and in particular at those places of the program which are also executed most often. Moreover, examination of $x[j]$ occurs much more frequently than reassignment of values to j. As a consequence, the principle of introduction of auxiliary data can again be applied to increase efficiency: a new variable

integer i

is used to represent the value so far denoted by $x[j]$. Consequently $x[j]: = i$ must always be executed before j is increased, and $i: = x[j]$ after j is decreased. This final step of program development leads to the reformulation of some of the above procedures as follows:

```
procedure testsquare;
    safe : = a[i]∧b[i+j]∧c[i−j];
procedure setqueen;
    a[i]: = b[i+j]: = c[i−j]: = false;
procedure removequeen;
    a[i]: = b[i+j]: = c[i−j]: = true;
procedure considerfirstcolumn;
    begin j : = 1; i : = 0 end;
procedure advancepointer; i : = i+1;
procedure considernextcolumn;
    begin x[j]: = i; j : = j+1; i : = 0 end;
Boolean procedure lastsquare;
    lastsquare : = i = 8.
```

The final program, using the procedures

```
testsquare
setqueen
regress
removequeen
```

and with the other procedures directly substituted, now has the form

```
j : = 1; i : = 0;
repeat
    repeat i : = i+1; testsquare
    until safe∨(i = 8);
    if safe then
        begin setqueen; x[j]: = i; j : = j+1; i : = 0 end
    else regress
until (j>8)∨(j<1);
if j>8 then PRINT(x) else FAILURE
```

It is noteworthy that this program still displays the structure of the version designed in the first step. Naturally other, equally valid solutions can be suggested and be developed by the same method of stepwise program refinement. It is particularly essential to demonstrate this fact to students. One alternative solution was suggested to the author by E. W. Dijkstra. It is based on the view that the problem consists of a stepwise extension of the board by one column containing a safely positioned queen, starting with a null-board and terminating with 8 columns. The process of extending the board is formulated as a procedure, and the natural method to obtain a complete board is by *recursion* of this procedure. It can easily be composed of the same set of more primitive instructions which were used in the first solution.

```
procedure Trycolumn(j);
  begin integer i; i: = 0;
    repeat i: = i + 1; testsquare;
      if safe then
      begin setqueen; x[j]: = i;
        if j < 8 then Trycolumn(j + 1);
        if ¬ safe then removequeen
      end
    until safe ∨ (i = 8)
  end
```

The program using this procedure then is

```
Trycolumn(1);
if safe then PRINT(x) else FAILURE
```

(Note that due to the introduction of the variable i local to the recursive procedure, every column has its own pointer of inspection i. As a consequence, the procedures

```
testsquare
setqueen
removequeen
```

must be declared locally within *Trycolumn* too, because they refer to the designating the scanned square in the *current* column.)

5 The generalized 8–queens problem

In the practical world of computing, it is rather uncommon that a program, once it performs correctly and satisfactorily, remains unchanged forever. Usually its users discover sooner or later that their program does not deliver all the desired results, or worse, that the results requested were not the ones really needed. Then either an extension or a change of the program is called for, and it is in this case where the method of stepwise program design and systematic structuring is most valuable and advantageous. If the structure and the program components were well chosen, then often many of the constituent instructions can be adopted unchanged. Thereby the effort of redesign and reverification may be drastically reduced. As a matter of fact, the *adaptability* of a program to changes in its objectives (often called maintainability) and to changes in its environment (nowadays called portability) can be measured primarily in terms of the degree to which it is neatly structured.

It is the purpose of the subsequent section to demonstrate this advantage in view of a generalization of the original 8-queens problem and its solution through an extension of the program components introduced before.

The generalized problem is formulated as follows:

Find *all* possible configurations of 8 hostile queens on an 8×8 chessboard, such that no queen may be taken by any other queen.

The new problem essentially consists of two parts:

1. Finding a method to generate further solutions.
2. Determining whether all solutions were generated or not.

It is evidently necessary to generate and test candidates for solutions in some *systematic manner*. A common technique is to find an *ordering of candidates* and a condition to identify the last candidate. If an ordering is found, the solutions can be mapped onto the integers. A condition limiting the numeric values associated with the solutions then yields a criterion for termination of the algorithm, if the chosen method generates solutions strictly in increasing order.

It is easy to find orderings of solutions for the present problem. We choose for convenience the mapping

$$M(x) = \sum_{j=1}^{8} x_j 10^{j-1}$$

An upper bound for possible solutions is then

$$M(x_{max}) = 88888888$$

and the "convenience" lies in the circumstance that our earlier program generating one solution generates the minimum solution, which can be regarded as the starting point from which to proceed to the next solution. This is due to the chosen method of testing squares strictly proceeding in increasing order of $M(x)$ starting with 00000000. The method for generating further solutions must now be chosen such that starting with the configuration of a given solution, scanning proceeds in the same order of increasing *M*, until either the next higher solution is found or the limit is reached.

6 The extended program

The technique of extending the two given programs finding a solution to the simple 8-queens problem is based on the idea of modification of the global structure only, and of using the same building blocks. The global structure must be changed such that upon finding a solution the algorithm will produce an appropriate indication—e.g., by printing the solution- —and then proceed to find the next solution until it is found or the limit is reached. A simple condition for reaching the limit is the event when the first queen is moved beyond row 8, in which case regression out of the first column will take place. These deliberations lead to the following modified version of the nonrecursive program:

```
considerfirstcolumn;
  repeat trycolumn;
    if safe then
    begin setqueen; considernextcolumn;
      if lastcoldone then
      begin PRINT(x); regress end
    end else regress
  until regressoutoffirstcol
```

Indication of a solution being found by printing it now occurs directly at the level of detection, i.e. before leaving the repetition clause. Then the algorithm proceeds to find a next solution whereby a shortcut is used by directly regressing to the prior column; since a solution places one queen in each row, there is no point in further moving the last queen within the eighth column.

The recursive program is extended with even greater ease following the same considerations:

```
procedure Trycolumn(j);
begin integer i;
  ⟨declarations of procedures testsquare, advancequeen,
  setqueen, removequeen, lastsquare⟩;
  i: = 0;
  repeat advancequeen; testsquare;
  if safe then
    begin setqueen; x[j]: = i;
      if ¬ lastcoldone then Trycolumn(j + 1) else PRINT(x);
      removequeen
    end
  until lastsquare
end
```

The main program starting the algorithm then consists (apart from initialization of a, b, and c) of the single statement *Trycolumn*(1).

In concluding, it should be noted that both programs represent the same algorithm. Both determine 92 solutions in the *same* order by testing squares 15720 times. This yields an average of 171 tests per solution; the maximum is 876 tests for finding a next solution (the first one), and the minimum is 8. (Both programs coded in the language PASCAL were executed by a CDC 6400 computer in less than one second.)

7 Conclusions

The lessons which the described example was supposed to illustrate can be summarized by the following points.

1. Program construction consists of a sequence of *refinement steps*. In each step a given task is broken up into a number of subtasks. Each refinement in the description of a task may be accompanied by a refinement of the description of the data which constitute the means of communication between the subtasks. Refinement of the description of program and data structures should proceed in parallel.

2. The degree of *modularity* obtained in this way will determine the ease or difficulty with which a program can be adapted to changes or extensions of the purpose or changes in the environment (language, computer) in which it is executed.

3. During the process of stepwise refinement, a *notation* which is natural to the problem in hand should be used as long as possible. The direction in which the notation develops during the process of refinement is determined by the language in which the program must ultimately be specified, i.e. with which the notation ultimately becomes identical. This langauge should therefore allow us to express as naturally and clearly as possible the structures of program and data which emerge during the design process. At the same time, it must give guidance in the refinement process by exhibiting those basic features and structuring principles which are natural to the machine by which programs are supposed to be executed. It is remarkable that it would be difficult to find a language that would meet these important requirements to a lesser degree than the one language still used most widely in teaching programming: FORTRAN.

4. Each refinement implies a number of *design decisions* based upon a set of design criteria. Among these criteria are efficiency, storage economy, clarity, and regularity of structure. Students must be taught to be conscious of the involved decisions and to critically examine and to reject solutions, sometimes even if they are correct as far as the result is concerned; they must learn to weigh the various aspects of design alternatives in the light of these criteria. In particular, they must be taught to revoke earlier decisions, and to back up, if necessary even to the top. Relatively short sample

problems will often suffice to illustrate this important point; it is not necessary to construct an operating system for this purpose.

5. The detailed elaborations on the development of even a short program form a long story, indicating that careful programming is not a trivial subject. If this paper has helped to dispel the widespread belief that programming is easy as long as the programming language is powerful enough and the available computer is fast enough, then it has achieved one of its purposes.

Acknowledgments. The author gratefully acknowledges the helpful and stimulating influence of many discussions with C. A. R. Hoare and E. W. Dijkstra.

References

The following articles are listed for further reference on the subject of programming: [Dijkstra 68e*, 72d*; Naur 69a*; Wirth 70*].

23
On a "Buzzword": Hierarchical Structure

David L. Parnas
University of North Carolina

Abstract   *This paper discusses the use of the term "hierarchically structured" to describe the design of operating systems. Although the various
uses of this term are often considered to be closely related, close examination of the use of the term shows that it has a number of quite different
meanings. For example, one can find two different senses of "hierarchy"
in a single operating system [Dijkstra 68a*] and [Habermann 67]. An
understanding of the different meanings of the term is essential, if a
designer wishes to apply recent work in software engineering and design
methodology. This paper attempts to provide such an understanding.*

Introduction

The phrase "hierarchical structure" has become a buzzword in the computer field. For many it has acquired a connotation so positive that it is
akin to the quality of being a good mother. Others have rejected it as being
an unrealistic restriction on the system [Wulf 74]. This paper attempts to
give some meaning to the term by reviewing some of the ways that the
term has been used in various operating systems (e.g., T.H.E. [Dijkstra
68a*], MULTICS [Graham 68], and the RC4000) and providing some
better definitions. Uses of the term, which had been considered equivalent
or closely related, are shown to be independent. Discussions of the advantages and disadvantages of the various hierarchical restrictions are included.

General properties of all uses of the phrase "hierarchical structure"

As discussed earlier [Parnas 71b*], the word "structure" refers to a partial
description of a system showing it as a collection of parts and showing
some relations between the parts. We can term such a structure *hierarchical*

if a relation or predicate on pairs of the parts $(R(\alpha, \beta))$ allows us to define levels by saying that

1. level 0 is the set of parts α such that there does not exist a β such that $R(\alpha, \beta)$, and
2. level i is the set of parts α such that
   (a) there exists a β on level i-1 such that $R(\alpha, \beta)$ and
   (b) if $R(\alpha, \gamma)$ then γ is on level i-1 *or lower.*

This is possible with a relation R only if the directed graph representing R has no loops.

The above definition is the most precise reasonably simple definition which encompasses all uses of the word in the computer literature. This suggests that the statement, "Our operating system has a hierarchical structure," carries no information at all. *Any* system can be represented as a hierarchical system with one level and one part; more importantly, it is possible to divide *any* system into parts and contrive a relation such that the system has a hierarchical structure. Before such a statement can carry any information at all, the way that the system is divided into parts and the nature of the relation must be specified.

The decision to produce a hierarchically structured system may restrict the class of possible systems, and may, therefore, introduce disadvantages as well as the desired advantages. In the remainder of this paper we shall introduce a variety of definitions for "hierarchical structure," and mention some advantages and disadvantages of the restriction imposed by these definitions.

1 The program hierarchy

E. W. Dijkstra in his paper on the T.H.E. system and in later papers on structured programming [Dijkstra 68a*, 68b*] has demonstrated the value of programming using layers of abstract machines. We venture the following definition for this program hierarchy. The parts of the system are subprograms, which may be called as if they were procedures.[1] We assume that each such program has a specified purpose (e.g., $FNO :: =$ find next odd number in sequence or invoke $DONE$ if there is none). The relation "uses" may be defined by $USES(p_j, p_k) =$ iff p_j calls p_k and p_j will be considered incorrect if p_k does not function properly.

With the last clause we intend to imply that, in our example, FNO does *not* "use" $DONE$ in the sense defined here. The task of FNO is to invoke $DONE$; the purpose and "correctness" of $DONE$ is irrelevant to FNO. Without excepting such calls, we could not consider a program to be

---

[1] They may be expanded as MACROS.

higher in the hierarchy than the machine which it uses. Most machines have "trap" facilities and invoke software routines when trap conditions occur.

A program divided into a set of subprograms may be said to be hierarchically structured when the relation "uses" defines levels as described above. The term "abstract machine" is commonly used because the relations between the lower level programs and the higher level programs is analogous to the relations between hardware and software.

A few remarks are necessary here. First, *we* do not claim that the only good programs are hierarchically structured programs. Second, we point out that the way that the program is divided into subprograms can be rather arbitrary. For *any* program some decompositions into subprograms may reveal a hierarchical structure, while other decompositions may show a graph with loops in it. As demonstrated in the simple example above, the specification of each program's purpose is critical!

The purpose of the restriction on program structure implied by this definition is twofold. First, the calling program should be able to ignore the internal workings of the called program; the called program should make no assumptions about the internal structure of the calling program. Allowing the called program to call its user might make this more difficult since each would have to be designed to work properly in the situations where it could be called by the other.

The second purpose might be termed "ease of subsetting." When a program has this "program hierarchy", the lower levels may always be used without the higher levels when the higher levels are not ready or their services are not needed. An example of nonhierarchical systems would be one in which the "lower level" scheduling programs made use of the "high level" file system for storage of information about the tasks that it schedules. Assuming that nothing useful could be done without the scheduler, no subset of the system that did not include the file system could exist. The file system (usually a complex and "buggy" piece of software) could not be developed using the remainder of the system as a "virtual machine."

For those who argue that the hierarchical structuring proposed in this section prevents the use of recursive programming techniques, we remind them of the freedom available in choosing a decomposition into subprograms. If there exists a subset of the programs, which call each other recursively, we can view the group as a single program for this analysis and then consider the remaining structure to see whether it is hierarchical. In looking for possible subsets of a system, we must either include or exclude this group of programs as a single program.

One more remark: please note that the division of the program into levels by the above discussed relation has no *necessary* connection with the division of the programs into modules as discussed in [Parnas 72f*]. This is discussed further later (Section 6).

2 The "Habermann hierarchy" in the T.H.E. system

The T.H.E. system was also hierarchical in another sense. In order to make the system relatively insensitive to the number of processors and their relative speeds, the system was designed as a set of "parallel sequential processes." The activities in the system were organized into "processes" such that the sequence of events within a process was relatively easy to predict, but the sequencing of events in different processes was considered unpredictable (the relative speeds of the processes were considered unknown). Resource allocation was done in terms of the processes and the processes exchanged work assignments and information. In carrying out a task, a process could assign part of the task to another process in the system.

One important relation between the processes in such a system is the relation "gives work to." In [Habermann 67], Habermann assumed that "gives work to" defined a hierarchy to prove "harmonious cooperation." If we have an operating system, we want to show that a request of the system will generate only a finite (and reasonably small) number of requests to individual processes before the original request is satisfied. If the relation "gives work to" defines a hierarchy, we can prove our result by examining each process separately to make sure that every request to it results in only a finite number of requests to other processes. If the relation is not hierarchical, a more difficult "global" analysis would be required.

Restricting "gives work to" so that it defines a hierarchy helps in the establishment of "well behavedness," but it is certainly not a necessary condition for "harmonious cooperation".[2]

In the T.H.E. system the two hierarchies described above coincided. Every level of abstraction was achieved by the introduction of parallel processes and these processes only gave work to those written to implement lower levels in the program hierarchy. One should not draw general conclusions about system structure on the basis of this coincidence. For example, the remark that "building a system with more levels than were found in the T.H.E. system is undesirable, because it introduces more queues" is often heard because of this coincidence. The later work [Dijkstra 72d*] on structured programming shows that the levels of abstraction are useful when there is only one process. Further, the "Habermann hierarchy" is useful when the processes are controlled by badly structured programs. Adding levels in the program hierarchy need not introduce new

---

[2] This restriction is also valuable in human organizations. Where requests for administrative work flow only in one direction things go relatively smoothly, but in departments where the "leader" constantly refers requests "downward" to committees (which can themselves send requests to the "leader") we often find the system filling up with uncompleted tasks and a correspondingly large increase in overhead.

processes or queues. Adding processes can be done without writing new programs.

The "program hierarchy" is only significant at times when humans are working with the program (e.g. when the program is being constructed or changed). If the programs were all implemented as macros, there would be no trace of this hierarchy in the running system. The "Habermann hierarchy" is a restriction on the runtime behavior of the system. The theorems proven by Habermann would hold even if a process that is controlled by a program written at a low level in the program hierarchy "gave work to" a process which was controlled by a program originally written at a higher level in the program hierarchy. There are also no detrimental effects on the program hierarchy provided that the programs written at the lower level are not written in terms of programs at the higher level. Readers are referred to Edwin Abbott's *Flatland, the Romance of Many Dimensions* (Dover, 1952).

3 Hierarchical structures relating to resource ownership and allocation

The RC4000 system (see [Brinch Hansen 70*]), enforced a hierarchical relation based upon the ownership of memory. A generalization of that hierarchical structure has been proposed in [Varney 72] and similar hierarchical relationships are to be found in various commercial operating systems, though they are not often formally described.

In the RC4000 system the objects were processes and the relation was "allocated a memory region to." Varney proposes extending the relation so that the hierarchical structure controlled the allocation of other resources as well. (In the RC4000 systems specific areas of memory were allocated, but that was primarily a result of the lack of virtual memory hardware; in most systems of interest now, we can allocate quantities of a resource without allocating the specific physical resources until they are actually used). In many commercial systems we also find that resources are not allocated directly to the processes which use them. They are allocated to administrative units, who, in turn, may allocate them to other processes. In these systems we do not find any loops in the graph of "allocates resources to", and the relation defines a hierarchy, which is closely related to the RC4000 structure.

This relation was not a significant one in the T.H.E. system, where allocating was done by a central allocator called a "banker." Again this sense of hierarchy is not strongly related to the others, and if it is present with one or more of the others, they need not coincide.

The disadvantages of a nontrivial hierarchy (the hierarchy is present in a trivial form even in the T.H.E. system) of this sort are: (1) poor resource utilization that may occur when some processes in the system are short of resources while other processes, under a different allocator in the hierarchy, have an excess; (2) high overhead that occurs when resources are tight. Requests for more resources must always go up all the levels of the hierarchy before being denied or granted. The central "banker" does not have these disadvantages. A central resource allocator, however, becomes complicated in situations where groups of related processes wish to dynamically share resources without influence by other such groups. Such situations can arise in systems that are used in real time by independent groups of users. The T.H.E. system did not have such problems and, as a result, centralized resource allocation was quite natural.

It is this particular hierarchical relation which the Hydra group rejected. They did not mean to reject the general notion of hierarchical structure as suggested in the original report ([Wulf 74] and private discussions).

4 Protection hierarchies à la MULTICS

Still another hierarchy can be found in the MULTICS system. The conventional two level approach to operating systems (low level called the supervisor, next level the users) has been generalized to a sequence of levels in the supervisor called "rings." The set of programs within a MULTICS process is organized in a hierarchical structure, the lower levels being known as the inner rings, and the higher levels being known as outer rings. Although the objects are programs, this relation is not the program hierarchy discussed in Section 1. Calls occur in both directions and lower level programs may use higher level ones to get their work done [Graham 68].

Noting that certain data are much more crucial to operation of the system than other data, and that certain procedures are much more critical to the overall operation of the system than others, the designers have used this as the basis of their hierarchy. The data to which the system is most sensitive are controlled by the inner ring procedures, and transfers to those programs are very carefully controlled. Inner ring procedures have unrestricted access to programs and data in the outer rings. The outer rings contain data and procedures that effect a relatively small number of users and hence are less "sensitive." The hierarchy is most easily defined in terms of a relation "can be accessed by" since "sensitivity" in the sense used above is difficult to define. Low levels have unrestricted access to higher levels, but not vice versa.

It is clear that placing restrictions on the relation "can be accessed by" is important to system reliability and security.

It has, however, been suggested that by insisting that the relation "can be accessed by" be a hierarchy, we prevent certain accessibility patterns that might be desired. We might have three segments in which A requires access to B, B to C, and C to A. No other access rights are needed or desirable. If we insist that "can be accessed by" define a hierarchy, we must (in this case) use the trivial hierarchy in which A, B, C are considered one part.

In the view of the author, the number of pairs in the relation "can be accessed by" should be minimized, but he sees no advantage in insisting that it define a hierarchy ([Parnas 73*; Price 73]).

The actual MULTICS restriction is even stronger than requiring a hierarchy. Within a process, the relation must be a complete ordering.

5 Hierarchies and "top-down" design methodology

About the time that the T.H.E. system work appeared, it became popular to discuss design methods using such terms as "top down" and "outside in" ([Parnas 67*, 69*; Randall 68*]). The simultaneous appearance of papers suggesting how to design a well-designed system led to the unfounded assumption that the T.H.E. system had been the result of a "top-down" design process. Even in more recent work [Baker 72] top-down design and structured programming are considered almost synonymous.

Actually "outside in" was a much better term for what was intended than was "top down"! The intention was to begin with a description of the system's user interface, and work in small, verifiable steps toward the implementation. The "top" in that hierarchy consisted of those parts of the system that were visible to the user. In a system designed according to the "program hierarchy" the lower level functions will be used by the higher level functions, but some of them may also be visible to the user (store and load, for example). Some functions on higher levels may not be available to him (restart system). Those participants in the design of the T.H.E. system with whom I have discussed the question (Dijkstra and Habermann), report that they did not proceed with the design of the higher levels first.

6 Hierarchical structure and decomposition into modules

Often one wants to view a system as divided into "modules" (e.g., with the purpose outlined in [Parnas 72f*, 72a*]). This division defines a relation "part of." A group of subprograms is collected into a module, groups of modules collected into bigger modules, etc. This process defines a relation "part of" whose graph is clearly loop-free. It remains loop-free even if we allow programs or modules to be part of several modules—the part never includes the whole.

Note that we may allow programs in one module to call programs in another module, so that the module hierarchy just defined need not have any connection with the program hierarchy. Even allowing recursive calls between modules does not defeat the purpose of the modular decomposition (e.g., flexibility), provided that programs in one module do not assume much about the programs in another.

7 Levels of language

It is so common to hear phrases such as "high level language," "low level language," and "linguistic level" that it is necessary to comment on the relation between the implied language hierarchy and the hierarchies discussed in the earlier sections of this paper. It would be nice if, for example, the higher level languages were the languages of the higher level "abstract machines" in the program hierarchy. Unfortunately, this author can find no such relation and cannot define the hierarchy that is implied in the use of those phrases. *In moments of scepticism* one might suggest that the relation is "less efficient than" or "has a bigger grammar than" or "has a bigger compiler than"; however, none of those phrases suggests an ordering, which is completely consistent with the use of the term. It would be nice if the next person to use the phrase "higher level language" in a paper would define the hierarchy to which he refers.

Summary

The computer system design literature now contains quite a number of valuable suggestions for improving the comprehensibility and predictability of computer systems by imposing a hierarchical structure on the programs. This paper has tried to demonstrate that, although these suggestions have been described in quite similar terms, the structure implied by those suggestions are not necessarily closely related. Each of the suggestions must be understood and evaluated (for its applicability to a particular system design problem) independently. Further, we have tried to show that, while each of the suggestions offers some advantages over an "unstructured" design, there are also disadvantages, which must be considered. The main purpose of this paper has been to provide some guidance for those reading earlier literature and to suggest a way for future authors to include more precise definitions in their papers on design methods.

Acknowledgments. The author acknowledges the valuable suggestions of Mr. W. Bartussek (Technische Hochschule, Darmstadt) and Mr. John Shore (Naval Research Laboratory, Washington, D.C.). Both of these gentlemen have made substantial contributions to the more precise formulation of many of the concepts in this paper; neither should be held responsible for the fuzziness, which unfortunately remains.

24

On the Design and Development of Program Families

David L. Parnas
University of North Carolina

Abstract *Program families are defined (analogously to hardware families) as sets of programs whose common properties are so extensive that it is advantageous to study the common properties of the programs before analyzing individual members. The assumption that, if one is to develop a set of similar programs over a period of time, one should consider the set as a whole while developing the first three approaches to the development, is discussed. A conventional approach called "sequential development" is compared to "stepwise refinement" and "specification of information hiding modules." A more detailed comparison of the two methods is then made. By means of several examples it is demonstrated that the two methods are based on the same concepts but bring complementary advantages.*

Introduction

We consider a set of programs to constitute a *family* whenever it is worthwhile to study programs from the set by *first* studying the common properties of the set and *then* determining the special properties of the individual family members. A typical family of programs is the set of versions of an operating system distributed by a manufacturer. While there are many significant differences between the versions, it usually pays to learn the common properties of all the versions before studying the details of any one. Program families are analogous to the hardware families promulgated by several manufacturers. Although the various models in a hardware family might not have a single component in common, almost everyone reads the common "principles of operations" manual before studying the special characteristics of a specific model. Traditional programming methods were intended for the development of a single program. In this paper, we propose to examine explicitly the process of developing a program family and to compare various programming techniques in terms of their suitability for designing such sets of programs.

Motivation for interest in families

Variations in application demands, variations in hardware configurations, and the ever-present opportunity to improve a program mean that software will *inevitably* exist in many versions. The differences between these versions are unavoidable and purposeful. In addition, experience has shown that we cannot always design all algorithms before implementation of the system. These algorithms are invariably improved experimentally after the system is complete. This need for the existence of many experimental versions of a system is yet another reason for interest in "multiversion" programs.

It is well known that the production and maintenance of multiversion programs is an expensive problem for software distributors. Often separate manuals and separate maintenance groups are needed. Converting a program from one version to another is a nontrivial (and hence expensive) task.

This paper discusses two relatively new programming methods which are intended explicitly for the development of program families. We are motivated by the assumption that if a designer/programmer pays conscious attention to the family rather than a sequence of individual programs, the overall cost of development and maintenance of the programs will be reduced.[1] The goal of this paper is to compare the methods, providing some insight about the advantages and disadvantages of each.

Classical method of producing program families

The classical method of developing programs is best described as *sequential completion*. A particular member of the family is developed completely to the "working" stage. The next member(s) of the family is (are) developed by modification of these working programs. A schematic representation of this process is shown by Fig. 1. In this figure a node is represented as a circle if it is an intermediate representation on the way to producing a program, but is not a working program itself. An *X* represents a complete (usable) family member. An arc from one node to another indicates that a program (or intermediate representation of a program) associated with the first node was modified to produce that associated with the second.

---

[1] Some preliminary experiments support this assumption [Parnas 72a*; Mills 72] but the validity of our assumption has not yet been proved in practice. Readers who do not want to read about programming techniques based on this unproved assumption should stop reading here.

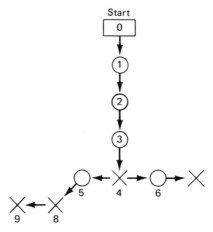

Figure 1   Representation of development by sequential completion. Note: nodes 5 and 6 represent incomplete programs obtained by removing code from program 4 in preparation for producing programs 1, 8, and 9. *Symbols*: □ is the set of initial possibilities; ○ is the incomplete program; × is the working program.

Each arc of this graph represents a design decision. In most cases each decision reduces the set of possible programs under consideration. However, when one starts from a working program, one generally goes through a reverse step, in which the set of possible programs is again increased (i.e., some details are not decided). Nodes 5 and 6 are instances of this.

When a family of programs is produced according to the above model, one member of the family can be considered to be an ancestor of other family members. It is quite usual for descendants of a given program to share some of its ancestor's characteristics which are not appropriate to the purpose of the descendants. In bringing the earlier version to completion, certain decisions were made which would not have been made if the descendant program had been developed independently. These decisions remain in the descendent program only because their removal would entail a great deal of reprogramming. As a result, later versions of the program have performance deficiencies, because they were derived by modifying programs designed to function in a different environment or with a different load.

New techniques

Figure 2 shows the common basic concept of newer methods. Using these methods one never modifies a completed program to get a new family member; one always begins with one of the intermediate stages and continues from that point with design decisions, ignoring the decisions made after that point in the development of the previous versions. Where

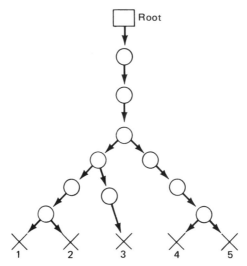

Figure 2   Representation of program development using "abstract decisions." *Symbols*: □ is the set of initial possibilities; O is the incomplete program; × is the working program.

in the classical method one can say that one version of the program is the ancestor of another, here we find that the two versions have a common ancestor [Dijkstra 72d*].

The various versions need not be developed sequentially. If the development of one branch of the tree does not use information from another branch, the two subfamilies could be developed in parallel. A second important note is that in these methods the order in which decisions are made has more significance than in the classical method. Recall that all decisions made above a branch point are shared by all family members below that point. In our motivation of the family concept we emphasized the value of having much in common among the family members. By deciding as much as possible before a branch point, we increase the "similarity" of the systems. Because we know that certain differences must exist between the programs, the aim of the new design methods is to allow the decisions, which can be shared by a whole family, to be made before those decisions, which differentiate family members. As Fig. 2 illustrates, it is meaningful to talk of subfamilies which share more decisions than are shared by the whole family.

If the root of the tree represents the situation before any decisions are made, then two programs, which have only the root as common ancestor, have nothing in common.

We should note that representing this process by a tree is an oversimplification. Certain design decisions can be made without consideration of others (the decision processes can be viewed as commutative operators). It is possible to use design decisions in several branches. For example, a number of quite different operating systems *could* make use of the same deadlock prevention algorithm, even if it was not one of the decisions made in a common ancestor.

Representing the intermediate stages

In the classical method of producing program families, the intermediate stages were not well defined and the incomplete designs were not precisely represented. This was both the cause and the result of the fact that communication between versions was in the form of completed programs. If either of the two methods discussed here is to work effectively, it is necessary that we have precise representations of the intermediate stages (especially those that might be used as branch points). Both methods emphasize precision in the descriptions of partially designed programs. They differ in the way that the partial designs are represented. We should note that it is not the final version of the program that is our real product (one seldom uses a program without modification); in the new methods it is the well-developed but still incomplete representation that is offered as a contribution to the work of others.

Programming by stepwise refinement

The method of "stepwise refinement"[2] was first formally introduced by [Dijkstra 72d*] and has since been further discussed by a variety of contributors [Wirth 71*; Wulf 72; Hoare 74a*]. In the literature the major emphasis has been on the production of correct programs, but the side effect is that the method encourages the production of program families. One of the early examples was the development of a program for generation of prime numbers in which the next to the last program still permitted the use of two quite different algorithms for generating primes. This incomplete program defined a family of programs which included at least two significantly different members.

In "stepwise refinement" the intermediate stages are represented by programs, which are complete except for the implementation of certain operators and operand types. The programs are written as if the operators and operands were "built in" the language. The implementation of these operators in the actual language is postponed to the later stages. Where the (implicit or explicit) definition of the operators is sufficiently abstract to permit a variety of implementations, the early versions of the program

[2] The reader should note that although stepwise refinement is often identified with "**goto** less programming," the use and abuse of the **goto** is irrelevant in this paper.

define a family in which there is a member for each possible implementation of the unimplemented operators and operands. For example, a program might be written with a declaration of a data type *stack* and operators *push* and *pop*. Only in later versions would the stack representation and procedures to execute *push* and *pop* be introduced. We illustrate the technique of stepwise refinement with two examples, which will be used in a later comparison.

EXAMPLE 1. *Dijkstra's Prime Program.* [Dijkstra 72d*] has described the development of a program to print numbers. The first step appears as follows:

> **begin variable** *table p*;
> > fill table *p* with first thousand prime numbers;
> > **print** *table p*
> **end**

In this program Dijkstra has assumed an operand type "table" and two operators. The representation of the table, the method of calculating the primes, and the printing format are all left undecided. In fact, the only binding decisions (common characteristics of the whole family of programs) are that *all* the primes will be developed before *any* are printed, and that we will always want the first thousand primes. Dijkstra then debates between implementing *table* or elaborating *fill table*. Eventually he decides that *table* should be implemented, and all members of the remaining family share the same table implementation. A branch of the family with an alternative table implementation is mentioned, but not developed. Later members of the family are developed by considering various possible methods of computing the prime numbers.

EXAMPLE 2. (*Wulf's KWIC Index Program*). [Wulf 72] presents a proposed stepwise refinement development of a KWIC index production program as follows:

> Step 1: *PRINTKWIC*
> We may think of this as being an instruction in a language (or machine), in which the notion of generating a KWIC index is primitive. Since this operation is not primitive in most practical languages, we proceed to define it:
> Step 2: *PRINTKWIC*: generate and save all interesting circular shifts; alphabetize the saved lines; print alphabetized lines.
> Again we may think of each of these lines as being an instruction in an appropriate language; and again, since they are not primitive in most existing languages, we must define them; for example:
> Step 3a: generate and save all interesting
> > circular shifts:

for each line in the input **do**
begin
generate and save all interesting shifts of "this line"
end

etc.

For purposes of later comparison, we note the decisions that must be shared by the remaining members of the family:

(1) all shifts will be stored;
(2) all circular shifts will be generated and stored before alphabetization begins;
(3) alphabetical ordering will be completed before printing is started;
(4) all shifts of the one line will be developed before any of the shifts for another line;
(5) "uninteresting" shifts will be eliminated at the time that the shifts are generated.

In the best-known examples of programming by stepwise refinement the definitions of the operators have been informal. All of the published examples have been designed as tutorial examples, and the operators are kept "classical" so that one's intuitive understanding of them suffices for the correct understanding of the program development. The only exception known to the author is [Henderson 72].[3] Formal definition of the operators can be included by application of the predicate insertion technique first introduced by Floyd for the purpose of program verification. As Dijkstra has suggested, we can think of the operators as "predicate transformers" (rules which describe how a predicate which describes the state of the program variables after application of the operator can be transformed into a predicate describing the state of the program variables before the operator is executed [Dijkstra 75a*]).

Technique of module specification

Another technique for the design of program families has been described in [Parnas 72d*, 72f*]. This method is distinguished from the method of stepwise refinement in that the intermediate representations are *not* incomplete programs. Instead, they are "specifications" of the externally visible collective behavior of program groups called modules.[4] These intermediate representations are not written in a programming language, and they never become part of the final system.

---

[3] In this example the method failed to produce a correct program because intuitive understanding of the operators was too vague.
[4] Naur has called a similar concept "action clusters" [Naur 69a*].

To illustrate this method we compare the development of the KWIC program described in [Parnas 72d*, 72f*] with the development by stepwise refinement discussed earlier in this paper.

In the method of "module specification" the design decisions which *cannot* be common properties of the family are identified and a module (a group of programs) is designed to hide each design decision. For our example, the following design decisions were identified:

(1) the internal representation of the data to be processed;
(2) the representation of the circular shifts of those lines and the time at which the shifts would be computed;
(3) the method of alphabetization to be used, and the time at which the alphabetization would be carried out;
(4) the input formats;
(5) the output formats;
(6) the internal representations of the individual words (a part of decision 1).

To hide the representation of the data in memory, a module was provided which allows its users to simply write *CHAR(line, word, c)* in order to access a certain character. Data were "stored" in this module by calling *SETCHAR(line, word, c, d)*. Other functions in the module would report the number of lines, the number of words in a given line, and the number of characters in a word. By the use of this group of programs the rest of the program could be written in a way that was completely independent of the actual representation.

A module quite similar in appearance to the one described above hid the representation of the circular shifts, the time at which they were computed, and even whether or not they were ever stored. (Some members of the program family reduced storage requirements by computing the character at a given point in the list of shifts whenever it was requested.) All these implementations shared the same external interface.

Still another pair of programs hid the time and method of alphabetization. This (2 program) module provided a function ITH(i) which would give the index in the second module for the ith line in the alphabetic sequence.

The decisions listed above are those which are not made, i.e., postponed. The decisions which were made are more difficult to identify. The design has placed restrictions on the way that program parts may refer to each other and has, in that way, reduced the space of possible programs.

The above description is intended as a brief review for those who already have some familiarity with the two methods. Those who are new to the ideas should refer to the original articles before reading further.[5]

---

[5] For symmetry we remark that while stepwise refinement was developed primarily to assist in the production of correct programs and has a pleasant side effect in the production of program families, module specification was developed for the production of program families but helps with "correctness" as discussed in [Price 73].

Comparison based on the KWIC example

To understand the differences in the techniques the reader should look at the list of decisions which define the family of KWIC programs whose development was started by Wulf. All of the decisions which are shared by the members of Wulf's family are hidden in individual modules by the second method and can therefore differentiate family members. Those decisions about sequencing of events are specified early in Wulf's development but have been postponed in the second method.

Lest one think that in the second method no decisions about implementation have been made, we list below some of the common properties of programs produced using the second method.

(1) All programs will have access to the original character string during the process of computing the KWIC index.
(2) Common words such as THE, AND, etc., would not be eliminated until the output stage (if ever).
(3) The output module will get its information one character at a time.

The astute reader sill have noted that these decisions are not necessarily good ones. Nonetheless, decisions have been made which allow work on the modules to begin and progress to completion without further interaction between the programmers. In this method the aim *of the early work* is not to make decisions about a program but to make it possible to postpone (and therefore easily change) decisions about the program. Later work should proceed more quickly and easily as a result [Parnas 72a*].

In the stepwise refinement method we progressed quickly toward a relatively narrow family (limited variations in the family). With modules we have prepared the way for the development of a relatively broad family.

Comparative remarks based on Dijkstra's prime program

We now take a second look at the Dijkstra development of the prime number program.

In his development Dijkstra is moved to make an early decision about the implementation of *table* in order to go further. All members of the family developed subsequently share that implementation. Should he decide to go back and reconsider that decision, he would have to reconsider all of the decisions made after that point. The method of module specification would have allowed him to postpone the table implementation to a later stage (i.e., to hide the decision) and thereby achieve a broader family.

Comparative remarks based on an operating system problem

We consider the problem of core allocation in an operating system. We assume that we have a list of free core areas and data that should be brought to core storage. Writing a program that will find a free spot and allocate the space to the program needing it is trivial. Unfortunately there are many such programs, and we cannot be certain which of them we want. The programs can differ in at least two important ways, policy and implementation of the mechanism. By "policy" we mean simply the rule for choosing a place, if there are several usable places; by "implementation of the mechanism" we mean such questions as, how shall we represent the list of free spaces, what operations must we perform to add a free space to the list, to remove a free space? Should the list be kept in a special order? What is the search procedure? etc.

The decisions discussed above are important in that they can have a major impact on the performance of a system. On the other hand, we cannot pick a "best" solution; there is no best solution!

On the policy side there have been numerous debates between such policies as "first fit"—allocate the first usable space in the list, "best fit"—find the smallest space that will fit, "favor one end of core," "modified best fit"—look for a piece that fits well but does not leave a hopelessly small fragment, etc. It is clear to most who have studied the problem that the "best" policy depends on the nature of the demand, i.e., the distribution of the requested sizes, the expected length of time that an area will be retained, and so on.

Choosing an implementation is even more complicated because it depends in part on the policy choice. Keeping a list ordered by size of fragment is valuable if we are going to seek a "best fit" but worse than useless for a policy which tends to put things as low in core as possible.

The following "structured programming" development of such an algorithm illustrates the construction of an abstract program which has the properties of all of those that we are interested in and does not yet prejudice our choice.

stage 1:
bestyet : = **null**;
while not all spaces considered **do**
    begin
        find next item from list of free spaces (*candidate*);
        bestyet : = *bestof*(*bestyet, candidate*)
    end;
if *bestyet* = **null** **then** *erroraction*;
allocate(*bestyet*); *remove* (*bestyet*)

Strictly following the principles of writing well-structured programs we should now verify that the above is correct or write down the conditions under which we can be certain that it is correct.

Correctness Assumptions

(1) *bestyet* is a variable capable of indicating a free space; **null** is a possible value of this variable indicating no space.

(2) "not all spaces considered" is a predicate that will be *true* as long as it is possible that a "better" space is still to be found but will be false when all possible items have been considered.

(3) variable *candidate* has the same type as bestyet.

(4) "find next item from list of free spaces" will assign to its parameter a value indicating one of the items on the free space list. If there are n such items on the list, n calls of the procedure will deliver each of the n items once.

(5) No items will be removed from or added to the list during the execution of the program.

(6) *bestof* is a procedure that takes two variables of the type of *bestyet* and returns (as a value of the same type) the better of the two possible spaces according to some unspecified criterium. If neither place is suitable, the value is **null**, which is always unsuitable.

(7) *error action* is what the program is supposed to do if no suitable place can be found.

(8) *remove* is a procedure that removes the space indicated by its parameter from the list of free spaces. A later search will not find this space.

(9) *allocate* is a procedure that gives the space indicated by its parameter to the requesting program.

(10) Once we have begun to execute this program, no other execution of it will begin until this one is complete (mutual exclusion).

(11) The only other program which might change the data structures involved is one that would add a space to the free space list. Mutual exclusion may also be needed here.

Design decisions in stage 1

Although this first program appears quite innocuous, it does represent some real design decisions which are best understood by considering programs which do *not* share the properties of the above abstract program.

(1) We have decided to produce a program in which one is not allowed to add to the free space list *during* a search for a free space.

(2) We have not allowed a program in which two searches will be conducted simultaneously.

(3) We are considering only programs where a candidate is not removed from the free space list while it is being considered. Perfectly reasonable programs could be written in which the "bestyet" was not on the list and was reinserted in the list when a better space was discovered.

(4) We have chosen not to use a program in which a check for possible allocation is made before searching the list. Some reasonable programs would have a check for the empty list, or even a check for the size of the largest available space before the loop so that no time would be spent searching for an optimum fit when no fit at all was possible. In our program, an assignment to *bestyet*, an evaluation of the termination condition, plus an evaluation of *bestyet* = **null** will take place every time the program is called.

The programs omitted from the family of programs which share the abstract program of stage 1 are not significant omissions. If they were, we would not have chosen to eliminate them at such an early state in our design. We have discussed them only so that the reader will see that writing the program of stage 1 has not been an empty exercise.

We now consider a subfamily of the family of programs defined in stage 1. In this subfamily we will decide to represent the list by a two-dimensional array in which each row represents an item in the free space list. We assume further that the first free space is kept in row 1, that the last is in row N, and that all rows between 1 and N represent valid free spaces. We make no assumptions about the information kept in each row to describe the free space or about the order of rows in the array. This allows us to write the following:

stage 2:
bestyet : = 0;
candidate : = 0;
while *candidate* ≠ *N* **do**
   begin
      candidate : = *candidate* + 1;
      bestyet : = *bestof* (*bestyet*, *candidate*)
   end;
if *bestyet* = 0 **then** *erroraction*;
allocate (*bestyet*);
remove (*bestyet*).

We have been able to allow variables *bestyet* and *candidate* to be integers to implement the test for "not all spaces considered" as an integer test on the value of *candidate* because of our assumptions. Our assumptions do not yet permit us to elaborate the operations on the table rows or to implement our policy decision in *bestof*. We cannot even implement *remove*, because we do not know if we are going to allocate all of the space found or allocate only that part needed and leave the rest on the free space list.

Stage 3

We now skip several stages in a "proper" structured programming development in order to show one of the possible "concrete" family members. In this program we have decided that the entries in each row of the array will give the first and last locations of each free space and that when we allocate a space we will allocate the whole space so as to avoid having to keep track of an ever increasing set of small fragments. We also assume a policy of "best fit" which means that we pick the smallest of the suitable free spaces.

```
bestyet : = 0;
candidate : = 0;
oldT : = ∞;
while candidate ≠ N do
      begin
          candidate : = candidate + 1;
          T : = end (candidate)-start (candidate);
          if T ⩾ request and T < oldT then begin
                  bestyet : = candidate;
                  oldT : = T end
      end;
if bestyet = 0 then erroraction;
allocate (bestyet);
N : = N − 1;
for I : = bestyet step 1 until N do begin
    end (I) : = end(I + 1);
    start (I) : = start (I + 1)
    end
```

To understand the value of structured programming in producing programming families, we now have to consider what would happen if, instead of the program developed in stage 3, we wanted a program in which (1) we did *not* allocate the *smallest suitable* space but only that part of it that was needed and (2) we represented the free spaces by giving the *start address* and the *length* rather than *start and end* addresses. We consider making this change in two situations.

Situation 1: We wrote the program shown in stage 3 in the classical way, i.e., we wrote that program directly without writing down the intermediate stages.

Situation 2: We used the structured programming development as shown above.

In situation 1 we would have to modify the programs shown in the section in *stage* 3. We would have nothing else. As you can see, it would take some effort to identify which lines in the program could remain and which could or should be changed. Even on this rather simple example it would require a fairly careful study of the program to determine which changes should be made unless the person making the changes was very familiar with the program (e.g., unless he personally had just written it).

In situation 2, however, we have the option of returning to the program labeled *stage 2*. All the assumptions made in *stage 2* are still valid and the program itself is still valid, only incomplete. Completing the program shown in *stage 2* in order to produce the new nonabstract program is as straightforward as the original modification of *stage 2* to get *stage 3*. It can be done by someone new. In this situation the new final program is obtained not by modifying the old working program but by modifying the closest common ancestor.

If the organization in charge of maintaining the system wishes to keep both versions in active use, they can use the *stage 2* documentation as valid documentation for both versions of the program and even consider some changes for both versions by studying *stage 2*.

This example was intended to demonstrate why structured programming is such a valuable tool for those who wish to maintain and develop families of programs such as operating systems. The reader must keep in mind that this is a small and simple example, the benefits would be even greater for larger programs developed in this way.

Although we have shown an advantage for development of program families by using structured programming, we have also revealed a fundamental problem. Progress at each stage was made by making design decisions. Going back to *stage 2* was possible in our case because we had in *stage 2* all those design decisions that we wanted to keep and none of those that we wanted to discard. Unless we were able to predict in advance exactly which decisions we would change and which we would keep, we are not likely to be so lucky in practice. In fact, even with the ability to see into the future, there might not be any decision making sequence which would allow us to backtrack without discarding the results of decisions which will remain unchanged. The results of perfectly valid design decisions may have to be recoded, because the code that implements those decisions was designed to interact with the code that is being changed.

It is to get around these difficulties that the division into "information hiding" modules can be introduced. Rather than continually refine step by step a single program, as is done in stepwise refinement, we break the program up into independent parts and develop each of them in ignorance of the implementation of the other. In contrast to classical programming methods, these parts are not the subprograms which are called from a main program; they are collections of subprograms.

In our example we would have a free space list module, an allocation module, and a selection criterion module. The free space list module would consist of

(1) the code that implemented variable *bestyet* and any other variable that could represent a place in a list as well as the representation of the constant **null**;

(2) the program "not all spaces considered";

(3) the program "find next item from the list of free spaces";

(4) the program *remove*;

(5) a program to add items to the free space list (this program is not called in the above program, but must be called elsewhere in the system and would be considered a part of the free space list module);

(6) programs to give the essential characteristics of a space on the list (e.g., *start* and *end* address).

The selection criterion module would consist of

(1) *bestof*;

(2) some other programs that will be called elsewhere, such as programs to choose a victim (a space to be removed from its owner and made available).

The allocation module consists of *allocate* and other programs not discussed above. Each of these modules would have to contain an initialization section which would be called from the main program so that the additional temporary variables introduced in implementing the programs would not be visible in the main program. For some implementations of a module the initialization section would be empty, but its call would be written in the main program so that the main program would not have to be changed if the new implementation included variables which had to be initialized.

This division into modules and independent implementation will only result in a working program if the external characteristics of each module were sufficiently well specified so that the code could be written without looking at the implementation of other modules [Parnas 72a*, 72d*]. This is clearly an extra effort which is not needed if only the stepwise refinement method is used. In return for this effort one would gain the ability to reverse the decision about table representation made in *stage 2* without even considering the code written to implement the policy introduced in *stage 3*. One also gains the ability to develop the two parts of the program without any communication between the groups developing each one. This can lead to a shorter development time and the ability to develop several versions of the system simultaneously.

How the module specifications define a family

Members of a family of programs defined by a set of module specifications can vary in three principal ways.

(1) *Implementation methods used within the modules*. Any combination of sets of programs which meets the module specifications is a member of the

program family. Subfamilies may be defined either by dividing each of the main modules into submodules in alternative ways, or by using the method of structured programming to describe a family of implementations for the module.

(2) *Variation in the external parameters*. The module specifications can be written in terms of parameters so that a family of specifications results. Programs may differ in the values of those parameters and still be considered to be members of the program family.

(3) *Use of subsets*. In many situations one application will require only a subset of the functions provided by a system. We may consider programs which consist of a subset of the programs described by a set of module specifications to be members of a family as well. This is especially important in the development of families of operating systems, where some installations will require only a subset of the system provided for another. The set of possible subsets is defined by the "uses" relation between the individual programs [Parnas 74b*].

Which method to use

By now it should be clear that the two methods are neither equivalent nor contradictory. Rather they are complementary. They are both based on the same basic ideas (see historical note which follows): (1) precise representations of the intermediate stage in a program design, and (2) postponement of certain decisions while continuing to make progress towards a completed program.

Stepwise refinement (as practiced in the literature) encourages one to make decisions about sequencing early, because the intermediate representations are all programs. Postponement of sequencing decisions until run time requires the introduction of processes [Dijkstra 68c*]. The method of module specification is not usually convenient for the expressing of sequencing decisions. (In our KWIC index project sequencing had to be described by writing a brief "structured" "Main Program," which was one of several possible ways that the modules could have been used to produce a KWIC index. It was written last!)

Stepwise refinement has the significant advantage that it does not add to the total amount of effort required to design the first complete family member. By keeping complexity in control, it usually reduces the total amount of effort. In contrast, the module specifications represent a very significant amount of extra effort. Experience has shown that the effort involved in writing the set of specifications can be greater than the effort that it would take to write one complete program. The method permits the production of a broader family and the completion of various parts of the system independently, but at a significant cost. It usually pays to apply the method only when one expects the eventual implementation of a wide selection of possible family members. In contrast, the method of stepwise refinement is always profitable.

Relation of the question of program families to program generators

A common step taken by industrial maintainers of multiversion programmers is the construction of system generation programs. These programs are given a great deal of data describing the hardware configuration and software needs of the users. Built into the generator is a description of a large family of programs and the generator causes one member of the family to materialize and be loaded on the target hardware.

The methods described in this paper are not intended to replace system generators, since these methods are applied in the design stage and generators are useful when a specific family member must be produced. Stepwise refinement and the method of module specification can simplify the work to be done by a system generation program.

System generators would be completely unnecessary if we wished to build a program which at run time could "simulate" any member of the family. Such a program would be relatively inefficient. By removing much of this variability at the time that the program is generated, increases in productive capacity are made possible.

Often a family of programs includes small members in which certain variables are fixed and larger members in which these factors may vary. For example, an operating system family may include some small members where the number of processes is fixed and other members where dynamic creation and deletion is possible. The programs developed for the larger members of the family can be used as part of the "generator," which produces a smaller member.

Concluding remarks

Another way of comparing the two methods is to answer the following often-heard questions.

(1) When should we teach structured programming or stepwise refinement to our students?
(2) When should we teach about modules and specifications?

To the first question we can respond with another question: "When should we teach unstructured programming?" The second question, however, requires a "straight answer": module design specifications should only be taught to students who have learned to program well and have decided to proceed further and learn methods appropriate to the production of software packages [Parnas 72a*].

One of the difficulties in applying the recent concepts of structured programming is that there are no criteria by which one may evaluate the structure of a system on an objective basis. Aspiring practitioners must go to a famous artist and ask for an evaluation. The "master" may then indicate whether or not he considers the system "tasteful."

The concept of program families provides one way of considering program structure more objectively. For any precise description of a program family (either an incomplete refinement of a program or a set of specifications or a combination of both) one may ask which programs have been excluded and which still remain.

One may consider a program development to be good if the early decisions exclude only uninteresting, undesired, or unnecessary programs. The decisions which remove desired programs would be either postponed until a later state or confined to a well delimited subset of the code. Objective criticism of a program's structure would be based upon the fact that a decision or assumption which was likely to change has influenced too much of the code either because it was made too early in the development or because it was not confined to an information hiding module.

Clearly this is not the only criterion which one may use in evaluating program structures. Clarity (e.g., ease of understanding, ease of verification) is another quite relevant consideration. Although there is some reason to suspect that the two measures are not completely unrelated, there are no reasons to assume that they will agree. For one thing, the "ease" measures mentioned above are functions of the understander or verifier, the set of programs being excluded by a design decision can be interpreted objectively. Of course, the question of which decisions are likely to require changing for some family members is again a question which requires judgment and experience. It is, however, a somewhat more concrete and more easily discussed question than ease of comprehension.

Historical note

In closing this comparison, I want to make a comment on the origin and history of some of the ideas found in this paper. I recently reread one of the papers in which Dijkstra introduced the ideas of structured programming [Dijkstra 72d*]. This paper is unusual in that it seems better each time you read it. The root of *both* methods of producing program families and the concept of family itself is in this original work by Dijkstra. The concept of the division into modules is somewhat differently formulated, but it is present in the concept of the design of the abstract machines; the notion of information hiding is implicit (in the discussion of the thickness of the ropes tying the pearls together). Module specification is not discussed. ([Naur 69a*] introduced a concept quite similar to that of the module when he discussed action clusters, but the concept of information hiding was not made specific and the example does not correspond exactly to what this principle would suggest.) For various reasons the concept of division into modules and the hiding of information seems to have attracted less attention, and later works by other authors [Wirth 71a*; Wulf 72] have emphasized only the stepwise refinement of programs, ignoring the order of the steps or the question of the thickness of the ropes.

Acknowledgments. I am grateful for opportunities to discuss the subject with members of I.F.I.P. Working Group 2.3 on Programming Methodology. These discussions have helped me to clarify the points in this paper. I am also grateful to W. Bartussek of the Technische Hochschule Darmstadt, for his thoughtful comments on an earlier version of this paper, to Dr. H. Mills of the IBM Federal Systems Division who found a rather subtle error in a recent draft, and to Dr. L. Belady of the IBM T. J. Watson Research Laboratory who made a number of helpful comments.

25
System Structure for Software Fault Tolerance

Brian Randell
University of Newcastle upon Tyne

Abstract *The paper presents, and discusses the rationale behind, a method for structuring complex computing systems by the use of what we term "recovery blocks," "conversations" and "fault-tolerant interfaces." The aim is to facilitate the provision of dependable error detection and recovery facilities which can cope with errors caused by residual design inadequacies, particularly in the system software, rather than merely the occasional malfunctioning of hardware components.*

1 Introduction

The concept of "fault-tolerant computing" has existed for a long time. The first book on the subject [Pierce 65] was published no less than ten years ago, but the notion of fault tolerance has remained almost exclusively the preserve of the hardware designer. Hardware structures have been developed that can "tolerate" faults, i.e., continue to provide the required facilities despite occasional failures, either transient or permanent, of internal components and modules. However, hardware component failures are only one source of unreliability in computing systems, decreasing in significance as component reliability improves, while software faults have become increasingly prevalent with the steadily increasing size and complexity of software systems.

In general, fault-tolerant hardware designs are expected to be correct, i.e., the tolerance applies to component failures rather than design inadequacies, although the dividing line between the two may on occasion be difficult to define. But all software faults result from design errors. The relative frequency of such errors reflects the much greater logical complexity of the typical software design compared to that of a typical hardware design. The difference in complexity arises from the fact that the "machines" that hardware designers produce have a relatively small number of possible internal states, whereas the designer of even a small software system has, by comparison, an enormous number of different states to consider; thus one can usually afford to treat hardware designs as being "correct," but often cannot do the same with software even after extensive validation efforts. (The difference in scale is illustrated by the fact that a software simulator of a computer, written at the level of detail required by the hardware designers to analyse and validate their logical design, is likely to be orders of magnitude smaller than the operating system supplied with that computer.)

If all design inadequacies could be avoided or removed this would suffice to achieve software reliability. (We here use the term "design" to include "implementation," which is in fact merely low-level design, concerning itself with detailed design decisions whose correctness nevertheless can be as vital to the correct functioning of the software as that of any high-level design decision.) Indeed many writers equate the terms "software reliability" and "program correctness." However, until *reliable* correctness proofs (relative to some correct and adequately detailed specification), which cover even implementation details, can be given for systems of a realistic size, the only alternative means of increasing software reliability is to incorporate provisions for software fault tolerance.

In fact there exist sophisticated computing systems, designed for environments requiring near-continuous service, which contain ad hoc checks and checkpointing facilities that provide a measure of tolerance against some software errors as well as hardware failures [Randell 71a*]. They incidentally demonstrate the fact that fault tolerance does not necessarily require diagnosing the cause of the fault or even deciding whether it arises from the hardware or the software. However there has as yet been comparatively little specific research into techniques for achieving software fault tolerance and the constraints they impose on computing system design.

Considerations such as these led to the establishment at the University of Newcastle upon Tyne of a project on the design of highly reliable computing systems, under the sponsorship of the Science Research Council of the United Kingdom. The aims of the project were and are "to develop, and give a realistic demonstration of the utility of, computer architecture and programming techniques which will enable a system to have a very high probability of continuing to give trustworthy service in the presence of hardware faults and or software errors, and during their repair. A major aim will be to develop techniques which are of general utility, rather than limited to specialised environments, and to explore possible trade-offs between reliability and performance."

A modest number of reports and papers have emanated from the project to date, including a general overview [Randell 74*]; papers concerned with addressing and protection [Lauer, H. C. 73, 74]; and a preliminary account of our work on error detection and recovery [Horning 74b*]. The present chapter endeavours to provide a rather more extensive discussion of our work on system error recovery techniques, and concentrates on techniques for system structuring which facilitate software fault tolerance. A companion paper [Anderson 76] presents a proof-guided methodology for designing the error detection routines that our method requires.

2 Fault tolerance in software

All fault tolerance must be based on the provision of *useful redundancy*, both for error detection and error recovery. In software the redundancy required is not simple replication of programs but redundancy of design.

The scheme for facilitating software fault tolerance that we have developed can be regarded as analogous to what hardware designers term "standby sparing." As the system operates, checks are made on the acceptability of the results generated by each component. Should one of these checks fail, a spare component is switched in to take the place of the erroneous component. The spare component is of course not merely a copy of the main component. Rather it is of independent design, so that there can be hope that it can cope with the circumstances that caused the main component to fail. (These circumstances will comprise the data the component is provided with and, in the case of errors due to faulty process synchronisation, the timing and form of its interactions with other processes.)

In contrast to the normal hardware standby sparing scheme, the spare software component is invoked to cope with merely the particular set of circumstances that resulted in the failure of the main component. We assume the failures of this component to be due to *residual* design inadequacies, and hence that such failures occur only in exceptional circumstances. The number of different sets of circumstances that can arise even with a software component of comparatively modest size is immense. Therefore the system can revert to the use of the main component for subsequent operations; in hardware this would not normally be done until the main component had been repaired.

The variety of undetected errors which could have been made in the design of a nontrivial software component is essentially infinite. Due to the complexity of the component, the relationship between any such error and its effect at run-time may be very obscure. For these reasons we believe that diagnosis of the original cause of software errors should be left to humans to do, and should be done in comparative leisure. Therefore our scheme for software fault tolerance in no way depends on automated diagnosis of the cause of the error; this would surely only result in greatly increasing the complexity and therefore the error-proneness of the system.

The recovery block scheme for achieving software fault tolerance by means of standby sparing has two important characteristics:

1. It incorporates a general solution to the problem of switching to the use of the spare component, i.e., of repairing any damage done by the erroneous main component, and of transferring control to the appropriate spare component.

2. It provides a method of physically structuring the software system which has the effect of ensuring that the extra software involved in error detection and in the spare components does not add to the complexity of the system and so reduce rather than increase overall system reliability.

3 Recovery blocks

Although the basic recovery block scheme has already been described elsewhere [Horning 74b*], it is convenient to include a brief account of it here. We will then describe several extensions to the scheme directed at more complicated situations than the basic scheme was intended for. Thus we start by considering the problems of fault tolerance, i.e., of error detection and recovery, within a single sequential process in which assignments to stored variables provide the only means of making recognizable progress. Considerations of the problems of communication with other processes, either within the computing system (e.g., by a system of passing messages or the use of shared storage) or beyond the computing system (e.g., by explicit input/output statements) is deferred until a later section.

The progress of a program is by its execution of sequences of the basic operations of the computer. Clearly error-checking for each basic operation is out of the question. Apart from questions of expense, absence of an awareness of the wider scene would make it difficult to formulate the checks. We must aim at achieving a tolerable quantity of checking and exploit our knowledge of the functional structure of the system to distribute these checks to best advantage. It is standard practice to structure the text of a program of any complexity into a set of blocks (by which term we include module, procedure, subroutine, paragraph, etc.) in order to simplify the task of understanding and documenting the program. Such a structure will allow one to provide a functional description of the purpose of the program text constituting a block. (This text may of course include calls on subsidiary blocks.) The functional description can then be used elsewhere in place of the detailed design of the block. Indeed, the structuring of the program into blocks and the specification of the purpose of each block is likely to precede the detailed design of each block, particularly if the programming is being performed by more than one person.

When executed on a computer, a program which is structured into blocks evokes a process which can be regarded as being structured into operations. Operations are seen to consist of sequences of smaller operations, the smallest operations being those provided by the computer itself. Our scheme of system structuring is based on the selection of a set of these operations to act as units of error detection and recovery, by providing extra information with their corresponding blocks, and so turning the blocks into *recovery blocks*.

The scheme is not dependent on the particular form of block structuring that is used or the rules governing the scopes of variables, methods of parameter passing, etc. All that is required is that when the program is executed the acts of entering and leaving each operation are explicit and that operations are properly nested. (In addition, although it is not required, considerable advantage can be taken of information which is provided indicating whether any given variable is local to a particular operation.) However, for convenience of presentation, we will assume that the program text is itself represented by a nested structure of ALGOL or PL/1-style blocks.

A recovery block consists of a conventional block which is provided with a means of error detection (an acceptance test) and zero or more standby spares (the additional alternates). A possible syntax for recovery blocks is as follows:

⟨recovery block⟩ : : =**ensure** ⟨acceptance test⟩ **by**
                         ⟨primary alternate⟩⟨other alternates⟩ **else error**
⟨primary alternate⟩ : : = ⟨alternate⟩
⟨other alternates⟩ : : = ⟨empty⟩|⟨other alternates⟩ **else by** ⟨alternate⟩
⟨alternate⟩ : : = ⟨statement list⟩
⟨acceptance test⟩ : : = ⟨logical expression⟩

The *primary alternate* corresponds exactly to the block of the equivalent conventional program and is entered to perform the desired operation. The *acceptance test*, which is a logical expression without side effects, is evaluated on exit from any alternate to determine whether the alternate has performed acceptably. A further *alternate*, if one exists, is entered if the preceding alternate fails to complete (e.g., because it attempts to divide by zero, or exceeds a time limit) or fails the acceptance test. However *before an alternate is so entered, the state of the process is restored* to that current just before entry to the primary alternate. If the acceptance test is passed, any further alternates are ignored, and the statement following the recovery block is the next to be executed. However, if the last alternate fails

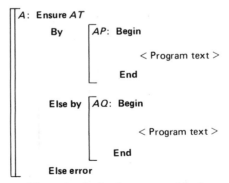

Figure 1   A simple recovery block.

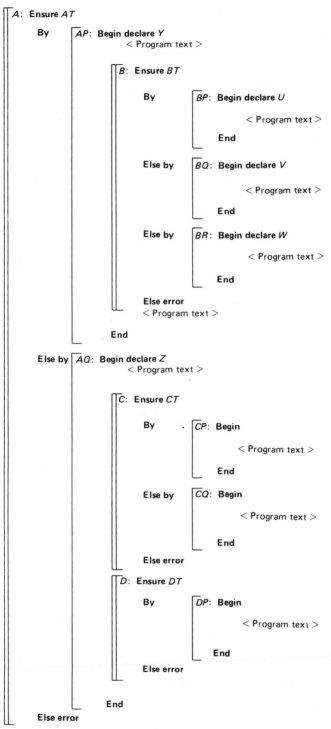

Figure 2 A more complex recovery block.

to pass the acceptance test, then the entire recovery block is regarded as having failed, so that the block in which it is embedded fails to complete, and recovery is then attempted at that level.

In the illustration of a recovery block structure in Figure 1, double vertical lines define the extents of recovery blocks, while single vertical lines define the extents of alternates, primary or otherwise. Figure 2 shows that the alternates can contain, nested within themselves, further recovery blocks.

Consider the recovery block structure shown in Figure 2. The acceptance test BT will be invoked on completion of primary alternate BP. If the test succeeds, the recovery block B is left and the program text immediately following is reached. Otherwise the state of the system is reset and alternate BQ is entered. If BQ, and then BR, do not succeed in passing the acceptance test, the recovery block B as a whole, and therefore primary alternate AP, are regarded as having failed. Therefore the state of the system is reset even further, to that current just before entry to AP, and alternate AQ is attempted.

Deferring for the moment questions as to how the state of the system is reset when necessary, the recovery block structure can be seen as providing a very general framework for the use of standby sparing which is in full accordance with the characteristics discussed earlier in Section 2. There is no need for, indeed no possibility of, attempts at automated error diagnosis because of the fact that the system state is reset after an error deleting all effects of the faulty alternate. Once the system state is reset, switching to the use of an alternate is merely a matter of a simple transfer of control.

The concept of a recovery block, in fact, has much in common with that of a sphere of control, as described by [Davies 73]. However, we have limited ourselves to preplanned error-recovery facilities, and base all error recovery on automatic reversal to a previously reached recovery point. Thus, once a process has "committed" itself by accepting the results of a recovery block, the only form of recovery we envisage involves a more global process reversal, to the beginning of a recovery block whose results have not yet been accepted. In contrast, Davies is prepared to allow for the possibility of recovery following commitment, by means of programmer-supplied "error compensation algorithms."

Although the scheme is related to those that are used in artificial intelligence-type backtracking programs [Hewitt 69], there are major differences. In our scheme backup, being caused by residual design inadequacies, occurs very infrequently and is due to unforeseeable circumstances, rather than very frequently and as an essential element of the basic algorithm.

The utility of the recovery block scheme for standby sparing in software rests on the practicability of producing useful acceptance tests and alternates and on the cost of providing means for resetting the system state. We will discuss each of these points in turn.

3.1 Acceptance tests

The function of the acceptance test is to ensure that the operation performed by the recovery block is to the satisfaction of the program which invoked the block. The acceptance test is therefore performed by reference to the variables accessible to that program, rather than variables local to the recovery block, since these can have no effect or significance after exit from the block. Indeed the different alternates will probably have different sets of local variables. There is no question of there being different acceptance tests for the different alternates. The surrounding program may be capable of continuing with any of a number of possible results of the operation, and the acceptance test must establish that the results are within this range of acceptability, without regard for which alternate can generate them.

There is no requirement that the test be, in any formal sense, a check on the absolute "correctness" of the operation performed by the recovery block. Rather it is for the designer to decide upon the appropriate level of rigor of the test. Ideally the test will ensure that the recovery block has met all aspects of its specification that are depended on by the program text that calls it—in practice, if only for reasons of cost and/or complexity, something less than this might have to suffice. (A methodological approach to the design of appropriate acceptance tests is described in [Anderson 76].)

Although when an acceptance test is failed all the evidence is hidden from the alternate which is then called, a detailed log is kept of such incidents, for off-line analysis. Some failures to pass the acceptance test may be spurious, because a design inadequacy in the acceptance test itself has caused an unnecessary rejection of the operation of an alternate. In fact the execution of the program of the acceptance test itself might suffer an error and fail to complete. Such occurrences, which hopefully will be rare, since the aim is to have acceptance tests which are much simpler than the alternates they check, are treated as failures in the enclosing block, and like all failures are also recorded in the error log. Thus the log provides a means of finding these two forms of inadequacy in the design of the acceptance test; the remaining form of inadequacy, that which causes the acceptance of an incorrect set of results, is of course more difficult to locate.

When an acceptance test is being evaluated, any nonlocal variables that have been modified must be available in their original as well as their modified form because of the possible need to reset the system state. For convenience and increased rigor, the acceptance test is enabled to access such variables either for their modified value or for their original (prior) value. One further facility available inside an acceptance test will be a means of checking whether any of the variables that have been modified

ensure   *ordered* (S) **and** $(sum\ (S) = sum\ (\textbf{prior}\ S))$
   by *Quickersort* (S)
   else by *Quicksort* (S)
   else by *Bubblesort* (S)
   else error

Figure 3 Fault-tolerant sort system.

have not yet been accessed within the acceptance test; this is intended to assist in detecting sins of commission, as well as omission, on the part of the alternate.

Figure 3 shows a recovery block whose intent is to sort the elements of the vector S. The acceptance test incorporates a check that the set of items in S after operation of an alternate are indeed in order. However, rather than incur the cost of checking that these elements are a permutation of the original items, it merely requires the sum of the elements to remain the same.

3.2 Alternates

The primary alternate is the one which is intended to be used normally to perform the desired operation. Other alternates might attempt to perform the desired operation in some different manner, presumably less economically, and preferably more simply. Thus as long as one of these alternates succeeds, the desired operation will have been completed, and only the error log will reveal any troubles that occurred.

However, in many cases one might have an alternate which performs a less desirable operation, but one which is still acceptable to the enclosing block in that it will allow the block to continue properly. (One plentiful source of both these kinds of alternates might be earlier releases of the primary alternate!)

Figure 4 shows a recovery block consisting of a variety of alternates. (This figure is taken from [Anderson 76]). The aim of the recovery block is to extend the sequence S of items by a further item i, but the enclosing

ensure *consistent−sequence* (S)
by *extend* (S): *with* (i)
else by *concatenate* $(S,\ construct\text{-}sequence\ (i))$
else by *warning* ('lost item')
else by $S: = construct−sequence\ (i)$;
  warning ('correction, lost sequence')
else by $S: = empty−sequence$;
  warning ('lost sequence and item')
else error

Figure 4 Recovery block with alternates with different results.

program will be able to continue even if afterwards S is merely "consistent." The first two alternates actually try, by different methods, to join the item i onto the sequence S. The other alternates make increasingly desperate attempts to produce at least some sort of consistent sequence, providing appropriate warnings as they do so.

3.3 Restoring the System State

By making the resetting of the system state completely automatic the programmers responsible for designing acceptance tests and alternates are shielded from the problems of this aspect of error recovery. No special restrictions are placed on the operations which are performed within the alternates, on the calling of procedures, or on the modification of global variables, and no special programming conventions have to be adhered to. In particular the error-prone task of explicit preservation of restart information is avoided. It is thus that the recovery-block structure provides a framework which enables extra program text to be added to a conventional program, for purposes of specifying error detection and recovery actions, with good reason to believe that despite the increase in the total size of the program its overall reliability will be increased.

All this depends on being able to find a method of automating the resetting of the system state whose overheads are tolerable. Clearly, taking a copy of the entire system state on entry to each recovery block, though in theory satisfactory, in practice would normally be far too inefficient. Any method of ensuring that a program be executed in such a fashion that sufficient information is saved for the program to be executable in reverse, instruction by instruction, would be similarly impractical.

Whenever a process has to be backed up it is to the state it had reached just before entry to the primary alternate; therefore the only values that have to be reset are those of nonlocal variables that have been modified. Since no explicit restart information is given, it is not known beforehand which nonlocal variables should be saved. Therefore we have designed various versions of a mechanism which arranges that nonlocal variables are saved in what we term a "recursive cache" as and when it is found that this is necessary, i.e., just before they are modified. The mechanisms do this by detecting, at run-time, assignments to nonlocal variables, and in particular by recognizing when an assignment to a nonlocal variable is the first to have been made to that variable within the current alternate. Thus precisely sufficient information can be preserved.

The recursive cache is divided into regions, there being one region for each nested recovery level, i.e., for each recovery block that has been entered and not yet left. The entries in the current cache region will contain the prior values of any variables that have been modified within the current recovery block, and thus in case of failure it can be used to back up the process to its most recent recovery point. The region will be discarded in its entirety after it has been used for backing up a process. However, if the recovery block is completed successfully some cache entries will be discarded; but those that relate to variables which are nonlocal to the enclosing environment will be consolidated with those in the underlying region of the cache.

A full description of one version of the mechanism has already been published [Horning 74b*], so we will not repeat this description here. We envisage that the mechanisms would be at least partly built in hardware— at any rate if, as we have assumed here, recovery blocks are to be provided within ordinary programs working on small data items such as scalar variables. If, however, one was programming solely in terms of operations on large blocks of data, such as entire arrays or files, the overheads caused by a mechanism built completely from software would probably be supportable. Indeed, the recursive cache scheme, which is essentially a means for secretly preventing what is sometimes termed "update in place," can be viewed as a generalization of the facility in CAP's "middleware" scheme [Randell 71a*] for preventing individual application programs from destructively updating common files.

The various recursive cache mechanisms can all work in terms of the basic unit of assignment of the computer, e.g., a 32-bit word. Thus they ensure that just those scalar variables and array elements which are actually modified are saved. It would of course be possible to structure a program so that all its variables are declared in the outermost block, so that within each recovery block each variable is modified, and so that a maximum amount of information is saved. In practice we believe that even a moderately well structured program will require comparatively little space for saved variables. Measurements of space requirements will be made on the prototype system now being implemented, but already we have some evidence for this from some simple experiments carried out by interpretively executing a number of ALGOL W programs. Even regarding each ALGOL block as a recovery block it was found that the amount of extra space that would be needed for saved scalar variables and array elements was in every case considerably smaller at all times than that needed for the ordinary data of the program.

The performance overheads of the different recursive cache mechanisms are in the process of being evaluated. Within a recovery block only the speed of store instructions is affected; and once a particular nonlocal variable has been saved, subsequent stores to that variable take place essentially at full speed. The overheads involved in entering and leaving recovery blocks differ somewhat between the various mechanisms, but two incur overheads which depend just linearly on the number of different nonlocal variables which are modified. It is our assessment that these overheads will also be quite modest. Certainly it would appear that the space and time overheads incurred by our mechanisms will be far smaller than would be incurred by any explicitly programmed scheme for saving and restoring the process state.

4 Error recovery among interacting processes

In the mechanism described so far, the only notion of forward progress is that of assignment to a variable. In order to reset the state of a process after the failure of an acceptance test, it was necessary only to undo assignments to nonlocal variables. In practice, however, there are many other ways of making forward progress during computations, e.g., positioning a disc arm or magnetic tape, reading a card, printing a line, receiving a message, or obtaining real-time data from external sensors. These actions are difficult or even impossible to undo. However, their effects must be undone in order not to compromise the inherent "recoverability" of state provided by the recursive cache mechanisms.

Our attempt to cope with this kind of problem is based on the observation that all such forms of progress involve interaction among processes. In some cases, one or more of these processes may be mechanical, human, or otherwise external, e.g., the process representing the motion of the card-reading machinery. In other cases, the progress can be encapsulated in separate but interacting computational processes, each of which is structured by recovery blocks. In this section, we will explore the effect of this latter type of interaction on the backtracking scheme, still restricting each process to simple assignment as the only method of progress. Then in Section 5 we will explore the more general problem.

Consider first the case of two or more interacting processes which have the requirement that if one attempts recovery from an error, then the others must also take recovery action "to keep in step."

For example, if one process fails after having received and destroyed information from another process, it will require the other process to resupply this information. Similarly a process may have received and acted upon information subsequently discovered to have been sent to it in error and so must abandon its present activity.

Maintaining, naturally, our insistence on the dangers of attempted programmed error diagnosis, we must continue to rely on automatic backing up of processes to the special recovery points provided by recovery block entries. Each process while executing will at any moment have a sequence of recovery points available to it, the number of recovery points being given by the level of dynamic nesting of recovery blocks.

An isolated process could only "use up" recovery points just one at a time by suffering a whole series of ever-more-serious errors. However,

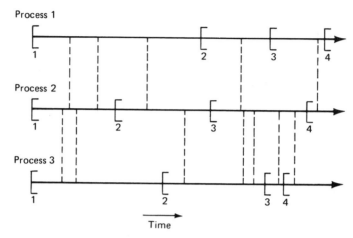

Figure 5   The domino effect.

given an arbitrary set of interacting processes, each with its own private recovery structure, a single error on the part of just one process could cause *all* the processes to use up many or even all of their recovery points, through a sort of uncontrolled domino effect.

The problem is illustrated in Figure 5, which shows three processes, each of which has entered four recovery blocks that it has not yet left. The dotted lines indicate interactions between processes (i.e., an information flow resulting in an assignment in at least one process). Should process 1 now fail, it will be backed up to its latest—i.e., its fourth—recovery point, but the other processes will not be affected. If process 2 fails, it will be backed up to its fourth recovery point past an interaction with process 1, which must therefore also be backed up to the recovery point immediately prior to this interaction, i.e., its third recovery point. However, if process 3 fails, all the processes will have to be backed up right to their starting points!

The domino effect can occur when two particular circumstances exist in combination:

1. The recovery block structures of the various processes are uncoordinated and take no account of process interdependencies caused by their interactions.
2. The processes are symmetrical with respect to failure propagation; either member of any pair of interacting processes can cause the other to back up.

By removing either of these circumstances, one can avoid the danger of the domino effect. Our technique of structuring process interactions into "conversations," which we describe next, is a means of dealing with point (1) above; the concept of multilevel processes, described in Section 5, will be seen to be based on avoiding symmetry of failure propagation.

4.1 Process conversations

If we are to provide guaranteed recoverability of a set of processes which by interacting have become mutually dependent on each other's progress, we must arrange that the processes cooperate in the provision of recovery points as well as in the interchange of ordinary information. To extend the basic recovery block scheme to a set of interacting processes, we have to provide a means for coordinating the recovery block structures of the various processes, in effect to provide a recovery structure which is common to the set of processes. This structure we term a *conversation*.

Conversations, like recovery blocks, can be thought of as providing firewalls (in both time and space) which serve to limit the damage caused to a system by errors. Figure 6 represents this view of a recovery block as providing a firewall for a single process. The downward pointing arrow represents the overall progress of the process. The top edge of the recovery block represents the environment of the process on entry, which is preserved automatically and can be restored for the use of an alternate. The bottom edge represents the acceptable state of the process on exit from the recovery block, as checked by the acceptance test, and beyond which it is assumed that errors internal to the recovery block should not propagate. (Of course the strength of this firewall is only as good as the rigor of the acceptance test.) The sides show that the process is isolated from other activities, i.e., that the process is not subject to external influences which cannot be recreated automatically for an alternate, and that it does not generate any results which cannot be supressed should the acceptance test

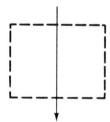

Figure 6   Recovery block in a sequential process.

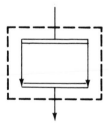

Figure 7   Parallel processes within a recovery block.

be failed. (These side firewalls are provided, by some perhaps quite conventional protection mechanism, to complement the top and bottom firewalls provided by the recursive cache mechanism and acceptance test.)

The manner in which the processing is performed within the recovery block is of no concern outside it, provided that the acceptance test is satisfied. For instance, as shown in Figure 7, the process may divide into several parallel processes within the recovery block. The recursive cache mechanisms that we have developed permit this and place no constraints on the manner in which this parallelism is expressed or on the means of communication between these parallel processes.

Any of the parallel processes could of course enter a further recovery block, as shown in Figure 8. However, by doing so it must lose the ability to communicate with other processes for the duration of its recovery block. To see this, consider the consequences of an interaction between the processes at points E and F. Should process Y now fail its acceptance test it would resume at point A with an alternate. But there is no way of causing process X to repeat the interaction at E without backing up both processes to the entry to their common recovery block at K. Thus communication, whether it involves explicit message-passing facilities, or merely reference to common variables, would destroy the value of the inner recovery block and hence must be prohibited.

A recovery block that spans two or more processes as is shown in Figure 9 is termed a conversation. Two or more processes which already possess the means of communicating with each other may agree to enter into a conversation. Within the conversation these processes may communicate freely between themselves but may not communicate with any other processes. At the end of the conversation *all the processes must satisfy their respective acceptance tests and none may proceed until all have done so.* Should any process fail, all the processes must automatically be backed up to the start of the conversation to attempt their alternates.

As is shown in Figure 9, it is possible that the processes enter a conversation at differing times. However all processes must leave the conversation together, since no process dare discard its recovery point until all processes have satisfied their respective acceptance tests. In entering a conversation a process does not gain the ability to communicate with any process with which it was previously unable to communicate; rather, entry to a conversation serves only to restrict communication, in the interests of error recovery.

As with recovery blocks, conversations can of course occur within other conversations so as to provide additional possibilities for error detection and recovery. However, conversations which intersect and are not strictly nested cannot be allowed. Thus structures such as that shown in Figure 10 must be prohibited, as can be demonstrated by an argument similar to that given in relation to Figure 8.

Figure 8 Interaction between processes at E and F must be prohibited.

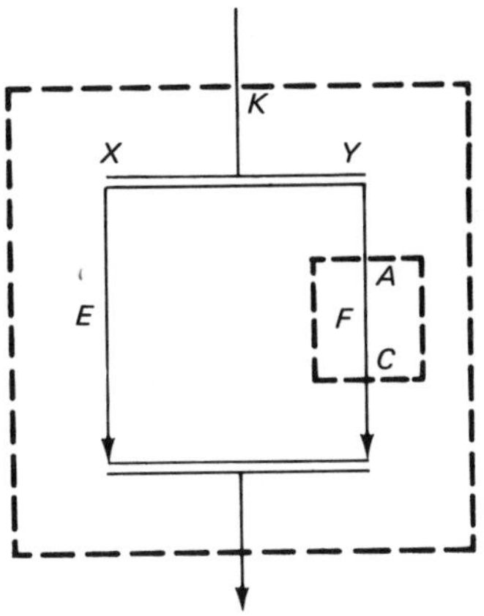

Figure 9 Parallel processes with conversations.

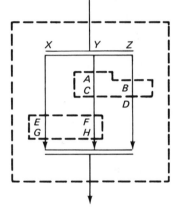

Figure 10 Invalid conversations that are not strictly nested.

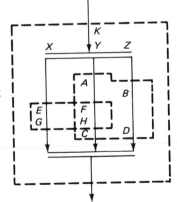

5 Multilevel systems

We turn now to a method of structuring systems which uses asymmetrical failure propagation in order to avoid the uncontrolled domino effect described in Section 4. In so doing we extend the scope of our discussions to cover more complex means of making recognizable progress than simple assignments. Moreover, we also face for the first time the possibility of reliability problems arising from facilities used to provide the means of constructing and executing processes and of using recovery blocks and conversations. The method of structuring which permits these extensions of our facilities for fault tolerance involves the use of what we (and others) term multilevel systems.

A multilevel system is characterized by the existence of a sequence of defined "abstract" or "virtual" machines which denote the internal interfaces between the various levels. A given virtual machine provides a set of apparently atomic facilities (operations, objects, resources, etc.). These can be used to construct the set of facilities that constitute a further (higher) virtual machine interface, possibly of a very different appearance. Each virtual machine is therefore an abstraction of the virtual machine below it. Since we are concerning ourselves with computer systems we in general expect each virtual machine to have the characteristics of a programmable computer. Thus it is capable of executing a program that specifies which operations are to be applied to which operands, and their sequencing.

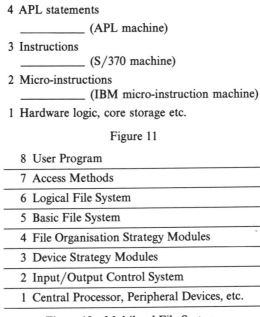

4 APL statements

_____ (APL machine)

3 Instructions

_____ (S/370 machine)

2 Micro-instructions

_____ (IBM micro-instruction machine)

1 Hardware logic, core storage etc.

Figure 11

8 User Program
7 Access Methods
6 Logical File System
5 Basic File System
4 File Organisation Strategy Modules
3 Device Strategy Modules
2 Input/Output Control System
1 Central Processor, Peripheral Devices, etc.

Figure 12   Multilevel File System.

Our use of the term "virtual machine" is quite general. In particular our concept of multilevel systems includes systems whose levels are entirely different from each other (as in Figure 11) as well as systems whose levels have much in common with each other (as in Figure 12)—for example, being constructed by applying a protection scheme on a single computer. However, in each case the operations that a given virtual machine provides can be regarded as atomic at the level above it and as implemented by the activity of the level immediately below the virtual machine interface. Thus from the viewpoint of level 8 of the system in Figure 12, the whole of the file accessing operation is performed by level 7. Indeed even the operation of addition, and the whole process of instruction fetching and decoding, can be regarded as being provided by level 7. This is the case no matter which actual level below level 7 is in fact responsible for the construction of these facilities out of more basic ones.

Some virtual machine interfaces allow the facilities they provide to be used without much, or even any, knowledge of the underlying structures used to construct these facilities. We will term virtual machine interfaces which have this characteristic *opaque* interfaces. Such virtual machine interfaces will be total (in the sense that a mathematical function which is defined for all possible arguments is total) and will have associated documentation which completely defines the interface. Being total and completely documented are necessary rather than sufficient conditions for a virtual machine interface to be usefully opaque, a characteristic which only well chosen ones possess in any great measure; but this is a subject which we will not pursue further here.

Opaque virtual machine interfaces facilitate the understanding of existing complex systems and the design of new ones. They do this by enabling the complexity of the system to be divided and conquered, so that no single person or group of persons has to master all the details of the design. They can therefore in themselves contribute to the overall reliability of a system by simplifying the tasks of its designers. However, if design errors are made, or operational failures of physical components occur, it will be found that existing methods of constructing opaque virtual machine interfaces are somewhat inadequate. The sought-after opacity of the interface will in many cases be lost, since error recovery (either manual or predesigned) will need an understanding of two or more levels of the system. Hence our interest in providing facilities for tolerating faults, including those due to design errors, which can be used by designers whose detailed understanding of the system is limited to that of a single level and the two virtual machine interfaces that bound it.

All this presupposes that the virtual machine interfaces have some physical realization in the operational system. Conceptual levels, though of value during system design and in providing documentation of the behavior of a reliable system, can play no part in failure situations; for example, the levels in the T.H.E. system [Dijkstra 68a*] have no relevance to the problem of coping with, say, an actual memory parity error. The

actual physical realization in existing multilevel systems can vary widely—from, for example, the provision of physically separate storage and
highways for microprograms and programs, to the use of a single control
bit to distinguish between supervisor and user modes of instruction execution. What we now describe are additional general characteristics and
facilities that we believe any such physical realization of a virtual machine
interface should possess in order to support our techniques for system fault
tolerance.

5.1 Errors above a virtual machine interface

Everything that appears to happen in a given level is in fact the result of
activity for which the level below is (directly or indirectly) responsible.
This applies not only to the ordinary operations performed at a level but
also to any recovery actions which might be required. Consider, for
example, a level i which uses our recovery block scheme to provide itself
with some measure of fault tolerance and which makes recognizable
progress by means of simple assignment statements. Then it is level $i-1$
which is responsible not only for the actual assignments, but also for any
saving of prior values of variables and reinstatement of them when
required.

Similarly, if the virtual machine which supports level i includes any
more exotic operations which change the system state as seen by level i,
e.g., magnetic tape rewind, then level $i-1$ will have the responsibility of
undoing their effects, e.g., repositioning the tape (whether level $i-1$
undertakes this responsibility itself or instead delegates it to level $i-2$ is
irrelevant).

Provided that level $i-1$ fulfills its responsibilities level i can thus
assume that error detection will automatically be followed by a return to
the most recent recovery point. This will occur whether the detection of a
level i error occurs at level i itself (e.g., by means of an acceptance test) or
below level i because of incorrect use by level i of one of the operations
provided to it by level $i-1$ (e.g., division by zero).

It should be noted that both progress and fallback, as recognizable in
the level above a virtual machine interface, are provided by progress on the
level below, i.e., the level $i-1$ keeps going forward, or at least tries to, even
if it is doing so in order to enable level i to (appear to) go backward.

For example, level i might read cards from an "abstract card reader"
while level $i-1$ actually implements this abstract card reader by means of
spooling. When level i encounters an error and tries to go backward, it
must appear to "unread" the cards read during the current recovery block.
But level $i-1$ implements this "unreading" by merely resetting a pointer in
its spool buffer—a positive or forward action on its part.

All this assumes level $i-1$ is trouble-free; what we must now discuss are
the complications caused by level $i-1$ being unable, for various reasons, to

maintain its own progress, and in particular that progress on which level i is relying.

5.2 Errors below a virtual machine interface

Needless to say, the programs which provide a virtual machine interface can, if appropriate, themselves incorporate recovery blocks for the purpose of local error detection and recovery. Thus when level $i-1$ makes a mistake, which is detected, while performing some operation for level i, if an alternate block manages to succeed where the primary alternate had failed, the operation can nevertheless be completed. In such circumstances the program at level i need never know that any error occurred. (For example, a user process may be unaware that the operating system had to make several attempts before it succeeded in reading a magnetic tape on behalf of the user process.) But if all the alternates of the outermost recovery block of the level $i-1$ program performing an operation for level i fail, so that the recovery capability at level $i-1$ is exhausted, then the operation must be rejected and recovery action undertaken at level i.

This case of an error detected at level $i-1$ forcing level i back to a recovery point in order to undertake some alternative action is very similar to the one mentioned earlier—namely, that of an error detected at level $i-1$ but stemming from the incorrect use of an operation by level i. The error log which is produced for later off-line analysis will indicate the difference between the two cases, but this information (let alone further information which might be needed for diagnostic purposes) will not be available to level i.

The situation is much more serious if level $i-1$ errs and exhausts any recovery capability it might have while performing an inverse operation on behalf of level i, i.e., if it fails to complete the act of undoing the effects of one or more operations that level i has used to modify its state. This possibility might seem rather small when the inverse operation is merely that of resetting the prior value of a scalar variable. However, when an inverse operation is quite complex (e.g., one that involves undoing the changes a process has caused to be made to complicated data structures in a large filing system), one might have to cope with residual design inadequacies as well as the ever-present possibility of hardware failure.

When an inverse operation cannot be completed, the level i cannot be backed up, so it has to be abandoned. This is perhaps the most subtle cause for level $i-1$ to abandon further attempts to execute a level i process; more familiar ones include the sudden inability of level $i-1$ to continue fetching and decoding level i instructions, locating level i operands, and so on, either because of level $i-1$'s own inadequacy, or that of the level $i-2$ machine on which it depends. (For example, level 3 of Figure 11, the APL interpreter, might find that the file in which it keeps the APL program belonging to a particular user was unreadable, a fault which perhaps was first detected at level 2 by the microprogram.)

There is one other important class of errors detected below a virtual machine interface which can be dealt with without necessarily abandoning level i, the level above the interface. After level i has passed an acceptance test, but before all the information constituting its recovery point has been discarded, there is the chance for level $i-1$ to perform any checking that is needed on the overall acceptability, in level $i-1$ terms, of the sequence of operations that has been carried out for level i.

For example, level i may have been performing operations which were, as far as it was concerned, disk storage operations. Level $i-1$ could in fact have buffered the information so stored. Before the present level of fallback capability of level i is discarded, level $i-1$ may wish to ensure that the information has been written to disk and checked. If level $i-1$ finds that it cannot ensure this, but instead encounters some problem from which it itself is unable to recover, then it can in essence cause level i to fail, and to fall back and attempt an alternate. This will be in the hope that whatever problem it was that level $i-1$ got into (on behalf of level i) this time, next time the sequence of operations that level i requests will manage to get dealt with to the satisfaction of level $i-1$ as well as of level i.

In fact, an interesting example of this case of level $i-1$ inducing a failure in level i occurs in the mechanization of conversations. Consider a level i process which is involved in a conversation with some other level i process and which, after completing its primary alternate, satisfies its acceptance test. At this moment level $i-1$ must determine whether the other process has also completed its primary alternate and passed its acceptance test. If necessary the process must be suspended until the other process has been completed, as discussed in Section 4. If the other process should fail, then the first process must also be forced to back up just as if it had failed its own acceptance test, even though it had in fact passed it.

5.3 Fault-tolerant virtual machine interfaces

We have so far discussed separately the problems of failures above and below a virtual machine interface. In fact, except for the highest level and the one that we choose to regard as the lowest level, every level is of course simultaneously below one virtual machine interface and above another such interface. Therefore each interface has the responsibility for organizing the interaction between two potentially unreliable levels in a multilevel system. The aim is to embody *within the interface* all the rules about interaction across levels that we have been describing, and so simplify the tasks of designing the levels on either side of the interface.

If this can be done, then it will be possible to design levels which are separated by opaque virtual machine interfaces independently of each other, even in the case where the possibility of failures is admitted. By enabling the design of error-recovery facilities to be considered separately

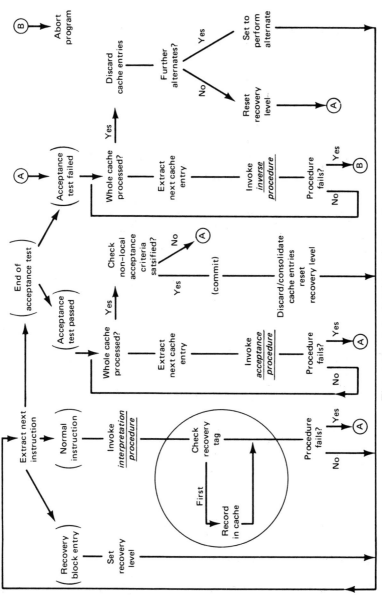

Figure 13   A fault-tolerant interpreter.

for different levels of the system, in the knowledge that the fault-tolerant interface will arrange their proper interaction, their design should be greatly simplified—a very important consideration if error-recovery facilities in complex systems are to be really relied upon.

Various different kinds of virtual machine interface are provided in current multilevel systems. These range from an interface which involves complete interpretation (e.g., the APL machine interface in Figure 11 and the lowest interface in Figure 12), to one where many of the basic facilities provided above the interface are in fact the same as those made available to the level immediately below the interface by some yet lower virtual machine interface (e.g., the other interfaces in Figure 12). These latter kinds of interfaces, because of their performance characteristics, can be expected to predominate in systems which have many levels; in theory the Multilevel File System (Figure 12) could be built using a hierarchy of complete interpreters, but this is of course wildly impractical.

It is not appropriate within the confines of this already lengthy chapter, which has concentrated on presenting the rationale behind our overall approach to structuring fault-tolerant systems, to give a fully detailed description of even a single kind, let alone the various different kinds, of fault-tolerant virtual machine interfaces. However, we have attempted, with Figure 13, to show the main features of a fault-tolerant interface of the complete interpreter kind. For purposes of comparison, Figure 14 shows the equivalent interface in a conventional complete interpreter.

The basic difference between a fault-tolerant interpreter and a conventional interpreter is that the fault-tolerant interpreter provides, in general, for each different type of instruction to be interpreted—not just a single

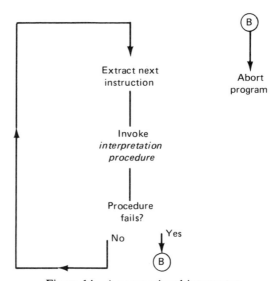

Figure 14   A conventional interpreter.

procedure but rather a set of three related procedures. These are as follows:

1. An *interpretation procedure*. This is basically the same as the single procedure provided in a conventional interpreter and provides the normal interpretation of the particular type of instruction. But within the procedure, the interface ensures that before any changes are made to the state of the interpreted process or the values of any of its variables, a test is made to determine whether any information should first be saved in order that fallback will be possible.
2. An *inverse procedure*. This will be called when a process is being backed up; it will make use of information saved during any uses of the interpretation procedure.
3. An *acceptance procedure*. This will be called when an alternate block has passed its acceptance test; it allows for any necessary tidying up and checking related to the previous use of the normal interpretation procedure.

When the instruction is one that does not change the system state, inverse and acceptance procedures are not needed. If the instruction is, for example, merely a simple assignment to a scalar, the interpretation procedure saves the value and the address of the scalar before making the first assignment to the scalar within a new recovery block. The inverse procedure uses this information to reset the scalar, and there is a trivial acceptance procedure. A nontrivial acceptance procedure would be needed if, for example, the interpreter had to close a file and perhaps do some checking on the filed information in order to complete the work stemming from the use of the interpretation procedure.

A generalization of the recursive cache, as described earlier in this chapter, is used to control the invocation of inverse and acceptance procedures. The cache records the descriptors for the inverse and acceptance procedures corresponding to interpretation procedures that have been executed and that have caused system state information to be saved. Indeed, each cache region can be thought of as containing a linear "program" rather than just a set of saved prior values. The "program" held in the current cache region indicates the sequence of inverse procedure calls that are to be "executed" in order to back up the process to its most recent recovery point. (If the process passes its acceptance test, the procedure calls in the "program" act as calls on acceptance procedures.) The program of inverse/acceptance calls is initially null but grows as the process performs actions which add to the task of backing it up. As with the basic recursive cache mechanism, the cache region will be discarded in its entirety after it has been used for backing up a process. Similarly, if the recovery block or conversation is completed successfully, some entries will be discarded; but those that relate to variables which are nonlocal to the enclosing environment will be consolidated with the existing "program" in the underlying region of the cache.

This, then, is a very brief account, ignoring various simple but important "mere optimizations," of the main characteristics of a failure-tolerant virtual machine interface of the complete-interpreter kind. Being so closely related to the basic recursive cache mechanism, it will perhaps be most readily appreciated by people who are already familiar with the published description [Horning 74b*] of the detailed functioning of one recursive cache mechanism.

6 Conclusions

The techniques for structuring fault-tolerant systems which we have described have been designed especially for faults arising from design errors, such as are at present all too common in complex software systems. However, we believe they are also of potential applicability to hardware, and in particular allow the various operational faults that hardware can suffer from to be treated as simple special cases. In fact the techniques we have sketched for fault tolerance in multilevel systems would appear to provide an appropriate means of integrating provisions for hardware reconfiguration into the overall structure of the system. Indeed, as a general approach to the structuring of a complex activity where the possibility of errors is to be considered, as others have previously remarked [Davies 73], there seems to be no *a priori* reason why the structuring should not extend past the confines of the computer system and apply to the environment and perhaps even the people surrounding the computer system.

The effectiveness of this approach to fault tolerant system design will depend critically on the acceptance tests and additional alternates that are provided. An experimental prototype system is currently being developed which should enable us to obtain experience in the use of this approach, to evaluate its merits, and to explore possible performance/reliability trade-offs. One lesson is, however, in our opinion already clear. If it is considered important that a complex system be provided with extensive error-recovery facilities whose dependability can be the subject of plausible *a priori* arguments, then the system structure will have to conform to comparatively restrictive rules. Putting this another way, it will not be sufficient for designers to argue for the use of very sophisticated control structures and intercommunication facilities on the grounds of performance characteristics and personal freedom of design, unless they can clearly demonstrate that these do not unduly compromise the recoverability of the system.

Acknowledgments. The work reported in this chapter is the result of the efforts of a number of people, all associated with the Science Research Council-sponsored project on system reliability at the University of Newcastle upon Tyne. Those most directly responsible for the techniques of system structuring which form the central theme of this paper are Jim Horning, Ron Kerr, Hugh Lauer, Mike Melliar-Smith and the author. (Professor Horning, of the University of Toronto, held a Senior Visiting Fellowship with the project during the summer of 1973.)

The author has great pleasure in acknowledging his indebtedness to all his colleagues on the project, several of whom—in particular Mike Melliar-Smith—provided many useful acceptance tests and alternates for the author's activity in preparing this paper.

26
Structured Analysis (SA): A Language for Communicating Ideas

Douglas T. Ross
SofTech, Inc.

Abstract   *Structured analysis (SA) combines blueprint-like graphic language with the nouns and verbs of any other language to provide a hierarchic, top-down, gradual exposition of detail in the form of an SA model. The things and happenings of a subject are expressed in a data decomposition and an activity decomposition, both of which employ the same graphic building block, the SA box, to represent a part of a whole. SA arrows, representing input, output, control, and mechanism, express the relation of each part to the whole. The paper describes the rationalization behind some 40 features of the SA language, and shows how they enable rigorous communication which results from disciplined, recursive application of the SA maxim: "Everything worth saying about anything worth saying something about must be expressed in six or fewer pieces."*

I Blueprint language

Neither Watt's steam engine nor Whitney's standardized parts really started the Industrial Revolution, although each has been awarded that claim, in the past. The real start was the awakening of scientific and technological thoughts during the Renaissance, with the idea that the lawful behavior of nature can be understood, analyzed, and manipulated to accomplish useful ends. That idea itself, alone, was not enough, however, for not until the creation and evolution of blueprints was it possible to express exactly how power and parts were to be combined for each specific task at hand.

Mechanical drawings and blueprints are not mere pictures, but a complete and rich language. In blueprint language, scientific, mathematical, and geometric formulations, notations, mensurations, and naming do not merely describe an object or process, they actually model it. Because of broad differences in subject, purpose, roles, and the needs of the people who use them, many forms of blueprint have evolved, but all rigorously present well structured information in understandable form.

Failure to develop such a communication capability for data processing is due not merely to the diversity and complexity of the problems we tackle, but to the newness of our field. It has naturally taken time for us to escape from naive "programming by priesthood" to the more mature approaches, such as structured programming, language and database design, and software production methods. Still missing from this expanding repertoire of evidence of maturity, however, is the common thread that will allow all of the pieces to be tied together into a predictable and dependable approach.

II Structured analysis (SA) language

It is the thesis of this paper that the language of structured analysis (SA), a new disciplined way of putting together old ideas, provides the evolutionary natural language appropriate to the needs of the computer field. SA is deceptively simple in its mechanics, which are few in number and have high mnemonic value, making the language easy and natural to use. Anybody can learn to read SA language with very little practice and will be able to understand the actual information content being conveyed by the graphical notation and the words of the language with ease and precision. But being a language, with rigorously defined semantics, SA is a tough taskmaster. Not only do well conceived and well phrased thoughts come across concisely and with precision, but poorly conceived and poorly expressed thoughts also are recognized as such. This simply *has* to be a fact for any language whose primary accomplishment is valid communication of understanding. If both the bad and the good were *not* equally recognizable, the understanding itself would be incomplete.

SA does the same for any problem chosen for analysis, for every natural language and every formal language are, by definition, included in SA. *The only function of SA is to bind up, structure, and communicate units of thought expressed in any other chosen language.* Synthesis is composition, analysis is decomposition. *SA is structured decomposition, to enable structured synthesis to achieve a given end.* The actual building-block elements of analysis or synthesis may be of any sort whatsoever. Pictures, words, expressions of any sort may be incorporated into and made a part of the structure.

The facts about Structured Analysis are as follows.

(1) It incorporates any other language; its scope is universal and unrestricted.
(2) It is concerned only with the orderly and well-structured decomposition of the subject matter.
(3) The decomposed units are sized to suit the modes of thinking and understanding of the intended audience.
(4) Those units of understanding are expressed in a way that rigorously and precisely represents their interrelation.
(5) This structured decomposition may be carried out to any required degree of depth, breadth, and scope while still maintaining all the above properties.

(6) Therefore, SA greatly increases both the quantity and quality of understanding that can be effectively and precisely communicated well beyond the limitations inherently imposed by the imbedded natural or formal language used to address the chosen subject matter.

The universality and precision of SA makes it particularly effective for requirements definition for arbitrary systems problems, a subject treated in some detail in a companion paper (see [Ross 77b*]). Requirements definition encompasses all aspects of system development prior to actual system design, and hence is concerned with the discovery of real user needs and communicating those requirements to those who must produce an effective system solution. Structured Analysis and Design Technique (SADT[1]) is the name of SofTech's proprietary methodology based on SA. The method has been applied to a wide range of planning, analysis, and design problems involving men, machines, software, hardware, database, communications procedures, and finances over the last few years, and several are cited in that paper. It is recommended that [Ross 77b*] be read prior to this paper to provide motivation and insight into the features of SA language described here.

SA is not limited to requirements definition nor even problems that are easily recognized as system problems. The end product of an SA analysis is a working model of a well-structured understanding, and that can be beneficial even on a uniquely personal level—just to "think things through." Social, artistic, scientific, legal, societal, political, and even philosophic subjects, all are subject to analysis, and the resulting models can effectively communicate the ideas to others. The same methods, approach, and discipline can be used to model the problem environment, requirements, and proposed solution, as well as the project organization, operation, budget, schedule, and action plan. Man thinks with language. Man communicates with language. SA structures language for communicating ideas more effectively. *The human mind can accommodate any amount of complexity as long as it is presented in easy-to-grasp chunks that are structured together to make the whole.*

III Outline of the demonstration

Five years ago I said in an editorial regarding software [Ross 71*]: "Tell me *why* it works, not *that* it works." That is the approach taken in this paper. This paper does not present a formal grammar for the SA language —that will come later, elsewhere. This paper also is not a user manual for either authors or readers of the language—a simple "how to" exposition. Instead, we concentrate here on the motivation *behind* the features of SA in an attempt to convey directly an appreciation for its features and power

[1] SADT is a trademark of SofTech, Inc.

even beyond that acquired through use by most SA practitioners. SA has been heavily developed, applied, taught, and used for almost three years already, but the design rationale behind it is first set down here.

SA (both the language and the discipline of thought) derives from the way our minds work, and from the way we understand real-world situations and problems. Therefore, we start out with a summary of principles of exposition—good storytelling. This turns out to yield the familiar top-down decomposition, a key component of SA. But more than that results, for consideration of how we view our space-time world shows that we always understand anything and everything in terms of *both* things *and* happenings. This is why all of our languages have *both* nouns *and* verbs —and this, in turn, yields the means by which SA language is universal, and can absorb any other language as a component part.

SA supplies rigorous structural connections to any language whose nouns and verbs it absorbs in order to talk about things and happenings, and we will spend some time covering the basics carefully, so that the fundamentals are solid. We do this by presenting, in tabular form, some 40 basic features, and then analyzing them bit by bit, using SA diagrams as figures to guide and illustrate the discussion.

Once the basics have thus been introduced, certain important topics that would have been obscure earlier are covered in some depth because their combinations are at the heart of SA's effectiveness. These topics concern constraints, boundaries, necessity, and dominance between modular portions of subject matter being analyzed. It turns out that constraints based on purpose and viewpoint actually *make* the structure. The depth of treatment gives insight into how we understand things.

The actual output of SA is a hierarchically organized structure of separate diagrams, each of which exposes only a limited part of the subject to view, so that even very complex subjects can be understood. The structured collection of diagrams is called an *SA model*. The demonstration here concludes with several special notations to clarify presentation and facilitate the orderly organization of the material. Since actual SA diagrams (some good, some illustrating poor style) are used as figure illustrations, the reader is exposed here to the style of SA even though the SA model represented by the collection of figures is not complete enough to be understandable by itself. Later papers will treat more advanced topics and present complete examples of SA use and practice in a wide variety of applications.

IV Principles of good storytelling

There are certain basic, known principles about how people's minds go about the business of understanding, and communicating understanding by means of language, which have been known and used for many centuries. No matter how these principles are addressed, they always end up with hierarchic decomposition as being the heart of good storytelling. Perhaps the most relevant formulation is the familiar: "Tell'em whatcha gonna tell'em. Tell'em. Tell'em whatcha told'em." This is a pattern of communication almost as universal and well-entrenched as Newton's laws of motion. It is the pattern found in all effective forms of communication and in all analyses of why such communication is effective. Artistic and scientific fields, in addition to journalism, all follow the same sequence, for that is the way our minds work.

Only something so obvious as not to be worth saying can be conveyed in a single stage of the communication process, however. In any worthwhile subject matter, Stage Two ("Tell'em") requires the parallel introduction of several more instances of the same pattern starting again with Stage One. Usually a story establishes several such levels of telling, and weaves back and forth between them as the need arises, to convey understanding, staying clear of excesses in either detail (boredom) or abstraction (confusion).

V The SA maxim

This weaving together of parts with whole is the heart of SA. The natural law of good communications takes the following, quite different, form in SA:

> "Everything worth saying about anything worth saying something about must be expressed in six or fewer pieces."

Let us analyze this maxim and see how and why it, too, yields hierarchically structured storytelling.

First of all, there must be something (anything) that is "worth saying something about." We must have some subject matter that has some value to us. We must have an interest in some aspect of it. This is called establishing the *viewpoint* for the model, in SA terminology. Then we must have in mind some audience we want to communicate with. That audience will determine what is (and is not) "worth saying" about the subject from that viewpoint. This is called establishing the *purpose* for the model, in SA terminology. As we will see, every subject has many aspects of interest to many audiences, so that there can be many viewpoints and purposes. But each SA model must have only one of each, to bound and structure its subject matter. We also will see that each model also has an established *vantage point* within the purpose-structured context of some other model's viewpoint, and this is how multiple models are interrelated so that they collectively cover the whole subject matter. But a single SA model considers only worthy thoughts about a single worthy subject.

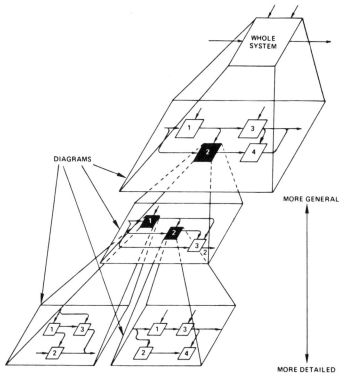

Figure 1   Structured decomposition.

The clincher, however, it that *every* worthy thought about that worthy subject must be included. The first word of the maxim is *everything*, and that means exactly that—absolutely nothing that fits the purpose and viewpoint can be left out. The reason is simple. By definition everything is the subject itself, for otherwise it would not *be* that subject—it would be a *lesser* subject. Then, if the subject is to be broken into six or fewer pieces every single thing must go into exactly one of those (nonoverlapping) pieces. Only in this way can we ensure that the subject stays the same, and does not degenerate into some lesser subject as we decompose it. Also, if overlapping pieces were allowed, conflicts and confusions might arise.

A "piece" can be anything we choose it to be—the maxim merely requires that the single piece of thought about the subject be broken into several (not too few, and not too many[2]) pieces. Now, certainly if the original single piece of thought about the subject is worthy, it is very unlikely that the mere breaking of it into six-or-fewer pieces exhausts that worth. The maxim still applies so that every one of them must similarly be

[2] Many people have urged me to relate the magic number "six" to various psychological studies about the characteristics of the human mind. I won't. It's neither scientific nor "magic." It is simply the *right* number. (Readers who doubt my judgement are invited to read for themselves the primary source [Miller 56].) The only proper reference would be to the little bear in the Goldilocks story. His portions always were "just right," too!

expressed in six-or-fewer *more* pieces—again and again—until the number of pieces has grown to suit the total worthiness. At a fine enough level of decomposition, it is not worth continuing. No further decomposition is required for completely clear understanding. Thus we see that the SA maxim must be interpreted *recursively*, and yields top-down hierarchic decomposition. The SA language allows this hierarchic structure to be expressed (see Fig. 1).

VI Expression

In the maxim, the word "express" covers both the rigorous grammar of SA language itself, as well as the grammar (however well or ill formed) of the natural language chosen to address the subject matter. By definition, SA language includes all other languages, and regardless of what language is embedded, the decomposition discipline (expressed by the SA language component of the combined language) ensures that at each stage, the natural language (whatever it may be) is used to address and express only every worthy thought about a more and more restricted piece of the worthy subject matter. Because of this orderly zeroing-in, SA certainly cannot decrease the effectiveness of that chosen language. In effect, the SA maxim is valid by definition, for whenever the subject matter has already been broken down to such a fine level that the SA decomposition would add nothing to what already would be done (as, for example, in jokes or some poetry) the chosen language stands by itself, not decreased in effectiveness.

Most of the time the conscious practice of Structured Analysis and its thought discipline improves people's ability to think clearly and find solutions. In the cases where this does not happen, however, Structured Analysis still "works," in the sense that the bad portions stand out more clearly and are understood to be bad and needing further attention. For the next step in our demonstration we consider thoughts, and the expression of thoughts in language.

VII Things and happenings

We live in a space-time world. Numerous philosophical and scientific studies, as well as the innate experience of every person, shows that we never have any understanding of any subject matter except in terms of our own mental constructs of "things" and "happenings" of that subject matter. It seems to be impossible for us to think about anything without having that subject automatically be bounded in our minds by a population of parts or pieces (concrete or abstract—but in any case "nominal" things, i.e., literally things to which we give names or nouns) which provide the basis for our even conceiving of the subject matter as a separate subject. Immediately, however, once we are aware of the things, we are aware of the happenings—the relationships, changes, and transformations which take place between and among those things and make the subject matter meaningful or interesting (the "verbial" things, to which we give action words or verbs).

The universality of things and happenings provides the next basic step of decomposition (after the still more fundamental decomposition of recognizing and isolating the purpose and viewpoint which established the "worth" of possible things to say about the "worth" of the subject matter). Every one of our languages, whether natural or artificial, formal or informal, has those two complementary aspects—nouns and verbs, operators and operands, etc.—to permit the expression of thoughts about the subject matter. Thus the means is provided to incorporate any other language into SA. The incorporation of other languages into SA is not forced, nor awkward.

SA language provides the same graphic notation for both the things and the happenings aspects of any subject. Every SA model has two dual aspects—a *thing* aspect, called the *data decomposition*, and a *happening* aspect, called the *activity decomposition*. The model is incomplete without both decompositions.

VIII Bounded subject matter

So we have now established the starting premises. The SA maxim forces gradual, top-down decomposition, leaving nothing out at any stage, and matching good storytelling exposition. The things and happenings (*data* and *activities*, in SA technical terms) match the nominal and verbial construction of any chosen language for directly addressing the subject, so we will never be "at a loss for words." Now we are ready to address the specifics—how SA language (mostly graphical, using boxes and arrows) actually allows well structured expression of well structured thought. We do this in stages: 1) we dump the entire body of the subject matter all at once into a table of some 40 separate items of notation and conventions—just to bound the subject itself; 2) we then start to pick our way through these topics, starting with those that define the basics of boxes and arrows; and 3) then we will use those basic expository capabilities to complete the consideration of the list.

In a prior, companion paper [Ross 75*], which had its roots in the same background that led to the development of SA, we described and illustrated a universal, standard pattern or process which appears to permeate all of software engineering and problem-solving in general. Since that pattern is so close to the natural phenomena of understanding which we are discussing here with respect to SA itself, we will use it to motivate, clarify, and structure the presentation. The idea of the pattern is captured in five words: (1) purpose; (2) concept; (3) mechanism; (4) notation; and (5) usage. Any systematic approach to a problem requires a concise purpose or objective that specifies which aspect of the problem is of concern. Within that purpose we formulate a valid conceptual structure (both things and happenings) in terms of which the problem can be analyzed and approached. We then seek out (or work out) the designs (mechanisms—concrete or abstract, but always including both data and activity aspects) which are capable of implementing the relevant concepts and of working together to achieve the stated purpose. (This combines three of the five words together.) Now, purpose, concepts, and mechanism, being a systematic approach to a *class* of problems, require a notation for expressing the capabilities of the mechanism and invoking its use for a particular problem in the class. Finally, usage rules are spelled out, explicitly or by example, to guide the use of the notation to invoke the implementation to realize the concept to achieve the specified purpose for the problem. The cited paper [Ross 75*] gives numerous carefully drawn examples showing how the pattern arises over and over again throughout systematic problem solving, at both abstract and concrete levels, and with numerous hierarchic and cross-linked interconnections.

IX The features of SA language

Fig. 2 is a tabulation of some 40 features or aspects of SA which constitute the basic core of the language for communication. For each feature, the purpose, concept, mechanism, and notation are shown. Usages (for the purposes of this paper) are covered only informally by the examples which follow. The reader should scan down the "purpose" column of Fig. 2 at this time, because the collection of entries there set the objectives for the bounded subject matter which we are about to consider. Note also the heavy use of pictures in the "notation" column. These are components of graphic language. But notice that most entries mix *both* English *and* graphic language into a "phrase" of SA notation. Clearly, any other spoken language such as French, German, or Sanskrit could be translated and substituted for the English terms, for they merely aid the understanding of the syntax and semantics of SA language itself.

In Fig. 2, the *name* and *label* portions of the "notation" column for rows 1 and 2, and the corresponding *noun* and *verb* indications in rows 6 and 7 are precisely the places where SA language absorbs other natural or formal languages in the sense of the preceding discussion. As the preceding sections have tried to make clear, *any* language, whether informal and natural or formal and artificial, has things and happenings aspects in the nominal and verbial components of its vocabulary. These are to be related to the *names of boxes* and *labels on arrows* in order to absorb those "foreign" languages into SA language.

Notice that is is not merely the nouns and verbs which are absorbed. Whatever richness the "foreign" language may possess, the full richness of the nominal and verbial expressions, including modifiers, is available in the naming and labeling portions of SA language. As we shall see, however, normally these capabilities for richness are purposely suppressed, for simplicity and immediacy of understanding normally require brevity and conciseness.

Fig. 2 has introduced our subject and has served to point out the precise way in which SA absorbs other languages, but this mode of discourse would make a long and rambling story. I therefore proceed to use SA itself to communicate the intended understanding of Fig. 2. This will not, however, be a perfect, or even a good example of SA communication in action, for the intent of this paper is to guide the reader to an understanding of SA, not to teach how to fully exploit SA diagrams and modeling. The SA diagrams presented here only as figures are incomplete and exhibit both good *and* bad examples of SA expressiveness, as well as showing all the language constructs. Our subject is too complex treat in a small model, but the figures at least present the reader with some measure of the flexibility of the language.

The reader is forewarned that there is more information in the diagrams than is actually referenced here in text which uses them as "figures." After the paper has been read, the total model can be studied for review and for additional understanding. Everything said here about the SA language and notations applies to each diagram, and most features are illustrated more than once, frequently before they are described in the text. Therefore, on first reading, please ignore any features and notations not explicitly referenced. Non-SA "first-reading" aids are isolated by a bold outline, in the diagrams.

In practical use of SofTech's SADT, a "reader/author cycle" is rigorously adhered to in which (similar to the code-reading phase of egoless structured programming) authors, experts, and management-level personnel read and critique the efforts of each individual SADT author to achieve a fully-acceptable quality of result. (It is in fact this rigorous adherence to quality control which enables production SA models to be relied upon. So far as possible *everything* worthy has been done to make sure that *everything* worthy has been expressed to the level required by the intended readership.)

	PURPOSE	CONCEPT		MECHANISM	NOTATION		NODE
1	BOUND CONTEXT	INSIDE/OUTSIDE		SA BOX	NAME		A11
2	RELATE/CONNECT	FROM/TO		SA ARROW	LABEL		A12
3	SHOW TRANSFORMATION	INPUT-OUTPUT		SA INTERFACE	INPUT --- OUTPUT		A13
4	SHOW CIRCUMSTANCE	CONTROL		SA INTERFACE	CONTROL		A14
5	SHOW MEANS	SUPPORT		SA MECHANISM	MECHANISM		A15
6	NAME APTLY	ACTIVITY HAPPENINGS	DATA THINGS	SA NAMES	ACTIVITY VERB	DATA NOUN	A211
7	LABEL APTLY	THINGS	HAPPENINGS	SA LABELS	NOUN	VERB	A212
8	SHOW NECESSITY	I-O	C-O	PATH			A213
9	SHOW DOMINANCE	C	I	CONSTRAINT			A214
10	SHOW RELEVANCE	ICO	ICO	ALL INTERFACES			A215
11	OMIT OBVIOUS	C-O	I-O	OMITTED ARROW			A216
12	BE EXPLICIT WITHOUT CLUTTER	PIPELINES, CONDUITS, WIRES		BRANCH	A / A / A		A221
13				JOIN	A / A / A		A221
14	BE CONCISE AND CLEAR	CABLES, MULTI-WIRES		BUNDLE	A / B / C(=A∪B)		A222
15				SPREAD	C=(A∪B) / A / B		A222
16	SHOW EXCLUSIVES	EXPLICIT ALTERNATIVES		OR BRANCH	A OR B / A / B		A223
17				OR JOIN	A / B / A OR B		A223
18	SHOW INTERFACES TO PARENT DIAGRAM	PARENT CHILD ARROWS PENETRATE		SA BOUNDARY ARROWS (ON CHILD)	NO BOX SHOWN		A231
19	SHOW EXPLICIT PARENT CONNECTION	NUMBER CONVENTION FOR PARENT, WRITE ICOM CODE ON CHILD BOUNDARY ARROWS		I C O	c1 c2 o2 (ON CHILD)		A232
20	SHOW UNIQUE DECOMPOSITION	DETAIL REFERENCE EXPRESSION (DRE)		C-NUMBER OR PAGE NUMBER OF DETAIL DIAGRAM	BOX ⊠—DRE		A233
21	SHOW SHARED OR VARIABLE DECOMPOSITION	DRE WITH (MODEL NAME)		SA CALL ON SUPPORT	BOX STUB—⊠—DRE		A234

Figure 2   SA language features.

	PURPOSE	CONCEPT	MECHANISM	NOTATION	NODE
22	SHOW COOPERATION	INTERCHANGE OF SHARED RESPONSIBILITY	SA 2-WAY ARROWS		A311
23	SUPPRESS INTERCHANGE DETAILS	ALLOW 2-WAY WITHIN 1-WAY PIPELINES	2-WAY TO 1-WAY BUTTING ARROWS		A312
24	SUPPRESS "PASS-THROUGH" CLUTTER	ALLOW ARROWS TO GO OUTSIDE DIAGRAMS	SA "TUNNELING" (WITH REFERENCES)	PARENT OFFSPRING	A313
25	SUPPRESS NEEDED-ARROW CLUTTER	ALLOW TAGGED JUMPS WITHIN DIAGRAM	TO ALL or FROM ALL	TO ALL	A314
26	SHOW NEEDED ANNOTATION	ALLOW WORDS IN DIAGRAM	SA NOTE	NOTE:	A32
27	OVERCOME CRAMPED SPACE	ALLOW REMOTE LOCATION OF WORDS IN DIAGRAM	SA FOOTNOTE	$(n=integer)$ n words n	A32
28	SHOW COMMENTS ABOUT DIAGRAM	ALLOW WORDS ON (NOT IN) DIAGRAM	SA META-NOTE	n $(n=integer)$	A32
29	ENSURE PROPER ASSOCIATION OF WORDS	TIE WORDS TO INTENDED SUBJECT	SA "SQUIGGLE"	label n (TOUCH REFERENT)	A32
30	UNIQUE SHEET REFERENCE	CHRONOLOGICAL CREATION	SA C-NUMBER	AUTHOR INITS INTEGER	A41
31	UNIQUE BOX REFERENCE	PATH DOWN TREE FROM BOX NUMBERS	SA NODE NUMBER (BOX NUMBERS)	A, D, OR M $\subseteq$ PARENT # $\subseteq$ BOX #	A42
32	SAME FOR MULTI-MODELS	PRECEDE BY MODEL NAME	SA MODEL NAME	MODEL NAME/NODE#	A42
33	UNIQUE INTERFACE REFERENCE	ICOM WITH BOX NUMBER	SA BOX ICOM	BOX# $\subseteq$ ICOM CODE	A43
34	UNIQUE ARROW REFERENCE	FROM - TO	PAIR OF BOX ICOMs	BOX ICOM$_1$ - BOX ICOM$_2$	A44
35	SHOW CONTEXT REFERENCE	SPECIFY A REFERENCE POINT	SA REF.EXP. "DOT"	A122.4I1 "WHICH SEE"	A45
36	ASSIST CORRECT INTERPRETATION	SHOW DOMINANCE GEOMETRICALLY (ASSIST PARSE)	STAIRCASE LAYOUT	DOMINANCE	A5
37	ASSIST UNDERSTANDING	PROSE SUMMARY OF MESSAGE	SA TEXT	NODE# $\subseteq$ T $\subseteq$ INTEGER	A5
38	HIGHLIGHT FEATURES	SPECIAL EFFECTS FOR EXPOSITION ONLY	SA FEOs	NODE# $\subseteq$ F $\subseteq$ INTEGER	A5
39	DEFINE TERMS	GLOSSARY WITH WORDS & PICTURES	SA GLOSSARY	MODEL NAME $\subseteq$ G $\subseteq$ INTEGER	A5
40	ORGANIZE PAGES	PROVIDE TABLE OF CONTENTS	SA NODE INDEX	NODE# ORDER	A5

X Purpose and viewpoint

Fig. 3 is an SA diagram[3] and, by definition, it is a meaningful expression in SA language. It consists of box and arrow graphical notation mixed with words and numbers. Consonant with the tutorial purpose of this paper, I will not, here, try to teach how to *read* a diagram. My tutorial approach aims only to lead to an understanding of what is *in* a diagram.

So we will just begin to examine Fig. 3. Start with the title, "Rationalize structured analysis features"—an adequate match to our understanding of the purpose and viewpoint of this whole paper. We seek to make rational the reasons behind those features. Next read the content of each of the boxes: "Define graphics; build diagram; use special notations; provide for referencing; organize material." These must be the six-or-fewer "parts" into which the titled subject matter is being broken. In this case there are five of them, and sure enough this aspect of SA follows exactly the time-tested outline approach to subject matter. Because our purpose is to have a graphics-based language (like blueprints), once we have decided upon some basics of graphic definition we will use that to build a diagram for some particular subject, adding special notations (presumably to improve clarity), and then because (as with blueprints) we know that a whole collection will be required to convey complex understanding in easy-to-understand pieces, we must provide for a way of referencing the various pieces and organizing the resulting material into what we see as an understandable whole.

Now, I have tried to compose the preceding long sentence about Fig. 3 using natural language constructs which, if not an exact match, are very close to terms which appear directly in Fig. 3. In fact, the reader should be able to find an exact correspondence between things which show in the figure and every important syntactic and semantic point in each part of the last sentence of the preceding paragraph, although the diagram has more to it than the sentence. Please reread that sentence now and check out this correspondence for yourself. In the process you will notice that considerable (though not exhaustive) use is made of information which is not *inside* the boxes, but instead is associated with the word-and-arrow structure of the diagram *outside* the boxes. This begins to show why, although SA in its basic backbone does follow the standard outline pattern of presentation, the box-and-arrow structure conveys a great deal more information than a simple topic outline (only the box *contents*) could possibly convey.

[3] The SADT diagram form itself is © 1975, SofTech, Inc., and has various fields used in the practice of SADT methodology.

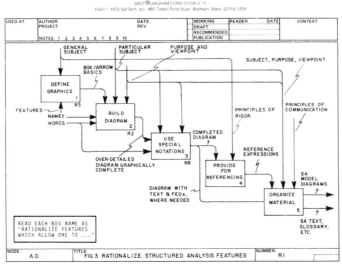

Figure 3   Rationalize SA features.

XI The first detail view

Figure 4 is another SA diagram. Simpler in structure than the diagram of Fig. 3, but nonetheless with much the same "look." The title, "Define graphics," is identical to the name inside the first box of Fig. 3, which is here being broken into five component worthy pieces, called the *nested factors* in SA terminology. Again the words written inside the boxes are legible, but are they understandable? How can "Bound context; relate/ connect; show transformation; show circumstance; show means," be considered parts of "Define graphs?" It is not very clear, is it? It would seem that something must be wrong with SA for the touted understandability turns out to be, in fact, quite obscure!

Look at Fig. 4 again and see if you don't agree that we have a problem —and see if you can supply the answer to the problem.

The problem is not with SA at all, but with our too-glib approach to it. SA is a rigorous language and thereby is unforgiving in many ways. In order for the communication of understanding to take place we ourselves must understand and conform to the rules of that rigor. The apparent obscurity should disappear in a twinkling once the following factor is pointed out: namely, *always be sure to do your understanding in the proper context*. In this case, the proper context was established by the title of Fig. 3, "Rationalize structured analysis features," and the purpose, to define graphical concepts and notations for the purpose of representing and

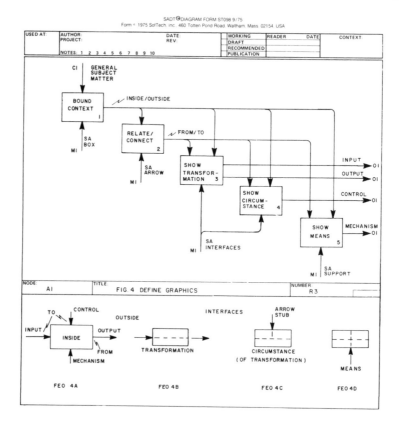

Figure 4   Define graphics.

conveying understanding of subject matters. Now, if we have all of that firmly implanted in our mind, then surely the name in Box 1 of Fig. 4 should be amply clear. Read, now, Box 4. 1[4] for yourself, and see if that clarity and communication of intended understanding does not take place.

You see, according to the diagram, the first feature of defining graphics is to "Bound the context"—precisely the subject we have just been discussing and precisely the source of the apparent obscurity which made SA initially appear to be on shaky ground. To aid first reading of the figures, a suggested paraphrasing of the intended context is given in a bold box on each of the other diagrams (see Fig. 3).

As we can see from the section of Fig. 4 labeled FEO 4A[5] the general subject matter is isolated from the rest of all subject matter by means of

---

[4] To shorten references to figures, "Box 4. 1" will mean "Box 1 of Fig. 4," etc. in the following discussion.

the SA box which has an inside and an outside (look at the box). The only thing we are supposed to consider is the portion of that subject matter which is *inside* the box—so the boundary of the box does bound the context in which we are to consider the subject.

XII The SA box as building block

We lack the backgound (at this point) to continue an actual reading of Fig. 4, because it itself defines the basic graphic notations used in it. Instead, consider only the sequence of illustrations (4A-4D) labeled FEO. FEO 4A shows that the fundamental building block of SA language notation is a box with four sides called INPUT, CONTROL, OUTPUT, and MECHANISM. As we have seen above, the bounded piece of subject matter is *inside* the box and, as we will see, the actual boundary of the box is made by the collection of *arrow stubs* entering and leaving the box. The bounded pieces are related and connected (Box 4.2) by SA arrows which go *from* an OUTPUT of one box *to* the INPUT or CONTROL of another box, i.e., such arrow connections make the *interfaces* between subjects. The names INPUT and OUTPUT are chosen to convey the idea that (see FEO 4B and Box 4.3) the box represents a *transformation* from a "before" to an "after" state of affairs. The CONTROL interface (see FEO 4C and Box 4.4) interacts and constrains the transformation to ensure that it applies only under the appropriate circumstances. The combination of INPUT, OUTPUT, and CONTROL fully specifies the bounded piece of subject, and the interfaces relate it to the other pieces. Finally, the MECHANISM *support* (not interface, see FEO 4D and Box 4.5) provide means for realizing the complete piece represented by the box.

We will see shortly why Fig. 4 contains no INPUT arrows at all, but except for that anomaly, this description should make Fig. 4 itself reasonably understandable. (Remember the context—"Rationalize the features of SA language which allow one to define graphic notation for...") The diagram (with FEO's and discussion) is the desired rationalization. It fits quite well with the idea of following the maxim. We don't mind breaking *everything* about a bounded piece of subject matter into pieces as long as we are sure we can express completely how all those pieces go back together to constitute the whole. Input, output, control, and mechanism provide that capability. As long as the right mechanism is provided, and the right control is applied, whatever is inside the box can be a valid

---

[5] This notation refers to the sequence of imbedded illustrations in Fig. 4 which are "For exposition only" (FEO).

transformation of input to output. We now must see how to use the "foreign" language names and labels of boxes and arrows. Then we can start putting SA to work.

XIII Using the basics for understanding

Figure 4, and especially FEO 4A, now that we have digested the meaning of the diagram itself, has presented the basic box-and-arrow-stubs-making-useful-interfaces-for-a-bounded-piece-of-subject-matter building block of SA. We now can start to use the input, output, control, and mechanism concepts to further our understanding. Knowing even this much, the power of expression of SA diagrams beyond that of simple outlining will start to become evident.

Figure 5, entitled "Build diagram," details Box 3.2. Referring back to Fig. 3 and recalling the opening discussion of its meaning (which we should do in order to establish in our mind the proper context for reading Fig. 5) we recall that the story line of Fig. 3 said that after Box 3.1 had defined the arrow and box basics, then we would build an actual diagram with words and names for a particular subject in accordance with a purpose and viewpoint chosen to convey the appropriate understanding. Looking at Box 3.2 in the light of what we have just learned about the box/arrow basics in Fig. 4, we can see that indeed the inputs are words and names, which will be transformed into a diagram (an over-detailed, but graphically complete diagram, evidently). Even though the mechanism

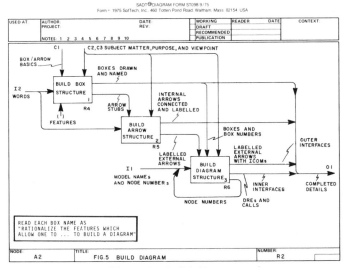

Figure 5   Build diagram.

is not specified, it is shown that this diagramming process will be controlled by (i.e., constrained by) the graphic conventions, subject, and viewpoint. Now refer to Fig. 5 with this established context and consider its three boxes:—"Build box structure; build arrow structure; build diagram structure." That matches our understanding that a diagram is a structure of boxes and arrows (with appropriate names and labels, of course). Study Fig. 5 yourself briefly, keeping in mind the points we have discussed so far. You should find little difficulty, and you will find that a number of the technical terms that were pure jargon in the tabulated form in Fig. 2 now start to take on some useful meaning. (Remember to ignore terms such as "ICOM" and "DRE," to be described later.)

If you have taken a moment or so to study Fig. 5 on your own, you probably have the impression things are working all right, but you are still not really sure that you are acquiring the intended level of understanding of Fig. 5. It seems to have too many loose ends semantically, even though it makes partial sense. If this is your reaction, you are quite right. For more detail and information is needed to make all the words and relationships take on full meaning. Fig. 5 does indeed tell *everything* about "Build diagram" in its three boxes, which are themselves reasonably understandable. But we need more information for many of the labels to really snap into place. This we will find in the further detailing of the three boxes. Context *orients* for understanding (*only* orients!); details *enable* understanding (and strengthen context).

Fig. 6 provides the detailing for Box 5.1. Expecially for this diagram, it is important to keep in mind the appropriate context for reading. It is not "*Draw* an SA diagram," but to motivate the *features* of SA. Thus, when we

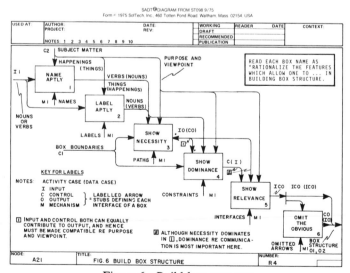

Figure 6   Build box structure.

read the title, "Build box structure," of Fig. 6, we must keep in mind that the worthy piece of subject matter is not *how* to build box structure, nor even the features which *create* box structure, but motivation for *explanation* of the features which allow box structure to represent the bounded context subject matter. This actually is a very sophisticated subject and normally we would only be diagramming it after we had already prepared rather complete models of the "how to" of SA so that many of the terms and ideas would already be familiar. In this paper however, the opening discussion must serve instead. The next four sections discuss Fig. 6.

XIV   Duality of data and activities

Recall that a complete SA model has to consider both the things and happenings of the subject being modeled. Happenings are represented by an activity decomposition consisting of activity diagrams and things are represented by data decomposition consisting of data diagrams. The neat thing about SA language is that both of these complementary but radically different aspects are diagrammed using exactly the same four-sided box notation. Fig. 7 illustrates this fact. The happening/activity and thing/data domains are completely dual in SA. (Think of an INPUT activity on a data box as one that creates the data thing, and of OUTPUT as one that

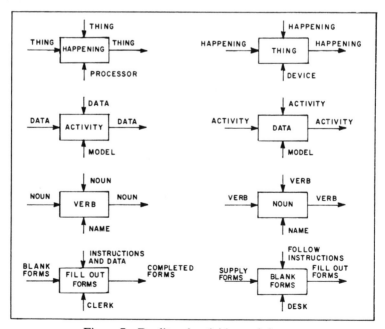

Figure 7   Duality of activities and data.

uses or references it.) Notice that mechanism is different in interpretation, but the role is the same. For a happening it is the *processor*, machine, computer, person, etc., which makes the happening happen. For a thing it is the *device*, for storage, representation, implementation, etc. (of the thing).

A quick check of Fig. 4 shows that mechanism's purpose is to show the means of realization, and that it is *not an interface* but is instead something called "support" in SA (described later in Section XXIII). For either activity or data modeling, a support mechanism is *a complete model*, with both data and activity aspects. As Fig. 7 shows, that complete "real thing" is *known by its name*, whereas things and happenings are identified by nouns and verbs (really nominal expressions and verbial expressions). With this in mind, we can see that the first two boxes in Fig. 6 motivate the naming and labeling features of SA to do or permit what Fig. 7 requires— boxes are named, and arrows are labeled, with either nouns or verbs as appropriate to the aspect of the model, and of course, in accordance with the intended purpose and viewpoint of the subject matter.

XV Constraints

We will consider next Boxes 6.3 and 6.4 together, and with some care, for this is one of the more subtle aspects of SA—the concept of a *constraint*— the key to well structured thought and well structured diagrams. The word *constraint* conjures up visions of opposing forces at play. *Something can be constrained only if there is something stronger upon which the constraining force can be based.* It might seem that from the ideas of SA presented so far, that that strong base will be provided by the rigorously defined bounded context of a box. Given a strong boundary, it is easy to envision forces saying either to stay inside the boundary or to stay outside the boundary. It is a pleasing thought indeed, and would certainly make strong structure in both our thinking and our diagrams. The only trouble is it does not work that way (or at least not immediately), but in fact it is just the opposite! In SA thinking *it is the constraints that make the boundaries, not the other way around.* This is a tricky point so we will approach it slowly. It is still true that a constraint, to be a constraint, has to have something to push against. If it is not the bounded-context boundary, then what is it?

The subtle answer is that *the purpose and viewpoint of the model provide the basis for all constraints* which in turn provide the strength and rigidity for all the boundaries which in turn create the inescapable structure which forces correct understanding to be communicated. This comes about through the concepts of *necessity* and *dominance*, which are the subjects of Boxes 6.3 and 6.4. Dominance sounds much like constraint, and we will

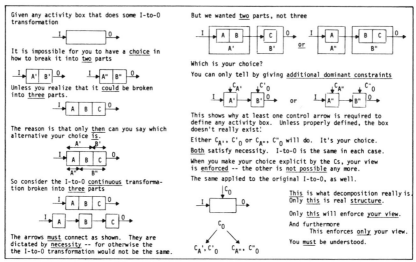

Figure 8 Dominance and necessity.

not be surprised to find it being the purveyor of constraint. But "necessity" has its own subtle twist in this, the very heart of SA. Therefore we must approach it, too, with some deliberation.

Figure 8 tells the story in concise form. Please read it now. Then please read it again, for all experience with SA shows that this simple argument seems to be very subtle and difficult for most people to grasp correctly. The reason is that the *everything* of the SA maxim makes the I-to-O *necessity* chain the *weakest possible structure*—akin to *no structure at all*. It merely states a fact that *must be true* for every SA box, because of the maxim. Therefore *dominant constraints*, expressed by the control arrows for activity boxes are, in fact, the *only* way possible, to impose structure. Furthermore, that enforcement of structure is unique and compelling—no other structure can be (mis-) understood in place of that intended by the SA author. This is, of course, all mediated by the effectiveness with which the SA author wields the chosen non-SA language used for names of boxes and labels on arrows, but the argument presented in this paper holds, nonetheless. This is because whenever the imprecision of the non-SA language intrudes, more SA modeling (perhaps even with new purpose and viewpoint for greater refinement, still, of objectives) is forced by the reader/author cycle of the SADT discipline.

XVI The rule of omission

Now consider Boxes 6.5 and 6.6, "Show relevance" and "Omit the obvious." These two ideas follow right along with the above discussion. Namely, in the case of activity diagramming, *if inputs are relevant* (i.e., if they make a strong contribution to understandability) *then they are drawn*. But on the other hand, since the important thing is the structure imposed by the control dominance and output necessity, and inputs *must* be supplied in any case for those outputs to result, *obvious inputs can and should be omitted from* the box structure of SA *activity diagramming*. In other words, whenever an obvious input is omitted in an activity diagram, the reader knows that (because of the SA maxim) whatever is needed will be supplied in order that the control and output which *are* drawn can happen correctly. Omitting the obvious makes the understandability and meaning of the diagram much stronger, because inputs when they *are* drawn are known to be important and nonobvious. Remember that SA diagrams are not wiring diagrams, they are vehicles for communicating understanding.

Although activity and data are dual in SA and use the same four-sided box notation, they are not quite the same, for the concept of dominance and constraint in the *data* aspect centers on *input* rather than control. In the data case, the weak chain of necessity is C-O-C-O-$\cdots$ not I-O-I-O-$\cdots$ as it is in the activity case. The reason comes from a deep difference between space and time (i.e., between things and happenings). In the case of the happening, the dominant feature is the control which says when to cut the transformation to yield a desired intermediate result, because the "freedom" of happenings is in time. In the case of things, however, the "freedom" which must be constrained and dominated concerns which version of the thing (i.e., which part of the data box) is the one that is to exist, regardless of time. The input activity for a data box "creates" that thing in that form and therefore it is the dominant constraint to be specified for a data box. An unimportant control activity will happen whenever needed, and may be omitted from the diagram.

Therefore, the rule regarding the obvious in SA is that *controls may never be omitted from activity diagrams and inputs may never be omitted from data diagrams*. Fig. 6 summarizes all of this discussion.

XVII Strengthening of boundaries

Recall that a constraint does need something to push on. What is that? The answer is the one originally proposed, but rejected. *Constraints are based on the boundary of a bounded context—but of the single box of the parent diagram which the current diagram details*. (A parenthesized hint that this would turn out to be the case *does* appear in the original rejection of the view that boundaries provide the base for constraints, above.) In other words, the constraints represented by the arrows on a diagram are *not* formed by the several boundaires of the boxes of *that* diagram, but all are based on the single boundary of the corresponding box in the *parent* diagram. As was stated above in Section XV, the constraints form the box boundary interfaces and define the boxes, not the other way around. The strength of those constraints comes from the corresponding "push" passed through from the parent. As the last "C_O" portion of Fig. 8 indicates, this hierarchic cascading of constraints is based entirely on the *purpose* of the model as a whole (further constrained in spread by the limited *viewpoint* of the model) as it is successively decomposed in the hierarchic layering forced by the six-or-fewer rule of the SA maxim.

All of this is a direct consequence of the *everything* of the SA maxim, and may be inferred by considering Fig. 8 recursively. The boundary of the top-most box of the analysis is determined entirely by the subject matter, purpose, and viewpoint of the agreed-upon outset understanding. ("Tell 'em whatcha gonna tell 'em.") Then each of the subsequent constraints derives its footing only insofar as it continues to reflect that subject, purpose, and viewpoint. And, each, in turn, provides the same basis for the next subdivision, etc. Inconsistencies in an original high-level interpretation are ironed out and are replaced by greater and greater precision of specific meaning.

Even though the basis for all of the constraint structure is the (perhaps ill-conceived, ambiguous, ill-defined) *outer* boundary, that boundary and the *innermost* boundary, composed of the collective class of all the boundaries of the finest subdivision taken together, are merely two representations of the *same* boundary—so that *strengthening of the inner boundary through extensive decomposition automatically strengthens the outer boundary*. It is as though the structured analyst (and each of his readers as well) were saying continually "My outermost understanding of the problem as a whole can only make sense, now that I see all this detail, if I refine my interpretation of it in this, this, and this precise way." This is the hidden power of SA at work. This is how SA greatly amplifies the precision and understandability of any natural or formal language whose nouns and verbs are imbedded in its box and arrow structure.

XVIII Arrow connections

Figure 6, which led to this discussion, detailed Box 5.1 "Build box structure"; Fig. 9 decomposes Box 5.2, "Build arrow structure." From Fig. 5 we see that the controlling constraints that dominate Box 5.2 are the subject matter, purpose, and viewpoint, as we would expect, along with the "arrow stubs" which resulted from building each box separately. The outputs are to be internal arrows connected and labeled, as well as labeled external arrows. A relevant (i.e., nonobvious) input is the collection of words—nouns or verbs—for making those labels.

With this context in mind, we are now ready to look at Fig. 9, "Build arrow structure." Here is an example of the use of non-English language to

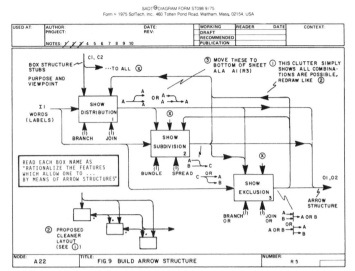

Figure 9   Build arrow structure.

label arrows. Small graphical phrases show the intended meaning of "branch" and "join" for distribution, and "bundle" and "spread" with respect to subdivision, as well as two forms of logical OR for exclusion. We have seen many examples of these in use in the diagrams already considered, so that the ideas should be quite transparent.

The little pictures as labels show how the labels attach to arrows to convey the appropriate meaning. In most good SA diagramming the OR's are used very sparingly—only when they materially assist understanding. In most circumstances, the fact that arrows represent constraints either of dominance or necessity supplies the required understanding in clearer form merely by topological connection. This also is the reason why there is no graphical provision for the other logical functions such as AND, for they are really out of place at the level of communication of basic SA language. In order for them to have an appropriate role, the total context of interpretation of an SA model must have been drawn down very precisely to some mathematical or logical domain at which point a language more appropriate to that domain should be chosen. Then logical terms in the nominal and verbial expressions in labels can convey the conditions. This is preferable to distorting the SA language into a detailed communication role it was not designed or intended to fulfill.

XIX   Boundaries

Figure 12, "Build diagram structure," will provide detailing for the third and last box of Fig. 5. It is needed as a separate consideration of this motivation model because the building of box structure (Box 5.1, detailed in Fig. 6) and arrow structure (Box 5.2, detailed in Fig. 9) only cover arrows between boxes in a single diagram—the *internal* arrows. Box 4.2 requires that *every* arrow which relates or connects bounded contexts must participate in both a *from* and a *to* interface. Every *external* arrow (shown as the second output of Box 5.2) will be missing either its source (from) or its destination (to) because the relevant boxes do not appear on this diagram. As the relationship between Boxes 5.2 and 5.3 in Fig. 5 shows, these labeled arrows are indeed a dominant constraint controlling Box 3, "Build diagram structure."

Figure 10 helps to explain the story. This is a partial view of three levels of nesting of SA boxes, one within the other, in some model (not an SA diagram). Except for three arrows, every arrow drawn is a complete from/to connection. The middle, second-level box has four fine-level boxes within it, and it in turn is contained within the largest box drawn in the figure. If we consider the arrows in the middle, second-level box, we note that only two of them are internal arrows, all the others being external. But notice also that every one of those external arrows (with respect to that middle-level box) are in fact *internal* with respect to the model as a whole. Each of those arrows does go from one box to another box—a lowest-level box in each case. In completing the connection, *the arrows penetrate the boundaries of the middle-level boxes* as though those boundaries were not there at all. In fact, there are only two real boundaries in all of Fig. 10—the two boundaries characteristic of every SA decomposition. These are 1) the *outer boundary* which is the outermost edge of Fig. 10, itself, and 2) the *inner boundary* which is the entire set of edges of all of the lowest-level boxes drawn in Fig. 10, considered as a single

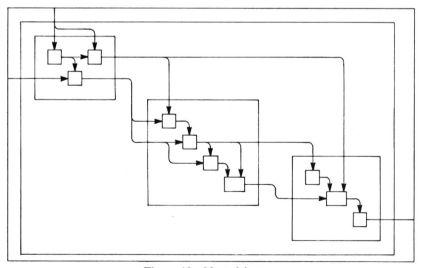

Figure 10   Nested factors.

boundary. As was stated above, the SA maxim requires that the outer boundary and the inner boundary must be understood to be *exactly the same* so that the subject is merely decomposed, not altered in any way.

XX Parents and children

To understand how the structuring of Fig. 10 is expressed in SA terms we must be clear about the relationship between boundaries and interfaces, boxes and diagrams, and the parent/child relationship. Fig. 11 lays all of this out. In the upper right appears the diagram for the largest box drawn in Fig. 10, and in the lower left appears the diagram for the central middle-level box which we were discussing. The first thing to notice is that the diagrams are here drawn as though they were punched out of Fig. 10, (like cutting cookies from a sheet of cookie dough). Although the dimensions are distorted, the note in the upper left points out that, by definition, *the diagram outer boundary is actually the same as the parent box boundary* (i. e., the current child diagram is the "cookie" removed from the sheet of dough and placed to one side).

Figure 11 also points out that, just as for the hierarchic decomposition as a whole, the *inner boundary of the parent diagram is the collection of all its child box boundaries considered as a single entity*. Notice the terminology

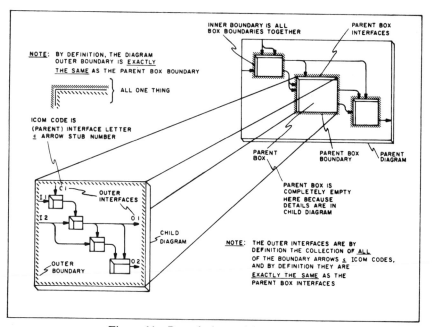

Figure 11   Boundaries and interfaces.

—with respect to the current child diagram, one of the boxes in the parent diagram is called the *parent box* of the child diagram. By definition of Fig. 4, that *parent box boundary* is the collection of *parent box interfaces and support* which compose it. Since we have just established that the outer boundary of the current diagram is the same as the corresponding parent box boundary, the parent box edges (interfaces *or* support) which compose the parent box boundary must somehow match the outer edges of the child diagram. This is the connection which we seek to establish rigorously.

By Fig. 10 we know that the external arrows of the child diagram penetrate through the outer boundary and are, in fact, the *same* arrows as are the stubs of the interfaces and support which compose the parent box boundary. Therefore, the connection which has to be made is clear from the definition. But for flexibility of graphic representation, *the external arrows of the current diagram need not have the same geometric layout, relationship, or labeling* as the corresponding stubs on the parent diagram, which are drawn on a completely different (parent) diagram.

In order to allow this flexibility, we construct a special code-naming scheme called *ICOM codes* as follows: An ICOM code begins with one of the letters I-C-O-M (standing for INPUT, CONTROL, OUTPUT, MECHANISM) concatenated with an integer which is obtained by considering that the stubs of the corresponding parent box edge are numbered consecutively from top to bottom or from left to right, as the case may be. With the corresponding ICOM code written beside the unattached end of the arrow in the current diagram, that arrow is no longer called "external," but is called a *boundary arrow*. Then *the four outer edges of the child diagram are, by definition, the four collections of ICOM boundary arrows* which are, by definition, exactly the same as the corresponding parent box edges, as defined by Fig. 4 and shown in Fig. 11. Thus even though the geometric layout may be radically different, the rigor of interconnection of child and parent diagrams is complete, and the arrows are continuous and unbroken, as required. Every diagram in this paper has ICOM codes properly assigned.

The above presentation is summarized in the first two boxes of Fig. 12 and should be clear without further discussion. Boxes 12.3 and 12.4 concern the SA language notations for establishing the relationships between the child and parent diagram cookies by means of a *detail reference expression* (DRE) or an SA *call*. We will consider these shortly. For now it is sufficient to note that the topics we have considered here complete the detailing of Fig. 5, "Build diagram"—how the box structure and arrow structure for individual diagrams are built, and then how the whole collection of diagrams is linked together in a single whole so that *everything* of the top-most cookie (treated as a cookie sheet from which other cookies are cut with zero width cuts) is completely understandable. Each individual diagram itself is only a portion of the cookie dough with an outer boundary and an inner boundary formed by the decomposition

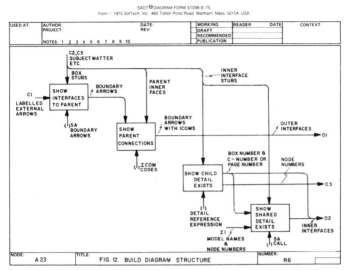

Figure 12   Build diagram structure.

operation. Nothing is either gained or lost in the process—so that the SA maxim is rigorously realized. Everything can indeed be covered for the stated purpose and viewpoint. We now complete our presentation of the remaining items in the 40 features of Fig. 2, which exploit further refinements of notation and provide orderly organization for the mass of information in a complete SA model.

XXI   Word notes

In SA language, not everything is said in graphical terms. Both words and pictures are also used. If the diagram construction notations we have considered so far were to be used exclusively and exhaustively, very cluttered and nonunderstandable diagrams would result. Therefore SA language includes further simplifying graphic notations (which also increase the expressive power of the language), as well as allowing nongraphic additional information to be incorporated into SA diagrams. This is the function of Fig. 13 which details Box 3.3. Fig. 13 points out that the (potentially) cluttered diagram is only graphically complete so that special *word* notations are needed. Furthermore, special arrow notations can supply more clarity, to result in a complete *and* understandable diagram.

We will not further detail Box 13.2. We merely point out that its output consists of three forms of verbal additions to the diagram. The first two—NOTES and $\boxed{n}$ footnotes—are actual parts of the diagram. The diagrams we have been examining have examples of each. The third category, $\widehat{n}$ metanotes, are *not* parts of the diagram themselves, but are

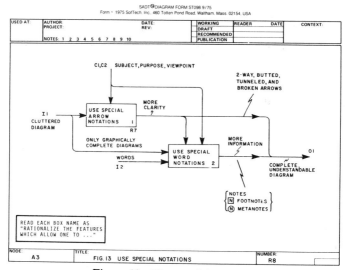

Figure 13   Use special notations.

instead notes *about* the diagram. The (n) metanotes have only an observational or referential relation to the actual information content of these diagrams and therefore they do not in any way alter or affect the actual representational function of the SA language, either graphical or verbal. There is no way that information in (n) metanotes can participate in the information content of the diagrams, and therefore they should not be used in an attempt to affect the interpretation of the diagrams themselves, but only for mechanical operations regarding the diagram's physical format or expression. Examples are comments from a reader to an author of a diagram suggesting an improved layout for greater understandability. A few examples are included on the diagrams in this paper. The $\boxed{n}$ footnotes are used exclusively for allowing large verbal expressions to be concisely located with respect to tight geometric layout, in addition to the normal footnoting function commonly found in textual information.

XXII Special graphic notations

Figure 14 provides the motivation for four very simple additions to the graphic notation to improve the understandability of diagrams. With respect to a specific aspect of the subject matter, two boxes sometimes really act as one box inasmuch as each of them shares one portion of a well-defined aspect of the subject matter. In this case, arrowheads with dots above, below, or to the right of the arrowhead are added instead of drawing two separate arrows as shown in FEO 14A. Two-way arrows are a form of bundling, however, *not* a mere shorthand notation for the two

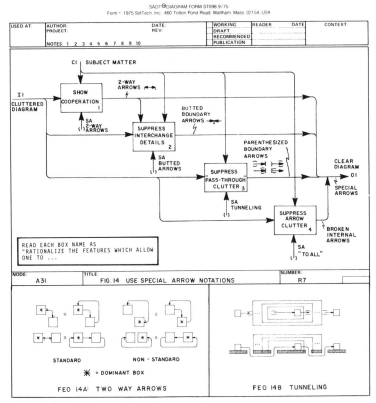

Figure 14   Use special arrow notations.

separate arrows. If the subject matters represented by the two separate arrows are not sufficiently similar, they should *not* be bundled into a two-way arrow, but should be drawn separately. Many times, however, the two-way arrow *is* the appropriate semantics for the relationship between two boxes. Notice that if other considerations of diagrams are sufficiently strong, the awkward, nonstandard two-way arrow notations shown also may be used to still indicate dominance in the two-way interaction.

SA arrows should always be thought of as conduits or pipelines containing multistranded cables, each strand of which is another pipeline. Then the branching and joining is like the cabling of a telephone exchange, including trunk lines. Box 14.2 is related to both two-way arrows and pipelines, and points out that a one-way pipeline stub at the parent level may be shown as a two-way boundary arrow in the child. This is appropriate since, with respect to the communication of understanding at the parent level, the relationship between boxes is one-way, whereas when details are examined, two-way cooperation between the two sets of detailing boxes may be required. An example is the boss-worker relation. The boss (at parent level) provides one-way command, but (at the child diagram level) a two-way interchange between worker and boss may be needed to clarify details.

Box 14.3 motivates an additional and very useful version of Box 6.6 ("Omit the obvious"). In this case, instead of omitting the obvious, we only postpone consideration of necessary detail until the appropriate level is reached. This is done by putting parentheses around the unattached end of an external arrow, or at the interface end of a parent box stub. The notation is intended to convey the image of an arrow "tunneling" out of view as it crosses a parent box inner boundary only to emerge later, some number of levels deeper in a child's outer interface, when that information is actually required. These are known as "tunneled" or "parenthesized" boundary arrows when the sources or destinations are somewhere within the SA model, and as (proper) *external* arrows when the missing source or destination is unspecified (i.e., when the model would need to be imbedded in some context larger than the total model for the appropriate connection to be made).

Finally, Box 14.4 is a seldom-used notation which allows internal arrows themselves to be broken by an ad hoc labeling scheme merely to suppress clutter. Its use is discouraged because of its lack of geometric continuity and because its use is forced only by a diagram containing so much information already that it is likely not to be clearly understood and should be redrawn. Examples occur in Fig. 9 just for illustration.

XXIII The reference language

Returning to Fig. 3, we now have considered all of the aspects of basic SA language which go into the creation of diagrams themselves, with the single exception of the detail reference expressions and SA call notation of Fig. 12, which were saved until this point since they relate so closely to Box 3.4, "Provide for referencing."

A complete and unique SA reference language derives very nicely from the hierarchically nested factors imposed by the SA maxim. Diagrams, boxes, interfaces, arrows, and complete contexts can be referenced by a combination of model names, *node numbers* (starting with A for activity or D for data, and derived directly from the box numbers), and ICOM codes. The insertion of a dot, meaning "which see" (i.e. "find the diagram and look at it"), can specify exactly which diagram is to be kept particularly in mind to provide the context for interpreting the SA language. Thus "A122. 4I1" means "in diagram A122, the first input of box 4"; "A1224. I1" means "in diagram A1224, the boundary arrow I4"; "A1224I1" means "the first input interface of node A1224." The SA language rules also allow such reference expressions to degenerate naturally to the minimum needed to be understandable. Thus, for example, the mechanism for showing that

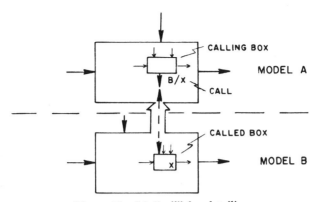

Figure 15   SA "call" for detailing.

the child detailing exists is merely to write the corresponding chronological creation number (called a *C-number*) under the lower right-hand corner of a box on the diagram, as a DRE. (A C-number is the author's initials, concatenated with a sequential integer—assigned as the first step whenever a new diagram sheet is begun.) When a model is formally published, the corresponding detail reference expression is normally converted into the page number of the appropriate detail diagram. The omission of a detail reference expression indicates that the box is not further detailed in this model. (For all the diagrams considered in this paper, the DRE's have been left in C-number form.)

The *SA call* notation consists of a detail reference expression preceded by a downward pointing arrow stub, and allows sharing of details among diagrams. It will not be covered in this paper beyond the illustration in Fig. 15, which is included here more to illustrate why mechanism support is not an interface (as has repeatedly been pointed out) than to adequately describe the SA call scheme. That will be the subject of a future paper, and is merely cited here for completeness. The SA call mechanism (see also [Ross 75*]) corresponds very closely to the subroutine call concept of programming languages, and is a key concept in combining multiple purposes and viewpoints into a single model of models.

XXIV Organizing the model

The final box of Fig. 3, Box 3.5, "Organize material," is not detailed in this model. Instead, we refer the reader back to the tabulation of Fig. 2 where the corresponding items are listed. In final publication form each diagram is normally accompanied by brief, carefully-structured *SA text* which, according to the reading rules, is intended to be read *after* the diagram itself has been read and understood. The SA text supplements but does not replace the information content of the diagram. Its purpose is to "tell 'em whatcha told 'em" by giving a walk-through through the salient features of the diagram, pointing out, by using the reference language, how the story line may be seen in the diagram. Published models also include glossaries of terms used, and are preceded by a *node index*, which consists of the node-numbered box names in indented form in node number sequence. Fig. 16 is the node index for the model presented in this paper, and normally would be published at the beginning to act as a table of contents.

RATIONALIZE SA FEATURES

A1   DEFINE GRAPHICS
    A11   Bound Context
    A12   Relate/Connect
    A13   Show Transformation
    A14   Show Circumstance
    A15   Show Means

A2   BUILD DIAGRAM
    A21   Build Box Structure
    A211   Name Aptly
    A212   Label Aptly
    A213   Show Necessity
    A214   Show Dominance
    A215   Show Relevance
    A216   Omit the Obvious
    A22   Build Arrow Structure
    A221   Show Distribution
    A222   Show Subdivision
    A223   Show Exclusion
    A23   Build Diagram Structure
    A231   Show Interfaces to Parent
    A232   Show Parent Connections
    A233   Show Child Detail Exists
    A234   Show Shared Detail Exists

A3   USE SPECIAL NOTATIONS
    A31   Use Special Arrow Notations
    A311   Show Cooperation
    A312   Supress Interchange Details
    A313   Supress "Pass-Through" Clutter
    A314   Supress Arrow Clutter
    A32   Use Special Word Notations

A4   PROVIDE FOR (UNIQUE) REFERENCING
    (A41   Sheet Reference)
    (A42   Box Reference)
    (A43   Interface Reference)
    (A44   Arrow Reference)
    (A45   Context Reference)

A5   ORGANIZE MATERIAL

Figure 16   Node index.

XXV Conclusion

The principle of good storytelling style (see Section IV) has been followed repeatedly in this paper. We have provided motivations for each of the 40 SA language features of structured analysis by relating each one to a need for clear and explicit exposition, with no loss, from an original bounded context. (The "node" column of Fig. 2 maps each feature to a diagram box in the other figures.) In the process, we have seen how the successive levels of refinement strengthen the original statement of purpose and viewpoint, to enforce unambiguous understanding. The best "tell 'em whatcha told 'em" for the paper as a whole is to restudy the SA model in the figures. (Space precludes even sketching the corresponding data decomposition.) The diagrams not only summarize and integrate the ideas covered in the paper, but provide further information, as well.

There are more advanced features of the SA language which will be covered in subsequent papers in the context of applications. In practice, SA turns out to depend heavily on the disciplined thought processes that lead to well-structured analyses expressed in well-structured diagrams. Additional rules and supporting methodology organize the work flow, support the mechanics of the methods, and permit teams of people to work and interact as one mind attacking complex problems. These are covered in SofTech's SADT methodology. The fact that SA incorporates by definition any and all languages within its framework permits a wide variety of natural and artificial languages to be used to accomplish specific goals with respect to understanding the requirements for solution. Then those requirements can be translated, in a rigorous, organized, efficient, and, above all, understandable fashion, into actual system design, system implementation, maintenance, and training. These topics also must of necessity appear in later papers, as well as a formal language definition for the ideas unfolded here.

Acknowledgments. The four-sided box notation was originally inspired[6] by the match between [Hori 72] activity cell and my own notions of Plex [Ross 61]. I have, of course, benefited greatly from interaction with my colleagues at SofTech, J. W. Brackett, J. E. Rodriguez, and particularly J. B. Goodenough gave helpful suggestions for this paper, and C. G. Feldmann worked closely with me on early developments. Some of these ideas have earlier been presented at meetings of the IFIP Work Group 2.3 on Programming Methodology.

[6]*Added in proof.* In writing the paper, "Origins of the APT language for automatically programmed tools" [Ross 78*], I found that the distinction between input and control, as well as the four-sided box, were known to me and used in December, 1956 in the first APT Interim Report. Structured Analysis and plex evidently arose together in my thinking at that time.

References

The following abbreviations are used in the references.

CACM	Communications of the ACM
JACM	Journal of the ACM
NACM	Proceedings of the National ACM Conference
SJCC	Proceedings of the AFIPS Spring Joint Computer Conference
FJCC	Proceedings of the AFIPS Fall Joint Computer Conference
NCC	Proceedings of the AFIPS National Computer Conference
IFIP	Proceedings of the IFIP Congress
IPL	Information Processing Letters
LNCS	Springer-Verlag Lecture Notes in Computer Science

WG2.3 Bibliography

This bibliography contains references to publications written by members of WG2.3 that relate to programming methodology. It was compiled from lists provided by WG2.3 members and from an extensive literature survey [Horning 77b*]. It is intended to describe the interests of the members, and that of WG2.3 itself.

Lest this appear to be too much of an attempt to bloat WG2.3's image, many references that obviously had no bearing on WG2.3 have been left out. For example, unless referenced in a paper in this volume, entries for publications before WG2.3's existence shouldn't appear. Thus, in addition to being authored by a member of WG2.3, each entry satisfies at least one of the following:

1. It was referenced in an article in this volume.
2. It covers work presented at a WG2.3 meeting.
3. It concerns some aspect of programming methodology and perhaps explicitly acknowledges the influence of WG2.3.
4. None of the above holds, but I as editor did not notice this.

The use of the word "with" in the list of authors of an entry (e.g., *Burstall, with J. Darlington*), means that the order of the authors in the publication itself differs from the order listed here.

Balzer, R. M.
- [67]   Dataless programming. *FJCC 1967*, 535–544.
- [71]   PORTS—a method for dynamic interprogram communication and job control. *SJCC 1971*, 485–489.
- [73a] A global view of automatic programming. *Proc. 3rd Int. Jnt. Conf. on AI* (Aug 1973), 494–499.
- [73b] CASAP: a testbed for program flexibility. *Proc. 3rd Int. Jnt. Conf. on AI* (Aug 1973), 601–605.
- [74a] with Greenfield, N., Kay, M., Mann, W., Ryder, W., Wilczynski, D. and Zobrist, A. Domain-independent automatic programming. *IFIP 1974*.
- [74b] A language-independent programmer's interface. *NCC 1974*, 365–370.
- [76a] Goldman, N., and Wile, D. On the transformational approach to programming. *Proc. Int. Conf. Software Eng. Oct 1976*, 337–344.
- [77a] Goldman, N., and Wile, D. Informality in program specification. *Proc. 5th Int. Jnt. Conf. on AI* (Aug 1977).
- [77b] Goldman, N., and Wile, D. Meta-evaluation as a tool for program understanding. *Proc. 5th Jnt. Conf. on AI* (Aug 1977).
- [77c] with Wile, D., and Goldman, N. Automated derivation of program control structure from natural language program description. *Symp. on AI and Prog. Lang., SIGPLAN Notices* **12** (Aug 1977), 77–84.

Brinch Hansen, P.
- [70]   The nucleus of a multiprogramming system. *CACM* **13** (April 1970), 238–250.
- [72a] Structured multiprogramming. *CACM* **15** (July 1972), 574–578.
- [72b] A comparison of two synchronizing concepts. *Acta Informatica* **1** (1972), 190–199.
- [72c] An outline of a course on operating system principles. In [Hoare 72c*], 29–36.
- [73a] *Operating Systems Principles*. Prentice–Hall, Englewood Cliffs, N.J., 1973.
- [73b] Testing a multiprogramming system. *Software—Practice and Experience* **3** (April 1973), 145–150.
- [73c] Concurrent programming concepts. *Computer Surveys* **5** (Dec 1973), 223–245.
- [74]   A programming methodology for operating system design. *IFIP 1974*, 394–397.
- [75a] Concurrent Pascal report. Information Science, Cal. Inst. of Technology, June 1975.
- [75b] The programming language Concurrent Pascal. *IEEE Trans. Software Eng.* **1** (June 1975), 199–207.
- [75c] Universal types in Concurrent Pascal. *IPL* **3** (July 1975), 165–166.
- [75d] Concurrent Pascal machine. Information Science, Cal. Inst. of Technology, Oct 1975.
- [75e] A real-time scheduler. Information Science, Cal. Inst. of Technology, Nov 1975.
- [76a] The job stream system. Information Science, Cal. Inst. of Technology, Jan 1976.
- [76b] The Solo operating system. *Software—Practice and Experience* **6** (April 1976), 141–205.
- [77]   *The Architecture of Concurrent Programs*. Prentice–Hall, Englewood Cliffs, N.J., 1977.

Burstall, R. M.
- [68]   Proving properties of programs by structural induction. Experimental Programming Reports, No. 17. DMIP, Edinburgh, 1968.
- [71]   Collins, J. S., and Popplestone, R. J. Programming in POP-2. Edinburgh Univ. Press, Edinburgh, 1971.

[72a] Some techniques for proving program correctness of programs which alter data structure. *Machine Intelligence* **7** (1972), 23–50.

[72b] Algebraic description of programs with assertions, verification and simulation. *ACM Conf. Proving Assertions About Programs 1972*, 7–14.

[75] and Thatcher, J. W. The algebraic theory of recursive program schemes. In *Category Theory Applied to Computation and Control, San Francisco, Cal., Feb 1974*. Springer–Verlag, Berlin, 1975, 126–131.

[76] with Darlington, J. A system which automatically improves programs. *Acta Informatica* **6** (1976), 41–60.

[77] and Darlington, J. A transformation system for developing recursive programs. *JACM* **24** (Jan 1977), 44–67.

Buxton, J. N.

[71] The nature and implications of software engineering. In Hugo, J. S. (ed.), *The Fourth Generation*. Infotech, Ltd., Berkshire, England, 1971, 227–238.

[74] Software engineering. In [Dahl 74*], 394–401.

[75] Naur, P. and Randell, B. (eds.) *Software Engineering*. Petrocelli, 1975. [Report on two NATO Conferences, held in Garmisch, Germany (Oct 68) and Rome, Italy (Oct 69).]

Dahl, O.-J.

[70] Myhrhaug, B. and Nygaard, K. *The SIMULA 67 Common Base Language*. Publication S-22, Norwegian Computing Center, Oslo, 1970.

[71] with Wang, A. Coroutine sequencing in a block structured environment. *BIT* **11** (1971), 425–449.

[72a] Hoare, C. A. R., and Dijkstra, E. W. *Structured Programming*. Academic Press, New York, 1972.

[72b] and Hoare, C. A. R. Hierarchical program structures. In [Dahl 72a*], 175–220.

[74] *Proc. 1974 CERN School of Computing, Godysund, Norway, Aug 1974*. CERN (Geneva) Report No. 74-23, Nov 1974.

[75] An approach to correctness proofs of semicoroutines. In *Mathematical Foundations of Computer Science. LNCS* 28, 1975, 157–174.

Dijkstra, E. W.

[62] Some meditations on advanced programming. *IFIP 1962*, 535–538.

[65] Solution of a problem in concurrent programming control. *CACM* **8** (Sept 1965), 569.

[68a] The structure of the THE multiprogramming system. *CACM* **11** (May 1968), 341–346.

[68b] Complexity controlled by hierarchical ordering of function and variability. In [Buxton 75*].

[68c] Cooperating sequential processes. In Genuys (ed.), *Programming Languages*. Academic Press, New York, 43–112.

[68d] Go to statement considered harmful, *CACM* **11** (March 1968), 147–148.

[68e] A constructive approach to the problem of program correctness. *BIT* **8** (1968), 174–186.

[71a] Concern for correctness as a guiding principle for program composition. In Hugo, J. S. (ed.), *The Fourth Generation*. Infotech, Ltd., Berkshire, England, 1971, 357–367.

[71b] A short introduction to the art of programming. Technological Univ., Eindhoven, EWD316, Aug 1971.

[71c] On a methodology of design. In *MC-25 Informatica Symposium*. Mathematisch Centrum, Amsterdam, 1971, 4.1–4.10.

[71d] Hierarchical ordering of sequential processes. *Acta Informatica* **1** (1971), 115–138. [Also in [Hoare 72c*], 79–93.]

[72a] A class of allocation strategies inducing bounded delays only. *SJCC 1972*, 933–936.

[72b] Reliability of programs. *Infotech State of the Art Report 7*, 1972, 217–232.
[72c] The humble programmer. *CACM* **15** (Oct 1972), 859–866.
[72d] Notes on structured programming. In [Dahl 72a*], 1–82.
[72e] Information streams sharing a finite buffer. *IPL* **1** (Oct 1972), 179–180.
[73a] A simple axiomatic basis for programming language constructs. Technological Univ., Eindhoven, EWD372, 1973.
[74a] Self-stabilizing systems in spite of distributed control. *CACM* **17** (Nov 1974), 643–644.
[74b] Synchronization and sequencing. *Informatie* (Netherlands) **16** (Dec 1974), 643–645. [In Dutch.]
[75a] Guarded commands, nondeterminacy and formal derivation of programs. *CACM* **18** (Aug 1975), 453–457.
[75b] Correctness concerns and, among other things, why they are resented. *Int. Conf. Reliable Software, SIGPLAN Notices* **10** (June 1975), 546–550.
[76a] *A Discipline of Programming*. Prentice–Hall, Englewood Cliffs, N.J., 1976.
[76b] *et al.* On-the-fly garbage collection: an exercise in cooperation. In *Language Hierarchies and Interfaces*. *LNCS* 46, 1976, 43–56.
[77] From craft to scientific discipline. *ICS 1977*.

Gries, D.
[73a] with Conway, R. *An Introduction to Programming: a Structured Approach Using PL/I and PL/C*. Winthrop, Cambridge, Mass., 1973. [2nd ed., 1975.]
[73b] Describing an algorithm by Hopcroft. *Acta Informatica* **2** (1973), 97–109.
[74] On structured programming—a reply to Smoliar. *CACM* **17** (Nov 1974), 655–657.
[76a] An exercise in proving parallel programs correct. In *Language Hierarchies and Interfaces*. *LNCS* 46, 1976, 57–81.
[76b] Some comments on programming language design. In Schneider, H.-J. and Nagl, M. (eds.), *Programmiersprachen 4. Fachtagung der GI*. Springer–Verlag, Berlin and New York, 1976, 235–252.
[76c] with Owicki, S. Verifying properties of parallel programs: an axiomatic approach. *CACM* **19** (May 1976). 279–285.
[76d] An illustration of current ideas on the derivation of correctness proofs and correct programs. *IEEE Trans. Software Eng.* **2** (Dec 1976), 238–244.
[76e] with Owicki, S. An axiomatic proof technique for parallel programs. *Acta Informatica* **6** (1976), 319–340.
[77a] and Gehani, N. Some ideas on data types in high level languages. *CACM* **20** (June 1977), 414–420.
[77b] Current ideas on programming methodology. In Wegner and Wulf (eds.), *The Impact of Research on Software Methodology*, to be published.
[77c] An exercise in proving parallel programs correct. *CACM* **20** (Dec 1977), 921–930.
[78a] The multiple assignment statement. *IEEE Trans. Software Eng.* **4** (Mar 1978), 87–93.

Guttag, J. V.
[75] The specification and application to programming of abstract data types. Ph.D. thesis, Computer Science Dept., Univ. of Toronto, 1975.
[76] Horowitz, E., and Musser, D. R. Abstract data types and software validation. USC Inf. Sci. Inst. Tech. Rpt. ISI/RR-76-48, 1976.
[77] Abstract data types and the development of data structures. *CACM* **20** (June 1977), 396–404.
[77b] Horowitz, E., and Musser, D. R. Some extensions to algebraic specifications. *Proc. LDRS, SIGPLAN Notices* **12** (March 1977), 63–67.
[77c] *et al.* Proof rules for the programming language EUCLID. USC Inf. Sci. Inst., May 1977.

[77d] and Horning, J. J. The algebraic specification of data types. *Acta Informatica* (1978).

Hoare, C. A. R.

[61] Algorithm 65, Find. *CACM* **4** (July 1961), 321.

[69] An axiomatic basis for computer programming. *CACM* **12** (Oct 1969), 576–580, 583.

[71a] Procedures and parameters: an axiomatic approach. In *Symposium on Semantics of Algorithmic Languages*. Springer–Verlag, Berlin and New York, 1971, 102–116.

[71b] Proof of a program: FIND. *CACM* **14** (Jan 1971), 39–45.

[71c] with Foley, M. Proof of a recursive program quicksort. *Computer J* **14** (Nov 1971), 391–395.

[72a] Proof of a structured program: the sieve of Eratosthenes. *Computer J* **15** (Nov 1972), 321–325.

[72b] The quality of software. *Software—Practice and Experience* **2** (April 1972), 103–105.

[72c] and Perrott, R. N. (eds.). *Operating Systems Techniques*. Academic Press, New York, 1972.

[72d] and Dahl, O.-J. Notes on data structuring. In [Dahl 72a*], 83–174.

[72e] and McKeag, R. M. A survey of store management techniques. In [Hoare 72c*], 117–131, 132–151.

[72f] Proof of correctness of data representations. *Acta Informatica* **1** (1972), 271–281.

[72g] Towards a theory of parallel programming. In [Hoare 72c*], 61–71.

[72h] with Clint, M. Program proving: jumps and functions. *Acta Informatica* **1** (1972), 214–224.

[72i] A note on the FOR statement. *BIT* **12** (1972), 334–341.

[72j] Prospects for a better programming language. *Infotech State of the Art Report 7: High Level Languages*, 1972, 327–343.

[72k] with Allison, D. C. S. Incomputability. *Computing Surveys* **4** (Sept 1972), 169–178.

[72l] The quality of software. *Software—Practice and Experience* **2** (1972), 103–105.

[73a] Parallel programming: an axiomatic approach. Stanford Univ., Dept. of Computer Science, 1973. [Also appeared in *Computer Languages*.]

[73b] Hints on programming language design. *ACM Symp. Princ. of Prog. Lang.*, *Oct 1973*, 1–30.

[73c] A structured paging system. *Computer J* **16** (Aug 1973), 209–215.

[73d] and Wirth, N. An axiomatic definition of the programming language PASCAL. *Acta Informatica* **2** (1973), 335–355.

[73e] Recursive data structures. Stanford Univ., Dept. of Computer Science, STAN-CS-73-400, Oct 1973.

[74a] Monitors: an operating system structuring concept. *CACM* **17** (Oct 1974), 549–557.

[74b] and Lauer, P. E. Consistent and complementary formal theories of the semantics of programming languages. *Acta Informatica* **3** (1974), 135–153.

[74c] Program correctness proofs. In *Formal Aspects of Computing Science*. Newcastle upon Tyne, Sept 1974, 7–45.

[75a] Data reliability. *Int. Conf. Reliable Software, SIGPLAN Notices* **10** (June 1975), 528–533.

[77] The engineering of software, a startling contradiction. *Computer Bull.* (1975).

Horning, J. J.

[73a] and Randell, B. Process structuring. *Computing Surveys* **5** (1973), 5–30.

[74a] What the compiler should tell the user. In Bauer and Eickel (eds.). *Compiler Construction, An Advanced Course. LNCS* 21, 1974, 525–548.

[74b] Lauer, H. C., Melliar-Smith, P. M., and Randell, B. A program structure for error detection and recovery. *Proc. Conf. on Operating Systems: Theoretical and Practical Aspects, April 1974*, 177–193.

[75a] with Gannon, J. D. The impact of language design on program reliability. *Int. Conf. Reliable Software, SIGPLAN Notices* **10** (June 1975), 10–22.

[75b] with Gannon, J. D. Language design for programming reliability. *IEEE Trans. Software Eng.* **1** (1975), 179–191.

[75c] Yes! High level languages should be used to write system software. *NACM 1975*, 206–208.

[76a] The software project as a serious game. In Wassermen (ed.), *Software Engineering Education: Needs and Objectives.* Springer–Verlag, Berlin and New York, 1976.

[76b] Some desirable properties of data abstraction facilities. *Proc. Conf. on Data: Abstraction, Definition and Structure, SIGPLAN Notices* **11** (March 1976), 60–62.

[77a] and Wortman, D. B. Software Hut: a computer program engineering project in the form of a game. *IEEE Trans. Software Eng.* **3** (July 1977).

[77b] with Greenspan, S. J. Programming methodology: an annotated bibliography for IFIP Working Group 2.3. CSRG-81, Univ. of Toronto, 1977.

[77c] *et al.* Notes on the design of EUCLID. *Proc. LDRS, SIGPLAN Notices* **12** (March 1977), 11–18.

[78] with Guttag, J. V. The algebraic specification of data types. *Acta Informatica* (1978).

Jackson, M. A.

[75] *Principles of Program Design.* Academic Press, New York, 1975.

[76a] Constructive methods of program design. In *Proc. ECI Conf., 1976. LNCS* 44, 1976, 236–262.

[76b] COBOL. *Proc. BCS Software Eng. Symp., 1976.*

Jones, C. B.

[70] with Henhapl, W. The block concept and some possible implementations, with proofs of equivalence. IBM, Vienna, TR25.104, April 1970.

[71a] with Henhapl, W. A run-time mechanism for referencing variables. *IPL* **1** (1971).

[71b] and Lucas, P. Proving correctness of implementation techniques. In Engler (ed.), *A Symposium on Algorithmic Languages.* Springer–Verlag Lecture Notes in Mathematics No. 188, 1971.

[72] Formal development of correct algorithms: an example based on Early's recognizer. *SIGPLAN Notices* **7** (Jan 1972).

[73a] with Allen, C. D. The formal development of an algorithm. IBM Hursley TR-12.110, March 1973.

[73b] Formal development of programs. IBM, Hursley TR12.117, June 1973.

[73c] with Hanford, K. V. Dynamic syntax: a concept for the definition of the syntax of programming languages. *Annual Review in Automatic Programming* **7** (1973), 115–142.

[74] with Bekic, H., Bjorner, D., Henhapl, W., and Lucas, P. Formal definition of a PL/I subset. IBM, Vienna TR25.139, Dec 1974.

[75] Formal definition in program development. In *Programming Methodology. LNCS* 23, 1975, 387–443.

[76a] Formal definition in compiler development. IBM, Vienna TR25.145, Feb 1976.

[76b] Some requirements of specification languages. IBM, Vienna LN25.3.108, Feb 1976.

[77a] Structured design and coding: theory versus practice. *Informatie* **19** (July 1977), 311–319.
[77b] Program specification and formal development. *Proc. ACM European Conf., April 1977*. [Invited tutorial.]

Lavrov, S. S.
  [71a] On problem solving on a computer and proving program correctness. *Prokl. Mat. i. Mekh.* Nauk (Publ.), USSR, 1971, 98–102. [In Russian.]
  [71b] Language foundations of computer applications. *Zh. Vychisl. Mat. i. Mat. Fiz.* **11(2)** (1971), 498–504. [In Russian.]

Lehman, M. M.
  [68] Mediocrity in middle management. Unpublished, 1968.
  [70] The programming process. IBM Res. Report RC 2722, Dec 1970.
  [71] with Belady, L. A. Programming system growth dynamics; or the meta-dynamics of systems in maintenance and growth. IBM Research Center, Yorktown Heights, No. RC 3546, Sept 1971.
  [72a] with Belady, L. A. An introduction to growth dynamics. In Freiberger (ed.), *Statistical Computer Performance*. Academic Press, New York, 1972, 503–511.
  [72b] with Belady, L. A. A system viewpoint of programming projects. *In Advances in Cybernetics and Systems*, I. Gordon and Breach, 1975, 15–28.
  [73] Computer usage control. *Computer J* **16** (May 1973), 106–110.
  [74] Programs, cities, students—limits to growth?. Inaugural Lecture, May 1974. In *Imperial College of Science and Technology Inaugural Lecture Series*, Vol. 9. London, 1970–1974, 211–229.

McIlroy, M. D.
  [68] Coroutines. Bell Laboratories, 1968.
  [72] and Boon, C. The outlook for software components. *Infotech State of the Art Report 11: Software Engineering*, 1972, 243–252.

McKeeman, W. M.
  [77] Respecifying the telegram problem. TR 77-2-001, Information Sciences, Univ. Calif. at Santa Cruz, Feb. 1977.

Mealy, G. H.
  [69] The system design cycle. In *2nd Symp. on Operating Systems Principles, Princeton* (Oct 1969), 1–7.

Naur, P.
  [60] (ed)., Report on the algorithmic language ALGOL 60. *CACM* **3** (May 1960), 299–314.
  [66] Proof of algorithms by general snapshots. *BIT* **6** (1966) 310–316.
  [69a] Programming by action clusters. *BIT* **9** (1969), 250–258.
  [69b] Buxton, J. N. and Randall, B. (eds.), *Software Engineering*. Petrocelli, 1975. [Report on two NATO Conferences, held in Garmisch, Germany (Oct 68) and Rome, Italy (Oct 69).]
  [72] An experiment in program development. *BIT* **12** (1972), 347–365.

Owicki, S.
  [75] Axiomatic proof techniques for parallel programs. Ph.D. thesis, Computer Science Dept., Cornell Univ., 1975.
  [76a] and Gries, D. Verifying properties of parallel programs: an axiomatic approach. *CACM* **19** (May 1976), 279–285.
  [76b] and Gries, D. An axiomatic proof technique for parallel programs. *Acta Informatica* **6** (1976), 319–340.

Parnas, D. L.
  [67] and Darringer. SODAS and methodology for system design. *FJCC 1967*, 449–474.
  [69] More on design methodology and simulation. *SJCC 1969*, 739–743.
  [71a] with Courtois, P. J. and Heymans, F. Concurrent control with readers and

writers. *CACM* **14** (Oct 1971), 667–668.

[71b] Information distribution aspects of design methodology. *IFIP 1971*.

[72a] Some conclusions from an experiment in software engineering. *FJCC 1972*, 325–329.

[72b] Sample man–machine interface specification—a graphics based line editor. In Haendler and Weizenbaum (eds.), *Display Use for Man Machine Dialog*. Carl Hauser Verlag, Munich, 1972.

[72c] with Courtois, P. J. and Heymans, F. Comments on a comparison of two synchronizing concepts. *Acta Informatica* **1** (1972), 375–376.

[72d] A technique for software module specification, with examples. *CACM* **15** (May 1972), 330–336.

[72e] and Habermann, A. N. Comment on deadlock prevention method. *CACM* **15** (Sept 1972), 840–841.

[72f] On the criteria to be used in decomposing systems into modules. *CACM* **15** (Dec 1972), 1053–1058.

[73] and Price, W. R. The design of the virtual memory aspects of a virtual machine. *Proc. ACM SIGARCH–SIGOPS Workshop on Virtual Computer Systems, March 1973*.

[74a] with Cooprider, L. W., Courtois, P. J., and Heymans, F. Information streams sharing a finite buffer: other solutions. *IPL* **3** (July 1974), 16–21.

[74b] On a "buzzword": hierarchical structure. *IFIP 1974*, 336–339.

[75a] Shore, J. E. and Elliot, W. D. On the need for fewer restrictions. In *Changing Compile-Time Environments. Proc. Inter. Computing Symp.* North–Holland, 1975, 45–48.

[75b] Software engineering or methods for the multi-person construction of multi-version programs. *Programming Methodology. LNCS* 23, 1975, 225–235.

[75c] and Handzel, G. More on specification techniques for software modules. T. H. Darmstadt, Fachbereich Informatik, Germany, Forschungsbericht BS I 75/1. [Feb 1975.]

[75d] On the solution of the cigarette smokers problem (without conditional statements). *CACM* **18** (March 1975), 181–183.

[75e] The influence of software structure on reliability. *SIGPLAN Notices* **10** (June 1975), 358–362; and Yeh (ed)., *Current Trends in Programming Methodology I*. Prentice–Hall, Englewood Cliffs, N.J., 1976, 111–119.

[75f] and Siewiorek, D. L. Use of the concept of transparency in the design of hierarchically structured systems. *CACM* **18** (July 1975), 401–408.

[76a] On the design and development of program families. *IEEE Trans. Software Eng.*, (March 1976), 1–9.

[76b] Shore, J. E. and Weiss, D. Abstract types defined as classes of variables. *Proc. Conf. on Data: Abstraction, Definition, and Structure, SIGPLAN Notices* **10** (June 1975), 22–24.

[76c] Handzel, G. and Wuerges, H. *IEEE Trans. Software Eng.*, **2** (Dec 1976), 301–307.

[76d] Shore, J. E., and Weiss, D. Abstract types defined as classes of variables, *Proc. Conf. on Data: Abstraction, Definition, Structure, SIGPLAN Notices* **10** (June 1975), 22–24.

[76e] and Wuerges, H. Response to undesired events in software systems. *Proc. Int. Conf. Software Eng., Oct 1976*, 437–446.

[77a] The use of precise specifications in the development of software. *IFIP 1977*, 861–868.

Randell, B.

[68] with Zurcher, F. W. Iterative multilevel modelling: a methodology for computing system design. *IFIP 1968*, 138–142.

[71a] Highly reliable computing systems. Tech. Rpt. 20, Univ. of Newcastle

upon Tyne, 1971.

[71b] Operating systems: the problems of performance and reliability. *IFIP 1971*, 1100–1109.

[74] Research on computing systems reliability at the University of Newcastle upon Tyne, 1972/73. Tech. Rpt. 57, Computing Lab, Univ. of Newcastle upon Tyne, Jan 1974.

[75a] System structure for software fault tolerance. *Int. Conf. on Reliable Software, SIGPLAN Notices* **10** (June 1975), 437–449.

[75b] Buxton, J. N., and Naur, P. (eds.), *Software Engineering*. Petrocelli, 1975. [Report on two NATO Conferences, held in Garmisch, Germany (Oct 68) and Rome, Italy (Oct 69).]

[77a] Lee, P. A., and Treleaven, P. C. Reliable computing systems. Tech Rpt. 102, Computing Lab, Univ. of Newcastle upon Tyne, May 1977, and *LNCS* **60**, 282–339.

Reynolds, J. C.

[70] GEDANKEN—a simple typeless language based on the principle of completeness and the reference concept. *CACM* **13**, (May 1970), 308–319.

[72] Definitional interpreters for higher order programming languages. *NACM 1972*, 717–740.

[74] Towards a theory of type structure. *Proc. Colloque sur la Programmation. LNCS* 19, 1974, 408–423.

[75] User-defined types and procedural data structures as complementary approaches to data abstraction. *Conf. on New Directions in Algorithmic Languages, IFIP, Aug 1975*, 157–168.

[78] Syntactic control of interference. *ACM Symp. Princ. Prog. Lang., Jan 1978*.

Ross, D. T.

[61] A generalized technique for symbol manipulation and numerical calculation. *CACM* **4** (March 1961), 147–150.

[70a] Uniform referents: an essential property for a software engineering language. In Tou (ed), *Software Engineering 1*. Academic Press, New York, 1970, 91–101.

[70b] Fourth generation software: A building block science replaces hand-crafted art. *Computer Decisions* **2** (April 1970), 32–38.

[71] It's time to ask why? *Software—Practice and Experience* **1** (Jan 1971), 103–104.

[75] Goodenough, J. B., and Irvine, C. A. Software engineering: process, principles, and goals. *Computer* (May 1975), 17–27.

[77a] Structured analysis (SA): a language for communicating ideas. *IEEE Trans. Software Eng.* **3** (Jan 1977), 16–34.

[77b] and Schoman, Jr., K. E. Structured analysis for requirements definition. *IEEE Trans. Software Eng.* **3** (Jan 1977), 6–15.

[78] Origins of the APT language for automatically controlled tools. *Proc. SIGPLAN History Prog. Lang. Conf., SIGPLAN Notices* **13** (Aug 1978).

Seegmueller, G.

[73] Systems programming as a discipline. *Proc. IFIP Conference on Programming Teaching Techniques, Zakopane, Poland*. North–Holland, 1973, 157–159.

[74a] System programming as an emerging discipline. *IFIP 1974*, 419–426.

[74b] *Einfuehrung in die Systemprogrammierung*. [*Introduction to Systems Programming*.] BI–Verlag, Mannheim, 1974. [In German).]

[76a] Language aspects in operating systems. In *Language Hierarchies and Interfaces. LNCS* 46, 1976, 266–292.

[76b] with Hegering, H.-G., Schneider, D., and Schwald, A. Systems program-

ming elements of the language ASTRA. *Proc. Eurocomp., London, Sept 1976.*

Sintzoff, M.
   [75a] Verification of assertions for functions. *Proc. IRIA Colloq. on Proving and Improving Programs, 1975,* 11–27. [In French.]
   [75b] and Van Lamsweerde, A. Constructing correct and efficient concurrent programs. *Proc. Int. Conf. on Reliable Software, SIGPLAN Notices* **10** (June 1975), 319–326.
   [75c] Composing specifications from information structures. *Conf. on New Directions in Algorithmic Languages, IFIP, Aug 1975,* 207–216.
   [76a] Eliminating blind alleys from backtrack programs. *Proc. 3rd Conf. Automata, Languages and Programming* (1976), 531–557.
   [77a] Inventing program construction rules. *Proc. IFIP Working Conf. on Constructing Quality Software, 1977.*
   [77b] et al. Mes premières constructions de programmes. *LNCS* 55, 1977. [In French.]

Teitelman, W.
   [70] Toward a programming laboratory. In [Buxton 75*].
   [72a] Do what I mean: the programmer's assistant. *Computers and Automation* **21** (April 1972), 8–11.
   [72b] Automated programming: the programmer's assistants. *FJCC 1972,* 917–921.
   [76] Clisp: conversational Lisp. *IEEE Trans. Computers* **25** (April 1976), 354–357.

Turski, W. M.
   [71] A model for data structures and its applications—Part I. *Acta Informatica* **1** (1971), 26–34.
   [72a] A model for data structures and its applications—Part II. *Acta Informatica* **1** (1972), 282–289.
   [72b] A correspondence between thesaurus-based and multi-attribute retrieval systems, *Information Storage and Retrieval* **8** (Dec 1972), 309–313.
   [74] Einige probleme der programmierung von elektronischen rechenmaschienen. *Wissenschaft und Menschheit* **10**, 1974, Urania–Verlag, Leipzig/Jana/Berlin, 324–331. [In German.]
   [75a] *Datenstrukturen.* Akademie Verlag, Berlin, 1975. [In German.]
   [75b] Software engineering—some principles and problems. *Mathematical Structures–Computational Mathematics–Mathematical Modelling.* Publ. House of the Bulgarian Academy of Sciences, Sofia, 1975. 485–491.
   [76] Data structure models in information science design. *Advances in Inf. Systems Science* **6** (1976), 115–159.
   [77a] *Computer Programming Methodology.* Heyden, Philadelphia, 1977.
   [77b] Changing nature of software problems. *Proc. Organizacja maszyn cyfrowych i mikroprogramowanie, Sept 1975,* 145–156.

Wirth, N.
   [66] and Hoare, C. A. R. A contribution to the development of ALGOL. *CACM* **9** (June 1966), 413–432.
   [70] Programming and programming languages. *Proc. Int. Computer Symp., Bonn, Germany, May 1970.*
   [71a] Program development by stepwise refinement. *CACM* **14** (April 1971), 221–227.
   [71b] The design of a Pascal compiler. *Software—Practice and Experience* **1** (Oct 1971), 309–333.
   [71c] The programming language Pascal. *Acta Informatica* **1** (1971), 35–63.
   [73a] *Systematic Programming: An Introduction.* Prentice–Hall, Englewood Cliffs, N.J., 1973.

[73b] From programming techniques to programming methods. In *Proc. Int. Computing Symp., Davos, Switzerland.* North–Holland, 1973.

[74a] On the composition of well-structured programs. *Computing Surveys* **6** (Dec 1974), 247–259.

[74b] and Jensen, K. *Pascal—User Manual and Report.* Springer–Verlag, Berlin and New York, 1974.

[75] An assessment of the programming language Pascal. *IEEE Trans. Software Eng.* **1** (June 1975), 192–198.

[76] Comment on a note on dynamic arrays in Pascal. *SIGPLAN Notices* **11** (Jan 1976), 37–38.

[77a] Modula: a language for modular multiprogramming. *Software—Practice and Experience* **7** (Jan 1977), 3–35.

[77b] Toward a discipline of real-time programming. *CACM* **20** (Aug 1977), 577–583.

Woodger, M.

[71] On semantic levels in programming. *IFIP 1971*, 402–407.

Reference II

The entries in this bibliography are those items referred to in the articles of this volume that do not appear in the WG2.3 Bibliography.

Ambler, A. P.

[71] and Burstall, R. M. LIB POLYSETS. POP-2 Program Library Specification, Dept. of Machine Intelligence, Univ. of Edinburgh, 1971.

Anderson, T. A.

[76] Provably safe programs. Tech. Rpt., Computing Lab. Univ. of Newcastle upon Tyne, 1976.

Ashcroft, E. A.

[71] and Manna, Z. Formalization of properties of parallel programs. *Machine Intelligence* **6** (1971), 17–41.

[73] Proving assertions about parallel programs. Computer Science Dept. Univ. of Waterloo, CS 73-01, 1973.

Baker, F. T.

[72] System quality through structured programming. *FJCC 1972*, 339–343.

Bauer, F. L.

[73] A course of three lectures on a philosophy of programming, Technische Univ., Muenchen, Oct 1973.

Baumann, R.

[64] *et al. Introduction to ALGOL.* Prentice–Hall, Englewood Cliffs, N.J., 1964.

Baumol, W. J.

[67] Macro-economics of unbalanced growth. *AM. Econ. Rev.* (June 1967), 415–426.

Birkoff, G.

[70] and Lipson, J. D. Heterogeneous algebras. *Journal of Combinatorial Theory* **8** (1970), 115–133.

Boon, W

[59] The word problem. *Annals of Mathematics* (1959), 207–265.

Box, G. E. P.

[70] and Jenkins, G. M. *Time Series Analysis.* Holden–Day, 1970, 17.

Boyer, R. S.

[75] and Moore, J. S. Proving theorems about LISP functions. *JACM* **22** (1975), 129–144.

Butterworth, D.
[74] Letter to the editor, *Datamation* (March 1974), 158.
Cadiou, J. M.
[73] and Levy, J. J. Mechanical proofs about parallel processes. *Proc. 14 Ann. IEEE Sym on Switching and Automata Theory* (1973), 34–48.
Campbell, R. H.
[74] and Habermann, A. N. *The Specification of Process Synchronization by Path Expressions. LNCS* **16**, 1974, 89–102.
Church, A.
[36] and Rosser, J. Some properties of conversion. *Trans American Math Society* **39** (1936), 472–482.
Clint, M.
[73] Program proving: coroutines. *Acta Informatica* **2** (1973), 50–63.
Cook, S. A.
[75] Axiomatic and interpretive semantics for an Algol fragment. Computer Science Dept., Univ. of Toronto, TR 79, 1975.
Cooper, D. C.
[66] The equivalence of certain computations. *Computer J* **9** (1966), 45–52.
Cox, D. R.
[66] and Lewis, P. A. W. *The Statistical Analysis of Series of Events*. Methuen, London, 1966, 38.
Darlington, J.
[72] A semantic approach to automatic program improvement. Ph.D. thesis, Dept. of Machine Intelligence, Univ. of Edinburgh, 1972.
[75] Application of program transformation to program synthesis. *Proc. IRIA Symp. on Proving and Improving Programs, Arc-et-Senans, 1975,* 133–144.
Davies, C. T.
[73] Recovery semantics for a DB/DC system. *NACM 1973,* 136–141.
DeBakker, J. W.
[68] Axiomatics of simple assignment statements. M.R.94, Mathematisch Centrum, Amsterdam, 1968.

Denning, P. J.
[73] Letter to the editor. *SIGPLAN Notices* **8** (Oct 1973), 5–6.
Donaldson, J.
[73] Structured programming. *Datamation* (Dec 1973), 53.
Ernst, G. W.
[67] and Newell, A. Generality and GPS. Carnegie Institute of Technology, 1967.
Evans, A.
[68] PAL—A language designed for teaching programming linguistics. *NACM 1968,* 395–403.
Fischer, A. E.
[73] and Fischer, M. J. Mode modules as representations of domains. *Proc. ACM Symp. Princ. of Prog. Lang. 1973,* 139–143.
Floyd, R. W.
[67] Assigning meanings to programs. *Proc. Amer. Math. Soc. Symp. in Applied Mathematics* **19** (1967), 19–31.
Garland, S. J.
[71] and Luckham, D. C. Program schemes, recursion schemes and formal languages. School of Engineering and Applied Science, Univ. of California, UCLA-ENG-7154, 1971.
Goguen, J. A.
[75] Thatcher, J. W., Wagner, E. G., and Wright, J. B. Abstract data-types as initial algebras and correctness of data representations. Proc. Conf. on Computer Graphics, *Pattern Recognition and Data Structure, May 1975.*

Graham, R. W.
  [68] Protection in an information processing utility. *CACM* **11** (May 1968), 365–369.
Habermann, A. N.
  [67] On the harmonious cooperation of abstract machines. Ph.D. thesis, Technical Univ., Eindhoven, The Netherlands, 1967.
  [72] Synchronization of communicating processes. *CACM* **15** (Mar 1972), 171–176.
  [73] Critical comments on the programming language Pascal. *Acta Informatica* **3** (1973), 47–57.
Harrison, M. C.
  [67] and Schwartz, J. T. SHARER, a time sharing system for the CDC 6600, *CACM* **10** (Oct 1967), 659–664.
Henderson, P.
  [72] and Snowden, R. An experiment in structured programming. *BIT* **12** (1972), 38–53.
Hermes, H.
  [65] *Enumerability, Decideability and Computability*. Academic Press, New York, 1965.
Hetzel, W C.
  [73] (ed.), *Program Test Methods*. Prentice–Hall, Englewood Cliffs, N.J., 1973.
Hewitt, C.
  [69] Planner: A language for proving theorems in robots. *Proc. Int. Joint Conf. on AI* (1969), 295–301.
Hopgood, F. R. A.
  [69] *Compiling Techniques*. Macdonald, London (and American Elsevier, N.Y.), 1969.
Hori, S.
  [72] Human-directed activity cell model. In *CAM-I, Long-Range Planning Final Rep*. CAM-I Inc., 1972.
Howard, J. H.
  [76] Proving Monitors. *CACM* **19** (May 1976), 273–279.
Igarashi, S.
  [64] An axiomatic approach to equivalence problems of algorithms with applications. Ph.D. thesis, Univ. of Tokyo, 1964.
Karp, R.
  [74] Letter to the editor, *Datamation* (March 1974), 158.
King, J. C.
  [69] A program verifier. Ph.D. thesis, Carnegie–Mellon Univ., 1969.
Kleene, S.
  [36] General recursive functions of natural numbers. *Math. Ann.* **112** (1936), 729–745.
Knuth, D. E.
  [73a] A review of "Structured programming". Computer Science Dept., Stanford Univ., STAN-CS-73-371, 1973.
  [73b] Selected topics in computer science. Lecture Note Series, Mathematical Institute, Univ. of Oslo, 1973.
Landin, P. J.
  [65] A correspondence between ALGOL 60 and Church's lambda-notation. *CACM* **8** (Feb–Mar 1965), 89–101, 158–165.
  [66] The next 700 programming languages. *CACM* **9** (March 1966), 157–166.
Laski, J.
  [68] Sets and other types. *ALGOL Bull.* **27** (1968), 41–48.
Lauer, H. C.
  [73] and Wyeth, D. A recursive virtual machine architecture. Rpt. 54, Computing Lab., Univ. of Newcastle upon Tyne, 1973.

[73b] Correctness in operating systems. Ph.D. thesis, Carnegie-Mellon Univ., 1973.

[74] Protection and hierarchical addressing structures. *Proc. Int. Workshop on Protection in Operating Systems, IRIA 1974*, 137–148.

Lauer, P. E.

[71] Consistent formal theories of the semantics of programming languages. IBM Laboratory Vienna, TR 25.121, 1971.

Lecarme, O.

[75] and Desjardins, P. More comments on the programming language Pascal. *Acta Informatica* **4** (1975), 231–243.

Lewis, C.

[73] and Rosen, B. Recursively defined data types. *Proc. ACM Symp. Princ. of Prog. Lang. 1973*, 125–238.

Lipton, R. J.

[74a] On synchronization primitive systems. Ph.D. thesis, Carnegie–Mellon Univ., 1974.

[74b] Reduction: a new method for proving properties of systems of processes. Yale Computer Science Res. Rpt. 30, 1974.

Liskov, B.

[72] A design methodology for reliable software systems. *FJCC 1972.*

[74] and Zilles, S. Programming with abstract data types. *Proc. ACM SIGPLAN Conf. Very High Level Languages, SIGPLAN Notices* **9** (April 1974), 50–60.

[77] *et al.* Abstraction mechanisms in CLU. *CACM* **20** (Aug 1977), 564–576.

Madnick, S. E.

[69] and Alsop, J. W., II. A modular approach to file system design. *SJCC 1969*, 1–13.

Majster, M. E.

[77] Limits of the algebraic specifications. *SIGPLAN Notices* **12** (Oct 1977), 37–41.

McCarthy, J.

[60] Recursive functions of symbolic expressions and their computation by machine, Pt.I. *CACM* **3** (Apr 1960), 184–195.

[63] Towards a mathematical theory of computation. *IFIP 1963.*

Meadows, D. H.

[72] *et al. The limits to growth.* Signet, 1972.

Miller, G. A.

[56] The magical number seven, plus or minus two: some limits on our capacity for processing information. *Psychol. Rev.* **63** (Mar 1956), 81–97.

Mills, H.

[71] Chief programmer team operations. IBM Tech. Rep. FSC 71-5108, 1971.

Milner, R.

[71] An algebraic definition of simulation between programs. CS205 Computer Science Dept., Stanford Univ., 1971.

Minsky, M.

[67] *Computation: Finite and Infinite Machines.* Prentice–Hall, Englewood Cliffs, N.J., 1967.

[70] Form and content in computer science. *JACM* **17** (April 1970), 197–215.

Morris, J. H.

[73] Types are not sets. *ACM Symp. Princ. of Prog. Lang., Oct 1973*, 120–124.

[74] Towards more flexible type systems. *Proc. Colloque sur la Programmation, LNCS* **19** (1974), 377–384.

Newton, G.

[75] Proving properties of interacting processes. *Acta Informatica* **4** (1975), 117–126.

Palme, J.
[73] Protected program modules in SIMULA 67. FOAP Report C8372-M3(E5), Res. Inst. of National Defense, Stockholm, Sweden, (1973).
Peterson, J. L.
[77] Petri nets. *Computing Surveys* **9** (Sept 1977), 223–252.
Pierce, W. H.
[65] *Failure-Tolerant Computer Design*. Academic Press, New York, 1965.
Polya, G.
[71] *How to Solve It*. Princeton Univ. Press, Princeton, N.J., 1971.
Price, W. R.
[73] Implications of a virtual memory mechanism for implementing protection in a family of operating systems. Ph.D. thesis, Carnegie–Mellon Univ., 1973.
Rohl, J. S.
[72] and Lin, J. A. A note on compiling arithmetic expressions. *Computer J* **15** (1972), 13–14.
Rosen, B.
[73] Tree manipulating systems and Church–Rosser theorems. *JACM* **20** (Jan 1973), 160–187.
[74] Correctness of parallel programs: the Church–Rosser approach. IBM Res. RC5107, T. J. Watson Research Center, Yorktown Heights, 1974.
Russell, B.
[08] Mathematical logic as based on the theory of types. *Amer. J. of Math.*, (1908).
Sheridan, P. B.
[59] The arithmetic translator–compiler of the IBM Fortran automatic coding system, *CACM* **2** (Sept 1959), 9.
Simon, H. A.
[62] The architecture of complexity. *Proc. Amer. Phila. Soc.* **106** (1962), 468–482.
[72] The heuristic compiler. In Simon, Siklossy (eds.), *Representation and Meaning*. Prentice–Hall, Englewood Cliffs, N.J., 1972.
Spitzen, J.
[75] and Wegbreit, B. The verification and synthesis of data structures. *Acta Informatica* **4** (1975), 127–144.
Standish, T. A.
[73] Data structures—an axiomatic approach. Bolt, Beranek, and Newman 2639 (Aug 1973).
Strong, H. R., Jr.
[70] Translating recursion equations into flow charts. *Proc. ACM Symp. Theory of Computing, 1970*, 184–197.
Topor, R. W.
[75] Interactive program verification using virtual programs. Ph.D. thesis, Dept. of Artificial Intelligence, Univ. of Edinburgh, 1975.
Varney, R. C.
[72] Process selection in a hierarchical operating system. *SIGOPS Operating Review* (June 1972).
Van Emden, M. H.
[77] Programming with verification conditions. Technical Report, Computer Science Dept., Univ. of Waterloo, 1977.
Van Wijngaarden, A.
[66] Numerical analysis as an independent science. *BIT* **6** (1966), 66–81.
[75] *et al*. Revised report on the algorithmic language ALGOL 68. *Acta Informatica* **5** (1975), 1–236.

Wulf, W.

[72] The GOTO controversy: a case against the GOTO. *SIGPLAN Notices* **7** (Nov 1972), 63–69.

[74] *et al.* Hydra: the kernel of a multiprogramming system. *CACM* **17** (June 1974), 337–345.

[77] Shaw, M., and London, R. L. Abstraction and verification in Alphard. Defining and specifying iteration and generators. *CACM* **20** (Aug 1977), 553–563.

Yanov, Yu I.

[58] Logical operator schemes. *Kybernetika* **1** (1958).

Zilles, S. N.

[75] Abstract specifications for data types. IBM Res. Lab. San Jose, Cal., 1975.

[78] Data algebra: a specification technique for data structures. Ph.D. thesis (forthcoming), M.I.T., 1978.

Computer Science from Springer-Verlag

Compiler Construction
An Advanced Course
Second Edition

Edited by **F.L. Bauer** and **J. Eickel**

1976. xiv, 638p. 123 illus. 2 tables. paper
(Springer Study Edition)

This text consists of papers carefully prepared by a group of experts for a workshop on compiler construction held in Munich in 1974 and repeated in 1975. The second edition contains an addendum by A.P. Ershov to the contribution by F.L. Bauer, as well as a new paper by D. Gries on "Error Recovery and Correction—An Introduction to the Literature."

Software Engineering
An Advanced Course

Edited by **F.L. Bauer**

1977. xii, 545p. paper
(Springer Study Edition)

Proceedings of an Advanced Course on Software Engineering, organized by the Mathematical Institute of the Technical University of Munich and the Leibniz Computing Center of the Bavarian Academy of Sciences, March, 1972.

Operating Systems
An Advanced Course

Edited by **R. Bayer, R.M. Graham**, and **G. Seegmüller**

1978. x. 593p. paper
(Lecture Notes in Computer Science, Vol. 60)

This volume contains the lectures which were given at the Advanced Course on Operating Systems, held in Munich in the summer of 1977 and repeated again in the spring of 1978. Emphasis is on areas of research in which progress has been made in the last few years. The following topics are covered: the object model abstract data types), protection, correctness, reliability, data base requirements and consequences of distributed processing.

Texts and Monographs in Computer Science

Suad Alagić and Michael A. Arbib
The Design of Well-Structured and Correct Programs
1978. x, 292p. 68 illus. cloth

Peter W. Frey, Ed.
Chess Skill in Man and Machine
1978. xii, 226p. 55 illus. cloth

Hans W. Gschwind and Edward J. McClusky
Design of Digital Computers
An Introduction
2nd Edition. 1975. viii, 548p. 375 illus. cloth

Brian Randell, Ed.
The Origins of Digital Computers
Selected Papers
2nd Edition. 1975. xvi, 464p. 120 illus. cloth

Arto Salomaa and M. Soittola
Automata-Theoretic Aspects of Formal Power Series
1978. x, 171p. cloth

Jeffrey R. Sampson
Adaptive Information Processing
An Introductory Survey
1976. x, 214p. 83 illus. cloth